Lecture Notes in Computer Science 15352

Founding Editors

Gerhard Goos
Juris Hartmanis

Editorial Board Members

Elisa Bertino, *Purdue University, West Lafayette, IN, USA*
Wen Gao, *Peking University, Beijing, China*
Bernhard Steffen, *TU Dortmund University, Dortmund, Germany*
Moti Yung, *Columbia University, New York, NY, USA*

The series Lecture Notes in Computer Science (LNCS), including its subseries Lecture Notes in Artificial Intelligence (LNAI) and Lecture Notes in Bioinformatics (LNBI), has established itself as a medium for the publication of new developments in computer science and information technology research, teaching, and education.

LNCS enjoys close cooperation with the computer science R & D community, the series counts many renowned academics among its volume editors and paper authors, and collaborates with prestigious societies. Its mission is to serve this international community by providing an invaluable service, mainly focused on the publication of conference and workshop proceedings and postproceedings. LNCS commenced publication in 1973.

Shiqi Yu · Wei Jia · Xiangbo Shu ·
Xiaotong Yuan · Jie Gui · Jinhui Tang ·
Caifeng Shan · Qingshan Liu
Editors

Biometric Recognition

18th Chinese Conference, CCBR 2024
Nanjing, China, November 22–24, 2024
Proceedings, Part I

Editors
Shiqi Yu
Southern University of Science
and Technology
Shenzhen, China

Xiangbo Shu
Nanjing University of Science
and Technology
Nanjing, China

Jie Gui
Southeast University
Nanjing, China

Caifeng Shan
Nanjing University
Nanjing, China

Wei Jia
Hefei University of Technology
Hefei, China

Xiaotong Yuan
Nanjing University
Nanjing, China

Jinhui Tang
Nanjing University of Science
and Technology
Nanjing, China

Qingshan Liu
Nanjing University of Posts
and Telecommunications
Nanjing, China

ISSN 0302-9743　　　　　　ISSN 1611-3349　(electronic)
Lecture Notes in Computer Science
ISBN 978-981-96-1067-9　　　ISBN 978-981-96-1068-6　(eBook)
https://doi.org/10.1007/978-981-96-1068-6

© The Editor(s) (if applicable) and The Author(s), under exclusive license to Springer Nature Singapore Pte Ltd. 2025

This work is subject to copyright. All rights are solely and exclusively licensed by the Publisher, whether the whole or part of the material is concerned, specifically the rights of translation, reprinting, reuse of illustrations, recitation, broadcasting, reproduction on microfilms or in any other physical way, and transmission or information storage and retrieval, electronic adaptation, computer software, or by similar or dissimilar methodology now known or hereafter developed.
The use of general descriptive names, registered names, trademarks, service marks, etc. in this publication does not imply, even in the absence of a specific statement, that such names are exempt from the relevant protective laws and regulations and therefore free for general use.
The publisher, the authors and the editors are safe to assume that the advice and information in this book are believed to be true and accurate at the date of publication. Neither the publisher nor the authors or the editors give a warranty, expressed or implied, with respect to the material contained herein or for any errors or omissions that may have been made. The publisher remains neutral with regard to jurisdictional claims in published maps and institutional affiliations.

This Springer imprint is published by the registered company Springer Nature Singapore Pte Ltd.
The registered company address is: 152 Beach Road, #21-01/04 Gateway East, Singapore 189721, Singapore

If disposing of this product, please recycle the paper.

Preface

Biometric technology, which enables automatic person recognition based on physiological or behavioral traits such as face, fingerprint, iris, gait, or signature, finds extensive applications in modern society. In recent years, biometric recognition systems have been widely deployed globally, spanning across law enforcement, government, and consumer sectors. Developing diverse and reliable approaches for trustworthy biometric applications has become imperative. In China, the proliferation of the Internet and smartphones among its vast population, coupled with substantial government investments in security and privacy protection, has led to the rapid growth of the biometric market. Consequently, biometric research in the country has garnered increasing attention. Researchers have been actively addressing various scientific challenges in biometrics, exploring diverse biometric techniques, and making significant contributions to the field. The Chinese Conference on Biometric Recognition (CCBR), an annual event held in China, serves as a pivotal platform for biometrics researchers. It provides an excellent opportunity to exchange knowledge, share progress, and discuss ideas related to the development and applications of biometric theory, technology, and systems.

CCBR 2024 took place in Nanjing from November 22–24, marking the 18th edition in a series of successful conferences held in prominent cities like Xuzhou, Beijing, Hangzhou, Xian, Guangzhou, Jinan, Shenyang, Tianjin, Chengdu, Shenzhen, Urumqi, Zhuzhou, and Shanghai since 2000. The conference received 82 submissions, each meticulously reviewed by a minimum of three experts from the Program Committee. Following a rigorous evaluation process, 52 papers were chosen for presentation (63.4% acceptance rate). These papers comprise these two volumes of the CCBR 2024 conference proceedings, which cover a wide range of topics: Fingerprint, Palmprint, and Vein Recognition; Face Detection, Recognition, and Tracking; Affective Computing and Human-Computer Interface; Gait, Iris, and Other Biometrics; Trust, Privacy, and Personal Data Security; Medical and Other Applications.

We would like to thank all the authors, reviewers, invited speakers, volunteers, and organizing committee members, without whom CCBR 2024 would not have been successful. We also wish to acknowledge the support of the China Society of Image and Graphics, the Chinese Association for Artificial Intelligence, the Institute of Automation of the Chinese Academy of Sciences, Springer, Nanjing University of Science and

Technology, Nanjing University, Nanjing University of Posts and Telecommunications, and Southeast University for sponsoring this conference.

November 2024

Jinhui Tang
Caifeng Shan
Qingshan Liu
Shiqi Yu
Wei Jia
Xiangbo Shu
Xiaotong Yuan
Jie Gui

Organization

Academic Advisory Committee

Anil K. Jain	Michigan State University, USA
Tieniu Tan	Nanjing University, China
David Zhang	Chinese University of Hong Kong (Shenzhen), China
Massimo Tistarelli	University of Sassari, Italy
Jingyu Yang	Nanjing University of Science and Technology, China
Jianhuang Lai	Sun Yat-sen University, China
Yunhong Wang	Beihang University, China

Industry Advisory Committee

Zhifei Wang	Information Center of Ministry of Human Resources and Social Security, China
Hongchuan Hou	First Research Institute of the Ministry of Public Security, China
Cong Liu	Iflytek Co., Ltd., China
Quanzeng You	Beijing Bytedance Technology Company, Ltd., China

General Chairs

Jinhui Tang	Nanjing University of Science and Technology, China
Caifeng Shan	Nanjing University, China
Qingshan Liu	Nanjing University of Posts and Telecommunications, China

Program Committee Chairs

Shiqi Yu Southern University of Science and Technology, China
Wei Jia Hefei University of Technology, China
Xiangbo Shu Nanjing University of Science and Technology, China
Xiaotong Yuan Nanjing University, China
Jie Gui Southeast University, China

Organizing Committee Chairs

Zhaofeng He Beijing University of Posts and Telecommunications, China
Xianye Ben Shandong University, China
Xinguang Xiang Nanjing University of Science and Technology, China
Yunlian Sun Nanjing University of Science and Technology, China
Jie Qin Nanjing University of Aeronautics and Astronautics, China

Publicity Chairs

Wenxiong Kang South China University of Technology, China
Hao Liu Ningxia University, China

Sponsorship Chairs

Xiushen Wei Southeast University, China
Lunke Fei Guangdong University of Technology, China

Publication Chairs

Qijun Zhao Sichuan University, China
Dan Zeng Sun Yat-Sen University, China

Forum Chairs

Zechao Li	Nanjing University of Science and Technology, China
Qi Li	Institute of Automation, Chinese Academy of Sciences, China
Yunlong Wang	Institute of Automation, Chinese Academy of Sciences, China
Zhe Jin	Anhui University, China
Jian Zhao	Northwestern Polytechnical University, China
Xin Liu	AutoDL, China
Peipei Li	Beijing University of Posts and Telecommunications, China

Contents – Part I

Fingerprint, Palmprint and Vein Recognition

OCT Fingerprint Fusion Combining Cross Attention and Quality Optimization 3
   Jianru Zhou, Haixia Wang, Yilong Zhang, and Haohao Sun

Beyond First-Order: A Multi-scale Approach to Finger Knuckle Print Biometrics 14
   Chengrui Gao, Ziyuan Yang, Andrew Beng Jin Teoh, and Min Zhu

Fingerprint Revocable Template Protection of Variable Window-Based Random Permutation && Check Code 25
   Zilong Xu, Weixin Bian, Yao Hu, and Feng Luo

Direction-Guided Sparse Representation Method for Finger Vein Recognition 36
   Lizhen Zhou, Lu Yang, Qinggang Meng, and Gongping Yang

Learning Compact Binary Codes for Few-Shot Finger Vein Recognition 46
   Jianian Hu, Shuyi Li, Lunke Fei, Shuping Zhao, and Lifang Wu

Privacy Protection in Palmprint Recognition via Pruning Frequency Channels 57
   Siyu Shi, Huikai Shao, and Dexing Zhong

A Federated Learning Framework for Lightweight Model Contrast for Finger Vein Recognition 68
   Guang Chen, Tianming Xie, Xu Yang, Feng Tian, and Wenxiong Kang

Palmprint Anti-spoofing via Frequency Enhancement and Selection 79
   Yani Ren, Huikai Shao, and Dexing Zhong

Spoofing Attacks Utilizing a More Realistic Contactless Palm Vein Correction Algorithm 89
   Jianbin Wang, Dacan Luo, Runzhang Chen, and Wenxiong Kang

An Image Super-Resolution Based Method for Palmprint Recognition 100
   Zekai Yang, Dacan Luo, Ming Zeng, Hao Wan, and Wenxiong Kang

FCNet: Adaptive Finger Trimodal Feature Crystal Construction
and Recognition 110
    *Zihao Zhao, Ziyun Ye, Binmeng Shi, Qi Liang, Xingzheng Zhu,
and Jinfeng Yang*

Unsupervised Fingerprint Registration: A Reinforcement Learning
Approach 121
    Jing Xing, Yuwei Jia, Zhe Cui, and Fei Su

Region of Interest Extraction for Palm in the Wild 131
    Haoheng Lin, Junqin Huang, Dacan Luo, Ming Zeng, and Wenxiong Kang

A GAN-Based Data Augmentation Method for Palm Vein Authentication 142
    Junqin Huang, Jiyi Huang, Haoheng Lin, Dacan Luo, and Wenxiong Kang

3D Palmprint MCI Synthesis for 2D-3D Heterogeneous Palmprint
Recognition 153
    Le Su, Lunke Fei, Shuping Zhao, Shuyi Li, and Jia Wei

Palmprint Recognition Method Based on Orientation Features: A Survey 164
    Hao Lu, Cunyu Sheng, and Wei Jia

Arm Vein Recognition Based on Multi-hop Graph Convolutional Networks 174
    Siyu Huang, Chaoying Tang, and Yuren Sun

Face Detection, Recognition and Tracking

Deepfake Video Detection Guided by Identity and Temporal Inconsistency 187
    Yufei Zhang, Bo Peng, Jing Dong, Weike You, and Wei Wang

Reflectance Recovery Guided Learning of Illumination-Invariant Features
for Person Re-Identification 200
    Xianbiao Chen and Xiaohua Xie

Exposing Deepfakes with Noise-Based Clues 210
    Shaocong Yang, Xiaolong Qi, Huiling Wang, Jian Wang, and Yunlian Sun

Adaptive Multi-modal Fusion Based Face Anti-spoofing with RGB-D
Images 220
    Zhan Teng, Wei Fang, Zhanli Liu, and Lixi Chen

Enhancing Deepfake Detection via Adversarial Generative Learning 231
    Zengqiang Chen, Xudong Wang, and Yuezun Li

Exposing Audio-Visual Forgeries in Frequency Domain 244
    Yuanfei Wan, Jian Wang, Jinrong Cui, and Yunlian Sun

Synergistic Alignment-Based Domain Adaptation For Gaze Estimation 254
    *Yushan Han, Haoxiang Ying, Honggang Zhu, Feiyang Gao,
    and Wanting Zhou*

Towards Fast Face Image Quality Assessment via Latent Diffusion Model 264
    *Zheyu Yan, Weisong Zhao, Xiangyu Zhu, Li Gao, Xiao-Yu Zhang,
    and Zhen Lei*

Unknown-Aware Diverse Prompt Learning for Open-Set Single Domain
Generalization-Based Face Anti-spoofing 275
    Fangling Jiang, Qi Li, Weining Wang, Bing Liu, and Zhenan Sun

Author Index 287

Contents – Part II

Face Detection, Recognition and Tracking

Multi-feature Consistency Learning for Face Forgery Detection 3
   Yikang Song, Zhentao Chen, and Junlin Hu

KAAN: Kolmogorov-Arnold Attention Networks for Object
Re-identification 13
   Simin Zhan, Jiajun Su, Pudu Liu, Jianqing Zhu, and Huanqiang Zeng

Implicit Feature Augmentation for Cloth-Changing Person
Re-identification 25
   Yongtang Bao, Hao Zheng, Caifeng Shan, and Peng Zhang

Micro-Expression Recognition via CNN and Multi-path Vision
Transformer Integrated with Spatiotemporal Separated Self-attention 35
   Yingying Guo, Tingxuan Xie, Wenqiang Jia, Sen Xu, and Xianye Ben

Affective Computing and Human-Computer Interface

Fusion of Heterogeneous Data for Enhanced Gesture Authentication: An
RGB-Event Stream Approach 49
   Binqiang Wang, Lihua Lu, Jinzhe Jiang, and Gang Dong

DualActNet: Exploiting SlowFast Architecture for Micro-action
Recognition 59
   *Churan Yu, Yiwei Ru, Zhenbo Xu, Huijia Wu, Hujiang Yang,
   and Zhaofeng He*

Reading Preference Analysis Through Eye-Tracking and Large Language
Models 69
   *Shuangshuang Ying, Dongsen Zhang, Huijia Wu, Churan Yu,
   Yongji Liu, and Zhaofeng He*

A Spatio-Temporal Transformer for Enhancing the Coherence on 3D
Human Motion Prediction 79
   Miner Xie, Lei Wang, and Feng Liu

Gait, Iris and Other Biometrics

Improved YOLOv8 Fall Detection Algorithm 93
    Bojie Liu and Daming Liu

Speaker Recognition Based on Locality Sensitive Hashing 103
    Yifan Wu, Erhua Zhang, Chunxia Hou, and Zhenmin Tang

Relax DARTS: Relaxing the Constraints of Differentiable Architecture
Search for Eye Movement Recognition 112
    Hongyu Zhu, Xin Jin, Hongchao Liao, Yan Xiang,
    Mounim A. El-Yacoubi, and Huafeng Qin

MILD: A Multimodal Biometric Recognition Framework Integrating
Large Foundation Models 123
    Huimin Lu, Qingxin Zhao, Zexing Zhang, Songzhe Ma, and Chenglin Lin

LipMVCL:Lipreading Based on Multi-view and Collaborative Learning 133
    Junyu Li, Yu Li, Shujie Li, and Feng Xue

Trustworthy, Privacy and Personal Data Security

Triplet-Bio: A Secure Cloud-Edge Collaborative Biometric Authentication
via Two-Factor Secret Sharing 145
    Hui Zhang, Ying Zhou, Xingbo Dong, Qingguo Meng, and Zhe Jin

A Lightweight Cancelable Biometric Template Protection Scheme 159
    Shuaichao Song, Songhui Guo, Yeming Yang, Miao Yu, and Ruiyang Ding

A Fuzzy Commitment Cryptosystem Based on One Permutation Hashing 177
    Ce Gao, Weiwei Wang, Yuxing Li, Zhicheng Cao, and Heng Zhao

A Federated Learning Framework Using FedProx Algorithm for
Privacy-Preserving Palmprint Recognition 187
    Jinrong Cui, Yinghua Li, Qiuli Zhang, Zhipeng He, and Shuping Zhao

Universal Face Manipulation Proactive Defense by Frequency-Driven
Imperceptible Adversarial Attack 197
    Jinchang Wen, Jian Wang, Yunlian Sun, and Massimo Tistarelli

Medical and Other Applications

Video Crowd Activity Recognition Based on Stereo Vision 209
    Gang Zhang, Cong Wang, and Yiwei Hu

Radar Respiratory and Heartbeat Signal Separation Algorithm Based on
Adaptive Cancellation 219
   Chen Cao, Weijie Xia, and Dongcai Guo

Recognizing Adenoid Hypertrophy from Facial Images with Multi-scale
Feature Fused State Space Model 228
   Shuai Ma, Jinrong He, Yao Wang, Yingzhou Bi, and Li Yang

Semantic Segmentation Active Learning with Scene Coverage CoreSet 238
   Hailun Liang, Sunyuan Qiang, Hui Ma, Jun Wan, and Yanyan Liang

PhysMamba: Efficient Remote Physiological Measurement with SlowFast
Temporal Difference Mamba 248
   Chaoqi Luo, Yiping Xie, and Zitong Yu

Robust Fast Supervised Discrete Hashing for Image Retrieval 260
   Minghua Wan, Yixuan Zhou, Guowei Yang, Hai Tan, and Zhangjing Yang

Unifying Large Language Models and Knowledge Graphs for Poultry
Diseases Diagnosis 272
   Shengxiang Xu, Liang Yao, Chenyu Huang, Guoxin Jiang, and Fan Liu

A Graph Structure-Feature Learning Network for Diagnosing Alzheimer's
Disease Based on Multi-modal Brain Biometric Feature 282
   Dongxu Shang, Huabin Wang, Mengxin Zhang, Yuhang Peng,
   Xingjian Ye, and Zilin Wang

Author Index 293

Fingerprint, Palmprint and Vein Recognition

OCT Fingerprint Fusion Combining Cross Attention and Quality Optimization

Jianru Zhou, Haixia Wang[✉], Yilong Zhang, and Haohao Sun

College of Computer Science and Technology, Zhejiang University of Technology, Hangzhou 310000, China
{zhoujianru,hxwang,zhangyilong,hhsun}@zjut.edu.cn

Abstract. Optical Coherence Tomography (OCT) is a non-invasive, high-resolution imaging technology that has recently been used in fingerprint acquisition. The captured external and internal fingerprints are robust to spoofing attacks and resistant to harsh skin conditions. The quality of the OCT fingerprints is limited by imaging mechanism and reconstruction. The paper proposes a fingerprint fusion network leveraging the concept that multiple fingerprints derived from OCT volume data can enhance one another. This network integrates cross-attention and quality optimization techniques to enhance the quality of OCT fingerprint images. Three fingerprints, two internal fingerprints and one external fingerprint reconstructed based on depth or intensity information, are utilized. The network introduces a cross-attention module and a quality index OCL to improve the feature representation capabilities and the retention of high-quality regions. Experimental results show that the fingerprint images obtained by the fusion method in this paper are superior in visual effects and quality scores. *abstract* environment.

Keywords: OCT · fingerprint · cross attention · quality index OCL · fusion network

1 Introduction

Fingerprint has been the primary focus of research in the field of biometric identification in recent decades due to its unique and enduring characteristics [1,2]. Conventional fingerprint is formed by external structures on the fingertip skin. In fact, the fingertip skin is primarily composed of epidermis and dermis, and there is a viable epidermis at the junction of them. The fluctuation of the epidermal layer is highly related to the structure of the viable epidermis [3]. The internal fingerprint formed by the viable epidermis acts as the mother template of the external fingerprint formed by the epidermis. The internal fingerprint is located within 2 mm under the skin of the fingertip [4]. It is not easily affected by external abrasion, scratch and dirt, and can effectively resist the fraud of fake fingerprints. Furthermore, the consistency between the external and the internal fingerprints has also been verified [5]. The internal fingerprint is capable of maintaining the integrity and continuity of the ridge and valley lines, and serves as a powerful complement to the external fingerprint.

Fingerprint sensing technologies have made significant progress in recent years [6]. For external fingerprints, total internal reflection (TIR) is an optical reflection system for surface imaging, which has been widely used in fingerprint capture due to its excellent fingerprint quality and low cost [7]. For internal fingerprints, optical coherence tomography (OCT) is based on the principle of low-coherence interference. It has the advantages of high-resolution, non-destructive and non-invasive imaging, and can capture three-dimensional data information under the skin of the fingertips [8], and can obtain internal fingerprint data from the viable epidermal layer of the finger. Not only that, OCT can obtain external fingerprint data from the epidermal layer of the finger. Chen et al. [9] have evaluated the feasibility of OCT for detecting reliable internal fingerprints. Chugh and Jain [10] have proved that OCT fingerprints can resist fake fingerprint attacks and bad fingertip conditions.

The external fingerprint image captured by traditional devices generally has a large effective area and high image contrast, but its anti-interference and anti-counterfeiting capabilities are weak. Internal fingerprints have strong anti-interference and anti-counterfeiting capabilities. However, the quality of OCT-captured fingerprint is usually limited by factors such as imaging mechanism and fingerprint reconstruction algorithms. Meanwhile, multiple fingerprints can be extracted by the OCT caputured volume data, including those from different depths as external and internal fingerprints, those from different reconstruction algorithms as fingerprints based on depth information and intensity information, etc. Therefore, fusing different fingerprint images captured by OCT is a way to improve fingerprint image quality. Darlow et al. [11] calculated the orientation certainty level (OCL) of the fingerprint image, and used a bias algorithm to fuse the OCT external and internal fingerprint images. Cui et al. [12] proposed an method that decomposes the source fingerprint image, adds OCL quality constraints, and finally performs fusion and reconstruction. Their methods place high demands on the collection equipment and have problems with internal and external fingerprint registration.

In recent years, OCT finger volume data extraction algorithms have been developed. Ding et al. [13] proposed a BCL-UNet to extract OCT finger volume data and reconstruct internal and external fingerprints using depth method and intensity method. These two reconstruction methods each have their own advantages. Based on this, we proposed a network based on encoder-decoder structure is proposed, called Triple Fingerprint Fusion Network(TFFNet). This network introduces a Cross Attention(CA) module in the image feature extraction stage. During the network training stage, it is combined with the fingerprint quality indicator OCL. And by fusing fingerprints reconstructed by multiple methods captured, a high-quality fused fingerprint is obtained. And by fusing OCT fingerprints reconstructed by multiple methods, a high-quality fused fingerprint is obtained. At the same time, this paper verifies the effectiveness of the proposed method through qualitative and quantitative analysis experiments, thereby proving that fused fingerprints can improve the quality of fingerprint images. And to a certain extent, it solves the problems encountered in the generation of fingerprints using OCT technology.

2 Related Work

Fingerprint images may have problems such as ridge breakage due to finger dryness, wear, scratches, etc. It is necessary to use fingerprint quality evaluation indexes to judge the quality of the collected fingerprint images. There have been many related studies on fingerprint quality evaluation, which can be summarized as methods based on global features [14–16], local features [17–19], and multi-features [20,21]. In conventional fingerprint quality evaluation, the whole fingerprint image is usually evaluated. However, in fingerprint fusion, local quality, that is, pixel-level quality values, are required. Therefore, in this paper, the OCL [22] is used to evaluate the fingerprint quality. OCL is used to measure the intensity of energy concentration along the main ridge flow direction. By performing principal component analysis on image blocks, the eigenvectors and eigenvalues are calculated to form an orthogonal basis, which is used to judge the quality of the fingerprint image. OCL quality index value is between 0 and 1. When the OCL quality index value is 1, it means that the ridges and valleys in the local block change uniformly in the same direction, and when the quality index value is 0, it means that the directions of the ridges and valleys in the local block are unclear. If the quality index value is 0, the fingerprint ridge and valley lines may not even exist.

3 The Proposed Method

3.1 Network Overview

This section introduces a fusion network called TFFNet, which is based on encoder and decoder for fusion of fingerprint images. The network contains three submodules, namely the Encoder, the Cross Attention (CA) feature fusion module, and the Decoder. Its network architecture is shown in Fig. 1. Through this network, a set of fingerprint images I_A, I_B and I_C, can be combined to generate a fused fingerprint image F. The network structure of TFFNet consists of Convolutional Layer (Conv), Deconvolutional Layer (DeConv), Batch Normalization Layer (BN), ReLU (Activation Function), and Fully Connected Layer (FC), and so on. Each in Fig. 1, the number below the block indicates the number of channels of the Conv or the DeConv, and the number above the block indicate the kernel size, stride, and padding size, respectively. In this network, the role of the encoder is to extract high-dimensional features from the input fingerprint image. The CA feature fusion module uses this feature information to perform feature fusion, allowing the relevant information in the three images to interact, and finally the decoder generates a high-quality fused fingerprint image. The Decoder consists of three modules, the first two of which are DeConv-BN-ReLU

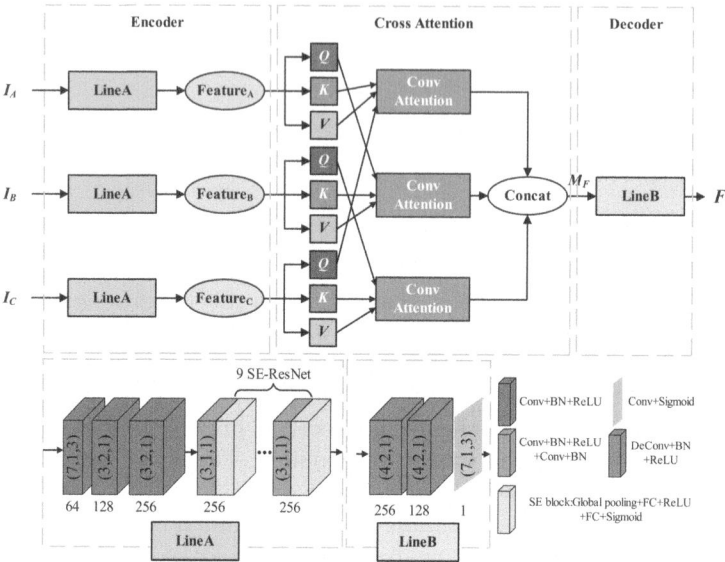

Fig. 1. TFFNet network structure diagram.

modules. These two modules use deconvolutional layers to upsample and deconvolution the cascaded feature maps M_F to restore the image size and reconstruct it. The last module is the Conv-Sigmoid block to produce a single-channel fused fingerprint image F.

3.2 CA Based Feature Fusion Module

In order to capture the features extracted by different branches and leverage their complementarity, we introduces a cross-attention based feature fusion module.

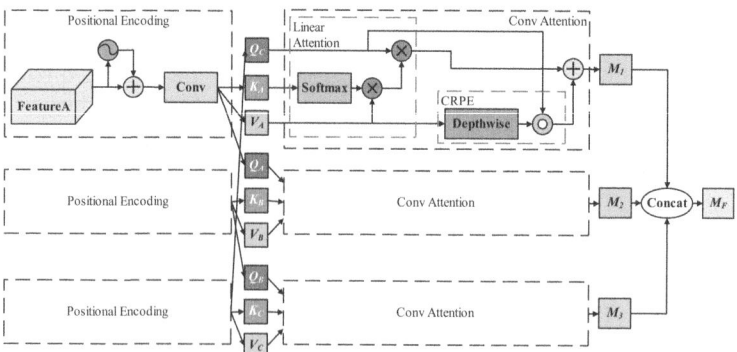

Fig. 2. Cross Attention module.

The architecture of this module is shown in Fig. 2. This module uses the linearized convolutional attention approach to enable interactive propagation. In this paper, The feature maps $Feature_A \in \mathbb{R}^{H \times W \times C_1}$, $Feature_B \in \mathbb{R}^{H \times W \times C_2}$, $Feature_C \in \mathbb{R}^{H \times W \times C_3}$ generated by the Encoder exist in tensor form. To meet the input requirements of the fusion network, we use traditional positional encoding methods to complement the position information and use 1×1 convolution operations to unify and reduce dimensionality along the channel dimension. Then, each feature map is mapped to three intermediate variables using three linear transformations: query vector Q, key vector K, and value vector V to achieve information interaction. By alternately using the linearly transformed query vectors Q_A, Q_B and Q_C from the three feature maps, coupling of features between $Feature_A$, $Feature_B$ and $Feature_C$ is achieved. The complete linearized Conv Attention module consists of two sub-modules, namely Linear Attention and convolutional relative position encoding(CRPE), which are used to complete interactive communication between different branches and generate interactive feature maps M_1, M_2 and M_3. Finally, the three interactional feature maps M_1, M_2 and M_3 are tensor concatenated to obtain the fused feature map M_F.

3.3 Loss Function

This paper proposes a custom loss function based on the Orientation Certainty Level (OCL) fingerprint quality metric to constrain the network learning process, thereby enhancing the network's ability to preserve the ridge-valley structure of fingerprints and optimize fingerprint quality. The OCL loss is specifically designed for the fingerprint image fusion task. Its goal is to guide the fusion network to capture regions of higher quality from each fingerprint while discarding regions of lower quality, ultimately optimizing the quality of the fused fingerprint image. The specific definition of OCL loss is as follows:

$$L_{OCL} = Mean(W_A I_A + W_B I_B + W_C I_C - F) \quad (1)$$

$$W_{i \in \{A,B,C\}} = \frac{ocl_i}{ocl_A + ocl_B + ocl_C} \quad (2)$$

In Eq. (6), $Mean(\cdot)$ denotes the mean value of image pixels. I_A, I_B and I_C denote the three different types of fingerprints and denotes the fused fingerprint. ocl_A, ocl_B and ocl_C respectively denote the weight proportions of the corresponding fingerprint's OCL quality map. The values of are distributed in the range of 0 to 1. When the fingerprint quality is higher, the value of the corresponding weight approaches 1; conversely, when the fingerprint quality is lower, the value of the corresponding weight approaches 0. The entire OCL loss is determined by the differences between the weighted sum of I_A, I_B, I_C and the fused fingerprint F.

4 Experiments

The fingerprint dataset used in this paper comes from dataset-A of ZJUT-EIFD [23], which contains 1280 fingerprint pairs.

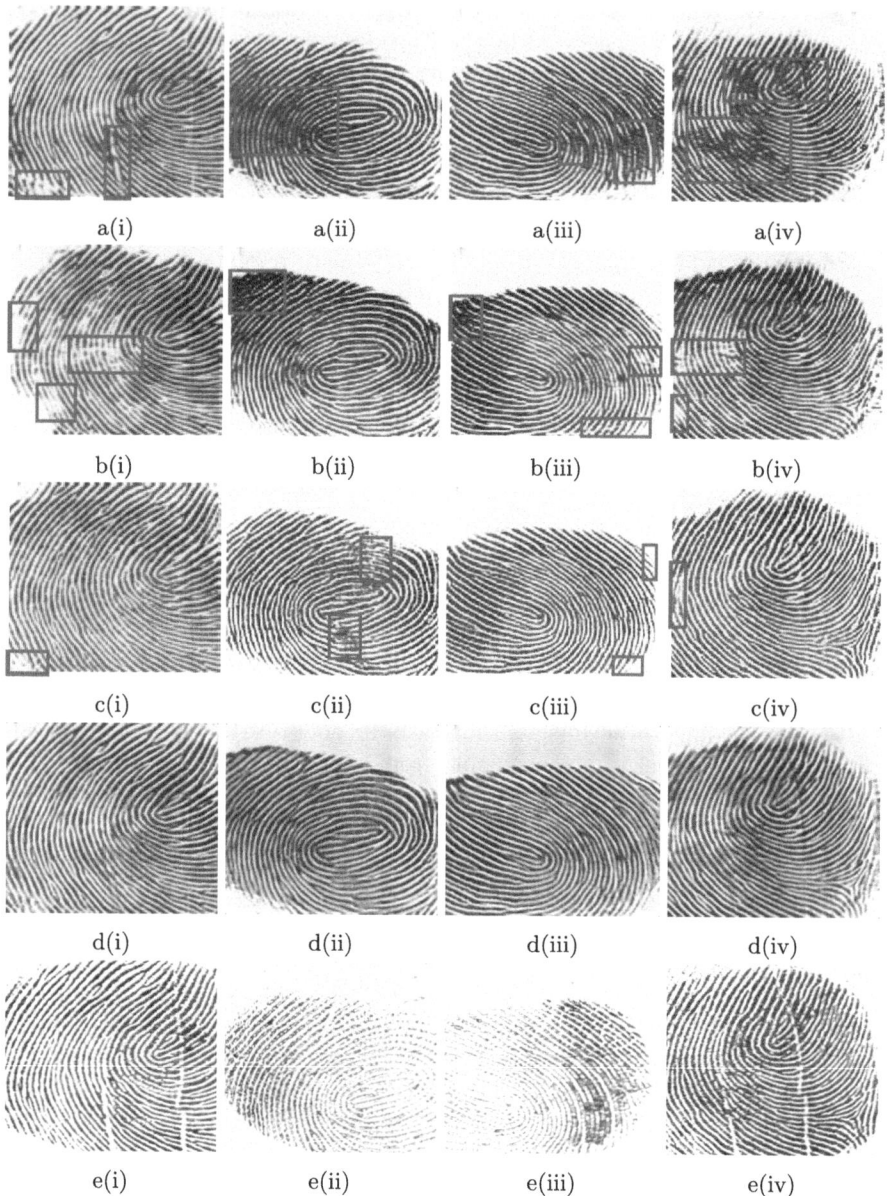

Fig. 3. Fingerprint image comparison. a(i)-a(iv) are DE, b(i)-b(iv) are DI, c(i)-c(iv) are GI, d(i)-d(iv) are TFFNet fused fingerprint images, e(i)-e(iv) are TIR fingerprint images.

4.1 Dataset

The external fingerprints captured by the TIR device are used only for the subsequent fingerprint quality comparison. For fingerprints captured by the OCT device, we select external fingerprints reconstructed using the depth method (DE), internal fingerprints reconstructed using the depth method (DI), and internal fingerprints reconstructed using the intensity method (GI) for experimentation. The training set consists of the latter 640 pairs of fingerprints (DE, DI, GI), while the test set consists of the former 640 pairs of fingerprints (DE, DI, GI).

4.2 Qualitative Fingerprint Quality Assessment

This section compares the fingerprint obtained by the proposed TFFNet fusion method with the fingerprint before fusion and the TIR external fingerprint. As shown in Fig. 3, a(i)-a(iv), b(i)-b(iv), c(i)-c(iv) are DE, DI, GI used for fusion, respectively. d(i)-d(iv) is the fusion result processed by the proposed TFFNet fusion method. e(i)-e(iv) is the TIR fingerprints. We can see that the TFFNet fusion method improves the fingerprint quality to a certain extent. The fusion method has a better repair effect on distorted fingerprints, and has significant improvements in visual effects, fingerprint effective area, and texture details. In details, for fingerprints with fuzzy areas, the fingerprint lines become clear and easy to distinguish through fusion processing. For fingerprints with information loss and ridge breakage, the missing parts are compensated through the fusion method, so that the fused fingerprint retains lots of fingerprint details.

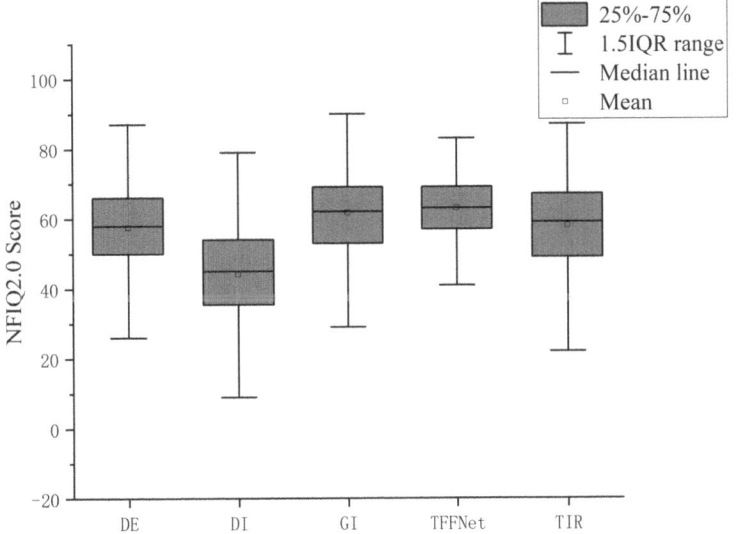

Fig. 4. Comparison of fingerprint qualities.

4.3 Quantitative Fingerprint Quality Assessment

We use the publicly available NIST Finger Image Quality (NFIQ) tool [21] to evaluate our fingerprints. NFIQ scores range from 0 to 100. The mean of the NFIQ scores aims to be high, while the variance aims to be low. The NFIQ scores of surface fingerprints and internal fingerprint databases are shown in Fig. 4.

The NFIQ scores are applied to the DE, DI, GI, fused fingerprints, and TIR external fingerprints datasets for quality assessment. The box plots of the NFIQ scores for the five fingerprint datasets are shown in Fig. 4. The results of the box plots indicate that DI has the poorest overall quality, with the lowest mean NFIQ scores. Except for TFFNet, the variance of the NFIQ scores for the remaining four types of fingerprint images is relatively large. Fingerprint images obtained by TFFNet fusion have the highest mean scores and the smallest variance in NFIQ scores, demonstrating that the fusion method proposed in this paper effectively retains high-quality information in fingerprint images while reducing the impact of low-quality areas.

4.4 Comparison Experiment

In this subsection, the proposed method TFFNet is compared with the fingerprint fusion method FPFNet [24]. The experiments are performed on 640 pairs of test datasets from Sect. 4.1 and quantitatively evaluated using NFIQ2.0 scores. The experimental results are shown in Table 1. It can be seen that the fingerprints fused by the TFFNet method have higher NFIQ scores which proves that the proposed method has better fusion performance.

Table 1. Comparison Experiment.

	TFFNet	FPFNet [24]
NFIQ 2.0	**62.89**	60.62

4.5 Ablation Experiment

In this section, three sets of ablation experiments were conducted to validate the effectiveness of the proposed cross-attention (CA) module and the OCL loss function. The NFIQ 2.0 scores of the fusion results were recorded and summarized in Table 2. From Table 2, it can be seen that the NFIQ 2.0 scores of the third column using CA+OCL are superior to those of the first column using only the OCL loss function without the CA module. This shows the effectiveness of the CA module. Regarding the OCL loss function, a comparison was made with the structural similarity loss function (SSIM). The NFIQ 2.0 values of the second column, which uses CA+SSIM, are lower, respectively, indicating the effectiveness of the OCL loss function.

Table 2. Results of ablation experiments.

	OCL	CA+SSIM	CA+OCL
NFIQ 2.0	60.83	59.00	**62.89**

5 Conclusion

This paper proposes a fingerprint image fusion network that uses cross-attention and quality optimization to improve the quality of the fused fingerprints. We use finger volume data captured by OCT device and reconstructed three types of fingerprint images using depth and intensity methods and fuse them. Through the cross-attention mechanism, the three branches interact and pay attention to each other's detailed information at the same time, thereby improving the representability of the features. At the same time, the quality index OCL is introduced as a loss function to constrain the fused image to retain high-quality areas and reduce low-quality areas. Experimental results show that this method can significantly improve the performance of fused fingerprints in terms of visual effects and NFIQ 2.0 scores, and perform well in terms of fingerprint matching performance. In addition, the image quality of the fingerprint data collected only by the OCT device, after being fused by this network, exceeds that of single fingerprints and external TIR fingerprints in terms of NFIQ2.0 scores. The work of this article provides reference and inspiration for the future identification of incomplete fingerprints, and provides solutions to the limitations encountered in the collection of OCT devices.

Funding Information. This work was supported in part by Natural Science Foundation of Zhejiang Province under Grant LR24F030003, National Natural Science Foundation of China under Grant 62376250, and Leading Innovation Team of Zhejiang Province under Grant 2021R01002.

References

1. Maltoni, D., Maio, D., Jain, A.K., Prabhakar, S., et al.: Handbook of Fingerprint Recognition, vol. 2. Springer (2009)
2. Jain, A.K., Pankanti, S., Prabhakar, S., Hong, L., Ross, A.: Biometrics: a grand challenge. In: Proceedings of the 17th International Conference on Pattern Recognition, ICPR 2004, vol. 2, pp. 935–942. IEEE (2004)
3. Bossen, A., Lehmann, R., Meier, C.: Internal fingerprint identification with optical coherence tomography. IEEE Photonics Technol. Lett. **22**(7), 507–509 (2010)
4. Shi, B., Meng, Z., Liu, T., Wang, L.: Identifying artificial fingerprint by using optical coherence tomography. J. Optoelectron. Laser **24**(12), 2404–2408 (2013)
5. Sun, H., et al.: Synchronous fingerprint acquisition system based on total internal reflection and optical coherence tomography. IEEE Trans. Instrum. Meas. **69**(10), 8452–8465 (2020)

6. Jing, H., Dong, W.: Research and application of pressure sensitive fingerprint acquisition system. In: 2010 First International Conference on Networking and Distributed Computing, pp. 57–59. IEEE (2010)
7. Liu, F., Zhang, D., Song, C., Lu, G.: Touchless multiview fingerprint acquisition and mosaicking. IEEE Trans. Instrum. Meas. **62**(9), 2492–2502 (2013)
8. Cheng, Y., Larin, K.V.: In vivo two-and three-dimensional imaging of artificial and real fingerprints with optical coherence tomography. IEEE Photonics Technol. Lett. **19**(20), 1634–1636 (2007)
9. Chen, P., Yu, Y., Ma, L., Wang, H., Liang, R.: Adaptive oct internal and external fingerprint extraction. J. Comput.-Aided Des. Comput. Graph. **31**(6), 961–970 (2019)
10. Chugh, T., Jain, A.K.: Oct fingerprints: resilience to presentation attacks, arXiv preprint arXiv:1908.00102 (2019)
11. Darlow, L.N., Connan, J., Singh, A.: Performance analysis of a hybrid fingerprint extracted from optical coherence tomography fingertip scans. In: 2016 International Conference on Biometrics (ICB), pp. 1–8. IEEE (2016)
12. Yin, M., Liu, X., Liu, Y., Chen, X.: Medical image fusion with parameter-adaptive pulse coupled neural network in nonsubsampled shearlet transform domain. IEEE Trans. Instrum. Meas. **68**(1), 49–64 (2018)
13. Ding, B., et al.: Surface and internal fingerprint reconstruction from optical coherence tomography through convolutional neural network. IEEE Trans. Inf. Forensics Secur. **16**, 685–700 (2020)
14. Qi, J., Abdurrachim, D., Li, D., Kunieda, H.: A hybrid method for fingerprint image quality calculation. In: Fourth IEEE Workshop on Automatic Identification Advanced Technologies (AutoID 2005), pp. 124–129. IEEE (2005)
15. Sharma, R.P., Dey, S.: Two-stage quality adaptive fingerprint image enhancement using fuzzy c-means clustering based fingerprint quality analysis. Image Vis. Comput. **83**, 1–16 (2019)
16. Lee, B., Moon, J., Kim, H.: A novel measure of fingerprint image quality using the fourier spectrum. In: Biometric Technology for Human Identification II, vol. 5779, pp. 105–112. SPIE (2005)
17. Poonia, P., Deshmukh, O.G., Ajmera, P.K.: Adaptive quality enhancement fingerprint analysis. In: 2020 3rd International Conference on Emerging Technologies in Computer Engineering: Machine Learning and Internet of Things (ICETCE), pp. 149–153. IEEE (2020)
18. Chen, T.P., Jiang, X., Yau, W.-Y.: Fingerprint image quality analysis. In: 2004 International Conference on Image Processing, ICIP 2004, vol. 2, pp. 1253–1256. IEEE (2004)
19. Syam, R., Mochamad, H., Purnomo, M.H.: Determining the dry parameter of fingerprint image using clarity score and ridge-valley thickness ratio. IAENG Int. J. Comput. Sci. **38**(4), 350–358 (2011)
20. Lim, E., Jiang, X., Yau, W.: Fingerprint quality and validity analysis. In: Proceedings of International Conference on Image Processing, vol. 1, p. I. IEEE (2002)
21. Li, Z., Han, Z., Fu, , B.: A novel method for the fingerprint image quality evaluation. In: 2009 International Conference on Computational Intelligence and Software Engineering, pp. 1–4. IEEE (2009)
22. Alonso-Fernandez, F., Fierrez-Aguilar, J., Ortega-Garcia, J.: A review of schemes for fingerprint image quality computation. arXiv preprint arXiv:2207.05449 (2022)

23. Sun, H., Wang, H., Zhang, Y., Liang, R., Chen, P., Feng, J.: Zjut-eifd: a synchronously collected external and internal fingerprint database. IEEE Trans. Pattern Anal. Mach. Intell. (2023)
24. Shi, M., Wang, H.: Internal and external fingerprint fusion combining cross attention and quality optimization. J. Chin. Comput. Syst. 1–8

Beyond First-Order: A Multi-scale Approach to Finger Knuckle Print Biometrics

Chengrui Gao[1,2], Ziyuan Yang[1], Andrew Beng Jin Teoh[2], and Min Zhu[1(✉)]

[1] College of Computer Science, Sichuan University, Chengdu 610045, China
cr@scu.stu.edu.cn, zhumin@scu.edu.cn
[2] School of Electrical and Electronic Engineering, Yonsei University, Seoul 03722, South Korea
bjteoh@yonsei.ac.kr

Abstract. Recently, finger knuckle prints (FKPs) have gained attention due to their rich textural patterns, positioning them as a promising biometric for identity recognition. Prior FKP recognition methods predominantly leverage first-order feature descriptors, which capture intricate texture details but fail to account for structural information. Emerging research, however, indicates that second-order textures, which describe the curves and arcs of the textures, encompass this overlooked structural information. This paper introduces a novel FKP recognition approach, the Dual-Order Texture Competition Network (DOTCNet), designed to capture texture information in FKP images comprehensively. DOTCNet incorporates three dual-order texture competitive modules (DTCMs), each targeting textures at different scales. Each DTCM employs a learnable texture descriptor, specifically a learnable Gabor filter (LGF), to extract texture features. By leveraging LGFs, the network extracts first and second order textures to describe fine textures and structural features thoroughly. Furthermore, an attention mechanism enhances relevant features in the first-order features, thereby highlighting significant texture details. For second-order features, a competitive mechanism emphasizes structural information while reducing noise from higher-order features. Extensive experimental results reveal that DOTCNet significantly outperforms several standard algorithms on the publicly available PolyU-FKP dataset.

Keywords: Finger Knuckle Print Recognition · Dual-order texture · Learnable Gabor filter · Competitive mechanism

1 Introduction

Biometric recognition is becoming increasingly prevalent across various application domains such as healthcare systems, public safety systems, and electronic banking [1]. The range of biometric technologies developed so far includes facial recognition, iris recognition, fingerprints, palmprints, and finger knuckle prints

(FKP), among others [2]. Recently, FKP has garnered increasing research attention due to its numerous advantages [3]. For example, unlike fingerprints, which may become damaged or worn from frequent handling of objects, the surface of FKP remains largely intact. Compared to facial recognition, FKP targets are smaller and more difficult to capture maliciously, thus offering greater privacy [5]. Additionally, the skin creases on the outer side of the FKP exhibit unique lines and wrinkles with rich textures and distinct features [4]. Furthermore, the data collection process for FKP is either non-contact or involves minimal contact, enhancing hygiene and making it a more user-friendly biometric modality.

In recent decades, numerous methods for FKP recognition have been developed. These approaches can be broadly categorized into two main types: (1) handcrafted methods and (2) deep learning methods. Since FKP images contain directional features similar to those in palmprints, many recent methods use palmprint encoding techniques [6]. Zhang et al. [7] encoded the dominant directional features of FKP images using a competitive code based on Gabor filter responses. The Gabor filter serves as a highly effective texture extractor for palmprint recognition [8]. These traditional descriptors are typically manually designed and leverage prior information. However, handcrafted algorithms often struggle to adapt to diverse modalities and varying image quality.

Deep learning methods, such as Convolutional Neural Networks (CNNs), have recently garnered significant attention in FKP recognition [9]. Many current CNN-based methods either utilize generic network models for training or directly adopt pre-trained models (such as VGGNet [10] and ResNet [11]) to extract deep features from databases. However, these generic models are primarily trained on large-scale image datasets (such as ImageNet), and the images in these datasets often exhibit a significant difference in feature distribution compared to those used in the FKP recognition task. Consequently, the performance of these models is often compromised. Thus, developing an effective neural network architecture tailored to the characteristics of FKP images is essential. For instance, Cheng et al. [12] achieved FKP recognition by investigating the learning of minimally dimensional discriminative feature vectors to represent FKP images. Li et al. [13] developed a Sparse and Discriminative Multi-modal Feature Coding (SDMFC) model for jointly learning specific and common features. Li et al. [14] proposed a Joint Discriminative Feature Learning (JDFL) model, which extracts discriminative binary codes from Gabor features for FKP recognition. However, these methods overlook the importance of multi-order feature learning despite its crucial role in thoroughly modeling spatial correlations, thereby ultimately enhancing recognition accuracy. As illustrated in Fig. 1, for FKP images, features processed by first-order learnable Gabor filters contain rich, detailed information. In contrast, those processed by second-order learnable Gabor filters encapsulate major structural features crucial for recognition.

To address the aforementioned issues, we introduce the Dual-Order Texture Competition Network (DOTCNet), an FKP recognition method that comprises three different scale branches, facilitating the propagation of multi-scale texture information and enhancing the features' nonlinear representation capabilities.

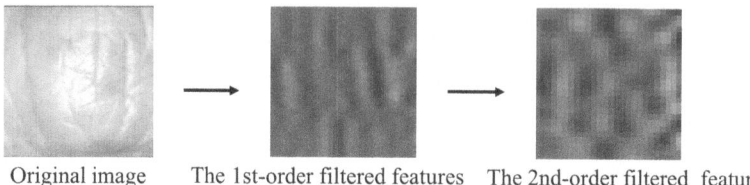

Original image　　　The 1st-order filtered features　　The 2nd-order filtered features

Fig. 1. The FKP image is processed by 1st/2nd order Gabor filters

Additionally, each branch incorporates a dual-order texture competitive module (DTCM) that employs diverse feature extraction techniques tailored to different feature orders in FKP images, thereby effectively capturing comprehensive texture and discriminative structure features. Specifically, first-order Gabor filtering is integrated with triplet attention mechanisms to enhance local and global features during the initial feature extraction phase. For second-order Gabor filtering, a competitive mechanism is utilized to select the optimal structure feature response, effectively eliminating redundant information, such as noise and irrelevant data, while preserving the important orientation of structure features. Then, we combine first-order and second-order features, allowing higher-dimensional feature vectors to be created and offering a more comprehensive texture description.

The main contributions of this article can be summarized as follows:

- We design the DTCM to utilize texture and structure information while avoiding additional noise fully. Attention and competitive mechanisms are leveraged on first-order and second-order features to focus on important characteristics.
- We propose an advanced FKP recognition method, DOTCNet, which combines the parallel texture-ordering feature extraction branches and the DTCM for comprehensive feature extraction.
- Experimental results on the open-access PolyU-FKP dataset substantiate the effectiveness of our method and demonstrate significant improvements in recognition performance.

2 Proposed Method

We propose DOTCNet, a network designed to enhance the global flow of multi-scale information. DOTCNet aims to achieve more refined multi-scale features and capture dual-order feature information from each scale, leading to a more comprehensive understanding of the data. The overall network architecture is shown in Fig. 2. This network consists of three branches, each containing the DTCM of different scales. For the DTCM, the first-order LGF captures features that contain rich details, while the second-order LGF captures features that contain the main structural elements. We use a spatial and channel-based attention mechanism for first-order features to extract local and global texture detail features comprehensively. Meanwhile, we focus only on the competitive relationships in the textural structure orientation of second-order features to avoid noise introduced by high-order filtering.

2.1 Multi-scale Network Structure

Different scales of DTCM are applied to the input FKP image, generating feature maps at various resolutions. This process constructs multi-scale features and integrates multi-scale contextual information. Specifically, DOTCNet is divided into three stages: Stage 1, Stage 2, and Stage 3. Features obtained from different scales of filters—large-scale, medium-scale, and tiny-scale—contain texture information at varying scales. Tiny-scale features often have relatively large spatial extents to capture more detailed texture information, whereas large-scale features contain strong semantic information. Information at different scales is interrelated and complementary. Global multi-scale features are then obtained by concatenating features from different scales. These concatenated features are processed through two fully connected layers to generate the final feature vector. The following expression illustrates this process:

$$F = \text{FC}\left(\text{FC}\left(\text{Concat}(F_{ls}, F_{ms}, F_{ts})\right)\right), \tag{1}$$

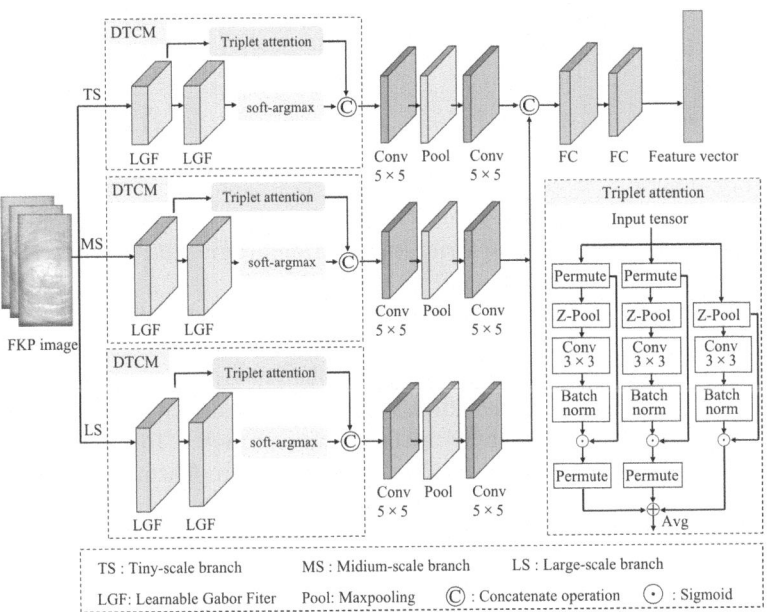

Fig. 2. The overview of the proposed DOTCNet.

where FC denotes the full connection layer, F_{ls}, F_{ms}, and F_{ts} represent the feature map generated by the different scale branches, Concat denotes the concatenate operation, and F represents the final vector feature.

2.2 Dual-Order Texture Competitive Module

For each DTCM, the process includes capturing the initial detail texture features through first-order LGF and the initial structure features through second-order LGF. Then, the attention and competition mechanisms are used for the two order features, respectively. Taking the large-scale branch as an example, dual-order features are generated by cascading first-order features and second-order features, and the expression is as follows:

$$F_{ls} = \text{Concat}(F_1, F_2), \quad (2)$$

where F_{ls} denotes the dual-order features in large-scale branch, F_1 represents the first-order detailed texture features, F_2 signifies the second-order structure features.

The Gabor filter feature extractor utilized in this paper is extensively employed in image processing because of its biological relevance and robust texture extraction capabilities. The Gabor filter is mathematically defined as follows:

$$g(x, y; \lambda, \theta, \phi, \sigma, \gamma) = \exp\left(-\frac{x'^2 + \gamma^2 y'^2}{2\sigma^2}\right) \exp\left(i\left(2\pi\frac{x'}{\lambda} + \phi\right)\right), \quad (3)$$

where $x' = x\cos\theta + y\sin\theta$ and $y' = -x\sin\theta + y\cos\theta$. (x, y) denotes the pixel position. λ denotes the wavelength of the sinusoidal plane wave component of the Gabor function. θ specifies the angle of the plane wave, while ϕ indicates the phase shift. Additionally, γ denotes the ellipticity of the Gaussian support of the Gabor function, and σ determines the standard deviation of the Gaussian filter within the Gabor function.

An effective Gabor filter requires an appropriate combination of parameters to match the given task. Previous studies [15] have typically used handcrafted methods for parameter selection, relying on inherent rules to set the parameters manually and cannot guarantee effectiveness for the current task. To overcome this limitation, we employ the LGF as the texture extractor [16], which facilitates learning optimal parameters $(\lambda, \sigma, \gamma)$ to extract texture features. In this paper, we employ the real part of the Gabor function, using Gabor filters with sizes of 7, 17, and 35 for tiny-scale, medium-scale, and large-scale textures. The filters are set to 12, 36, and 6, respectively.

The First-Order Detailed Texture Feature Extraction. We first use first-order LGF to extract the edge and texture information of the image preliminarily. The expression is as follows:

$$\chi = \text{LGF}(X), \tag{4}$$

where X represents the input FKP image, χ is the initial detail texture features through first-order LGF, and LGF(·) is the LGF operation.

For the generated feature χ, we establish dimensional dependencies through rotation operations and residual transformations, capture cross-dimensional interactions to calculate attention weights, and encode channel and spatial information through the triplet attention module [17]. The architecture of the triplet attention module is shown in Fig. 2. Given an input feature $\chi \in \mathbb{R}^{C \times H \times W}$, we obtain the (C, H)-branching identity $\hat{\chi}_1$ by rotating it 90° anti-clockwise along the H axis. We rotate χ 90° anti-clockwise along the W axis to obtain the (C, W) branch feature map $\hat{\chi}_2$. χ is the input of the (H, W) branch. Then, the Z-Pool process connects each branch's average pooling and maximum pooling results, which can be expressed as:

$$\hat{\chi}_i^* = \text{Z\_Pool}(\hat{\chi}_i) = [\text{MaxPool}(\hat{\chi}_i), \text{AvgPool}(\hat{\chi}_i)], \tag{5}$$

where $\hat{\chi}_i^*$ means the feature map through the Z-Pool process.

Finally, the interaction of spatial and channel attention across different dimensions can be represented as:

$$F_1 = \frac{1}{3}(\overline{\hat{\chi}_1 \sigma(\psi_1(\hat{\chi}_1^*))} + \overline{\hat{\chi}_2 \sigma(\psi_2(\hat{\chi}_2^*))} + \chi\sigma(\psi_3(\chi^*))), \tag{6}$$

where F_1 represents the first-order detailed texture feature, σ represents the sigmoid activation function. ψ_1, ψ_2, and ψ_3 represent the standard two-dimensional convolutional layers defined by kernel size 3 in the three branches of triplet attention. The overline represents rotating the input tensor 90° clockwise.

The Second-Order Structure Feature Extraction. After the process above, the first-order LGF captures detailed features and ensures a balance between local and global information through the attention mechanism. Building on this, the second-order LGF further strengthens important structural features, making the final feature representation more discriminative. The specific expression is as follows:

$$g = \text{LGF}(F_1), \tag{7}$$

where F_1 represents the generated first-order texture feature, g means the initial structure features through second-order LGF.

To capture the crucial structure information, soft competitive code (SCC) [18] is introduced to extract the ordering relationship as the feature using the Softmax function. The process is formulated as follows:

$$F_2 = \text{softmax}(g) \tag{8}$$

where F_2 is the input of the competitive mechanism, respectively. Softmax(·) denotes the competition extraction process along the channel dimension.

3 Experiments and Results

3.1 Datasets and Experimental Settings

This section introduces the PolyU Finger Knuckle Print Database (PolyU-FKP) used for experimental analysis [19]. The database comprises FKP images collected by the Hong Kong Polytechnic University using a low-resolution camera in a peg-free environment. The dataset involves 148 individuals and includes images of the left index FKP, left middle FKP, right index FKP, and right middle FKP. The images were captured in a contactless mode with a resolution of 110 × 220 pixels in BMP format. For each FKP image, there are 12 images. We randomly selected six samples from each FKP to create the FKP training set while reserving the remaining samples for the FKP testing phase.

Our method is implemented using the PyTorch framework and optimized with the Adam optimizer [20], utilizing a learning rate of 0.01 and a batch size 1024. The experiments are conducted on an NVIDIA GTX 3090 GPU. In this paper, we develop a loss function by integrating cross-entropy loss with contrastive loss [21]. For comparison, other deep learning methods are implemented by replacing the network while keeping all other parameters consistent.

3.2 Recognition Performance

We compared the proposed method with the classical FKP recognition methods BOCV [6], ResNet18 [11], DenseNet101 [23], VGG16 [10], Compnet [18], and PCANet-FKP [22]. Moreover, we also implemented two advanced texture description methods, CO3Net [24] and CCNet [25]. Through experiments conducted on the PolyU-FKP dataset (comprising left index FKP, left middle FKP, right index FKP, and right middle FKP), we evaluated the performance of these methods. Table 2 presents the FKP recognition performance of various models

Table 1. Comparison of the proposed method with state-of-the-art methods.

Methods	EER(%)				
	Left index	Left middle	Right index	Right middle	Total
BOCV [6]	8.753	8.712	8.845	8.667	8.657
ResNet18 [11]	5.349	4.392	5.545	4.657	3.484
DenseNet101 [23]	5.686	5.968	5.799	6.708	4.725
VGG16 [10]	6.550	4.842	6.250	4.649	4.039
Compnet [18]	2.558	3.228	4.940	3.498	2.934
PCANet-FKP [22]	4.542	2.614	4.054	3.307	2.431
CO3Net [24]	4.748	4.354	5.405	5.291	4.294
CCNet [25]	2.477	3.059	3.941	3.042	2.622
Ours	**2.327**	**2.571**	**2.909**	**2.664**	**2.186**

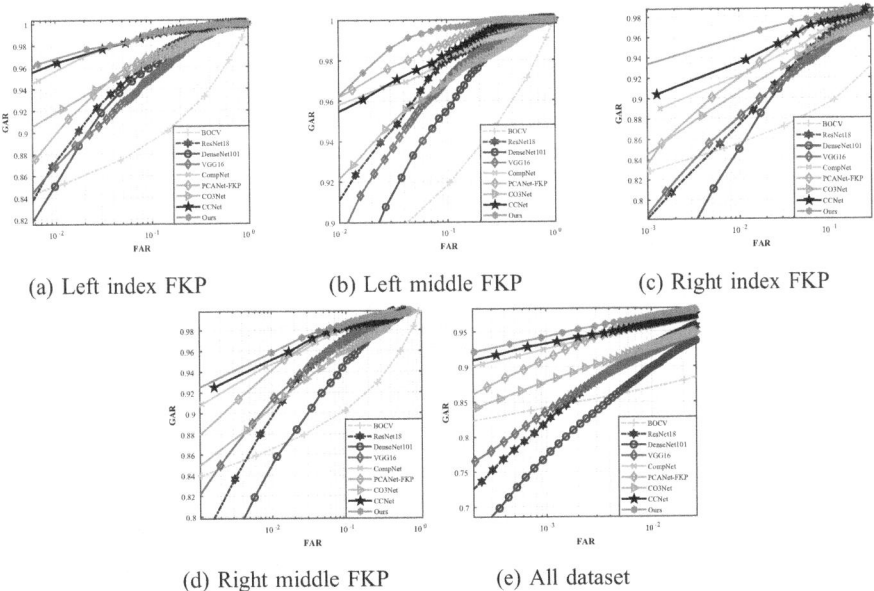

(a) Left index FKP (b) Left middle FKP (c) Right index FKP

(d) Right middle FKP (e) All dataset

Fig. 3. The ROC curves of the proposed and compared methods on PolyU-FKP.

on the dataset. For instance, our method achieved an Equal Error Rate (EER) of 2.186 on the overall FKP dataset, which is significantly lower than the second-ranked PCANet-FKP, representing an improvement of 11.2%. Our method also demonstrated superior EER performance across the PolyU-FKP dataset subset. Overall, the proposed method achieved the lowest EER across all test datasets, indicating superior accuracy and robustness in FKP recognition tasks.

To further validate the effectiveness of our method, we plotted the corresponding Receiver Operating Characteristic (ROC) curves, as shown in Fig. 3. The closer the curve is to the top left corner of the plot, the better the performance of the corresponding algorithm. These curves illustrate that our method exhibits superior performance across different thresholds, significantly outperforming other comparative methods. Compared with traditional techniques and other deep learning-based approaches, our method achieves the lowest EER values and the most optimal ROC curves on the PolyU-FKP dataset, showcasing its robustness and efficacy (Table 3).

3.3 Ablation Experiments

The Efficiency of Multi-scale Branches. To validate the necessity of multi-scale branches in recognition performance, we conducted several ablation experiments on the PolyU-FKP dataset. The entire experimental process ensured consistent network layers to ensure result comparability. The experimental results are shown in Table 1. First, we tested the recognition performance using only the

Table 2. Accuracies (%) and EERs (%) obtained with different scale branches on PolyU-FKP.

Large-scale	Midium-scale	Tiny-scale	ACC(%)	EER(%)
✓	×	×	98.84	4.308
×	✓	×	99.40	2.949
×	×	✓	99.32	2.980
✓	✓	×	99.37	2.702
×	✓	✓	99.51	2.338
✓	✓	✓	**99.60**	**2.186**

Table 3. Accuracies (%) and EERs (%) obtained with different mechanisms on PolyU-FKP.

1st-order feature		2nd-order feature		ACC(%)	EER(%)
TAM	CM	TAM	CM		
✓	✓	×	×	99.37	2.881
✓	✓	✓	✓	99.49	2.610
✓	×	✓	×	99.51	2.570
×	✓	×	✓	99.49	2.585
×	✓	✓	×	99.54	2.468
✓	×	×	✓	**99.60**	**2.186**

large, medium, and tiny individual branches separately. The experimental results showed that the medium-scale branch outperformed the large-scale and tiny-scale branches, performing the best. Next, based on the medium-scale branch, we added the large-scale and tiny-scale branches for combination testing. The results indicated that the combination of medium-scale and tiny-scale branches outperformed the combination of medium-scale and large-scale branches, further validating the importance of the tiny-scale branch in the multi-scale structure. Based on the performance of the three branches in the experiments and the analysis of their importance, we allocated appropriate network layers to each branch. Specifically, the large-scale branch was assigned six layers, the medium-scale branch 36 layers, and the tiny-scale branch 12 layers. This allocation of network layers effectively improved the model's recognition performance.

The Efficiency of Dual-Order Texture Extraction. We conduct ablation experiments to evaluate the importance of dual-order texture features and the contributions of the Triplet Attention Mechanism (TAM) and the Competition Mechanism (CM) for first-order and second-order textures. These experiments isolate and elucidate the impact of each mechanism on overall model performance. The configurations of the ablation experiments on the PolyU-FKP dataset are as follows: (1) Only retaining the first-order texture extraction, (2) TAM and CM for both first-order and second-order textures, (3) TAM for both first-order and second-order textures, (4) CM for both first-order and second-order textures, (5) CM for first-order texture and TAM for second-order texture, and (6) TAM for first-order texture and CM for second-order texture.

As shown in Table 2, configuration (1) is compared with (2), and it is concluded that retaining dual-order features is significantly better than retaining only first-order features. The highest performance was observed in configuration (5), indicating that TAM effectively captured the essential features of first-order textures. In contrast, the CM was more suitable for handling the complexity and feature differentiation in second-order textures. This suggests that first-order textures benefit more from TAM's focused attention on salient features, whereas second-order textures require effectively differentiating between significantly varying directional structure features.

4 Conclusion

In this paper, we propose a novel FKP recognition network termed DOTCNet. This network incorporates multi-scale branches and the DTCM to achieve comprehensive feature extraction. For DTCM, detailed texture features are captured by the first-order LGF. At the same time, inter-dimensional dependencies are established through rotational operations and residual transformations within the triplet attention mechanism, preserving the cross-dimensional texture features. Subsequently, structural features are captured by the second-order LGF and processed via a competitive mechanism to differentiate feature directions. Finally, the dual-order features are concatenated to achieve comprehensive feature extraction. To validate the effectiveness of the proposed method, we conducted extensive experiments on the open-access dataset. The experimental results indicate that our method has significant advantages over several other methods. This work notably treats left FKP images and right FKP images as distinct identities. However, establishing consistency in the templates for left and right FKP images, as well as exploring cross-matching between them, presents an intriguing research direction.

References

1. Yang, Z., Teoh, A.B.J., Zhang, B., et al.: Physics-driven spectrum-consistent federated learning for palmprint verification. Int. J. Comput. Vision 1–16 (2024)
2. Hattab, A., Behloul, A.: Face-iris multimodal biometric recognition system based on deep learning. Multimedia Tools Appl. **83**(14), 43349–43376 (2024)
3. Su, L., Fei, L., Zhang, B., et al.: Complete region of interest for unconstrained palmprint recognition. IEEE Trans. Image Process. (2024)
4. Fei, L., Zhang, B., Wen, J., et al.: Jointly learning compact multi-view hash codes for few-shot FKP recognition. Pattern Recogn. **115**, 107894 (2021)
5. Yang, Y., Fei, L., Alshehri, A.H., et al.: Joint multi-type feature learning for multi-modality FKP recognition. Eng. Appl. Artif. Intell. **126**, 106960 (2023)

6. Guo, Z., Zhang, D., Zhang, L., et al.: Palmprint verification using binary orientation co-occurrence vector. Pattern Recogn. Lett. **30**(13), 1219–1227 (2009)
7. Zhang, D., Lu, G., Zhang, L., et al.: Finger-knuckle-print verification. Adv. Biometrics 85–109 (2018)
8. Gao, C., Yang, Z., Ng, T.S., et al.: Cross-Chirality Palmprint Verification: Left is Right for the Right Palmprint. arXiv preprint arXiv:2409.13056 (2024)
9. Li, S., Fei, L., Zhang, B., et al.: Hand-based multimodal biometric fusion: a review. Inf. Fusion 102418 (2024)
10. Hong, H.G., Lee, M.B., Park, K.R.: Convolutional neural network-based finger-vein recognition using NIR image sensors. Sensors **17**(6), 1297 (2017)
11. Kim, W., Song, J.M., Park, K.R.: Multimodal biometric recognition based on convolutional neural network by the fusion of finger-vein and finger shape using near-infrared (NIR) camera sensor. Sensors **18**(7), 2296 (2018)
12. Cheng, K.H., Kumar, A.: Accurate 3D finger knuckle recognition using auto-generated similarity functions. IEEE Trans. Biometrics Behav. Identity Sci. **3**(2), 203–213 (2021)
13. Li, S., Zhang, B., Fei, L., et al.: Learning sparse and discriminative multimodal feature codes for finger recognition. IEEE Trans. Multimedia **25**, 805–815 (2021)
14. Li, S., Zhang, B., Fei, L., et al.: Joint discriminative feature learning for multimodal finger recognition. Pattern Recogn. **111**, 107704 (2021)
15. Aliraid, R., Ouamane, A.: A novel descriptor (LGBQ) based on gabor filters. Multimedia Tools Appl. **83**(4), 11669–11686 (2024)
16. Chen, P., Li, W., Sun, L., et al.: LGCN: learnable gabor convolution network for human gender recognition in the wild. IEICE Trans. Inf. Syst. **102**(10), 2067–2071 (2019)
17. Misra, D., Nalamada, T., Arasanipalai, A.U., et al.: Rotate to attend: convolutional triplet attention module. In: IEEE/CVF Winter Conference on Applications of Computer Vision, pp. 3139–3148 (2021)
18. Liang, X., Yang, J., Lu, G., et al.: Compnet: competitive neural network for palmprint recognition using learnable gabor kernels. IEEE Signal Process. Lett. **28**, 1739–1743 (2021)
19. Zhang, L., Zhang, L., Zhang, D.: Finger-knuckle-print: a new biometric identifier. In: IEEE International Conference on Image Processing, pp. 1981–1984 (2009)
20. Kingma, D.P., Ba, J.: Adam: a method for stochastic optimization. arXiv preprint arXiv:1412.6980 (2014)
21. Gao, C., Yang, Z., Zhu, M., et al.: Scale-aware competition network for palmprint recognition. In: IEEE International Conference on Acoustics, Speech and Signal Processing, pp. 4580–4584 (2024)
22. Attia, A., Mazaa, S., Akhtar, Z., et al.: Deep learning-driven palmprint and finger knuckle pattern-based multimodal person recognition system. Multimedia Tools Appl. **81**(8), 10961–10980 (2022)
23. Song, J.M., Kim, W., Park, K.R.: Finger-vein recognition based on deep densenet using composite image. IEEE Access **7**, 66845–66863 (2019)
24. Yang, Z., Xia, W., Qiao, Y., et al.: CO3Net: coordinate-aware contrastive competitive neural network for palmprint recognition. IEEE Trans. Instrum. Meas. (2023)
25. Yang, Z., Huangfu, H., Leng, L., et al.: Comprehensive competition mechanism in palmprint recognition. IEEE Trans. Inf. Forensics Secur. (2023)

Fingerprint Revocable Template Protection of Variable Window-Based Random Permutation && Check Code

Zilong Xu[1,2], Weixin Bian[1,2(✉)], Yao Hu[1,2], and Feng Luo[1,2]

[1] School of Computer and Information, Anhui Normal University, Wuhu 241002, Anhui, China
bwx2353@ahnu.edu.cn
[2] Anhui Provincial Key Laboratory of Network and Information Security, Wuhu 241002, Anhui, China

Abstract. The Uniformly Random Permutation Hashing (URP-IoM) algorithm demonstrates reliable performance and irreversibility in biometric template protection. However, URP-IoM, through random permutation and Hadamard product computation, fails to retain the local features of the original feature vector, which can negatively impact recognition rates and result in varying performance across different datasets. Addressing the impact of biometric template revocability on recognition rates and performance, this paper proposes a novel revocable template method for fingerprint biometrics, called Variable Window-Based Random Permutation IoM Hashing&&Check Code (VWP-IoM&&CC). This method first generates variable windows and check codes based on the Euclidean features of the user password and original feature vector, then records the maximum index of the Hadamard product under the variable window. Finally, it combines the maximum index value with the check code. Experimental results show that the VWP-IoM&&CC algorithm improves recognition rates and performance in FVC2002 and FVC2004 (DB1, DB2), and also meets the requirements of revocability and unlinkability.

Keywords: cancelable template protect · security and privacy · Euclidean Locality Sensitive Hashing · fingerprint

1 Introduction

With the development of recognition technology, an increasing number of identity authentication systems are gradually relying on users' biometric characteristics to verify personal identity, replacing traditional token and password authentication. However, while the application of biometric features is widespread, their

---

Supported by the Natural Science Foundation of Anhui Province (Grant No. 2108085MF206) and the National Natural Science Foundation of China (Grant No. 61976006).

© The Author(s), under exclusive license to Springer Nature Singapore Pte Ltd. 2025
S. Yu et al. (Eds.): CCBR 2024, LNCS 15352, pp. 25–35, 2025.
https://doi.org/10.1007/978-981-96-1068-6_3

uniqueness and irrevocability pose significant risks. If biometric data is stolen by malicious individuals, it can lead to irreversible damage [1]. To address the security and privacy concerns in biometric recognition systems, a feasible solution is cancelable biometrics [2]. This technique involves mapping biometric features into a transformed domain through irreversible changes, with matching performed within this domain. Different biometric templates can be obtained by changing parameters. In 2001, Ratha et al. [3] introduced the concept of Cancelable Biometrics (CB). In 2015, Patel et al. [4] further defined cancelable biometrics as the purposeful, repeatable distortion of biometric information through irreversible transformations for template comparison in the transformed domain. CB must meet the requirements of irreversibility, unlinkability, revocability, and performance.

Jin et al. [5] proposed two algorithms based on sensitive hash functions: the Gaussian Random Projection-based Index-of-Max Hashing (GRP-IoM) and the Uniform Random Permutation-based IoM Hashing (URP-IoM). These schemes possess reliable irreversibility and good unlinkability. However, the URP-based template uses a fixed window k value, which makes it difficult to maintain local features and is significantly affected by different fingerprint databases [6]. To avoid the impact of a fixed window k value while maintaining the revocability, irreversibility, unlinkability, and performance of the template, a new method based on generic salt cancelable biometric templates was proposed, called Variable Window-Based Random Permutation IoM Hashing& & Check Code (VWP-IOM&&CC). This scheme preserves both local and global attributes of biometric features, aligns with the definition of locality-sensitive hashing, and reduces template errors.

2 Proposed Scheme

The IOM hashing takes fixed-length fingerprint vectors as input. This section first briefly introduces the generation of fingerprint vectors, then explains the method and implementation of Variable Window-Based Random Permutation IoM Hashing & &Check Code (VWP-IOM & CC).

In this paper, fingerprint vectors are extracted using the method proposed in [7]. The construction of fingerprint vectors involves three main steps: first, minutiae descriptors are extracted using the Minutiae Cylinder Code (MCC) [8]. Then, KPCA (Kernel Principal Component Analysis) is applied, using a fixed-length representation technique to convert the extracted feature descriptors into fixed-length vectors. Finally, feature binarization is performed. Since IOM hashing uses real-valued vectors as input, the binarized features are discarded.

Locality-Sensitive Hashing (LSH) is a technique used to find similar data in high-dimensional spaces. The basic idea is to map similar data items into the same hash buckets, with the number of buckets being much smaller than the number of input items, thereby allowing for quick location of similar data during a search. The primary goal of LSH is to maximize the probability of "collisions" for similar items. A family of LSH functions maps data points from

$\mathbb{R}^d$ to "buckets" $b \in B$, i.e., $\mathbb{R}^d \xrightarrow{h_i} b$. For any two given points $X, Y \in \mathbb{R}^d$, the following conditions hold:

$$\mathbb{P}_{h \in H}[h_i(X) = h(Y)] \leq P_1 \quad \text{if} \quad S(X,Y) < R_1$$

$$\mathbb{P}_{h \in H}[h_i(X) = h(Y)] \geq P_2 \quad \text{if} \quad S(X,Y) > R_2 \tag{1}$$

where $P_2 > P_1$, $S(\cdot)$ is a similarity function, and $H = \{h : \mathbb{R}^d \to U\}$ where U is the hash metric space dependent on the similarity function S. The index i refers to the number of hash functions $h(\cdot)$.

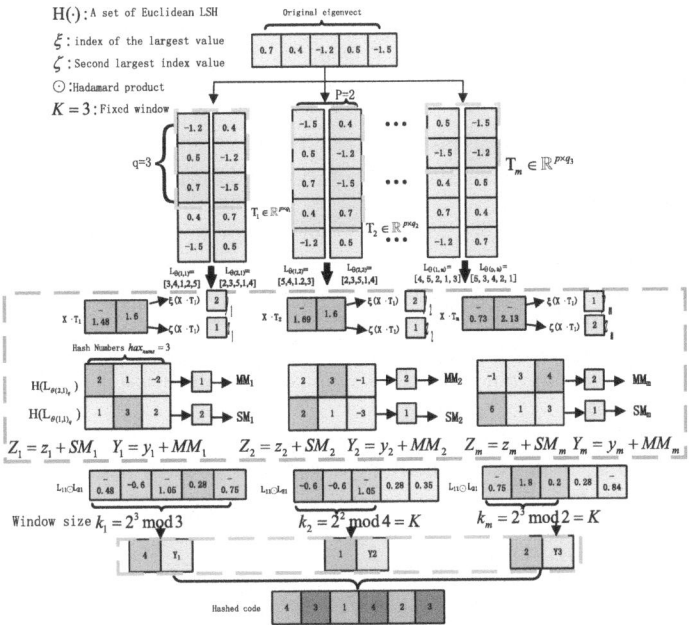

Fig. 1. Variable Window-Based Random Permutation IoM Hashing && Check Code

Based on the theory of Locality-Sensitive Hashing (LSH), Jin et al. [5] proposed the URP-IoM algorithm. First, the user token matrix is combined with the original feature vector to generate a random permutation vector $L(p,m)$. Second, each group of random permutation vectors undergoes a Hadamard product. Finally, the top few positions of the resulting vector, based on window size, are selected, and the indices of their maximum values are obtained. However, this method only considers the maximum index of a fixed window size k, which introduces some errors and performs poorly on different fingerprint databases. To preserve more properties of the original features, the VWP&&CC method generates a variable k value based on fingerprint information as the window size for the Hadamard product operation, capturing macroscopic information.

Then, Euclidean LSH [9] is used to calculate the check code and check the local information. These two maximum indices and the check code form the VWP hash code. This approach effectively retains the properties of the original feature vector, enhancing the stability of the hashing result. The framework of the VWP-IOM algorithm is shown in Fig. 1. The specific steps are as follows:

Algorithm 1: Variable Window-Based Random Permutation IoM Hashing && Check Code

---

Input: Feature vector $\hat{x}$, dimension **d**, order of Hadamard product p, number of random permutations m, element count **q**, number of hash functions hax_{nums}
For each permutation set $\theta_{(l,i)} \mid l = 1, \ldots, p; i = 1, \ldots, m$
For random sequences $Q_{(q_i)} \mid q_i \in [2, d]; i = 1, \ldots, m$
Step 1: Permute the feature vector $\hat{x}$ using permutation $\theta_{(i,l)}$, obtaining permuted vector $L_{\theta(p,i)}$.
Step 2: Initialize the i^{th}th hash code $t_i = 0$.
Step 3: Hadamard product vector generation and output check code
for $i = 1$ to m
 for $l = 1$ to p:
  temp$[l]$ $=< \hat{x}_{q_i}, L_{\theta(l,i)_{q_i}} >$
 end for
 y_i = maxvalue-index(temp), z_i = secvalue-index(temp) $y_i, z_i \in [1, p]$.
 mmi, smi = Hashvec($L_{\theta(y_i,i)_q}, hax_{nums}$), Hashvec($L_{\theta(z_i,i)_q}, hax_{nums}$)
 MMi, SMi = maxvalue-index(mmi), maxvalue-index(smi)
 Y_i = MMi + y_i.
 Z_i = SMi + z_i.
 Transform Z_i to $k_i = 2^{Z_i}$ mod (q_i).if $k_i \leq 1$ or $\geq d$,$k_i = K$
 for $j = 1$ to k_i
  Set $\overline{x}(j) = \prod_{l=1}^{p} (L_{\theta(1,l)}(j))$.
  If $\overline{x}(j) > \overline{x}(t_i)$ then set $t_i = j$.
 end for
end for
Output the hash codes: $t_{URP} = \{t_i \in [1, k_i] \mid i = 1, \ldots, m\}$.
Output the check codes: $t_{cc} = \{Y_i \in [1, hax_{nums}] \mid i = 1, \ldots, m\}$.

---

1. Random Mapping and Permutation: Generate a random matrix $A \in \mathbb{R}^{d \times d}$ based on the user's token, with the same dimension as the original fingerprint vector x. Compute the inner product of the original feature vector and the random matrix A to obtain the mapped vector $\hat{x} \in \mathbb{R}^d$. Generate a random sequence $Q_{(q_i)} \mid q_i \in [2, d]; i = 1, \ldots, m$ based on the permutation token.
2. Generate Permutation Set: Generate the permutation set $\theta_{(l,i)}$ based on the permutation token, where $L_{\theta(l,i)} \mid l = 1, \ldots, p$ are the permuted vectors of $\hat{x} \in \mathbb{R}^d$.
3. Generate Random Window: Obtain the first q_i elements from the original vector and the permuted vectors $\mathbf{x}, L_{\theta(1,i)}, \ldots, L_{\theta(p,i)}$. Compute the inner

products $< \mathbf{x}_{q_i}, L\theta(1,i)_{q_i} >, \ldots, < \mathbf{x}_{q_i}, L\theta(p,i)_{q_i} >$ and identify the indices of the maximum and the second maximum values, $y_i, z_i \in [1, p]$. Hash $L\theta(y_i, i)q$ and $L\theta(z_i, i)q$ using hax_{nums} hash functions to get the indices of the maximum values ($MMi, SMi \in [1, hax_{nums}]$). Compute $Y_i = MMi + y_i$ and $Z_i = SMi + z_i$. Calculate the random window $k_i = 2^{Z_i} \mod (q_i)$ and if $k_i \leq 1$ or $\geq d$, $k_i = K$

4. Hadamard Product Vector Generation: Generate the p-order Hadamard product vector by performing element-wise multiplication on the p permuted vectors: $\overline{\mathbf{x}}(j) = \prod_{l=1}^{p} (L_{\theta(1,l)}(j)) \in \mathbb{R}^d$.
5. For each $\overline{\mathbf{x}}$, select the first k_i elements.
6. Record Maximum Value Index: Record the index of the maximum value among the first k_i elements, and store the index as $t \in [1, k_i]$.
7. Repeat steps 2 to 6 for different permutation sets $\theta_{(l,i)} \mid l = 1, \ldots, p$. Construct the Variable Window-Based IoM hash codes $t_{VWP} = t_i \in [1, k_i] \mid i = 1, \ldots, m$ and the check codes $tcc = Y_i \in [1, hax_{nums}] \mid i = 1, \ldots, m$.

2.1 Matching of IoM Hashed Codes

The VWP-IOM&&CC hashing follows a ranked LSH method, ensuring a high collision probability for two fingerprint vectors with high similarity in the transformed domain. Conversely, if the two vectors are significantly different, the collision probability decreases. For example, consider two hash codes, the registration instance $t^e = \{t_i^e | i = 1 \ldots m\}$ and the verification instance $t^q = \{t_i^q | i = 1 \ldots m\}$. Let $S(t^e, t^q)$ denote the collision probability of the two hash codes. If $\mathbb{P}[t_i^e = t_i^p] - S(t^e, t^q) \leq \tau$ for $i = 1 \ldots m$, and if τ is sufficiently small, it indicates a higher collision probability and greater similarity between the two hash codes. Otherwise, the collision probability decreases, indicating less similarity.

For VWP-based IoM, $S_{VWP}(\cdot, \cdot)$ is a rank correlation measure. In other words, rank correlation refers to a measure of ordinal association based on the relative ordering of values within a given range. The rank correlation expression function PO can be formulated as:

$$S_{VWP}(t^e, t^q) = PO(t^e, t^q) \approx \frac{\sum_{i=0}^{m-1} \left(\frac{R_i(t^e, t^q)}{k_i - 1} + \frac{R_i(t^e, t^q)}{hax_{nums} - 1} \right)}{d/k_i + d/hax_{nums}} \quad (2)$$

where $R_i(t^e, t^q)$ represents the number of items at the i-th position in t^e and t^q that have the same order relationship.

In Eq. 2, the index i can enumerate the maximum in a permutation window of size k_i as follows: within this window, one can choose $k - 1$ entries that are smaller than the entry at position i, and that are common to both t^e and t^q. This also indicates the collision probability of a pair of URP-based hash codes. Similarly, the matching score is obtained simply by counting the number of items with the same order relationship in t^e and t^q and dividing by $2m$.

3 Experimental Results and Analysis

To evaluate the performance of the proposed revocable biometric template, we conducted experimental assessments using four publicly available fingerprint datasets: FVC2002 DB1, FVC2002 DB2, FVC2004 DB1, and FVC2004 DB2. Each dataset comprises 800 grayscale fingerprint images collected from 100 different fingers (corresponding to 100 users), with 8 samples taken from each finger. Following the methodology outlined in reference [4], the first 3 fingerprints of each finger were utilized as the training set, while the subsequent 5 fingerprints were used for testing. This resulted in 500 samples ($100 \times 5 = 500$ samples) of fixed-length biometric feature strings, each of length 299. According to the literature, each dataset allows for the generation of 1000 ($100 \times C_5^2$) genuine match scores and 4950 (C_{100}^2) impostor match scores, calculated based on five different keys (tokens) to compute the average Equal Error Rate (EER).

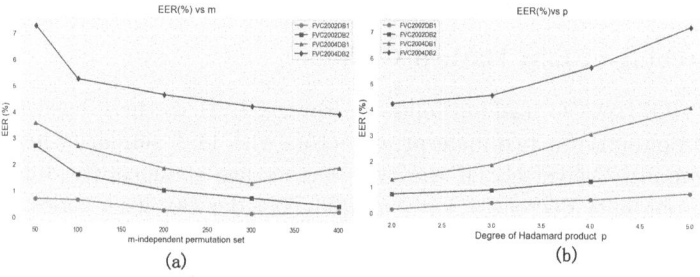

Fig. 2. (a) The curves of "EER (%) vs m-independent permutation set" for FVC2002 and FVC2004 (DB1, DB2). (b) The curves of "EER (%) vs p-Degree of Hadamard product" for FVC2002 and FVC2004 (DB1, DB2).

3.1 The Parameters Of VWP-IoM&&CC

The impact of the order p of the Hadamard product, the number of permutation sequences m, and the number of hash functions: For the URP-based IoM, we first study the impact of the number of permutation sequences m and the order p of the Hadamard product on performance from the perspective of EER. In the experiments, we vary the value of m from 50, 100, 200, 300, to 400 while fixing p at 2, and the value of hax_{nums} at 16. We then vary the value of p from 2, 3, 4, to 5 while fixing m at 300 and hax_{nums} at 16.

Figure 2 shows the "EER(%)-vs-k" and "EER(%)-vs-p" curves on FVC2002 (DB1, DB2) and FVC2004 (DB1, DB2). We can observe that:

1. As expected, an increase in m leads to better EER, and it tends to stabilize with larger m. The randomization process can be considered as part of the hash function, so the constructed random permutation vectors approximate a Gaussian distribution with sufficiently large m.

2. Similarly, the smaller the value of p, the lower the EER. As shown in Algorithm 1, $\overline{\mathbf{x}}(j) = \prod_{l=1}^{p}\left(L_{\theta(1,l)}(j)\right)$. Increasing the value of p increases the distortion caused by noise. Therefore, it is expected that performance will degrade as p increases.
3. The performance of hax_{nums} mainly depends on the performance of Euclidean LSH. In the experiments, we fixed $m = 300$ and $p = 2$, and varied the values of (hax_{nums}, q) from $(8, 3)$, $(10, 4)$, $(12, 5)$, $(14, 6)$, to $(16, 7)$. We found that the overall EER values did not change significantly, so within a certain range, we can set the value of hax_{nums} within a reasonable range to enhance efficiency and greatly reduce computational and storage costs.

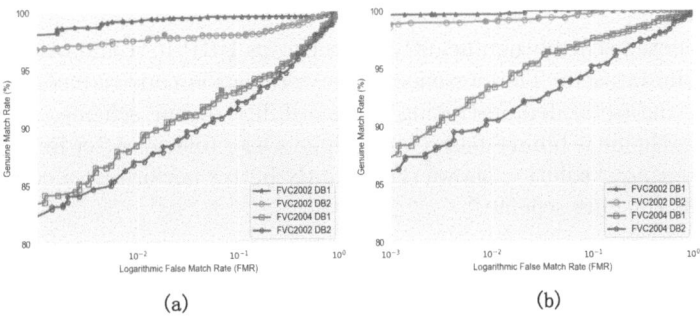

Fig. 3. (a) ROC Curves of URP-IOM on Four Datasets, (b) ROC Curves of the Proposed Method on Four Datasets

Table 1. Performance Accuracy (Average EER %) and Comparison

Scheme	EER (%) for FVC2002		EER (%) for FVC2004	
	DB1	DB2	DB1	DB2
MCC(Original) [5]	0.60	0.59	3.79	5.22
URP-IoM [3]	0.43	2.10	4.15	8.20
GRP-IoM [3]	0.22	0.47	4.74	4.1
Bloom filter [10]	2.3	1.8	13.4	8.1
WSE Hashing [11]	0.2	0.62	2.6	7.12
Abdullahi [3]	0.38	1.16	2.42	7.13
Proposed ($m = 300, p = 2, hax_{mums} = 16$)	0.26	0.72	2.78	4.23
Proposed (genuine token)	0.11	0.24	0.88	1.56

3.2 Performance Evaluation

In this section, we conduct performance experiments on FVC2002 (DB1, DB2) and FVC2004 (DB1, DB2) using the best parameters adjusted in the previous section, simulating scenarios where user tokens are stolen. Table 1 presents the experimental results and compares them with other schemes. Figure 3 shows the ROC curves of URP-IoM and the proposed scheme using the same parameters. It can be observed that:

1. Compared to the original fingerprint vector MCC, the accuracy of the VWP-IoM-based hashing scheme is well maintained. Furthermore, the performance remains stable whether the token is stolen or the genuine token is used. This suggests that the security and privacy requirements for external tokens can be relaxed.
2. The proposed scheme significantly outperforms URP-IoM and other schemes on certain datasets. The presence of the verification code reduces instability in noisy datasets, demonstrating the feasibility of our scheme. "The WSE Hashing scheme is binary-based and employs user tokens. After implementing user tokens, our solution shows significantly better performance compared to the WSE Hashing scheme."

3.3 Safety Analysis

Unlinkability. In this section, we use the method proposed by Gomez-Barrero et al. [12] to evaluate system unlinkability by calculating local metrics $D_\leftrightarrow(s)$ and global metrics $D_\leftrightarrow^{sys}$ based on the distribution of paired/non-paired sample scores. The paired sample score distribution is calculated from the similarity matches between templates generated by the same user using different keys. In this study, the paired sample scores are generated by using different samples from the same finger of the same user with 5 different keys, resulting in a total of $100 \times C_5^2 \times 5 \times 4 = 16000$ Mated scores. The non-paired sample score distribution refers to the similarity matches between templates derived from different users using the same key. In this study, the non-paired sample scores are generated by using different users' fingerprints of the same ID finger with 5 different keys, resulting in a total of $5 \times C_{100}^2 \times 5 = 123750$ Non-Mated scores. Both $D_\leftrightarrow(s)$ and $D_\leftrightarrow^{sys}$ values range from $[0, 1]$, with smaller values indicating better unlinkability. As shown in Fig 4a, the $D_\leftrightarrow^{sys}$ value in our scheme is nearly zero, and the distribution curves of the matched and non-matched scores almost overlap. Therefore, the proposed scheme demonstrates the property of unlinkability.

Revocability. According to the revocability requirement, if biometric templates are compromised, new biometric templates can be generated by modifying the transformation parameters. For each user, 51 different templates are generated using 51 different keys and the user's first feature vector. The first template (assumed to be the compromised one) is matched against the remaining 50 templates (assumed to be updated templates), yielding a total of

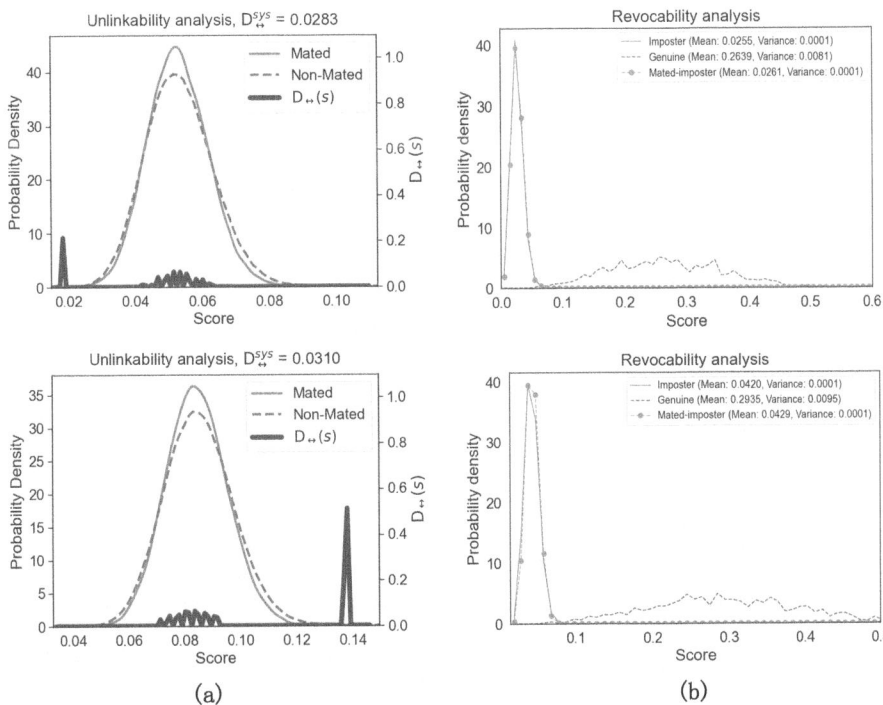

Fig. 4. (a) Unlinkability analysis by the distribution of Mated-scores and Non-mated scores on FVC2002 FVC2004 DB1. (b) Revocability analysis by the distribution of genuine, imposter and Mated-imposter scores on FVC2002 FVC2004 DB1.

5000 (50 × 100) Mated-genuine scores. The distributions of the genuine match scores, imposter match scores, and paired match scores are shown in Fig. 4b. It can be observed that the paired genuine match score curve overlaps significantly with the imposter match score curve, while the paired genuine match score curve is distinct from the genuine match score curve. This indicates that the biometric templates generated by transforming the same biometric feature with different transformation parameters are not identical. Therefore, the proposed method meets the revocability requirement.

Irreversibility Irreversibility refers to the computational difficulty of recovering fingerprint feature vectors from substitution seeds or random matrices. Suppose an attacker manages to obtain the hashed codes, tokens, and permutation seeds, and is aware of the algorithm and its corresponding parameters such as m, p, and hax_{nums}. For the VWP-IoM&&CC in discrete index form, there is no indication that an attacker can directly infer the original information of the finger vein features (real-valued features) from the stolen hashed codes. Moreover, even if the attacker knows the token (substitution seeds and projection matrix), it would not help in recovering the fingerprint feature vectors because there is no direct relationship between the token and the finger vein vectors. The attack model can only directly guess the real values, which offers no advantage.

4 Conclusion

This paper proposes a dual-factor cancelable fingerprint template protection algorithm combining Variable Window IoM and check codes, termed VWP-IoM&&CC. Both theoretical and experimental results demonstrate that, due to the advantageous properties of random projection and locality-sensitive hashing, as well as the inclusion of local Euclidean features, this approach effectively preserves the original biometric characteristics. Compared to other methods and URP-IoM, the recognition rate of the template is significantly improved. According to the experimental results, VWP-IoM&&CC also meets the standards for revocable biometric template protection.

References

1. Yin, X., Wang, S., Zhu, Y., et al.: A novel length-flexible lightweight cancelable fingerprint template for privacy-preserving authentication systems in resource-constrained IoT applications. IEEE Internet Things J. **10**(1), 877–892 (2022)
2. Dong, X., Park, J., Jin, Z., et al.: On the security risk of pre-image attack on cancelable biometrics. J. King Saud Univ.-Comput. Inf. Sci. **36**(5), 102060 (2024)
3. Ratha, N.K., Connell, J.H., Bolle, R.M.: Enhancing security and privacy in biometrics-based authentication systems. IBM Syst. J. **40**(3), 614–634 (2001)
4. Patel, V.M., Ratha, N.K., Chellappa, R.: Cancelable biometrics: a review. IEEE Signal Process. Mag. **32**(5), 54–65 (2015)
5. Jin, Z., Hwang, J.Y., Lai, Y.L., et al.: Ranking-based locality sensitive hashing-enabled cancelable biometrics: index-of-max hashing. IEEE Trans. Inf. Forensics Secur. **13**(2), 393–407 (2017)
6. Ghammam, L., Karabina, K., Lacharme, P., et al.: A cryptanalysis of two cancelable biometric schemes based on index-of-max hashing. IEEE Trans. Inf. Forensics Secur. **15**, 2869–2880 (2020)
7. Jin, Z., Lim, M.H., Teoh, A.B.J., et al.: Generating fixed-length representation from minutiae using kernel methods for fingerprint authentication. IEEE Trans. Syst. Man Cybern. Syst. **46**(10), 1415–1428 (2016)
8. Cappelli, R., Ferrara, M., Maltoni, D.: Minutia cylinder-code: a new representation and matching technique for fingerprint recognition. IEEE Trans. Pattern Anal. Mach. Intell. **32**(12), 2128–2141 (2010)
9. Datar, M., Immorlica, N., Indyk, P., et al.: Locality-sensitive hashing scheme based on p-stable distributions. In: Proceedings of the Twentieth Annual Symposium on Computational Geometry, pp. 253–262 (2004)
10. Abe, N., Yamada, S., Shinzaki, T.: Irreversible fingerprint template using minutiae relation code with bloom filter. In: 2015 IEEE 7th International Conference on Biometrics Theory, Applications and Systems (BTAS), pp. 1–7. IEEE (2015)
11. Kong, X.J., Li, X.J., Jin, Z., et al.: One-factor revocable biometric authentication method. Acta Automatica Sinica **47**(5), 1159–1170 (2021)

12. Gomez-Barrero, M., Galbally, J., Rathgeb, C., et al.: General framework to evaluate unlinkability in biometric template protection systems. IEEE Trans. Inf. Forensics Secur. **13**(6), 1406–1420 (2017)
13. Abdullahi, S.M., Lv, K., Sun, S., et al.: Cancelable fingerprint template construction using vector permutation and shift-ordering. IEEE Trans. Dependable Secure Comput. **20**(5), 3828–3844 (2022)

Direction-Guided Sparse Representation Method for Finger Vein Recognition

Lizhen Zhou[1], Lu Yang[2(✉)], Qinggang Meng[3], and Gongping Yang[3]

[1] Department of Information, ZiBo Normal College, Zibo 255130, China
[2] School of Computer Science and Technology, Shandong Jianzhu University, Jinan 250101, China
hizlz@126.com
[3] School of Software, Shandong University, Jinan 250101, China

Abstract. The extended sparse representation method is robust to image deformation and has shown promising performance in finger vein recognition. However, its large number of dictionary atoms results in high memory usage and long computation time. To address these issues, we propose a direction-guided sparse representation (DGSR) method for finger vein recognition. Our method computes the guidance direction based on rough matching results between the testing and training images, and then selects the corresponding dictionary atoms, reducing the dictionary size and computation time. Additionally, this method uses vein backbones, which are robust to noise, as image features in sparse representation. Experimental results on the open finger vein database from Hong Kong Polytechnic University demonstrate the effectiveness of the proposed method.

Keywords: Finger vein recognition · Sparse representation · Direction

1 Introduction

Finger vein recognition is a promising biometric identification method with two key advantages over traditional technologies [1]. First, finger veins are internal features, making them not easily affected by external influences and difficult to steal. Second, vein images can only be captured from living individuals, which effectively prevents spoofing attacks.

Traditional finger vein recognition methods primarily rely on image processing techniques and feature extraction algorithms [2]. Vein pattern extraction approaches, such as Repeated Line Tracking (RLT) [3], Maximum Curvature Points (MaxiC) [4], Gabor filters [5], and the Anatomy Structure Analysis-based Method (ASAVE) [6,7], focus on extract unique finger vein patterns. Local descriptor-based methods include Local Binary Pattern (LBP) [8] and its variants, as well as methods that obtain binary codes through learning [9,10]. Dimensionality reduction techniques like Principal Component Analysis (PCA) [11] and Linear Discriminant Analysis (LDA) [12] have shown promising results.

Deep learning-based finger vein recognition methods have also achieved good recognition performance [13]. For example, Shaheed et al. [14] introduced a pretrained Xception model based on deep separable convolutional neural networks for finger vein recognition. To enhance system security, Yang et al. [15] proposed a Finger-Vein Recognition and Anti-Spoofing Network (FVRAS-Net). Additionally, to address issues such as computational complexity and poor real-time performance, Shen et al. [16] developed a lightweight finger vein recognition and matching algorithm. However, deep learning methods still face challenges in terms of high computational complexity and limited timeliness, restricting their widespread application in practical scenarios.

Sparse representation theory has also been widely applied in finger vein recognition. Shazeeda et al. [17,18] proposed Mutual Sparse Representation Classification (MSRC) and methods based on Nearest Centroid Neighbor (NCN). Yang et al. [7] introduced the Sparse Reconstruction Error Constrained Low-Rank Representation (SRLRR) method, and Zhao et al. [19] developed the Progressive Sparse Representation Classification (PSRC) method for single-sample finger vein recognition. Shi et al. [20] adopted a hierarchical sparse representation method to tackle the cross-sectional finger vein recognition challenge.

Among methods based on sparse representation, the extended sparse representation method employs a sliding window approach to construct more dictionary atoms that reflect intra-class changes, thus representing possible intra-class differences. Specifically, this method uses a sliding window that moves across the training images in both horizontal and vertical directions with a predefined step size, generating image blocks to form a comprehensive dictionary. However, the large number of dictionary atoms in the extended sparse representation method leads to excessive memory usage and long computation time, consequently restricting its practical application.

To address these issues, this paper proposes a finger vein recognition method based on direction-guided sparse representation (DGSR). Unlike previous methods, which construct dictionaries using all image blocks produced by sliding windows in both horizontal and vertical directions, DGSR determines the guidance direction based on coarse match results between testing images and training images. It selects specific image blocks in the guidance direction as dictionary atoms. This approach uses fewer dictionary atoms compared to previous methods, resulting in more efficient sparse representation classification.

2 Proposed Method

The process of DGSR for finger vein recognition is illustrated in Fig. 1. We will mainly introduce the steps of obtaining the guidance direction and selecting dictionary atoms.

2.1 Obtaining the Guidance Direction

Since random finger placement on the acquisition device can lead to differences in images of the same finger, the two images to be matched must be aligned to

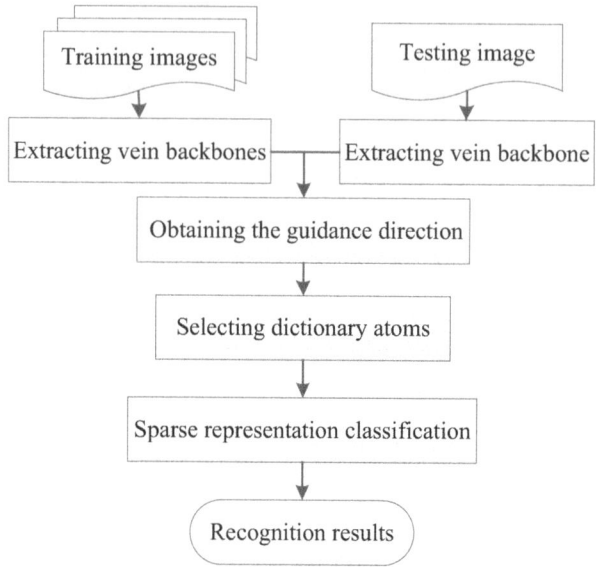

Fig. 1. Flowchart of the proposed method

achieve a high matching score. The following example discusses the matching of two images in the horizontal direction. This principle similarly applies to the vertical direction.

Quality-robust vein backbones are used as image features [6]. Let f and g represent the vein backbones of the testing and training images, respectively. As shown in Fig. 2, due to image deformation, three scenarios may occur when matching f and g:

(1) f has no displacement relative to g, and the central region of f is aligned with the central region of g, resulting in the highest matching score.
(2) f moves to the left relative to g, and the central region of f is aligned with the left region of g, resulting in the highest matching score.
(3) f moves to the right relative to g, and the central region of f is aligned with the right region of g, resulting in the highest matching score.

According to the above discussion, when the two images are displaced, matching along the direction of displacement typically results in a higher matching score. Based on this idea, the testing image is matched with various regions of the training image, and the displacement direction that yields the highest matching score is chosen as the guidance direction. The dictionary atoms are then selected along this direction, as it is closer to the testing image. The specific steps for obtaining the guidance direction are given as follows:

(1) Preprocessing. For the testing image f, we obtain its corresponding central region f^c. For the training image g, a window of the same size as f^c is

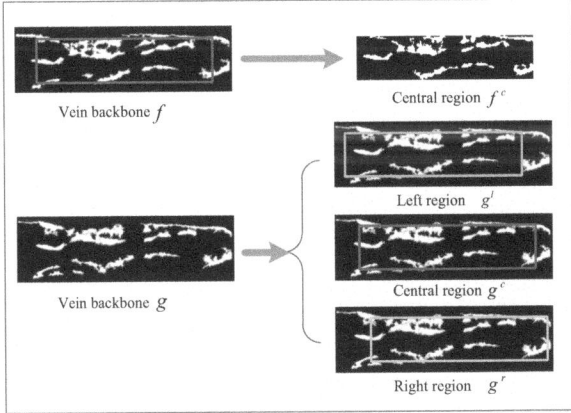

Fig. 2. Matching of two vein backbones

used to obtain the central region g^c, left-side region g^l, right-side region g^r, upper-side region g^u, and lower-side region g^d.

(2) Calculate the Maximum Matching Score. Equation (1) is used to compute the matching score s^c between g^c and f^c:

$$s^c = 1 - dis(f^c, g^c) \qquad (1)$$

where $dis(f^c, g^c)$ represents the Euclidean distance between f^c and g^c. Then, the same formula is used to calculate the matching scores s^l, s^r, s^u, and s^d between f^c and g^l, g^r, g^u, and g^d. Finally, the maximum matching score S is obtained using Eq. (2):

$$S = \max(s^c, s^l, s^r, s^u, s^d) \qquad (2)$$

(3) Obtain the Guidance Direction. The guidance direction p is determined from the maximum matching score. If $S = s^c$, there is no translation between the testing image and the training image, so $p = C$. If $S = s^l$, the training image moves leftward relative to the testing image, so $p = L$. Similarly, if $S = s^r$, the training image moves rightward relative to the testing image, so $p = R$. Likewise, if $S = s^u$, the training image moves upward relative to the testing image, so $p = U$. Conversely, if $S = s^d$, the training image moves downward relative to the testing image, so $p = D$.

The process of obtaining the guidance direction can be summarized in Algorithm 1.

Algorithm 1. Obtain the Guidance Direction

Input: Testing image vein backbone f, training image vein backbone g
Output: Guidance direction p
Step1: Obtain the central regions f^c and g^c, and the offset regions g^l, g^r, g^u, g^d.
Step2: Calculate the maximum matching score S using Equation (2).
Step3: Obtain the guidance direction.
        IF $S = s^c$
        $p = C$
        ELSEIF $S = s^l$
        $p = L$
        ELSEIF $S = s^r$
        $p = R$
        ELSEIF $S = s^u$
        $p = U$
        ELSEIF $S = s^d$
        $p = D$
        ENDIF

Return: p

2.2 Selecting Dictionary Atoms

In the generation of direction-guided dictionary atoms, a sliding window with the same size as the central region f^c of the testing image is defined. During the matching between the testing image f and the training image g, the sliding window is moved along direction p with a step size t to select dictionary atoms.

The sliding window movement area is shown in Fig. 3. We illustrate the selection of dictionary atoms in the horizontal direction as an example. If $p = C$, the window slides within the region $A_2B_2C_2D_2$. As shown in Fig. 3(a), the distance from each edge of $A_2B_2C_2D_2$ to the edges of the vein image is d. If $p = L$, the window slides within the region $A_1B_1C_1D_1$, and the distance from the right boundary of $A_1B_1C_1D_1$ to the right edge of the vein image is $2d$. If $p = R$, the window slides within the region $A_3B_3C_3D_3$, and the distance from the left boundary of $A_3B_3C_3D_3$ to the left edge of the vein image is $2d$.

2.3 Sparse Representation Classification

We calculate the sparse representation coefficients of the testing image based on the selected dictionary atoms. Using these coefficients, the testing image is reconstructed, and its category is determined by minimizing the reconstruction error. The sparse coefficients are obtained by solving the following optimization problem:

$$\min ||y - XA||_2^2 + \gamma ||A||_1 . \tag{3}$$

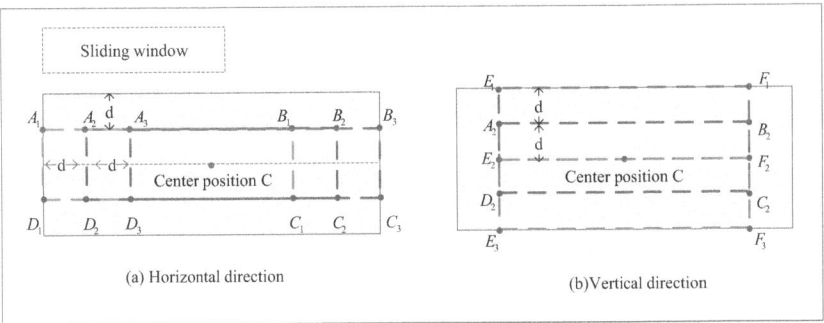

Fig. 3. Sliding window movement sketch

Here, y represents the testing image, γ is a regularization parameter that balances the reconstruction error term and the sparsity constraint term, A denotes the sparse coefficient matrix, and X represents the training image set.

Let δ_i represent the sparse coefficient vector for the i-th class of finger vein images, which is then used to reconstruct the testing image:

$$r_i = ||y - X\delta_i(\overline{a})||_2^2 \ . \tag{4}$$

If $r_k = \min r_i$, the testing image y belongs to class k.

3 Results and Discussion

3.1 Experiment Settings

The experiments use the open finger vein database from Hong Kong Polytechnic University. A total of 156 volunteers participated in two imaging stages. In the first stage, 156 volunteers provided 1872 images from 312 fingers. In the second stage, 105 volunteers provided 1260 images from 210 fingers. Due to the varying number of participants, the number of images per finger varied. For our experiments, we use the 1872 images from the first stage, with 936 images for training and 936 images for testing.

All experiments are conducted in MATLAB 2018 on a computer with an Intel i5-4590 3.30 GHz CPU and 16 GB of memory. The performance of the method is evaluated using the recognition rate, which measures the accuracy of classifying finger vein images.

3.2 Comparison of Dictionary Size and Processing Time

This experiment aims to verify the advantages of DGSR in terms of dictionary size and processing time. The Extended Sparse Representation (ESR) method, which generates dictionary atoms using a sliding window moving in both horizontal and vertical directions, is used for comparison. Both methods utilize finger vein backbone images as features with identical parameter settings. In the experiment, ESR generates 49 dictionary atoms per training image, while DGSR generates only 25 dictionary atoms, reducing the dictionary size by nearly 50%. It indicates that DGSR significantly reduces the dictionary size and saves memory space.

To verify the advantage of DGSR in processing time, Table 1 presents the average processing time for the main steps of different methods. Although DGSR involves additional steps for obtaining directional guidance and selecting dictionary atoms, which take an extra 0.02 s, it requires only 0.65 s to compute the sparse coefficients for a single testing image, significantly less than ESR. The classification step in DGSR method takes 0.38 s, which is also less than the 0.96 s required by the ESR method.

Table 1. Comparison of main steps calculation time of different methods.

Method	Guidance + Dictionary Selection (s)	Sparse Coefficient (s)	Classification (s)
ESR	0	2.15	0.96
DGSR	0.02	0.65	0.38

Overall, compared to the ESR method, although the DGSR method requires some additional time for obtaining directional guidance and selecting dictionary atoms, the total processing time for a single testing image is less than that of the ESR method. This is mainly due to the significantly smaller dictionary size in DGSR, leading to reduced time for computing sparse coefficients and classification.

3.3 Parameter Settings

This experiment evaluates the impact of the region parameter d in sliding window movement on finger vein recognition performance. In this experiment, the sliding window step t is 3 pixels.

Table 2. Recognition performance with different d values

d	Number of Atoms	Recognition Rate (%)	Drop Rate (%)
$0t$	49	99.36	0
$1t$	25	99.25	0.11
$2t$	9	97.44	1.81

As shown in Table 2, under the initial settings, when $d = 0t$, the movement region overlaps with the image, and each training image generates a maximum of 49 dictionary atoms. This achieves the highest recognition rate of 99.36%, but it results in higher memory usage. When $d = 1t$, the number of dictionary atoms decreases from 49 to 25, significantly reducing the number of atoms, while the recognition rate remains at 99.25%, with only a slight drop of 0.11%. However, when $d = 2t$, the number of dictionary atoms further decreases from 25 to 9, and the recognition rate drops to 97.44%, with a larger drop of 1.81%. This indicates that generating only 9 dictionary atoms per training image may not be sufficient to effectively represent the testing image, leading to a significant performance loss.

To balance performance and memory usage, $d = 1t$ is chosen in this study. In this setting, the number of dictionary atoms is significantly reduced, and the recognition rate remains at 99.25%.

3.4 Comparison of Different Methods

This experiment compares the DGSR method with mainstream finger vein recognition methods, including: (1) Local descriptor methods: Local Binary Pattern (LBP) and Local Line Binary Pattern (LLBP). (2) Vein patterns methods: Repeated Linear Tracking (RLT), Maximum Curvature Points (MaxiC), and Gabor filtering. (3) Sparse representation methods: Mutual Sparse Representation (MSRC), Sparse Representation (SR), and Extended Sparse Representation (ESR). The recognition rates are shown in Table 3.

Table 3. Recognition rates of different methods.

Category	Method	Recognition Rate (%)
Local descriptors methods	LBP	96.58
	LLBP	93.59
Vein patterns methods	RLT	87.18
	MaxiC	88.03
	Gabor	96.79
Sparse representation methods	MSRC	94.55
	SR	93.75
	ESR	99.36
Proposed method	DGSR	99.25

The results show that DGSR has a significant advantage in recognition rate compared to methods based on local descriptors and vein patterns. This is due to DGSR's directional guidance strategy, which selects multiple image blocks as dictionary atoms using a sliding window and effectively utilizing image information and enabling a more accurate linear representation of the testing image. Additionally, using finger vein backbones as features enhances discrimination and robustness, and further improves recognition performance.

Among sparse representation methods, DGSR shows high recognition performance. Compared to traditional methods like MSRC and SR, both ESR and DGSR show higher recognition rates, with 99.36% and 99.25% respectively. This indicates that the sliding window method for obtaining dictionary atoms improves recognition rates. By extracting multiple image blocks from an image, the constructed dictionary more accurately represents testing images. In contrast, methods using the entire image as dictionary atoms limit representation capability, reducing recognition rates for some testing images. Although DGSR has significantly fewer dictionary atoms than ESR, its recognition rate has not dropped significantly. This suggests that dictionary atoms obtained through directional guidance effectively represent testing images.

4 Conclusion

In this paper, we propose the DGSR method for finger vein recognition. Our approach uses direction guidance to select specific image blocks as dictionary atoms, achieving a more efficient sparse representation. Experiments conducted on the open finger vein database from the Hong Kong Polytechnic University demonstrate that this method not only reduces the number of dictionary atoms and shortens the sparse representation computation time, but also maintains a high recognition rate. However, there is still room for improvement. The current method primarily focuses on optimizing the dictionary atoms generated by the guidance direction. Studying other effective methods for dictionary atom optimization would be a valuable direction for future research.

Acknowledgments. This work was supported in part by the National Natural Science Foundation of China under Grant 62076151, the Taishan Scholar Project of Shandong Province under Grant tsqn202211182 and Youth Innovation Team of Shandong Province Higher Education Institutions under Grant 2022KJ205.

References

1. Hou, B., Zhang, H., Yan, R.: Finger-vein biometric recognition: a review. IEEE Trans. Instrum. Meas. **71**, 1–26 (2022)
2. Sidiropoulos, G.K., Kiratsa, P., Chatzipetrou, P., Papakostas, G.A.: Feature extraction for finger-vein-based identity recognition. J. Imaging **7**(5), 89 (2021)
3. Miura, N., Nagasaka, A., Miyatake, T.: Feature extraction of finger-vein patterns based on repeated line tracking and its application to personal identification. Mach. Vis. Appl. **15**, 194–203 (2004)
4. Miura, N., Nagasaka, A., Miyatake, T.: Extraction of finger-vein patterns using maximum curvature points in image profiles. IEICE Trans. Inf. Syst. **90**(8), 1185–1194 (2007)
5. Kumar, A., Zhou, Y.: Human identification using finger images. IEEE Trans. Image Process. **21**(4), 2228–2244 (2011)
6. Yang, L., Yang, G., Yin, Y., Xi, X.: Finger vein recognition with anatomy structure analysis. IEEE Trans. Circuits Syst. Video Technol. **28**(8), 1892–1905 (2018)

7. Yang, L., Yang, G., Wang, K., Hao, F., Yin, Y.: Finger vein recognition via sparse reconstruction error constrained low-rank representation. IEEE Trans. Inf. Forensics Secur. **16**, 4869–4881 (2021)
8. Huang, Y., Yang, X., Zhou, M.: Improved LBP finger vein recognition based on RoI. Transducer Microsyst. Technol. **42**(04), 143–147 (2023)
9. Liu, H., Yang, G., Yang, L., Yin, Y.: Learning personalized binary codes for finger vein recognition. Neurocomputing **365**, 62–70 (2019)
10. Li, S., Ma, R., Fei, L., Zhang, B.: Learning compact multirepresentation feature descriptor for finger-vein recognition. IEEE Trans. Inf. Forensics Secur. **17**, 1946–1958 (2022)
11. Wu, J.D., Liu, C.T.: Finger-vein pattern identification using principal component analysis and the neural network technique. Expert Syst. Appl. **38**(5), 5423–5427 (2011)
12. Da Wu, J., Liu, C.T.: Finger-vein pattern identification using SVM and neural network technique. Expert Syst. Appl. **38**(11), 14284–14289 (2011)
13. Shadhar, A.M.: The finger vein recognition using deep learning technique. Wasit J. Comput. Math. Sci. **1**(2), 1–7 (2022)
14. Shaheed, K., et al.: DS-CNN: a pre-trained Xception model based on depth-wise separable convolutional neural network for finger vein recognition. Expert Syst. Appl. **191**, 116288 (2022)
15. Yang, W., Luo, W., Kang, W., Huang, Z., Wu, Q.: Fvras-net: an embedded finger-vein recognition and antispoofing system using a unified CNN. IEEE Trans. Instrum. Meas. **69**(11), 8690–8701 (2020)
16. Shen, J., et al.: Finger vein recognition algorithm based on lightweight deep convolutional neural network. IEEE Trans. Instrum. Meas. **71**, 1–13 (2021)
17. Shazeeda, S., Rosdi, B.A.: Finger vein recognition using mutual sparse representation classification. IET Biometrics **8**(1), 49–58 (2019)
18. Shazeeda, S., Rosdi, B.A.: Nearest centroid neighbor based sparse representation classification for finger vein recognition. IEEE Access **7**, 5874–5885 (2018)
19. Zhao, P., et al.: Single-sample finger vein recognition via competitive and progressive sparse representation. IEEE Trans. Biometrics Behav. Identity Sci. **5**, 209–220 (2022)
20. Shi, X., Yang, L., Guo, J., Ma, Y.: Cross-area finger vein recognition via hierarchical sparse representation. In: Chinese Conference on Pattern Recognition and Computer Vision, pp. 86–96. Springer, Singapore (2023)

Learning Compact Binary Codes for Few-Shot Finger Vein Recognition

Jianian Hu[1], Shuyi Li[1(✉)], Lunke Fei[2], Shuping Zhao[2], and Lifang Wu[1]

[1] School of Information Science and Technology, Beijing University of Technology, Beijing, China
syli2022@bjut.edu.cn
[2] School of Computer Science and Technology, Guangdong University of Technology, Guangdong, China

Abstract. In recent years, as a means of identity authentication, the finger-vein pattern has gradually attracted widespread attention in the academia and industry due to its unique biological characteristics, high stability, and wide applicability. Although some progress has been made in finger-vein recognition, most existing methods typically rely on much experience and require numerous labelled training samples. In order to break through this limitation, this paper develops a novel Compact Binary Code Learning (CBCL) method for few-shot finger vein identification. Specifically, a set of linear projection functions are jointly learned by training finger-vein images to convert texture information features into discriminant binary codes. Subsequently, the learned binary codes are weighted and summed to real values to generate the feature map, which realizes the adaptive learning and coding of the finger vein features. Following this, we calculate the local block histograms of each feature map and integrate them into a feature vector as the final feature representation. For testing, the texture features of the finger vein testing images are mapped to binary features for matching based on a pre-trained projection matrix. Experiments results on two SDUMLA and CAUC finger-vein databases show that the proposed CBCL method is superior to the current state-of-the-art finger vein recognition method, demonstrating its powerful feature representation ability in few-shot learning.

Keywords: Finger-vein identification · Projection functions · Compact binary code · Few-shot learning

1 Introduction

Biometrics is a technology that accurately identifies individuals based on each person's unique physiological characteristics [1]. By reason that finger-vein (FV) is located beneath the skin tissue, finger-vein recognition has higher security, higher accuracy, and better stability than other traits, such as face, ear, and fingerprint [2]. Recently, finger-vein biometrics has been well applied to various authentication scenarios, including banking and finance, access control, and device login etc. [3,4].

So far, researchers have proposed a variety of feature extraction methods to meet the needs of different application scenarios [5,6], which can be roughly classified into two categories: global features-based method and local features-based method. Typical global features-based methods include principal component analysis (PCA) [7] and linear discriminant analysis (LDA) [8]. In addition, there have been extensive studies and applications of exploiting local features to express the rich vein features. As one of the most popular and significant local features-based methods, local binary pattern (LBP) [9,10], maximum curvature [11], Gabor wavelets [12], and local graph structure (LGS) [13] have been widely applied in the finger-vein recognition community. Although recent advances have been made in finger-vein recognition, most of them are hand-crafted by design based on experience and knowledge, which are more suitable for identifying categories under the closed-set protocol. More recently, some deep learning-based finger vein recognition methods have emerged [14,15]. However, due to the small sample size of the existing finger vein databases, these deep learning-based finger vein recognition methods have been limited in the practical application. It has been proven that binary features are more effective to some intra-class changes (such as illumination and rotation variations), which can be well applied to few-shot learning. Therefore, the binary feature learning methods project the input data into discriminative space, which have been successfully applied for finger-vein and other biometrics tasks. For instance, Fei et al. [16] presented JMvFL for hand-print recognition including both finger-knuckle-print (FKP) and palmprint recognition. This method automatically and jointly learns multi-view discriminant features of hand-print. In addition, Fei et al. [17] presented a few-shot learning-based feature extraction method for finger knuckle print recognition. The proposed method outperforms the state-of-the-art FKP descriptors with few-shot training samples. Beyond that, various sparsity techniques (e.g., l_1 norm and $l_{2,1}$ norm) have been embedded into the existing learning models, obtaining satisfactory classification performances. Li et al. [18] proposed an adaptive discriminant and sparsity feature descriptor (DSFD) for FV feature extraction, which used the l_2 norm to constrain the projection matrix. Wen et al. [19] combined LDA and the $l_{2,1}$ norm to constrain the projection matrix, which is able to simultaneously perform feature extraction and feature selection.

Inspired by the binary feature learning and the $l_{2,1}$ norm, this paper introduces a novel Compact binary codes learning (CBCL) algorithm for few-shot finger-vein recognition. Figure 1 illustrates the detailed framework of the proposed CBCL. Firstly, we extract the texture local difference vector(TLDV) by Local Binary Pattern(LBP), and then use the proposed CBCL to learn a set of mapping functions to convert the TLDV into the discriminative binary codes. Then, the learned binary features are integrated into the real-valued features. Next, we calculate the block-by-block histograms and stitch them together into a global histogram as a matching final feature for finger-vein recognition.

The main contributions of this paper are as follows: (1) A new data-driven binary feature learning model (CBCL) is proposed, which can automatically extract and encode finger-vein features. (2) The proposed CBCL constrains the observations of each finger-vein sample and uses the $l_{2,1}$ norm makes the projection matrix more sparse and discriminative. (3) Experimental results showed that our CBCL is superior to the existing methods in open-set finger vein recognition.

2 Proposed Approach

Let $\boldsymbol{X} = [x_1, x_2, ..., x_n] \in \mathbb{R}^{d \times m}(m = np)$ is a set of n finger-vein samples, where $x_n \in \mathbb{R}^{d \times p}$ is the texture local difference vector (TLDV) extracted from the n-th finger-vein ROI image by using the Local Binary Pattern(LBP) templates. d represents the dimension of the TLDV features and p denotes the image size ($row \times column$) of an image. By using LBP, we compare the gray value relationship between the target pixel and its neighborhood pixels to generate a unique LBP code that reflects the local texture pattern of the area. Figure 2 illustrates how to extract the TLDV from a local patch of a finger-vein image. In Fig. 2, for each target pixel, we empirically select the 5×5 adjacent pixels and Given a finger-vein patch, we first obtain the response results by convolving the original image and LBP templates. Next, the TLDV for each target pixel is generated by calculating the difference between the center pixel and the neighborhood pixel. Assuming CBCL jointly learns k mapping functions of $\boldsymbol{P} = [p_1, p_2, ..., p_k] \in \mathbb{R}^{d \times d}$ associated with the TLDV features x_n to accurately approximate the binary features. Then, CBCL can automatically learn the binary code instead of using the empirical thresholding method. Let p_k is the learned projection vector for the kth function, the binary code $y_{n,k}$ of x_n can be obtained by quantifying it as

$$y_{n,k} = \text{sgn}(p_k^T x_n + q_n), \quad (1)$$

where $y_{n,k} \in \{0, 1\}^k$ is the kth learned binary codes and q_n denotes the projection regularization of the nth sample. If the value of $z \geq 0$, sgn(z) equals to 1, otherwise, sgn(z) equals to -1. Let $Q = [q_1, q_2, ..., q_n]$, $Y = [y_1, y_2, ..., y_n]$, the objective function of (1) can be rewritten in matrix form as:

$$Y = \text{sgn}(P^T X + Q), \quad (2)$$

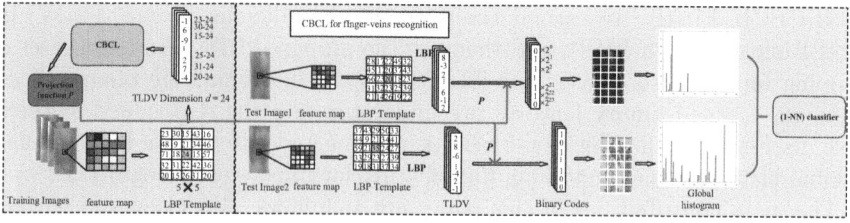

Fig. 1. The basic idea of CBCL for finger-vein recognition.

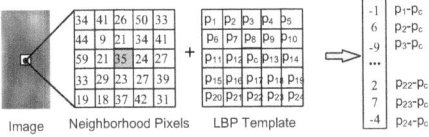

Fig. 2. An example of how to obtain the TLDV in a finger-vein image.

2.1 The Proposed CBCL

By introducing constraints earlier, this model aims to hold the following properties: (1) The Euclidean distance of the projected intra-class samples should be minimized, at the same time, the Euclidean distance of the projected inter-class samples should be maximized. (2) The sparse feature selection matrix is helpful to select more important and compact features, and the separability of the data can be improved by the constraints on the $l_{2,1}$ norm. In this case, the overall objective function can be represented as:

$$\min_{p_k,q_n} \sum_{k=1}^{K} (\sum_{i,j \in \text{Intra-class}} \|y_{i,k} - y_{j,k}\|^2 - \sum_{i,j \in \text{Inter-class}} \|y_{i,k} - y_{j,k}\|^2)$$
$$+ \lambda_1 \|P\|_{2,1} + \frac{\lambda_2}{2} R(Y,Q), s.t. y_{n,k} = \text{sgn}(p_k^T x_n + q_n) \quad (3)$$

where **Intra − class** denotes the samples from the same category and **Inter − class** represents the samples from different categories. $R(Y,Q)$ is a regularization term to avoid overfitting.

Suppose C is a binary matrix that expresses the relationships between the intra-class and inter-class images. Specifically, if the two images belong to same category (**Intra − class**), C is set to 1, otherwise, C is set to -1. Let $Y = [y_1, y_2, ..., y_n]$ be the projected binary matrix, Eq. (3) can be rewritten in matrix form as:

$$\min_{P,Q} \|Y \cdot C\|_F^2 + \lambda_1 \|P\|_{2,1} + \frac{\lambda_2}{2} R(Y,Q), s.t. Y = \text{sgn}(P^T X + Q) \quad (4)$$

where λ_1 and λ_2 are two positive weighting parameters to balance the contributions of the relative constraint terms, $\|P\|_{2,1} = \sum_{i=1}^{d} \sqrt{\sum_{j=1}^{d} p_{i,j}^2}$ denotes the $l_{2,1}$ norm.

Within Eq. (4), the proposed CBCL aim to learn the projection matrix P, the projection error Q, and two hyperparameters. By minimizing the objective population function, we achieve two core goals: one is to minimize the error in the projection process, and the other is to minimize the distance between the same category of data and maximize the distance between different categories of data.

2.2 Optimization

To find the local optimal solution of Eq. (4), we use Alternating Direction Method of Multipliers(ADMM) to iteratively update each variable in sequence until the objective function converges. By introducing the Lagrange multipliers M, Eq. (4) can be converted into the following augmented Lagrange function:

$$\mathcal{L}(P,Q,Y,M) = \|Y \cdot C\|_F^2 + \lambda_1 \|P\|_{2,1} + \frac{\lambda_2}{2}(\|Y\|_F^2 + \|Q\|_F^2) \\ + <M, Y - P^T X - Q> + \frac{\delta}{2}\|Y - P^T X - Q\|_F^2. \quad (5)$$

where $M \in \mathbb{R}^{n \times d}$, $\delta > 0$ is a penalty parameter.

Update Q: When P, Y is fixed, problem (5) becomes

$$\mathcal{L}(Q) = \frac{\lambda_2}{2}\|Q\|_F^2 + \|Y - P^T X - Q + \frac{M}{\delta}\|_F^2. \quad (6)$$

Let the partial derivative of $\mathcal{L}(Q)$ with respect to Q to 0, we obtain

$$Q = \frac{2}{2 - \lambda_2}(Y - P^T X + \frac{M}{\delta}), Q = max(0, Q) \quad (7)$$

Update P: When Q, Y is fixed, problem (5) becomes

$$\mathcal{L}(P) = \lambda_1 \|P\|_{2,1} + \|Y - P^T X - Q + \frac{M}{\delta}\|_F^2. \quad (8)$$

Let the partial derivative of $\mathcal{L}(P)$ with respect to P to 0, we obtain

$$P = (\lambda_1 D + 2XX^T)^{-1} X \cdot U^T. \quad (9)$$

where $U = Y - Q + \frac{M}{\delta}$, D is defined as $D = \begin{bmatrix} \frac{1}{\|P_1\|_2} & \cdots & 0 \\ 0 & \cdots & 0 \\ 0 & 0 & \frac{1}{\|P_k\|_2} \end{bmatrix}$.

Update Y: When P, Q is fixed, problem (5) becomes

$$\mathcal{L}(Y) = \|Y \cdot C\|_F^2 + \frac{\lambda_2}{2}\|Y\|_F^2 + \|Y - P^T X - Q + \frac{M}{\delta}\|_F^2. \quad (10)$$

Let the partial derivative of $\mathcal{L}(Y)$ with respect to Y to 0, we obtain

$$Y = \frac{\lambda_2 + 4}{2}(P^T X + Q - \frac{M}{\delta}), Y = max(0, Y) \quad (11)$$

Update M and δ:

$$M = M + \delta(Y - P^T X - Q) \quad (12)$$

$$\delta = min(\rho, \delta, \delta_{max}) \quad (13)$$

where ρ and δ_{max} are constants.

By continuously updating variables and ultimately converging Eq. (5) or a preset maximum number of iterations is achieved, we can learn the mapping function P.

2.3 CBCL-Based Finger-Vein Recognition

In this subsection, we provide a detailed introduction of the proposed CBCL for finger vein recognition. For the given training and testing samples, we first use the LBP to calculate the TLDV. Then, CBCL are used to learn a projection matrix from the training samples. Based on this learned projection matrix, the TLDV features of testing images are converted into m-bit binary codes, each of which is quantified by a weight of 2^{m-1}. For example, a 6-bit binary sequence [1 0 1 1 0 0] is converted to a real value by $0\times 2^0 + 0\times 2^1 + 1\times 2^2 + 1\times 2^3 + 0\times 2^4 + 1\times 2^5 = 44$). Subsequently, we divide this real-value map into multiple non-overlapping 16×16 blocks. For each block, we extract its local histograms and combine them into a feature vector with a dimension of $256\times p$, where p represents the total number of blocks. Finally, we use the nearest neighbor (1-NN) classifier for matching by calculating the Euclidean distance between the extracted feature vectors of the two samples.

3 Experiments and Analysis

3.1 Datasets

In this section, we conducted the finger-vein identification experiments on two commonly used finger-vein datasets. (1) SDUMLA-fv [20] is a public finger vein dataset created by Shandong University, which is divided into 636 categories. This SDUMLA-fv dataset is collected from the left and right hands of 106 volunteers, with 3 fingers in each hand divided into one category, i.e. $106 \times 2 \times 3 = 636$. The size of the ROI images in this dataset has been cropped to 120×233 pixels. (2) CAUC-fv [21] was established by the Civil Aviation University of China, which consists of 5,850 images captured from 585 fingers of 195 individuals. Each individual collected the index, middle, and ring fingers of a hand. Each finger acquired ten finger-vein images. The size of the ROI images in this database has been cropped to 91×200 pixels.

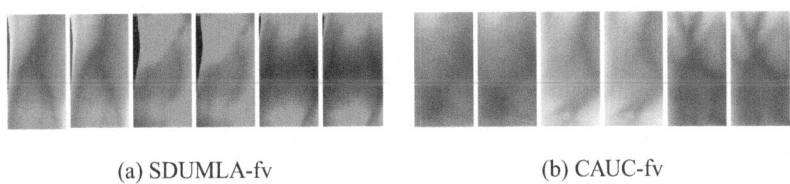

(a) SDUMLA-fv (b) CAUC-fv

Fig. 3. Some typical ROI images selected from the two datasets.

Figure 3 shows some samples of the finger-vein ROI images. In order to save storage space, the size of the finger-vein images was uniformly resized into 55×110 pixels in the two databases.

3.2 Finger-Vein Identification

Finger-vein identification is a one-to-many matching process to identify an individual. To evaluate the identification performance of the proposed algorithm, We carried out the open-set finger-vein identification experiments on two finger-vein datasets, including SDUMLA-fv [20] and CAUC-fv [21]. We provided the comparison results with the typical hand-crafted descriptors of GLBP [9], LLBP [10], Competitive [22], LLDP [23], WLGS [13], as well as the deep learning methods of VGG-F [24] and CNN-based [15]. Additionally, the advanced feature learning method JMvFL [16] and the state-of-the-art finger-vein recognition methods of DSFD [18] and CMrFD [25] also were implemented. All comparison approaches use the same matching protocol and run ten times to calculate the average identification accuracy. Table 1 shows the rank-one average accuracy (ARR) and standard deviations on the two finger-vein datasets, correspondingly. It can be clearly seen from the table that our proposed CBCL method still consistently outperforms other methods. The ARRs of our method can achieve 99.2745% on SDUMFL-fv and 100% on CAUC-fv (with Tr. = 3). This is because the data-adaptive feature learning of CBCL is more suitable for solving the open-set finger-vein biometrics problem than the manually designed descriptors.

Table 1. The rank-one identification results (%) of different methods on the SDUMLA-fv and CAUC-fv dataset.

Methods	SDUMLA-fv (Tr.=2)	SDUMLA-fv (Tr.=3)	CAUC-fv (Tr.=2)	CAUC-fv (Tr.=3)
GLBP	86.3902 ± 0.5217	90.1442 ± 0.6213	97.8502 ± 0.0845	98.9216 ± 0.0584
LLBP	83.1240 ± 0.8782	84.0286 ± 1.3243	96.4226 ± 0.1213	97.3634 ± 0.1556
Competitive	75.6202 ± 1.5616	77.3240 ± 1.0277	96.4549 ± 0.5439	96.8126 ± 0.3947
LLDP	75.7163 ± 1.2406	76.6700 ± 1.6542	95.5906 ± 0.2117	96.5643 ± 0.1739
WLGS	94.1224 ± 0.6531	95.2335 ± 0.7016	98.7932 ± 0.0925	99.1208 ± 0.0685
VGG-F	94.4256 ± 0.8942	94.8023 ± 0.0766	95.8621 ± 0.2603	97.2346 ± 0.0122
CNN-based	96.4426 ± 0.8025	96.8041 ± 1.1012	96.8178 ± 0.0149	97.9738 ± 0.0146
DSFD	97.8465 ± 1.4239	98.5922 ± 0.5876	99.8235 ± 0.1024	99.8649 ± 0.1246
JMvFL	97.2406 ± 1.6321	98.2603 ± 1.6459	99.8006 ± 0.2946	99.8509 ± 0.0533
CMrFD	93.3721 ± 1.6512	96.4344 ± 2.4522	99.5931 ± 0.1120	99.7002 ± 0.0831
CBCL(ours)	**98.5780 ± 0.8060**	**99.2745 ± 0.5271**	**100 ± 0**	**100 ± 0**

3.3 Parameters Selection

In the CBCL method, the key parameters λ_1 and λ_2 of the objective function are used to adjust the influence of different constraints. In order to explore the effect of these two parameters on performance, we conducted extensive experiments in this section, with parameters of 0.0001, 0.001, 0.01, 0.1, 1, 10, 100, 1000, and 10000. On the SDUMLA-fv dataset, we performed parameter tuning experiments. The results show that when λ_1 is in the range of [0.0001, 10000] and λ_2 is in the range of [10, 100], the system performance is stable and good. However, when λ_2 is in the range of [1000, 10000], the average accuracy decreases rapidly. Under other combinations of parameters, the performance of the system is moderate but not stable enough. For the SDUMLA-fv dataset, we recommend the optimal combination of parameters as $\lambda_1 = 1000$ and $\lambda_2 = 0.001$. Similarly, experimental results show that the system can show stable and good recognition performance on the CAUC-fv dataset when λ_1 is in the range of [0.0001, 10000] and λ_2 is in the range of [0.0001, 1000]. However, when λ_2 exceeds 1000, the average accuracy decreases significantly. For the CAUC-fv dataset, we determined that the optimal parameter combination was $\lambda_1 = 10000$ and $\lambda_2 = 0.01$. Figure 4 shows the average accuracy (%) versus parameters λ_1 and λ_2 on the (a) SDUMLA-fv and (b) CAUC-fv.

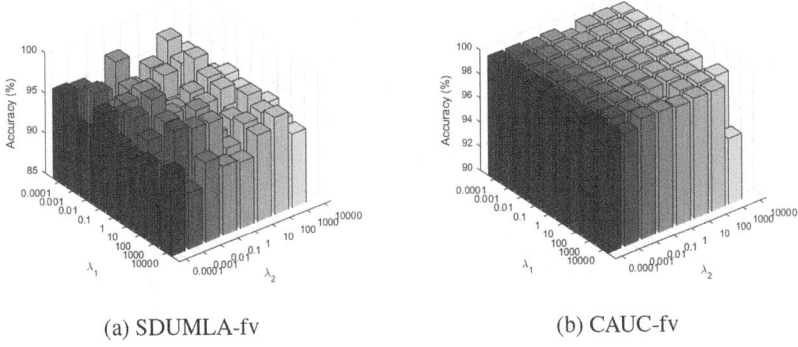

(a) SDUMLA-fv (b) CAUC-fv

Fig. 4. The average accuracy (%) versus parameters λ_1 and λ_2 on two databsets.

3.4 Convergence Study

For the previously proposed CBCL optimization problem, we use the iterative update rule to find the optimal solution. A series of experiments are carried out to verify the convergence performance of CBCL. In the experiment, we had a maximum of 90 iterations. Figure 5 illustrates the variation of the objective function value with the number of iterations, especially on the two-finger vein dataset. As can be seen from the graph, the value of the objective function decreases rapidly at the beginning and then tends to stabilize. In particular, the proposed CBCL converges extremely quickly on the two finger vein datasets, usually within 10 iterations.

3.5 Ablation Study

In order to verify the validity of different constraints in the objective function of CBCL, we compare the performance of different constraints in Table 2. When no

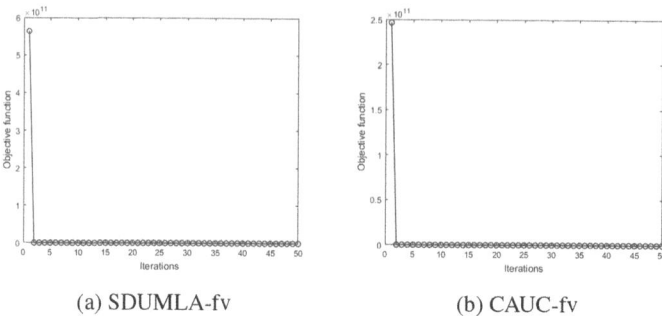

(a) SDUMLA-fv (b) CAUC-fv

Fig. 5. Objective function value versus the number of iterations on the two datasets.

sparsity constraint is applied ($\lambda_1 = 0$), the performance of CBCL changes to a certain extent. Similarly, when no regularization constraint is applied ($\lambda_2 = 0$), the performance of CBCL is affected. From the data in Table 2, it is clear that the removal of these two constraints will lead to a decrease in recognition accuracy, regardless of the two finger-vein database (SDUMLA-fv and CAUC-fv). This result proves that regularization constraint and sparsity constraint are essential to improve the recognition performance of CBCL. It is worth noting that on the two datasets of SDUMLA-fv and CAUC-fv, the recognition accuracy of CBCL decreases more significantly after removing the regularization constraint ($\lambda_2 = 0$) than that of the sparsity constraint ($\lambda_1 = 0$). This results may be since the regularization constraint has a more significant effect on improving the recognition accuracy than the sparsity constraint.

Table 2. Influences of different constraint terms.

Datasets	CAUC	SDUMLA
no sparsity ($\lambda_1 = 0$)	96.1437 ± 1.1365	95.4803 ± 1.5322
no regularization ($\lambda_2 = 0$)	95.3484 ± 1.3724	95.0551 ± 1.3448
CBCL(ours)	**100 ± 0**	**98.5780 ± 0.8060**

4 Conclusion

In this paper, we introduce a new data-driven method for open-set finger-vein recognition. Different from the manual design of feature descriptors that rely on additional prior knowledge, the proposed CBCL (Constrained Binary Coding Learning) realizes the adaptive learning and coding of finger-vein features by introducing the $l_{2,1}$ norm, so as to ensure the recognition of features. In terms of feature extraction, the CBCL method uses Gabor convolution response to capture directional difference features. In the process of feature learning, we apply constraints to the observations of the training samples, taking into account projection regularization and sparsity attributes. These features distinguish CBCL from other binary feature learning methods. Through the experimental verification of two publicly available finger-vein datasets, CBCL has excellent performance in recognition performance, surpassing the existing state-of-the-art finger-vein recognition methods.

References

1. Yang, J., Shi, Y., Jia, G.: Finger-vein image matching based on adaptive curve transformation. Pattern Recognit. **66**, 34–43 (2017)
2. Yang, L., Yang, G., Xi, X., Su, K., Chen, Q., Yin, Y.: Finger vein code: from indexing to matching. IEEE Trans. Inf. Forensics Secur. **14**(5), 1210–1223 (2018)
3. Li, S., Zhang, B.: Joint discriminative sparse coding for robust handbased multimodal recognition. IEEE Trans. Inf. Forensics Secur. **16**, 3186–3198 (2021)
4. Yang, L., Yang, G., Wang, K., Hao, F., Yin, Y.: Finger vein recognition via sparse reconstruction error constrained low-rank representation. IEEE Trans. Inf. Forensics Secur. **16**, 4869–4881 (2021)
5. Liu, H., Yang, G., Yang, L., Yin, Y.: Learning personalized binary codes for finger vein recognition. Neurocomputing **365**, 62–70 (2019)
6. Li, S., Zhang, B., Fei, L., Zhao, S.: Joint discriminative feature learning for multimodal finger recognition. Pattern Recognit. **111**, 107704 (2021)
7. Wu, J.-D., Liu, C.-T.: Finger-vein pattern identification using principal component analysis and the neural network technique. Expert Syst. Appl. **38**(5), 5423–5427 (2011)
8. Zhao, X., Guo, J., Nie, F., Chen, L., Li, Z., Zhang, H.: Joint principal component and discriminant analysis for dimensionality reduction. IEEE Trans. Neural Networks Learn. Syst. **31**(2), 433–444 (2020)
9. Peng, J., Li, Q., EL-Latif, A.A.A., Wang, N., Niu, X.: Finger vein recognition with gabor wavelets and local binary patterns. IEICE Trans. Inf. Syst. **96**(8), 1886–1889 (2013)
10. Lu, Y., Xie, S.J., Yoon, S., Park, D.S.: Finger vein identification using polydirectional local line binary pattern. In: International Conference on ICT Convergence, pp. 61–65 (2013)
11. Miura, N., Nagasaka, A., Miyatake, T.: Extraction of finger-vein patterns using maximum curvature points in image profiles. IEICE Trans. Inf. Syst. **90**(8), 1185–1194 (2007)
12. Yang, J., Shi, Y., Yang, J.: Finger-vein recognition based on a bank of gabor filters. In: Zha, H., Taniguchi, R., Maybank, S. (eds.) ACCV 2009. LNCS, vol. 5994, pp. 374–383. Springer, Heidelberg (2010). https://doi.org/10.1007/978-3-642-12307-8_35
13. Li, S., Zhang, H., Jia, G., Yang, J.: Finger vein recognition based on weighted graph structural feature encoding. In: Zhou, J., et al. (eds.) CCBR 2018. LNCS, vol. 10996, pp. 29–37. Springer, Cham (2018). https://doi.org/10.1007/978-3-319-97909-0_4
14. Zhang, R., Yin, Y., Deng, W., Li, C., Zhang, J.: Deep learning for finger vein recognition: a brief survey of recent trend. arXiv, vol. abs/2207.02148 (2022). https://api.semanticscholar.org/CorpusID:250279864

15. Das, R., Piciucco, E., Maiorana, E., Campisi, P.: Convolutional neural network for finger-vein-based biometric identification. IEEE Trans. Inf. Forensics Secur. **14**(2), 360–373 (2019)
16. Fei, L., Zhang, B., Teng, S., Guo, Z., Li, S., Jia, W.: Joint multiview feature learning for hand-print recognition. IEEE Trans. Instrum. Meas. **69**(12), 9743–9755 (2020)
17. Fei, L., Zhang, B., Wen, J., Teng, S., Li, S., Zhang, D.: Jointly learning compact multi-view hash codes for few-shot FKP recognition. Pattern Recognit. **115**, 107894 (2021). https://www.sciencedirect.com/science/article/pii/S0031320321000819
18. Li, S., Zhang, B.: An adaptive discriminant and sparsity feature descriptor for finger vein recognition. In: Proceedings of IEEE ICASSP 2021, pp. 2140–2144 (2021)
19. Wen, J., Fang, X., Cui, J., Fei, L., Yan, K., Chen, Y., Xu, Y.: Robust sparse linear discriminant analysis. IEEE Trans. Circuits Syst. Video Technol. **29**(2), 390–403 (2019)
20. Yin, Y., Liu, L., Sun, X.: SDUMLA-HMT: a multimodal biometric database. In: Sun, Z., Lai, J., Chen, X., Tan, T. (eds.) CCBR 2011. LNCS, vol. 7098, pp. 260–268. Springer, Heidelberg (2011). https://doi.org/10.1007/978-3-642-25449-9_33
21. Li, S., Zhang, H., Shi, Y., Yang, J.: Novel local coding algorithm for finger multi-modal feature description and recognition. Sensors **19**(9), 1–15 (2019)
22. Yang, W.M., Huang, X.L., Zhou, F., Liao, Q.M.: Comparative competitive coding for personal identification by using finger vein and finger dorsal texture fusion. Inf. Sci. **268**, 20–32 (2014)
23. Luo, Y.T., et al.: Local line directional pattern for palmprint recognition. Pattern Recognit. **50**, 26–44 (2016)
24. Simonyan, K., Zisserman, A.: Very deep convolutional networks for large-scale image recognition (2014). https://arxiv.org/abs/1409.1556
25. Li, S., Ma, R., Fei, L., Zhang, B.: Learning compact multirepresentation feature descriptor for finger-vein recognition. IEEE Trans. Inf. Forensics Secur. **17**, 1946–1958 (2022)

Privacy Protection in Palmprint Recognition via Pruning Frequency Channels

Siyu Shi[1], Huikai Shao[1,2,3(✉)], and Dexing Zhong[1,4,5]

[1] School of Automation Science and Engineering, Xi'an Jiaotong University, Xi'an 710049, Shaanxi, China
[2] State Key Laboratory for Novel Software Technology, Nanjing University, Nanjing, People's Republic of China
shaohuikai@xjtu.edu.cn
[3] Xi'an Yizhanghui Technology Co., Xi'an 712000, Shannxi, China
[4] Pazhou Laboratory, Guangzhou 510335, China
[5] Research Institute of Xi'an Jiaotong University, Zhejiang 311215, China

Abstract. Palmprint recognition is an emerging biometric technology with many advantages. However, there is some sensitive personal information in palmprint images. Once accessed by unauthorized malicious third parties, it may lead to privacy breaches. Current palmprint recognition methods focus on recognition accuracy but ignore the privacy protection issue. In this paper, we propose a novel privacy-protecting palmprint recognition method, named Pruning Frequency Channels (PFC). Based on the difference in image perception between the human eye and the model, we eliminate the privacy information in palmprint images by pruning the low-frequency components that can be perceived by humans. Subsequently, we propose a pruning strategy for determining the pruned channels based on the energy of the frequency channels. We explore the impact of the energy ratio threshold on PFC performance and find an energy ratio threshold that is universal to different datasets. Adequate experiments conducted on multiple databases show that our PFC method can perform better than other methods and effectively hide personal privacy information with almost no damage to recognition accuracy.

Keywords: Palmprint recognition · Privacy protection · Frequency learning

1 Introduction

Biometrics based on physiological or behavioral characteristics for identity authentication brings us many conveniences in our daily lives [1,2]. As one of the promising biometric technologies, palmprint recognition has attracted the attention of many researchers [3]. There have been many effective palmprint recognition methods proposed for different scenarios. For example, Fei *et al.*

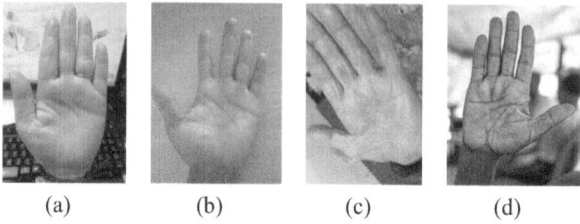

(a)   (b)   (c)   (d)

Fig. 1. Privacy information in palmprint images. (a) is a female palm, (b) is a male palm, (c) is the palm of an old lady, and (d) is the palm of a manual laborer.

[4] proposed a spectrum-invariant feature learning method for cross-spectral palmprint recognition. Some work has focused on the security and protection of palmprint recognition, such as palmprint template protection [5], palmprint anti-spoofing detection [6], and palmprint reconstruction attack [7].

In this paper, we focus on another scenario of data and security protection in palmprint recognition, *i.e.*, privacy protection in palmprint images. Currently, palmprint recognition in practical applications typically needs to be done online to get around local resource limitations and achieve high recognition accuracy. Palmprint images are collected by local devices and then uploaded to a third-party service provider, which uses Convolutional Neural Networks (CNN) for feature extraction and matching. Nevertheless, as shown in Fig. 1, the palmprint images contain some soft features, including skin color, age, gender, race, health status, and even occupation. These soft features could have been excluded from the identification. However, they have a tight connection to user privacy. Unauthorized collection and use of palmprint images by service providers may lead to serious consequences. In addition to these unregulated service providers, malicious users and hackers also pose a significant threat to privacy leakage. Therefore, in this paper, we propose a novel approach called Pruning Frequency Channels (PFC) to protect privacy information by converting palmprint images into data that cannot be interpreted by the eye.

Privacy protection in palmprint recognition is to maximize the concealment of personal privacy information in palmprint images while minimizing the reduction of recognition performance. We accomplish this goal by taking advantage of the difference in perception of images between human eyes and models: human eyes mainly perceive the low-frequency components of images because only they carry signals of significant magnitude for human eyes to recognize; while models can recognize images based on their high-frequency components [8]. Therefore, privacy-preserving palmprint recognition can be achieved by pruning the low-frequency components of images and training the neural network solely with the high-frequency components. As shown in Fig. 2, to facilitate the extraction and pruning of low-frequency components of images, we firstly apply Block Discrete Cosine Transform (BDCT) to convert palmprint image into 64 frequency channels. Then, we construct an effective strategy to prune the low-frequency channels that are closely related to privacy based on the energy of the channels.

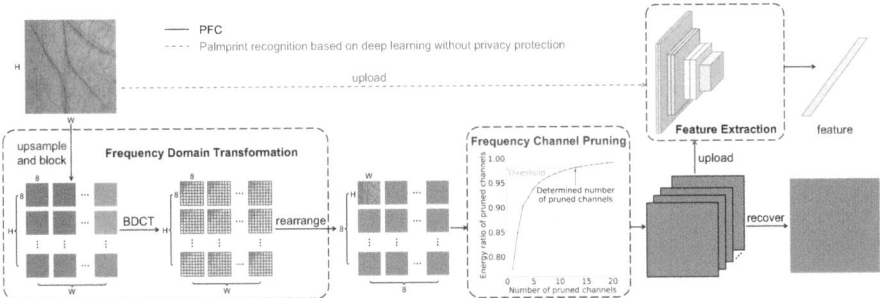

Fig. 2. Overview of PFC. The frequency domain transformation module converts the palmprint image to frequency channels. The frequency channel pruning module prunes appropriate frequency channels. The feature extraction module takes the remaining frequency channels as input and extracts the palmprint feature.

Finally, the remaining frequency channels are fed into the feature extractor. As a result, we can achieve only a slight degradation in the performance of palmprint recognition while ensuring that the image recovered from the remaining frequency channels after pruning contains almost no privacy information.

The contributions of this paper are summarized as follows:

1. A novel PFC method is proposed for privacy protection in palmprint recognition. The palmprint image is converted into a form indistinguishable to the naked eye to protect privacy without unduly compromising accuracy.
2. An advanced strategy for pruning frequency channels appropriately and effectively based on frequency channel energy is designed, which can overcome the shortcomings of pruning fixed frequency channels.
3. Adequate experiments are conducted on three benchmark databases. The results show that our method is effective in preserving the privacy features of palmprint images and can maintain acceptable accuracy.

2 Related Work

Most palmprint recognition methods focus on accuracy in various scenarios. There is some work beginning to look at privacy protection for palmprint recognition. Shao et al. [9] introduced federal learning into palmprint recognition and proposed Federal Metric Learning to address the issue of data privacy and data islands. Sardar et al. [5] proposed a Bio-Cryptosystem method for template protection in palmprint recognition. Liu et al. [10] proposed a Dynamic Random Invisible Watermark Embedding model to embed a watermark in each palmprint image and determine if the image is attacked by verifying the presence or absence of the watermark. However, there has been no research on the privacy protection of palmprint images, which is also very important in palmprint recognition.

Another line of related work is frequency learning. Transforming images from the spatial domain to the frequency domain for processing is a widely used and effective technique. For instance, the JPEG standard [11] employs the Discrete Cosine Transform (DCT) [12] to convert image data into the frequency domain, thereby achieving efficient image compression. Studies [13,14] have shown that the performance of image classification directly within the frequency domain is only slightly inferior compared to traditional classification methods carried out in the spatial domain. Ji et al. [8] further revealed a key finding: even when a few low-frequency components are removed, neural networks can still rely on the remaining frequency components to perform image recognition with high accuracy. Based on this, Mi et al. [15] pruned a fixed portion of the low-frequency components of face images and processed the remaining frequency components to perform privacy-preserving face recognition. However, different from it, our method prunes non-fixed channels according to the frequency distributions of different original images, which is more efficient and generalized.

3 Method

In this section, we will describe the framework of our proposed method for privacy protection in palmprint recognition. As illustrated in Fig. 2, our approach is primarily composed of three modules: a frequency domain transformation module, a low-frequency channel pruning module, and a feature extraction module.

3.1 Frequency Domain Transformation

For a better illustration, it is first necessary to establish some basic concepts: $\langle X, y \rangle$ denotes a data sample of a palmprint image and its corresponding label, where X is the spatial domain image and y represents the label. $\mathbf{x}$ denotes the frequency composition of X and x_i denotes its individual frequency channels. $f(\cdot; \theta)$ denotes the recognition model parameterized by θ. $\mathcal{T}(\cdot)$ denotes the frequency domain transformation and $\mathcal{T}^{-1}(\cdot)$ denotes its inverse transform. $l(\cdot, \cdot)$ is a generic loss function. In this paper, Additive Angular Margin Loss (ArcFace) [16] is adopted as $l(\cdot, \cdot)$, but other similar loss functions can also be used. ArcFace is an effective loss function in face recognition and can be defined as:

$$L_{ArcFace} = -\frac{1}{N} \sum_{i=1}^{N} \log \frac{e^{s(\cos(\theta_{y_i}+m))}}{e^{s(\cos(\theta_{y_i}+m))} + \sum_{j=1, j \neq y_i}^{n} e^{s \cos \theta_j}}, \quad (1)$$

where y_i denotes the class of the i-th sample, θ_j is the angle between the weight and the feature, m is an additive angular threshold, and s is a scaling factor. The batch size and the class number are N and n, respectively.

Our core idea is to utilize the difference in image perception between human eyes and models to train the neural network using only the high-frequency components of the palmprint image to achieve privacy protection. Therefore, we need to first convert the palmprint image to the frequency domain and then find a frequency decomposition of $\mathbf{x} = \{\mathbf{x}_l, \mathbf{x}_h\}$, where $\mathbf{x}_l$ and $\mathbf{x}_h$ are the low- and high-frequency channels, respectively, and then prune $\mathbf{x}_l$. We use BDCT as the basis of frequency domain transformation because it can decompose the spatial domain information of an image into a series of frequency channels, usually 64.

Specifically, suppose X is a grayscale image with only one spatial channel, and its shape is (H, W). We firstly use bilinear interpolation to perform an 8-fold upsampling on X, converting its shape to $(8H, 8W)$. Then, we adjust the value range of X to [-128, 127] to meet the requirements of BDCT input. Next, we divide X into $H \times W$ pixel blocks with the shape of $(8, 8)$. Subsequently, we apply a normalized, two-dimensional type-II DCT to convert each pixel block into an 8×8 frequency block with frequency coefficients ranging from -1024 to 1023. For an image block of shape (N, N), its normalized, two-dimensional type-II DCT can be represented as:

$$F(u,v) = \frac{2}{N^2} \cdot C(u) \cdot C(v) \sum_{x=0}^{N-1} \sum_{y=0}^{N-1} f(x,y) \cos\left[\frac{(2x+1)u\pi}{2N}\right] \cos\left[\frac{(2y+1)v\pi}{2N}\right], \quad (2)$$

where $f(x, y)$ is the pixel value of the original image block at coordinates (x, y) and $F(u, v)$ is the frequency coefficient of the frequency block at coordinates (u, v). $C(u)$ and $C(v)$ are normalization factors in the row and column directions. When $u = 0$, $C(u) = 1/\sqrt{2}$, otherwise $C(u) = 1$, and the same is true for $C(v)$. Finally, we reorganize all coefficients from the same frequency in each frequency block into a frequency channel shaped as (H, W) to obtain 64 frequency channels. As a result, X is turned into $\mathbf{x}$ of the form $(64, H, W)$, and each frequency channel in $\mathbf{x}$ retains the spatial structure information of the original X.

3.2 Pruning Low-Frequency Channels

Existing frequency-domain-based privacy protection methods for face recognition usually prune a fixed number of low-frequency channels [8,15]. However, the characteristics of palmprint images collected under various conditions through different devices are quite different, making it difficult to determine a universal number of pruned low-frequency channels, as shown in Sect. 4.5.

To combat this challenge, we design a method to quickly determine the number of low-frequency channels that should be pruned for different datasets. Recall that we rely on the difference in perception of visual information between human eyes and models to protect the privacy of palmprint recognition. Therefore, to determine the appropriate number of low-frequency channels to be pruned is essentially to determine which visual information should be removed: if the visual information mainly perceived by human eyes is not sufficiently removed, human eyes will be able to obtain personal privacy based on the remaining visual information; if too much visual information is removed, the model will have difficulty in recognizing palmprint based on the remaining visual information. Please note that the reason why human eyes mainly perceive visual information in the low-frequency channels is that only they have high amplitudes for human eyes to recognize. Therefore, we can determine which frequency channels contain the visual information mainly perceived by human eyes based on their amplitudes.

We use the channel energy $e(\cdot)$ to measure the amplitude of a frequency channel, which is the average value of amplitudes of all elements:

$$e(x) = \frac{1}{HW} \sum_{i=0}^{H-1} \sum_{j=0}^{W-1} \left| x^{i,j} \right| . \tag{3}$$

For a given palmprint dataset, we can easily calculate the average energy of each frequency channel. Then, we can set an energy ratio threshold t, and select σ frequency channels with the highest average energy as the pruned channels $\mathbf{x}_l$, where σ is the smallest integer that makes $\sum_{x \in \mathbf{x}_l} e(x) \geq t \sum_{x \in \mathbf{x}} e(x)$ hold.

After determining the appropriate pruned channels, we only need to change the number of input channels of the feature extractor to the number of remaining frequency channels, and then provide the remaining frequency channels $\mathbf{x}_h$ to the model. We can then use $\arg\min_\theta l(f(\mathbf{x}_h, \theta), y)$ to train the model.

4 Experiments and Results

4.1 Database

PolyU multispectral palmprint database was collected under blue light, green light, red light, and near-infrared light [17]. It can be considered as four independent datasets, denoted as PolyU-Blue, PolyU-Green, PolyU-Red, and PolyU-NIR. The images are cropped into ROIs with the size of 128 × 128 like [17].

Tongji palmprint database was collected in a contactless manner [18]. During acquisition, the position of the hand and the brightness of the lights were carefully adjusted. The ROI images of size 128 × 128 extracted from [18] are used in this paper. Throughout this paper, we abbreviate this database as Tongji.

Chinese Academy of Sciences Institute of Automation (CASIA) palmprint image database is a popular constrained palmprint dataset [19]. In this paper, we extract ROI images of size 128 × 128. Throughout this paper, we abbreviate this database as CASIA.

4.2 Implementation Details

In experiments, each category of palmprint images from each dataset is divided into training, validation, and testing sets at ratios of 60%, 15%, and 25%, respectively. ResNet18 [20] is selected as the backbone network. The energy ratio threshold t is set to 0.981. Adam optimizer is applied to train the entire model from scratch, with a batch size set to 128. Palmprint identification and verification are carried out to evaluate our method. For palmprint identification, the first palmprint image of each class in the test set is used as the registration image, and the remaining images are query images. For palmprint verification, all of the palmprint images in the test set are matched with each other. Then, the Equal Error Rate (EER) is calculated. To evaluate the privacy-preserving performance, we pad all pruned frequency channels with zero and apply the inverse transform of block DCT to restore the frequency channels provided to the model back into the spatial domain image, i.e., the recovered image $X' = \mathcal{T}^{-1}(\{\mathbf{0}, \mathbf{x}_h\})$.

Table 1. Performance of palmprint identification and verification.

Dataset	Accuracy (%)		EER (%)	
	Baseline	PFC	Baseline	PFC
PolyU-Blue	99.90	99.70	0.0029	0.1898
PolyU-Green	99.90	100.00	0.0180	0.1051
PolyU-Red	100.00	99.60	0.0048	0.1610
PolyU-NIR	100.00	99.80	0.0248	0.0585
Tongji	99.92	99.83	0.0341	0.0584
CASIA	95.03	94.68	1.9591	3.1241

4.3 Experimental Results

Recognition Performance. In order to evaluate the effectiveness of our PFC, experiments are conducted on six palmprint datasets. Table 1 shows the results, where "Baseline" means the feature extractor is directly trained by using the original grayscale palmprint ROI images. From the results, it can be seen that the maximum accuracy gap between PFC and the baseline is 0.4%, with an average accuracy gap of only 0.19%. The maximum EER gap is 1.165% and the average EER gap is only 0.27%. It indicates that the recognition performance of PFC is very close to the baseline.

Privacy Protection Performance. Figure 3 shows a set of examples of the original palmprint ROI images in the six datasets and the corresponding palmprint images recovered after PFC processing. It can be seen that, although there are significant differences in the visual features of the palmprint images in the six datasets, PFC effectively eliminates the vast majority of the human eye recognizable features of the images in all datasets and realizes excellent privacy protection, which demonstrates the excellent versatility of our method.

4.4 Energy Ratio Threshold Tuning

There is a key parameter in PFC, *i.e.*, energy ratio threshold t. We test the recognition performance and privacy protection of PFC on six datasets as t varies from 0.9400 to 0.9888, and find that if t is less than 0.9733, the privacy information cannot be adequately protected on some datasets; if t is greater than 0.9841, the accuracy of the model will significantly decrease on some datasets. When t varies between 0.9733 and 0.9846, the variation of the average recognition accuracy of the model on the six datasets is as shown in Table 2. It is evident that when $0.9798 \leq t < 0.9819$, PFC can achieve optimal recognition performance while fully protecting privacy information.

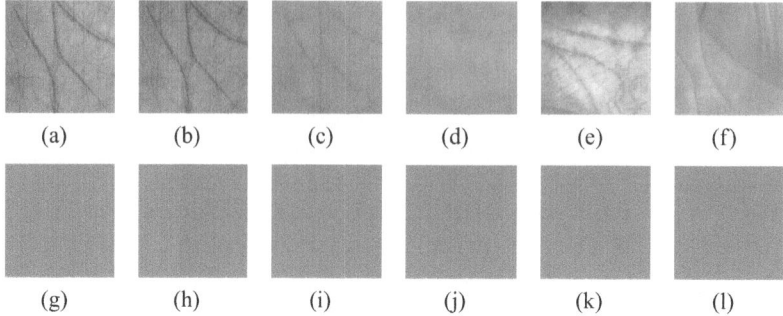

Fig. 3. Examples of original palmprint images in (a) PolyU-Blue, (b) PolyU-Green, (c)PolyU-Red, (d) PolyU-NIR, (e) Tongji and (f) CASIA and recovered images in (g) PolyU-Blue, (h) PolyU-Green, (i)PolyU-Red, (j) PolyU-NIR, (k) Tongji and (l) CASIA.

Table 2. Average accuracy on six datasets when t varies from 0.9733 to 0.9846.

The range of values of t	Accuracy (%)	The range of values of t	Accuracy (%)
$0.9733 \leq t < 0.9757$	98.74	$0.9797 \leq t < 0.9798$	98.84
$0.9757 \leq t < 0.9764$	98.76	$0.9798 \leq t < 0.9819$	98.94
$0.9764 \leq t < 0.9768$	98.81	$0.9819 \leq t < 0.9823$	98.89
$0.9768 \leq t < 0.9775$	98.84	$0.9823 \leq t < 0.9824$	98.92
$0.9775 \leq t < 0.9783$	98.88	$0.9824 \leq t < 0.9833$	98.82
$0.9783 \leq t < 0.9796$	98.84	$0.9833 \leq t < 0.9841$	98.81
$0.9796 \leq t < 0.9797$	98.81	$0.9841 \leq t < 0.9846$	98.61

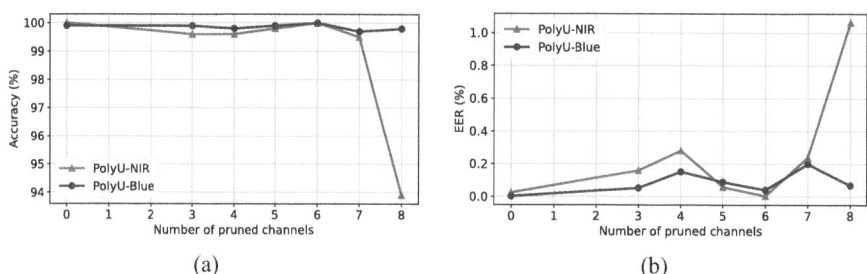

Fig. 4. Variation curves of (a) accuracy and (b) EER on PolyU-Blue and PolyU-NIR when the number of pruned channels changes.

4.5 Comparison with Other Methods

Pruning Fixed Frequency Channels. To prove the drawbacks of pruning fixed low-frequency channels, we selected two datasets, PolyU-NIR and PolyU-Blue, to test the recognition performance of the model trained with $\arg\min_\theta l(f(\mathbf{x}_h, \theta), y)$ as well as the privacy preservation effect when the number

Table 3. Comparison of different methods for palmprint identification and verification

Dataset	Accuracy (%)			EER (%)		
	Baseline	PFC	DCTDP	Baseline	PFC	DCTDP
PolyU-Blue	99.90	99.70	99.60	0.0029	0.1898	0.1947
PolyU-Green	99.90	100.00	99.30	0.0180	0.1051	0.3333
PolyU-Red	100.00	99.60	99.70	0.0048	0.1610	0.1984
PolyU-NIR	100.00	99.80	99.90	0.0248	0.0585	0.0363
Tongji	99.92	99.83	99.60	0.0341	0.0584	0.0893
CASIA	95.03	94.68	92.80	1.9591	3.1241	3.7891

of pruned low-frequency channels is gradually increased from 3 to 8. When the number of pruned low-frequency channels is less than 8, the privacy preservation effect on the PolyU-Blue dataset is not very satisfactory, as palmprints can be seen in the recovered images. However, as shown in Fig. 4(a–b), when the number of pruned low-frequency channels is 8, the model's recognition performance on the PolyU-NIR dataset is severely reduced. It can be seen that the appropriate number of pruned low-frequency channels for one palmprint dataset may not necessarily be suitable for other palmprint datasets.

Using Privacy-Preserving Face Recognition Method Directly. Based on our knowledge, there is currently no method for privacy protection of palmprint recognition. Therefore, we migrate a privacy-preserving face recognition method with good performance proposed in [21], directly to palmprint recognition to compare with our method, denoted as DCTDP. It first transforms the image to the frequency domain, then removes the DC component, and finally predicts based on the perturbed frequency components. The results in Table 3 show that the performance of DCTDP is slightly lower than that of PFC. In addition, DCTDP retains more frequency channels and requires training learnable privacy budgets, which means its model size is larger than PFC. Besides, compared with PFC, the privacy budget of DCTDP needs to be adjusted through multiple experiments on different datasets, resulting in higher training costs.

5 Conclusion

In this paper, we propose a privacy-preserving palmprint recognition method, PFC. It uses the block discrete cosine transform to convert the palmprint images into frequency channels, then pruned a part of the low-frequency channels according to the energy of the frequency channels, and finally trains the model to recognize based on the remaining frequency channels. A large number of experiments have shown that PFC can effectively hide personal privacy information with little damage to the performance of palmprint recognition.

Acknowledgments. This work was supported in part by National Natural Science Foundation of China under Grant 62206218 and Grant 62376211, in part by Key Research and Development Program of Shaanxi under Grant 2024GX-YBXM-158, in part by Zhejiang Provincial Natural Science Foundation of China under Grant LTGG23F030006, in part by Young Talent Fund of Association for Science and Technology in Shaanxi, China, under Grant XXJS202231, in part by Xi'an Science and Technology Project under Grant 23ZCKCGZH0001, and in part by Shaanxi Postdoctoral Research Project Funding.

References

1. Fu, C., Zhou, X., He, W., He, R.: Towards lightweight pixel-wise hallucination for heterogeneous face recognition. IEEE Trans. Pattern Anal. Mach. Intell. **45**(7), 9135–9148 (2023)
2. Grosz, S.A., Jain, A.K.: AFR-Net: attention-driven fingerprint recognition network. IEEE Trans. Biom. Behav. Identity Sci. **6**(1), 30–42 (2024)
3. Shao, H., Zou, Y., Liu, C., Guo, Q., Zhong, D.: Learning to generalize unseen dataset for cross-dataset palmprint recognition. IEEE Trans. Inf. Forensics Secur. **19**, 3788–3799 (2024)
4. Fei, L., Wong, W.K., Zhao, S., Wen, J., Zhu, J., Xu, Y.: Learning spectrum-invariance representation for cross-spectral palmprint recognition. IEEE Trans. Syst. Man Cybern. Syst. **53**(6), 3868–3879 (2023)
5. Sardar, A., Umer, S., Rout, R.K., Khan, M.K.: A secure and efficient biometric template protection scheme for palmprint recognition system. IEEE Trans. Artif. Intell. **4**(5), 1051–1063 (2023)
6. Yao, D., Shao, H., Zhong, D.: Palmprint anti-spoofing based on domain-adversarial training and online triplet mining. In: ICIP, pp. 1235–1239 (2023)
7. Yang, Z., Leng, L., Zhang, B., Li, M., Chu, J.: Two novel style-transfer palmprint reconstruction attacks. Appl. Intell. **53**(6), 6354–6371 (2023)
8. Mi, Y., et al.: Duetface: collaborative privacy-preserving face recognition via channel splitting in the frequency domain. In: 30th ACM International Conference on Multimedia (MM), pp. 6755–6764 (2022)
9. Shao, H., Liu, C., Li, X., Zhong, D.: Privacy preserving palmprint recognition via federated metric learning. IEEE Trans. Inf. Forensics Secur. **19**, 878–891 (2024)
10. Liu, C., Zhong, D., Shao, H.: Data protection in palmprint recognition via dynamic random invisible watermark embedding. IEEE Trans. Circuits Syst. Video Technol. **32**(10), 6927–6940 (2022)
11. Wallace, G.K.: The JPEG still picture compression standard. Commun. ACM **34**(4), 30–44 (1991)
12. Chen, W.H., Smith, C., Fralick, S.: A fast computational algorithm for the discrete cosine transform. IEEE Trans. Commun. **25**(9), 1004–1009 (1977)
13. Gueguen, L., Sergeev, A., Liu, R., Yosinski, J.: Faster neural networks straight from JPEG. In: NIPS, pp. 3937–3948 (2018)
14. Xu, K., Qin, M., Sun, F., Wang, Y., Chen, Y., Ren, F.: Learning in the frequency domain. In: CVPR, pp. 1737–1746 (2020)
15. Mi, Y., et al.: Privacy-preserving face recognition using random frequency components. In: ICCV, pp. 19616–19627 (2023)
16. Deng, J., Guo, J., Xue, N., Zafeiriou, S.: Arcface: additive angular margin loss for deep face recognition. In: ICCV, pp. 4690–4699 (2019)

17. Zhang, D., Guo, Z., Lu, G., Zhang, L., Zuo, W.: An online system of multispectral palmprint verification. IEEE Trans. Instrum. Meas. **59**(2), 480–490 (2010)
18. Zhang, L., Li, L., Yang, A., Shen, Y., Yang, M.: Towards contactless palmprint recognition: a novel device, a new benchmark, and a collaborative representation based identification approach. Pattern Recognit. **69**, 199–212 (2017)
19. Sun, Z., Tan, T., Wang, Y., Li, S.Z.: Ordinal palmprint representation for personal identification representation read representation. In: CVPR, pp. 279–284 (2005)
20. He, K., Zhang, X., Ren, S., Sun, J.: Deep residual learning for image recognition. In: CVPR, pp. 770–778 (2016)
21. Ji, J., et al.: Privacy-preserving face recognition with learnable privacy budgets in frequency domain. In: ECCV, pp. 475–491 (2022)

A Federated Learning Framework for Lightweight Model Contrast for Finger Vein Recognition

Guang Chen[1,2], Tianming Xie[1], Xu Yang[2], Feng Tian[2], and Wenxiong Kang[1(✉)]

[1] School of Automation Science and Engineering, South China University of Technology, Guangzhou 510641, China
`jidiangaopeichen@126.com`
[2] GRGBanking Equipment Co., Ltd., Guangzhou 510663, China

Abstract. The training efficacy of finger vein models is influenced by varied device image acquisition characteristics, collector gestures, and contact modes. However, conventional approaches relying on vast data volumes face challenges in the finger vein domain due to stringent security and privacy concerns, limiting data availability. This study proposes a federal learning framework for vein recognition model training, introducing FedFvMCo, a model of contrastive learning among participants. By comparing global and local lightweight model parameters under data convergence limitations, FedFvMCo enhances cross-domain finger vein recognition performance and model generalization. Incorporating an attention mechanism into the lightweight model further optimizes its application in resource-constrained intelligent devices. This framework is validated using four public datasets, demonstrating improved model performance and independence from data convergence constraints. This method can be extended to different modes of biometrics recognition.

Keywords: Federal learning · finger veins · contrast learning · training framework

1 Introduction

Finger vein recognition employs the absorption of deoxyhemoglobin in near-infrared wavelength light to differentiate veins from other human tissues based on their distinct absorption properties. This technique primarily identifies veins in the human hand, including finger, palm, and dorsal hand veins [1,2]. In financial equipment, stringent security and privacy requirements necessitate that vein models adapt to various manufacturers, models, and configurations without centralizing sensitive data within the system. Additionally, the limited computing resources of intelligent equipment and finger vein modules impose strict requirements on model training and interference, complicating the engineering implementation of finger vein systems.

To solve the problem that it is difficult to train the digital vein model due to the high privacy requirement and the sparse data of a single individual.To address the challenges of data convergence and limited computing resources while meeting heterogeneous data adaptation requirements, this study proposes a federated learning framework for lightweight model contrast of finger vein identification model called Model-Contrastive Federated Learning Framework for Finger Vein Recognition (FedFvMCo). The framework involves designing a base model for lightweight finger vein recognition and using the aggregated global lightweight model and the participant local lightweight model to realize collaborative model training across multiple participants. This approach facilitates the finger vein authentication model across diverse manufacturers, devices, and regions. The proposed approach comprises three steps: participant-independent training, federated aggregation and update, and participant contrast training. In the first step, all participants independently train on their local data. In the second step, the updated finger vein recognition models of participants are integrated. An updated finger vein recognition model is formed based on the contributions of the participants and sent back to the participants for federal training. In the third step, the difference between the aggregated updated service party model and the local model is computed as the loss. This loss is combined with the loss from the next independent training of the finger vein recognition model to update the local model. The three steps are repeated until the model converges. The primary contributions of this paper are as follows:

1) We propose a multi-participant model comparison federated learning framework FedFvMCo. This framework enables multi-field adaptation training of the model without converging finger vein image data from multiple participants, enhancing model adaptability and identification accuracy. **2)** We adopt a momentum aggregation strategy for multi-participant weights to improve model robustness and training efficiency during federated learning; **3)** We address sparse information in finger vein images by embedding an attention mechanism in the lightweight model, ensuring performance maintenance of the federal learning and training basic model under lightweight conditions. **4)** We conduct analyses using datasets collected by different devices. We perform experiments on individual datasets, pooled datasets, and federated training. The experimental findings validate the efficacy of the proposed FedFvMCo method.

The rest of this paper is organized as follows. Section 2 describes the methodology of our approach. Section 3 reports the experiments evaluations. Finally, Sect. 4 concludes the findings of the paper.

2 Method

In this study, the model training setup includes a service provider and N participants $P_1, ..., P_N$ with non-independent and equally distributed data.

The study proposes the Model-Contrastive Federated Learning Framework for Finger Vein Recognition (FedFvMCo), addressing the challenges of aggregating heterogeneous finger vein data for joint training through a coherent framework. As shown in Fig. 1, the framework comprises three steps: participant-independent training, federated aggregation update, and participant contrast training.

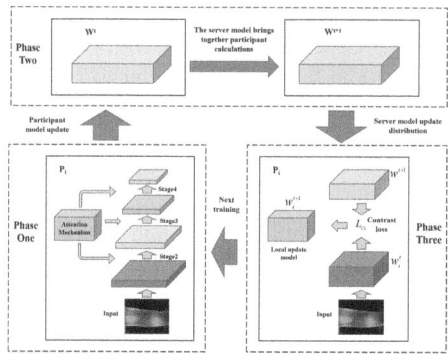

Fig. 1. Framework of adaptive learning method of lightweight finger vein model.

2.1 Independent Training Phase-Lightweight Finger Vein Identification Based on Attentional Mechanism

Vein model algorithms face limitations in storage space, computing resources, and computing resources. Common base models are often large, consume significant computing resources. Optimizing and selecting a lightweight base model tailored to the characteristics of digital veins is imperative. Finger vein recognition primarily relies on key grain information in one-view vein images. Compared with the resource-intensive self-attention mechanism, combining channel and spatial attention reduces computing resources while maintaining performance, making it more suitable for intelligent devices.

ShufflenetV2 network [3] extracts the characteristics of finger vein using its lightweight design, meeting the requirements of heterogeneous intelligent device identification. However, noise, suboptimal acquisition equipment, and fingerprint interference impact the acquisition of the training dataset, Resulting in unclear data that interferes with model training. To address this issue, we propose an algorithmic model based on the attention mechanism, as depicted in Fig. 3. This model integrates the attention mechanism into the commonly used algorithm for middle finger vein recognition.

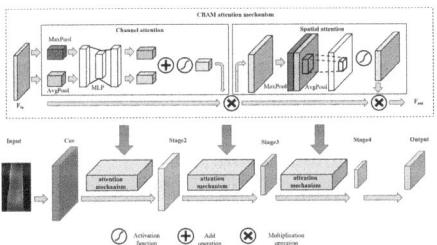

Fig. 2. Schematic diagram of the lightweight backbone model improvement.

The network structure of the CBAM attention mechanism is illustrated in Fig. 2. In the channel attention block, the input features undergo maximum pooling (MaxPool) and average pooling (AvgPool). The resulting channel features from these two feature graphs are weighted using a multi-layer perceptron (MLP), yielding weighted maximum pooling and average pooling features. These features are then added and activated:

$$F_{\text{out}} = M_S\left(M_C(F_{\text{in}}) * F_{\text{in}}\right) * M_C(F_{\text{in}}) * F_{\text{in}} \tag{1}$$

where F_{in} and F_{out} denote the input and output features, respectively; $*$ represents the multiplication, $M_S()$ and $M_C()$ signify the mapping functions of the spatial attention module and channel attention module respectively.

The attention mechanism model effectively suppresses noise in finger vein images and enhances focus on vein patterns. CBAM attention mechanism can emphasize spatial features, such as feature maps and pixel-level vein textures, and channel features with greater expressive ability. This model enhances the network's recognition capabilities, optimizes parameters and computational efficiency, and allows seamless integration into the existing network architectures as a plug-and-play module. Therefore, this study adopts the CBAM attention mechanism for experiments and analysis.

2.2 Federated Aggregation Update Phase-Multi-Participant Cooperation Model Momentum Aggregation Strategy

During model training, the service party distributes the initial model and the training task to all participants in the network and uploads their local training update models as per the service party's deployment. The process consists of two stages: top-down and bottom-up. The service party uses information exchange among the participants to update the model of the service party and achieves local optimal aggregation.

Model aggregation primarily adopts addition and aggregation techniques. Participants train or update their models, aggregated using a defined logic. Aggregation can apply to the entire model or specific parts, adjustable based on the model segmentation method. Common approaches include model averaging, synchronous stochastic gradient descent (SGD) method [4], and elastic average SGD method [5]. Model averaging, as employed in the FedAvg method [6], involves synchronizing model parameters across all participant nodes and updating them via weighted average computation. The updated model is then transmitted back to participants from the service party through system broadcasting or point-to-point communication.

This method constructs the middle layer of the global target model, building model sequence for update server aggregation. The party updates the model sequence for local model comparison by the participants. Similar to contrastive learning, we builds a discrete dictionary from the high-dimensional sequence of server aggregation and dynamically updates the dictionary with momentum calculation, forming a contrast-oriented momentum aggregation strategy:

$$w_q = \frac{1}{N} \sum_{k=1}^{N} W_{t+1}^k \qquad (2)$$

where N denotes the number of participants, and k signifies the k-th participant of the iteration. The value of N changes dynamically with the number of participants in each round, accommodating variations in participant involvement during training and enhancing the system's robustness.

$$w_{t+1} = mw_t + (1 - m) \cdot w_q \qquad (3)$$

where m denotes the momentum coefficient, w_t representing model parameters at time t after the last iteration and w_q representing the aggregation from each participant. However, in actual implementations, uneven local data distributions and asynchronous update speeds among participants can impact the generalization of the average aggregation model, particularly in training finger vein models with limited data. To address this issue, we improve the model aggregation method by constructing a discrete model dictionary and employing a momentum aggregation approach, enhancing the model's expression capability across different participants.

2.3 Participant Contrast Phase-Local Global Model Contrast Representation Update Method

In this study, participants' models are updated through clustering. Current research explores the implementation of unsupervised and self-supervised comparative learning methods [7] in federated learning, combining the classification loss from each participant based on learning with the aggregated loss of the service providers. While comparative learning [8,9] has been extensively studied, its application in digital vein analysis remains underdeveloped, necessitating improvements to ensure accurate vein clustering. Comparative learning aims to bring representations of similar data closer and distancing those of different categories. This approach minimizes the distance between representations learned by local models and the global model and maximizes the distance between the local model and the previous local model.

Before model construction, a key challenge is selecting positive and negative samples. Existing contrast learning approaches typically use instance contrast, where a sample (x, Y) is transformed in a positive pair (xT, YT) through enhancement or other techniques, while different samples serve as negative samples. Contrast loss parameters are then iteratively updated. In federated learning, the direct exchange of training data among participants is not feasible; thus, the comparison method cannot be used directly. However, trained model parameters and some features can be transmitted after encryption. By aggregating model parameters from participants to the service party and comparing them with local participant parameters, a contrastive loss is determined by the participant locally to realize the comparison training of the model.

This study focuses on supervised learning settings and proposes model contrastive learning to compare the representations learned by various models. Each round involves the server sending the global model to the parties, receiving local models from the parties, and updating the global model through weighted averaging. The local loss in this study is illustrated in Fig. 3. During local training, each party updates the global model using its local data with random gradient descent. The local loss comprises two components: a cross-entropy loss ℓ_{sup} typical in supervised learning and a novel contrastive loss ℓ_{con} term (model-contrastive loss) proposed in this study (Eq. 4):

$$\ell_{\text{con}} = -\log\left\{\frac{\exp[\text{sim}(z, z_{\text{glob}})/\tau]}{\exp[\text{sim}(z, z_{\text{glob}})/\tau] + \exp[\text{sim}(z, z_{\text{prev}})/\tau]}\right\} \quad (4)$$

where τ denotes the temperature coefficient, (z, z_{glob}) and (z, z_{glob}) represents positive and negative sample pairs, respectively. The loss of input (x, y) is defined as follows. sim() represents similarity.

$$l = l_{\text{sup}}\left[\omega_i^t, (x, y)\right] + \mu l_{\text{con}}\left[\omega_i^t; \omega_i^{t-1}; \omega^t; x\right] \quad (5)$$

where μ signifies the hyperparameter controlling the model's contrastive loss weight. The final computation yields:

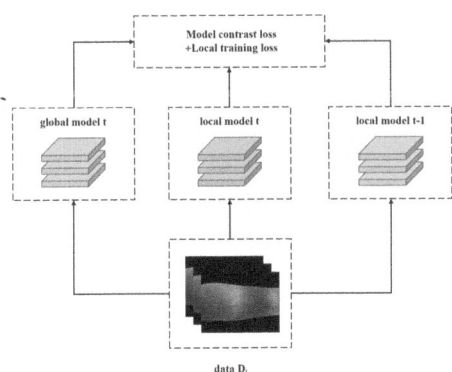

Fig. 3. Schematic representation of the participant local model contrast training.

$$\min_{w_i^t} \mathbb{E}_{(x,y) \sim D^i} \left[\ell_{\sup} \left(w_i^t; (x,y) \right) + \mu \ell_{\text{con}} \left(w_i^t; w_i^{t-1}; w^t; x \right) \right] \tag{6}$$

3 Experimental Setup and Analysis

3.1 Description of the Experimental Data

The dataset used in this study is available for academic research purposes. It includes various biometric datasets, including palm print, finger vein, palm vein, iris, and face. The authors acknowledge the team that provided these open-source datasets, including BIP at the South China University of Technology, Joint Laboratory of Intelligent Computing and Intelligent Systems, Wuhan University, University of Science Malaysia, and Jeonbuk National University of Korea.

3.2 Setting of the Experimental Environment

The experiments were conducted on two GPU servers, each equipped with an Intel Xeon Processor CPU with eight cores of 32G and a GPU server with two Nvidia RTX T4 16 GB cards. PyTorch was used to implement FedFvMCo and other baselines. The local model was trained for 300 epochs, whereas federated learning methods default to 2 epochs per communication round of 100. The regularization loss coefficient μ for FedFvMCo and Fedprox is tuned from 0.01, 0.1, 1,5, 10, with the best results selected as 1 and 0.01, respectively.

3.3 Backbone Network Model Experiment

The lightweight backbone networks: MobileNet V2 [10], ResNet18 [11], ResNet50 [12], DenseNet121 [13], and ShuffleNet V2 [3], have strong performance in image classification and recognition tasks. However, their effectiveness varies in finger vein recognition due to the unique characteristics of this application. Several studies have evaluated the performance of these publicly available backbone networks in finger vein recognition (Table 1).

Table 1. Influence of various backbone networks on model performance (ERR%) [13]

Backbone	SDUMLA-HMT	FV-USM	MMCBNU_6000	HKPU	SCUT-RIFV
MobileNet V2	0.82	0.48	0.21	0.22	0.19
ResNet-50	0.80	0.45	0.21	0.18	0.23
DenseNet-121	0.73	0.33	0.14	0.19	0.15
ShuffleNet	0.6	0.18	0.12	0.17	0.2

Analyzing backbone networks across different datasets reveals that the best model performance is achieved on the MMCBNU-6000 (from JBNU) dataset, followed by the FV-USM (from UTM) dataset and the HKPU dataset, with the poorest performance observed on the SDUMLA-HMT (from SDU) dataset. The evaluation included five models: MobileNet V2 [10], ResNet-18, ResNet-50, DenseNet-121 [13], and Modified ShuffleNet V2 [3]. Among these models, Modified ShuffleNet V2 demonstrated superior performance by combining low-level and high-level features to improve ShuffleNet V2 and train the cross-entropy loss function. Experiments validate that optimizing ShuffleNet V2 as the backbone network is feasible for enhancing the identification performance of finger veins.

3.4 Analysis of the Model Ablation Experiments

In our ablation study, ShuffleNet is used as the backbone network for federated learning among participants to train and validate the model across four datasets. We conducted three experiments. In the "Self-train" experiment ShuffleNet is independently applied to each dataset. The experimental findings verify that the training effect of an independent data training model serves as the primary experimental basis for each respective dataset. In the "Co-train" experiment, data from each dataset is combined to train a model for each participant. While the model converged directly according to the dataset, the improvement in model generalization to each dataset is not significant. In the "FedFvMCo" experiment, the model targeted the finger vein by improving model comparison. The results demonstrate significant accuracy enhancements in data identification and model generalization (Table 2).

Table 2. Results of the FedFvMCo ablation experiments

Ablation experiment	SDUMLA	FV-USM	MMCBNU6000	HKPU	SCUT-RIFV
Self-train	87.93%	87.20%	92.83%	88.40%	97.75%
Co-train	90.84%	86.18%	93.00%	92.67%	99.70%
FedFvMCo	100%	99.73%	97.33%	100%	99.70%

3.5 Training Accuracy Comparison of Different Aggregation Models

Model accuracy on the SCUT-RIFV dataset is assessed using three federated learning algorithms: FedAvg, FedProx, FedFvMCo ($\mu = 1$), and FedFvMCo ($\mu = 10$), across three communication rounds (25, 50, and 100) and three local rounds (2, 5, and 10). Accuracy, expressed as a percentage, measures model performance on the test set. The results are detailed in Tables 3 and 4.

Table 3 indicates that FedFvMCo (particularly with $\mu =10$) demonstrates superior performance across all three communication rounds and maintains high accuracy in short-term and long-term training. This finding showcases that FedFvMCo is more adaptable to model heterogeneity and non-independent identically distributed data within the federated learning framework. Compared to

Table 3. Accuracy comparison of diverse communication rounds for the three training methods

Method	Local rounds of Epoch = 2		
	25 Wheels	50 Boxes	100 Wheels
FedAvg	97.8%	98.8%	99.3%
FedProx	98.9%	99.2%	99.3%
FedFvMCo ($\mu = 1$)	98.6%	99.5%	100%
FedFvMCo ($\mu = 10$)	99.0%	99.8%	100%

Table 4. Comparison of the best accuracy of different local rounds for the methods

data set	The communication round is Rounds = 25		
Local rounds, Epochs	2	5	10
FedAvg	99.3%	99.2%	99.1%
FedProx	99.3%	99.8%	99.5%
FedFvMCo ($\mu = 1$)	100%	99.5%	99.6%

FedAvg and FedProx, FedFvMCo yields higher accuracy, and performs better at 25 rounds, highlighting improved communication efficiency and validating the advantages of FedFvMCo in federated learning scenarios.

From Table 4, FedFvMCo achieves or approaches the highest accuracy with shorter and longer local rounds, demonstrating its effectiveness in federated learning scenarios. Compared to FedAvg and FedProx, FedFvMCo exhibits greater adaptability and stability in handling model heterogeneity and non-independent identically distributed data. FedFvMCo outperforms the other methods at 10 epochs, proving its ability to mitigate negative effects in such cases.

3.6 Comparison of Model Training Efficiency

We analyze the accuracy and speed of three federated learning algorithms: FedAvg, FedProx, and FedFvMCo, on the SCUT-RIFV datasets using 25, 50, and 100 communication rounds.

Table 5 highlights the number of rounds required by FedProx to achieve the same accuracy as the other two models at 50 rounds. It is observed that FedFvMCo significantly reduces the number of communication rounds, yielding higher communication efficiency than the other methods. Among the three levels of data imbalance, FedFvMCo consistently achieves the highest accuracy. When the imbalance is reduced, FedAvg performs worse than FedProx, while FedFvMCo outperforms FedProx. FedFvMCo maintains the highest accuracy and relatively stable performance across varying data imbalance, validating its robustness.

Table 5. Speed of different approaches to achieve the optimal accuracy of FedProx

method	SCUT-RIFV	
	number of epochs	velocity
FedAvg	35	1.43×
FedProx	50	1×
FedFvMCo	25	2×

4 Conclusion

This study proposes the FedFvMCo framework, a federated learning model that leverages the characteristics of the multiple vein image participants model and integrates a lightweight model with an embedded attention mechanism. It enhances the adaptability and accuracy of vein recognition models without requiring convergence on the vein data. In addition, the momentum aggregation strategy for multi-participant weights is optimized to enhance training efficiency in federated learning across various domain data. Experiments were conducted using four datasets collected by different devices, with separate training, pooled training, and federated training. The experimental results validate the performance improvement and effectiveness of the proposed FedFvMCo approach.

References

1. Zhenan, S., Ran, H., Liang, W., et al.: Overview of biometrics research. J. Image Graph. **26**(6), 1254–1329 (2021)
2. Huang, J., Zheng, A., Saad Shakeel, M., Yang, W., Kang, W.: FVFSNet: frequency-spatial coupling network for finger vein authentication. IEEE Trans. Inf. Forensics Secur. **18**, 1322–1334 (2023)
3. Ma, N., Zhang, X., Zheng, H.-T., Sun, J.: ShuffleNet V2: practical guidelines for efficient CNN architecture design. In: Ferrari, V., Hebert, M., Sminchisescu, C., Weiss, Y. (eds.) Computer Vision – ECCV 2018. LNCS, vol. 11218, pp. 122–138. Springer, Cham (2018). https://doi.org/10.1007/978-3-030-01264-9_8
4. Zinkevich, M., Weimer, M., Li, L., Smola, A.: Parallelized stochastic gradient descent. Adv. Neural Inf. Process. Syst. **23** (2010)
5. Zhang, S., Choromanska, A.E., LeCun, Y.: Deep learning with elastic averaging SGD. Adv. Neural Inf. Process. Syst. **28** (2015)
6. Chen, Y., et al.: Partnership-based collaborative learning approach from decentralized data. In: 2021 IEEE 15th International Conference on Big Data Science and Engineering (BigDataSE), pp. 103–110. IEEE (2021)
7. Li, Q., He, B., Song, D.: Model-contrastive federated learning. In: Proceedings of the IEEE/CVF Conference on Computer Vision and Pattern Recognition, pp. 10713–10722 (2021)
8. He, K., Fan, H., Wu, Y., Xie, S., Girshick, R.: Momentum contrast for unsupervised visual representation learning. In: Proceedings of the IEEE/CVF Conference on Computer Vision and Pattern Recognition, pp. 9729–9738 (2020)

9. Khosla, P., et al.: Supervised contrastive learning. Adv. Neural. Inf. Process. Syst. **33**, 18661–18673 (2020)
10. Sandler, M., Howard, A., Zhu, M., Zhmoginov, A., Chen, L.-C.: MobileNetV2: inverted residuals and linear bottlenecks. In: Proceedings of the IEEE Conference on Computer Vision and Pattern Recognition, pp. 4510–4520 (2018)
11. He, K., Zhang, X., Ren, S., Sun, J.: Deep residual learning for image recognition. In: Proceedings of the IEEE Conference on Computer Vision and Pattern Recognition, pp. 770–778 (2016)
12. Huang, G., Liu, Z., Van Der Maaten, L., Weinberger, K.Q.: Densely connected convolutional networks. In: Proceedings of the IEEE Conference on Computer Vision and Pattern Recognition, pp. 4700–4708 (2017)
13. Zheng, H., Hu, Y., Liu, B., Chen, G., Kot, A.C.: A new efficient finger-vein verification based on lightweight neural network using multiple schemes. In: Farkaš, I., Masulli, P., Wermter, S. (eds.) ICANN 2020, Part I. LNCS, vol. 12396, pp. 748–758. Springer, Cham (2020). https://doi.org/10.1007/978-3-030-61609-0_59

Palmprint Anti-spoofing via Frequency Enhancement and Selection

Yani Ren[1], Huikai Shao[1,2,3], and Dexing Zhong[1,4,5(✉)]

[1] School of Automation Science and Engineering, Xi'an Jiaotong University, Xi'an 710049, Shaanxi, China
bell@xjtu.edu.cn
[2] State Key Lab. for Novel Software Technology, Nanjing University, NanJing 210000, Jiangsu, China
[3] Xi'an Yizhanghui Technology Co., Xi'an 712000, Shannxi, China
[4] Pazhou Lab, Guangzhou 510335, China
[5] Research Institute of Xi'an Jiaotong University, Zhejiang 311215, China

Abstract. Palmprint recognition has attracted considerable interest from researchers as a convenient and secure biometric identification technology. The majority of research on palmprint recognition focuses on enhancing recognition accuracy and speed. However, the security aspects of palmprint recognition are rarely considered. This paper proposed a palmprint anti-spoofing method, called Frequency Enhancement and Selection (FES), based on frequency-domain features. Firstly, the palmprint images are transformed using the discrete cosine transform to obtain frequency-domain features. These features are then enhanced by the frequency-domain enhancement module. Finally, the frequency channels for classification are filtered based on the gate module. In this paper, experiments are conducted on a palmprint anti-spoofing database, and the experimental results demonstrate that our method can obtain the anti-spoofing accuracy of 99.81% and can outperform other methods.

Keywords: Palmprint recognition · Anti-spoofing · Frequency learning

1 Introduction

With the rapid advancement of biometric recognition technology, numerous techniques have emerged and been applied in real life, such as fingerprint, facial, and palmprint recognition. Among them, palmprint and palm vein recognition have gained popularity due to their convenience and security [1]. Palmprint recognition stands out for its rich texture information, non-contact collection, and high privacy protection [2]. Although the technology has made significant strides in accuracy and speed, challenges regarding model security persist. Anti-spoofing technology is crucial in ensuring that biometric systems recognize a living body rather than static images or simulations. In palmprint recognition, forged biometric data could pose threats to users' safety and property. Therefore, developing an effective palmprint anti-spoofing method is essential for the practical application of this technology.

A palmprint anti-spoofing method needs to identify a stable and highly discriminative feature that is not affected by the collection environment. Furthermore, considering that palmprint recognition algorithms will be deployed on embedded devices with limited memory and computational power, it is essential to consider resource constraints when designing the palmprint anti-spoofing algorithm. Based on these issues, this paper proposes Frequency Enhancement and Selection (FES) method for palmprint anti-spoofing.

The main contributions can be summarized as follows:

(1) FES method is proposed for palmprint recognition. The frequency-domain features of images are used for liveness detection, which is effective for palmprint recognition to enhance anti-spoofing accuracy.
(2) The images are extracted to the frequency-domain information by discrete cosine transform and the frequency-domain information is enhanced by frequency enhancement module. The information is then filtered by the gate module, from which the information is selected to participate in the subsequent network inference.
(3) Experiments are conducted on the palmprint anti-spoofing database, which show that the performance of frequency enhancement and selection method of palmprint anti-spoofing tasks is superior to other methods.

2 Related Work

2.1 Palmprint Recognition

The primary process of palmprint recognition includes image acquisition, Region of Interest (ROI) extraction, feature extraction, and matching [3]. The most critical steps are palmprint image ROI extraction and feature extraction/matching [4]. Traditional ROI extraction methods rely on geometric distances and palm contours to locate key points, as demonstrated by Zhang et al. [5]. With the rise of convolutional neural networks (CNNs), end-to-end learning has eliminated the need for manual feature extraction, making CNNs adaptable to various datasets and achieving great results in palmprint recognition [6]. Feature extraction methods include structure-based, code-based, and subspace-based algorithms [7].

2.2 Anti-spoofing

The development of anti-spoofing algorithms has mainly targeted fingerprint and facial recognition. For fingerprint, Yuan et al. [8] proposed a method combining multi-scale Local Phase Quantization (LPQ) and Principal Component Analysis (PCA), with a support vector machine for classification. In facial anti-spoofing, local feature descriptors such as LBP [9] and SIFT [10] are used to extract facial features, focusing on image color, texture, and noise. Zhang et al. [11] separated liveness features from content features. Additionally, infrared information from thermal images can distinguish genuine biometric features from fakes, as replayed images and electronic screens lack thermal signatures [12]. Based on this, a palmprint anti-spoofing method via frequency enhancement and selection is proposed.

3 Method

As shown in Fig. 1, we propose a Frequency Enhancement and Selection method for palmprint recognition anti-spoofing. Palmprint images are transformed from RGB to YCbCr color space, then converted to frequency domain via Discrete Cosine Transform (DCT). The frequency-domain information is enhanced through FEM. The YCbCr colour space facilitates the subsequent convolutional neural network to extract the main information from the image. The frequency channels filtered by the Gate module are reorganised and normalised before CNN inference. This reduces the computational requirements for input dimensions, communication bandwidth and validity detection.

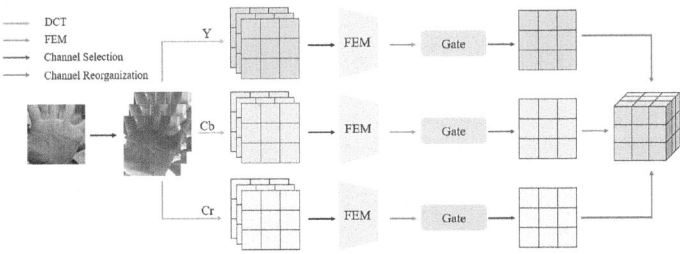

Fig. 1. Famework of FES method.

3.1 Discrete Cosine Transform

Discrete Cosine Transform (DCT) is a method for converting a signal from the time domain to the frequency domain. It decomposes the image signal into low-frequency components, which carry most of the energy, and high-frequency components, which represent detailed information. In this paper, palmprint images are first transformed from RGB to YCbCr color space, then 8×8 DCT is applied to the Y, Cb, and Cr channels separately. The DCT process is defined as:

$$F(u,v) = \frac{2}{N}C(u)C(v) \sum_{i=0}^{N-1}\sum_{j=0}^{N-1} f(i,j) \cos[\frac{(2i+1)u\pi}{2N}] \cos[\frac{(2j+1)v\pi}{2N}]$$

$$C(u) = \begin{cases} \frac{1}{\sqrt{N}}, u=0 \\ \frac{\sqrt{2}}{\sqrt{N}}, u \neq 0 \end{cases}, C(v) = \begin{cases} \frac{1}{\sqrt{N}}, v=0 \\ \frac{\sqrt{2}}{\sqrt{N}}, v \neq 0 \end{cases}. \quad (1)$$

where $f(i,j)$ represents the the pixel value at position (i,j) of the original transformed image, N represents the image dimension, which is 8 in this case, and $F(u,v)$ is the pixel value at position (u,v) in the coefficient matrix after DCT. $C(u)$, $C(v)$ are scaling factors.

Based on this idea, we use a generalized doubly stochastic matrix for the encryption function. After DCT, components of the same frequency from 8×8 blocks are grouped into a single channel, preserving their spatial relationships.

3.2 Frequency Enhancement Module

This paper designs a Frequency Enhancement Module (FEM) to enhance frequency-domain features after DCT, as shown in Fig. 2. The features are divided into low-frequency and high-frequency features, which are fed into the FEM separately. High-frequency signals capture detailed image parts, such as edges and textures, while low-frequency signals represent overall structure. Enhancing both frequency bands separately allows the deep learning network to use information from both bands for classification, rather than relying on one. The FEM computes attention scores, refines features with a 3 × 3 convolution kernel, and applies ReLU activation to introduce nonlinearity, improving augmentation and model generalization. Finally, the enhanced features are concatenated and reorganized, maintaining the original feature dimensions $H/8 \times W/8 \times 64C$.

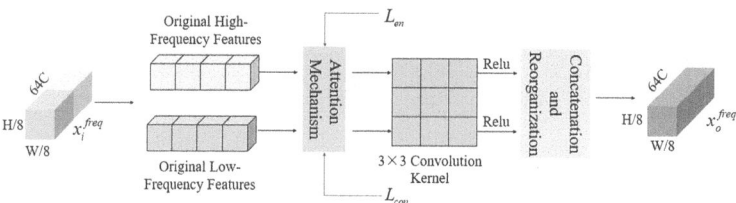

Fig. 2. Workflow of FEM. DCT-derived frequency features x_i^{freq} are split, processed with attention scores, refined by 3 × 3 convolution, activated by ReLU, and concatenated, maintaining input dimensions to enhance model generalization.

We use loss function to evaluate the enhancement effect of the FEM combining reconstruction loss L_{con} and frequency-domain enhancement loss L_{en}. L_{con} uses Mean Squared Error (MSE) to measure the difference between the enhanced frequency-domain features x_o^{freq} and the original features x_i^{freq} which ensures that the enhanced features remain close to the original frequency-domain features during the enhancement process. L_{con} is defined as:

$$L_{con} = MSE(x_i^{freq}, x_o^{freq}). \quad (2)$$

L_{en} measures the effect of frequency enhancement by comparing the differences between the images before and after enhancement. The objective of L_{en} is to augment image detail and sharpness by prompting the model to diminish the overall discrepancy between x_o^{freq} and x_i^{freq}. Given that detail and sharpness are predominantly influenced by high frequency components, L_{en} indirectly fosters the enhancement of high frequency features and is defined as:

$$L_{en} = MAE(x_i^{freq}, x_o^{freq}). \quad (3)$$

L_{FEM} combines these two losses using a weighted average, which can be defined as:

$$L_{FEM} = \alpha L_{con} + (1 - \alpha) L_{en}. \quad (4)$$

where the parameter α is used to adjust the weights between the reconstruction loss and the frequency enhancement loss, which strikes a balance between preserving the fundamental content of the feature (low L_{con}) and enhancing its details (low L_{en}).

3.3 Channel Selection Module

We propose a learnable channel selection mechanism for the classification task, as shown in Fig. 3. The Gate module assigns a binary score to each channel: 1 for channels that benefit classification and 0 for others. Channels with a score of 0 are discarded. The selected channels are reorganized and used as input features, changing the data dimensions from $H/8 \times W/8 \times 64C$ to $H/8 \times W/8 \times K$.

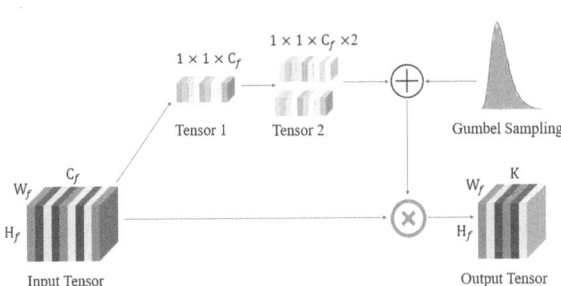

Fig. 3. Mechanism of the gate module for channel selection.

As shown in Fig. 3, The input frequency tensor undergoes average pooling and a 1×1 convolution layer to obtain a tensor with the shape $1 \times 1 \times C$, referred to as tensor 1. Tensor 1 is multiplied by a trainable parameter to generate tensor 2 with the shape $\times 1 \times C \times 2$. Tensor 2 is normalized using Gumbel Softmax [13], sampling probability values of 0 or 1, naking the sampling process to be differentiable.

The sampled probability values are multiplied channel-wise with the input tensor to obtain the final output tensor, with dimensions determined by the hyperparameter K.

Based on the analysis, an RGB image with dimensions $H \times W \times C$ is transformed into frequency-domain features of $H/8 \times W/8 \times 64C$ through DCT. After processing with the frequency-domain information enhancement and gate module, the feature size becomes $H/8 \times W/8 \times K$. Typically, an RGB image with dimensions $224 \times 224 \times 3$, when processed by FES, results in frequency-domain features of size $28 \times 28 \times K$. The existing network only needs to modify the input layer to K channels, retaining subsequent convolution and pooling operations to perform inference.

4 Experiments and Results

4.1 Dataset

XJTU-MPD-Replay [14] database is based on MPD [15], which is established using related equipment to display and capture palmprint images. The palmprint images are displayed on display devices and captured using capture devices to construct the palmprint liveness detection database. For each original palmprint image, five different combinations of display and capture devices were used, named f1 to f5. The XJTU-MPD-Replay database contains a total of six sub-datasets: one real palmprint dataset and five fake palmprint datasets, with each sub-dataset containing 16,000 palmprint images. Some typical palmprint samples are shown in Fig. 4.

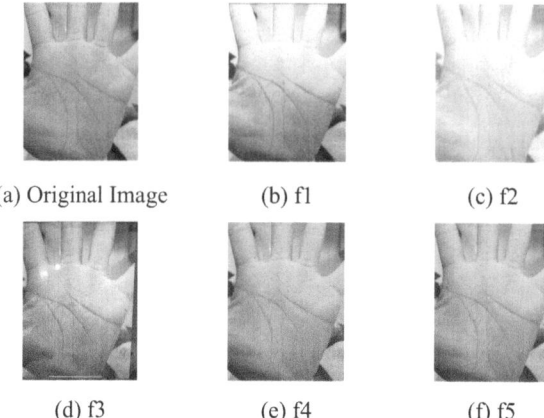

Fig. 4. XJTU-MPD-Replay database sample examples.

We defined two testing protocols based on commonly used testing methods in face anti-spoofing research. These two testing schemes correspond to different data set partitioning methods of the XJTU-MPD-Replay database. The specific details are shown in Table 1.

Protocol I is focused on testing the basic anti-spoofing performance of the palmprint liveness detection model. The XJTU-MPD-Replay database is vertically segmented, and all palmprint images of each category (palmprint ID in the table) are divided into training, validation, and test sets. These three data sets overlap in image categories.

Protocol II aims to test the generalization ability of the palmprint liveness detection model. The XJTU-MPD-Replay database is horizontally split based on palmprint ID, and divided into training, validation, and test sets according to a specified ratio. These three data sets do not overlap in image categories.

In the Table 1, "a" and "b" represent two different partitioning ratios. In testing protocol X.a, the ratio of the training set to the test set is 3:1, while in protocol X.b, the ratio is 1:1. The validation set data remains constant in both protocols.

4.2 Implementation Details

This paper evaluates the model using metrics such as model accuracy, Attack Presentation Classification Error Rate (APCER), Bona Fide Presentation Classification Error Rate (BPCER), and Average Classification Error Rate (ACER). Model accuracy denotes the accuracy of the model anti-spoofing.

In liveness detection binary classification, data is categorized as: TP (True Positives) for correctly predicted positives, TN (True Negatives) for correctly predicted negatives, FP (False Positives) for negatives incorrectly predicted as positives, and FN (False Negatives) for positives incorrectly predicted as negatives.

APCER measures the error rate when an attack is wrongly classified as a real palm. A lower APCER indicates better attack detection. It is defined as:

$$APCER = \frac{FP}{TN + FP}. \tag{5}$$

Table 1. Details of XJTU-MPD-Replay database partitioning

Testing rotocols	Dataset	Palm ID	Number of Real Palmprint Images	Number of Fake Palmprint Images
I.a	Training	1-200	9600	48000
	Validation	1-200	3200	16000
I.b	Training	1-200	3200	16000
	Validation	1-200	6400	32000
II.a	Training	1-200	3200	16000
	Validation	1-200	6400	32000
	Training	1-120	9600	48000
	Validation	121-160	3200	16000
II.b	Training	161-200	3200	16000
	Validation	1-80	6400	32000
	Training	121-160	3200	16000
	Validation	80-120, 161-200	6400	32000

NPCER represents the error rate when a real palmprint is classified as fake. A lower NPCER indicates a stronger ability to detect real palmprints. NPCER is defined as:

$$NPCER = \frac{FN}{TP + FN}. \quad (6)$$

ACER is the average of APCER and NPCER, serving as a comprehensive metric for system performance. A lower ACER indicates better model performance.

4.3 Experimental Results

Experiments were conducted on the XJTU-MPD-Replay palmprint database. The results are shown in Table 2. Overall, FES achieved excellent performance in the palmprint anti-spoofing task, with recognition accuracy exceeding 97% across all four testing protocols, successfully distinguishing between real palmprints and fake images.

Table 2. Performance of FES on XJTU-MPD-Replay palmprint database.

Test Protocols	Accuracy (%)	APCER	NPCER	ACER
I.a	99.81	0.0005	0.0089	0.0047
I.b	99.64	0.0036	0.0039	0.0037
II.a	97.06	0.0048	0.1522	0.0785
II.b	97.70	0.0012	0.1322	0.0667

To validate the performance of FES, we selected several classic face liveness detection methods for comparison, using RGB images while keeping all other experimental parameters consistent. The results are presented in Table 3.

Table 3. Performance of different methods

Test Protocols	Methods	Accuracy (%)	APCER	NPCER	ACER
I.a	FeatherNets [16]	98.50	0.0140	0.0210	0.0175
	PatchNet [17]	99.58	0.0022	**0.0045**	**0.0034**
	FGDNet [18]	99.08	0.0307	0.0049	0.0178
	FES	**99.81**	**0.0005**	0.0089	0.0047
I.b	FeatherNets [16]	97.44	0.0180	0.0620	0.0400
	PatchNet [17]	99.27	0.0351	**0.0016**	0.0183
	FGDNet [18]	98.92	0.0281	0.0074	0.0178
	FES	**99.64**	**0.0036**	0.0039	**0.0037**
II.a	FeatherNets [16]	94.61	0.0520	0.0640	0.0580
	PatchNet [17]	97.02	0.0580	**0.0250**	**0.0410**
	FGDNet [18]	95.30	0.1400	0.0290	0.0840
	FES	**97.06**	**0.0048**	0.1522	0.0785
II.b	FeatherNets [16]	96.05	0.0200	0.1400	0.0790
	PatchNet [17]	**98.16**	0.0500	**0.0120**	0.0310
	FGDNet [18]	97.35	0.0355	0.0248	**0.0302**
	FES	97.70	**0.0012**	0.1322	0.0667

FeatherNets [16] is a lightweight network for face liveness detection, reducing hardware requirements for embedded devices. PatchNet [17] approaches face anti-spoofing as a patch recognition problem, introducing a new loss function to boost robustness. Fine-Grained Detection Network (FGDNet) [18] uses pixel-level segmentation to partition the face and employs multi-channel region swapping to diversify training data, enhancing generalization.

Table 3 shows that FES outperforms other methods across various protocols. In Protocol I.a, it achieves the highest accuracy at 99.81% and the lowest APCER, indicating its effectiveness in meeting strict anti-spoofing standards for real-world palmprint recognition.

In open-set validation Protocol II, all methods show reduced performance. In Protocol II.b, PatchNet achieves the highest recognition accuracy at 98.16%, 0.46% above FES. While FES excels in APCER, its NPCER metric lags behind other algorithms.

5 Conclusion

This paper addresses RGB palmprint image misjudgments caused by lighting and environmental factors. We propose FES for palmprint recognition anti-spoofing. FES converts palmprint images into frequency-domain and uses a fine-tuned deep learning network for detection. To improve feature representation, we designed a Frequency Enhancement Module that employs channel attention mechanisms. Additionally, a Gate Module selects the most significant channels, reducing network input and optimizing performance. Experiments on the XJTU-MPD-Replay database show that FES outperforms other methods in liveness detection.

Acknowledgments. This work was supported in part by National Natural Science Foundation of China under Grant 62206218 and Grant 62376211, in part by Key Research and Development Program of Shaanxi under Grant 2024GX-YBXM-158, in part by Zhejiang Provincial Natural Science Foundation of China under Grant LTGG23F030006, in part by Young Talent Fund of Association for Science and Technology in Shaanxi, China, under Grant XXJS202231, in part by Xi'an Science and Technology Project under Grant 23ZCKCGZH0001, in part by Shaanxi Postdoctoral Research Project Funding and in part by Fundamental Research Funds for the Central Universities under Grant xzy012023061.

References

1. Zhao, S., Fei, L., Wen, J.: Multiview-learning-based generic palmprint recognition: a literature review. Mathematics **11**(5), 1261 (2023)
2. Fei, L., Wong, W.K., Zhao, S., Wen, J., Zhu, J., Xu, Y.: Learning spectrum-invariance representation for cross-spectral palmprint recognition. IEEE Trans. Syst. Man Cybern. Syst. **53**(6), 3868–3879 (2023)
3. Guo, Q., Shao, H., Liu, C., Wan, J., Zhong, D.: Homomorphic encryption-based privacy protection for palmprint recognition. In: Jia, W., et al. (eds.) CCBR 2023. LNCS, vol. 14463, pp. 363–371. Springer, Singapore (2023). https://doi.org/10.1007/978-981-99-8565-4_34
4. Shao, H., Zou, Y., Liu, C., Guo, Q., Zhong, D.: Learning to generalize unseen dataset for cross-dataset palmprint recognition. IEEE Trans. Inf. Forensics Secur. **19**, 3788–3799 (2024)
5. Zhang, D., Kong, W.-K., You, J., Wong, M.: Online palmprint identification. IEEE Trans. Pattern Anal. Mach. Intell. **25**(9), 1041–1050 (2003)
6. Sharifani, K., Amini, M.: Machine learning and deep learning: a review of methods and applications. World Inf. Technol. Eng. J. **10**(07), 3897–3904 (2023)
7. Zhong, D., Du, X., Zhong, K.: Decade progress of palmprint recognition: a brief survey. Neurocomputing **328**, 16–28 (2019)
8. Yuan, C., Sun, X., Lv, R.: Fingerprint liveness detection based on multi-scale LPQ and PCA. China Commun. **13**(7), 60–65 (2016)
9. Boulkenafet, Z., Komulainen, J., Hadid, A.: Face anti-spoofing based on color texture analysis. In: IEEE International Conference on Image Processing, Quebec, pp. 2636–2640. IEEE (2015)
10. Patel, K., Han, H., Jain, A.K.: Secure face unlock: Spoof detection on smartphones. IEEE Trans. Inf. Forensics Secur. **11**(10), 2268–2283 (2016)
11. Zhang, K.-Y., et al.: Face anti-spoofing via disentangled representation learning. In: Vedaldi, A., Bischof, H., Brox, T., Frahm, J.M. (eds.) ECCV 2020. LNCS, vol. 12364, pp. 641–657. Springer, Cham. (2020). https://doi.org/10.1007/978-3-030-58529-7_38

12. Zhang, Z., Yi, D., Lei, Z., Li, S.Z.: Face liveness detection by learning multispectral reflectance distributions. In: 2011 IEEE International Conference on Automatic Face & Gesture Recognition (FG), Santa Barbara, pp. 436–441. IEEE (2011)
13. Herrmann, C., Bowen, R.S., Zabih, R.: Channel selection using gumbel softmax. In: Vedaldi, A., Bischof, H., Brox, T., Frahm, JM. (eds.) ECCV 2020. LNCS, vol. 12372, pp. 241–257. Springer, Cham (2020). https://doi.org/10.1007/978-3-030-58583-9_15
14. Liu, C., Shao, H., Zhong, D.: PalmSecMatch: a data-centric template protection method for palmprint recognition. Displays **84**, 102771 (2024)
15. Zhang, L., Li, L., Yang, A., Shen, Y., Yang, M.: Towards contactless palmprint recognition: a novel device, a new benchmark, and a collaborative representation based identification approach. Pattern Recogn. **69**, 199–212 (2017)
16. He, D., et al.: Lightweight network-based multi-modal feature fusion for face anti-spoofing. Vis. Comput. **39**(4), 1423–1435 (2023)
17. Wang, C., Lu, Y., Yang, S., Lai, S.: PatchNet: a simple face anti-spoofing framework via fine-grained patch recognition. In: Proceedings of the IEEE/CVF Conference on Computer Vision and Pattern Recognition, New Orleans, pp. 20281–20290. IEEE (2022)
18. Qiao, T., Wu, J., Zheng, N., Xu, M., Luo, X.: FGDNet: fine-grained detection network towards face anti-spoofing. IEEE Trans. Multimedia **25**, 7350–7363 (2022)

Spoofing Attacks Utilizing a More Realistic Contactless Palm Vein Correction Algorithm

Jianbin Wang[1,2], Dacan Luo[2], Runzhang Chen[2], and Wenxiong Kang[2](✉)

[1] School of Mathematics and Statistics, Zhaoqing University, Zhaoqing, China
[2] School of Automation Science and Engineering, South China University of Technology, Guangzhou, China
auwxkang@scut.edu.cn

Abstract. Palm vein recognition research is progressing rapidly, underscoring the growing urgency for security studies in this field. A pivotal component of this research, anti-spoofing is currently hindered primarily by the scarcity of spoofing datasets. The scarcity stems from the immature methods employed in generating more realistic spoofing samples in contactless environments. This paper proposed an innovative method that enables generating convincingly realistic spoofing samples feasible. We observe considerable luminance distribution discrepancies between the actual palm and its captured image which are caused by non-uniform illumination. Through modeling and theoretical analysis, the issue of non-uniform illumination in contactless palm vein imaging is effectively addressed and remedied, subsequently enables the generation of more realistic spoofing samples. The experimental results demonstrate that the fabricated spoofing samples exhibit notable realism, with deception rates spanning from 87.37% to 88.83%, thereby verifying the viability of the proposed method.

Keywords: palm vein · ROI · luminance distribution · spoofing attack

1 Introduction

The application of biometric in information security domain is very popular now [1]. Vein recognition, a new research focus of biometrics, has attracted many researchers' attention [2]. Due to a dual benefit of convenience and user-friendly, palm veins (PV) are commonly employed as keys or identifiers in a variety of security contexts, including access control, online payments, and account authentication. This eliminates the need to carry physical tokens, which are prone to loss, theft, or unauthorized duplication. Palm vein recognition can offer an enhanced level of security and reliability than fingerprint and facial recognition. This is attributed to the fact that vein patterns, situated beneath the skin's surface, are inherently more challenging to replicate and damage.

Vein recognition systems necessitate rigorous security measures. Nonetheless, it is apparent that research in security lags considerably behind the rapid progress observed in feature extraction, data augmentation, and other relevant domains. Tome, P., et al. [3,4] have shown that printed version of bona bide samples can cheat the recognition system with a high probability. Nguyen, H. H., et al. [5] and Shaheed, K., et al. [6] introduce several other possible attacks or threats to a vein recognition system.

To date, there has been a dearth of contactless PV spoofing datasets reported in the literature. The main reason is that technological constraints often compromise the realism of the data when constructing datasets, particularly within the contactless PV domain, thereby hindering the creation of effective spoofing datasets. To address this gap, this manuscript proposes an innovative method that enhances the realism of raw PV images, thereby generating convincingly realistic spoofing PV images. This approach can promote the development of PV anti-spoofing research.

2 Related Work

2.1 Anti-spoofing in Veins Biometrics

The primary focus of the spoofing attacks detection (SAD) study is on developing effective methods to defend against spoofing attacks. Qiu, X. W., et al. [7] proposed a TV-LBP method which uses Total Variation Decomposition and LBP for detecting attacks, and the method outperformed all other methods at that time. In the literature [8], a method named MHOG (multi-scale histogram of oriented gradients) is proposed for presentation attack detection (PAD) and yields the second-best result after TV-LBP. In this literature [9], twelve algorithms were proved to be vulnerable for PA, but fusion of similarity scores from these methods is capable of detecting PA. More work is summarized in the literature [10]. In this manuscript, the terms "PA" and "SA" are used interchangeably.

The aforementioned SAD methods relies on feature engineering. With the rise of deep learning technology, researchers have used various deep learning networks to establish SAD methods [11]. Xinwei, Q., et al. [12] designed a CNN named FPNet for finger vein (FV) PAD, yields the excellent results on two publicly accessible FV datasets. Yang, W. L., et al. [13] propose a lightweight CNN called the Finger-Vein Recognition and AntiSpoofing Network (FVRAS-Net), which integrates recognition task and anti-spoof task into a unified CNN model by utilizing a multitask learning approach and achieves high security and strong real-time performance. In addition, a challenging finger-vein database with images depicting severe axial finger rotation is built for more rigorous validation of the proposed system. Shaheed, K., et al. [14] proposed a novel depthwise separable CNN with residual connection and a linear support vector machine for the automatic detection of FV presentation attacks. This method attained a error rate of 0.00% for SAD on two publicly accessible datasets.

2.2 Spoofing in Veins Biometrics

Spoofing ways are rarely studied, perhaps for moral reasons. Spoofing samples are usually created using printers, but some researchers explored innovative approaches. Schuiki, J., et al. [9] employ wax to generate new PA samples which cause high threat to vein pattern based algorithms, while exerting a relatively minor effect on key-point and texture-based algorithms. In the literature [15], spoofing attack samples of ICG, black silicone tubes, and pencil drawings were produced to verify the detection performance of their proposed anti-spoofing strategy.

Constructing more realistic spoofing datasets is instrumental in advancing the anti-spoofing research of PV recognition. Given the dearth of extensive research on the fabrication of SA samples, we delve into the exploration of generating printed variants of SA samples by restoring more realistic contactless PV images.

3 Methodology

3.1 Analysis and Modeling of Sample Acquisition

3.1.1 Luminance Distribution of Real Contactless Palm Vein

A simple visual inspection of actual palm indicates that if under a uniformly illuminated environment, there are minor fluctuations in the luminance of the palm skin, along with palm prints and veins. The captured image should exhibit these subtleties. This observation is confirmed by Fig. 1, which displays a PV image selected from the CAISA datasets under relatively uniform illumination within a restricted space. The contour lines reveal the luminance variation in the center region of the palm is small, with an almost imperceptible gradient change.

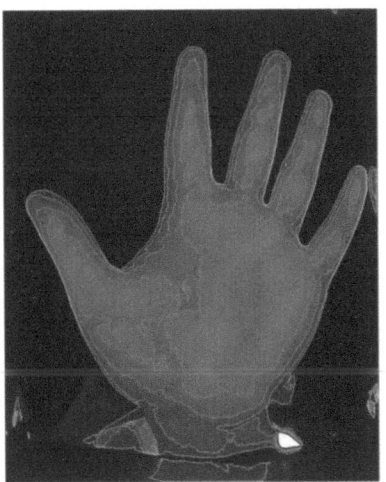
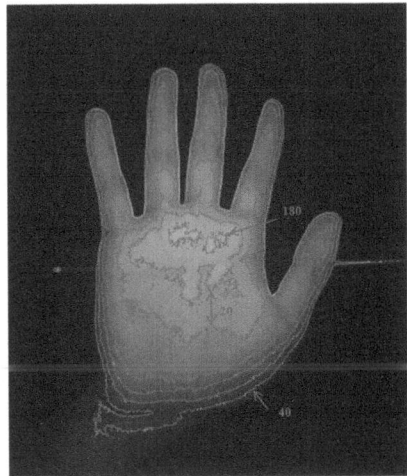

Fig. 1. Luminance contour lines of a real palm vein from CASIA [16].

Fig. 2. Luminance contour lines of a real palm vein captured by us.

In contrast, the captured contactless PV image in unrestricted space, is inconsistent with the aforementioned observation, it is apparent that there are significant differences in luminance distribution. As shown in Fig. 2, the luminance contour lines vary from 40 to 180 in steps of 20. The luminance of the image peaks near its center, whereas decreases towards its periphery. This big gradient of diminishing luminosity from the center to the periphery suggests that the illumination is not uniform and the realism of the palm is weakened.

3.1.2 Luminance Attenuation Patterns To investigate luminance attenuation patterns within the NIR optical field, we printed a unique gray level, denoted as c, onto a sheet of paper, placed it horizontally under the camera and subsequently captured a image labeled as g. These two gray images are shown at the top of Fig. 3. The attenuation value for each pixel in the image is determined by the ratio g(x, y)/c, thereby generating an attenuation value surface. This surface represents the attenuation pattern for the given distance and gray level.

An attenuation pattern of the NIR optical field is illustrated at the bottom of Fig. 3. The image shows that luminance value peaks near the center, gradually decreases from the center to the periphery. This observation explains why the realism of PV image decreased. The pattern of luminance gradient descent is in accordance with what is depicted in Fig. 2.

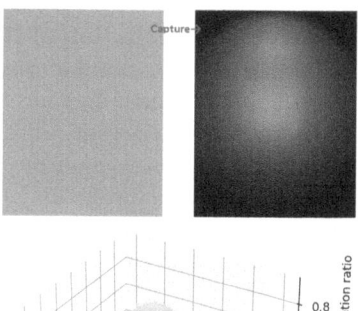

The study further investigated the effects of distance and gray level on the attenuation patterns. The distance variable was varied from 8 cm to 14 cm in steps of 1 cm, while the gray level was varied from 120 to 240 in steps of 30. However, the complex interplay between orientation and inclination on the attenuation patterns has not been thoroughly investigated, and these factors would be crucial for generating a more realistic SA sample.

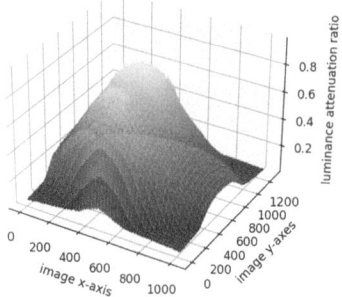

Fig. 3. Luminance attenuation pattern (grayscale = 180, distance = 9 cm).

3.1.3 Problem Modeling

$$g1(x,y) = f(p_{x,y}, d_{x,y}). \quad (1)$$

$$g1'(x,y) = g1(x,y) + noise(x,y). \quad (2)$$

$$g2(x,y) = f(g1'_{x,y}, d'_{x,y}). \quad (3)$$

Based on prior analysis, it is evident that using the first captured image for a direct print-and-reenact SA would likely increase the deviation observed during the second capture. To address this issue, we employ Eqs. 1–3 to qualitatively elucidate the principles governing the acquisition process of both the raw and SA images. We label the real PV image as the first acquisition image, $g1$, which represents the output of function f, reflecting the palm and its distance. Then, $g1$ is printed on a paper and becomes $g1'$ which include noise introduced by printer. We assume the noise can be ignored if print quality is very high. Finally, we get $g2$ (i.e. SA) by capturing $g1'$ image. Due to luminance non-uniformity of the optical field, $g1$ has a significant luminance distribution difference compared to a real palm, resulting in the recaptured SA image ($g2$) exhibiting more pronounced luminance attenuation.

Knowing the specific mathematical form of function f would simplify the problem significantly. However, this is not an easy task. If we let $d^*_{x,y} \to d_{x,y}$ and $g1^* \to p$, $g1^*$ is a corrected version of $g1$, we have $g2^* \approx f(g1^*, d*_{x,y}) \to f(p_{x,y}, d_{x,y}) = g1$, then we have $g2^* \to g1$. This implies that the first acquisition image $g1$ is corrected or adjusted appropriately, thereby enabling the SA image to serve as a more precise approximation of real image ($g1$). Consequently, we devised an algorithm to correct $g1$ by leveraging luminance attenuation patterns.

3.1.4 Correction Algorithm

We design special experiment (refer to Sect. 5.1 for detail) to get the attenuation patterns of NIR optical filed, i.e. att_4d shown in Fig. 4. Then, we devise an algorithm to correct first acquisition images. The algorithm first obtains a candidate list (g1_list) of possible corrected images through the implementation of a dual-nested loop structure. Then, the output of $g1^*$ is determined by selecting maximal average luminance. The algorithm works for most of the first acquisition images, but fails sometimes if the palm is not held nearly parallel to the camera because the attenuation patterns are estimated on a horizontal surface assumption.

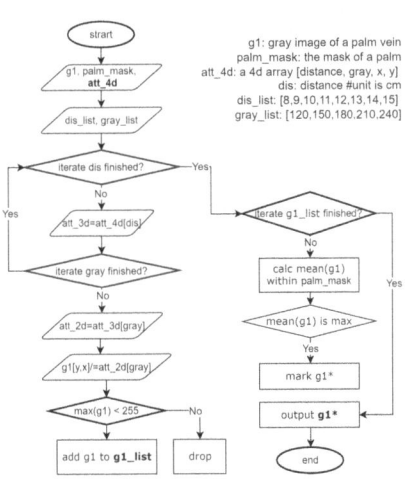

Fig. 4. Flowchart of first acquisition image correction algorithm.

4 Experiment and Analysis

4.1 Data Collection and Process

The acquisition of a palm vein using the reflection method. It should be noted that several LED on the surface of the device emit NIR light at 850 nm to enhance the visibility of palm veins. To eliminate background interference, an optical filter is placed in front of the camera lens, which blocking any light except NIR light.

The SA images are also captured by the image acquisition system. To facilitate the acquisition process, the device is inverted and mounted on a computer vision experimental platform, with the printed paper placed on the bottom tray, as shown in Fig. 5. The distance between the camera and the paper can be adjusted flexibly.

4.1.1 Optimal Selection of Equipment and Materials for The Preparation of Spoofing Data
The equipment and materials used to prepare spoofing data are mainly printers and paper. The market offers primarily two classes of printer: Ink-jet printers and toner-based laser printers. Each category contains a large number of brands, and the printing quality also varies. Additionally, the variety of printable paper available encompasses

Fig. 5. SA image acquisition.

diverse materials, colors, and textures. Conceptually, given n types of printers and m types of paper, there is n * m types of SA samples.

Through continuous attempt, we finally select three high-end printers - Canon, Ricoh, and Konica Minolta - along with two types of paper: standard A4 printing paper and Munken Paper.

4.1.2 Spoofing Data Collection and Process
Upon successfully attaining the attenuation patterns of NIR optical field, we proceed to correct the first captured images utilizing the algorithm detailed in Sect. 3.1.4. This corrected image is then printed, and the copy is subsequently re-captured to generate the spoof image. Figure 6 illustrates this process: sub-image (a) represents the first captured image, (b) represents the corrected image, and (c) represents the spoof (second acquisition) image. Comparing images (a) and (c), it is evident that the spoof image closely resembles the real one. The ROI image is then extracted from the palm vein image using an algorithm developed by our lab. For detailed steps, please refer to the literature [17]. This similarity is also evident in both the real and spoofing ROI as shown in Fig. 7.

In constructing SA datasets, we utilized our self-built contactless PV dataset, which includes 500 subjects, each captured nine times in a single session. The PV images are 1024×768 in size. We then corrected real PV images to generate more realistic SA images.

When using Canon and Ricoh printers on A4 paper, the PV image exhibits bright spots, especially when the camera is in close proximity to the paper and the toner concentration is high. In contrast, the ROI experiences less exposure. This study is dedicated to generating a spoof dataset of the ROI.

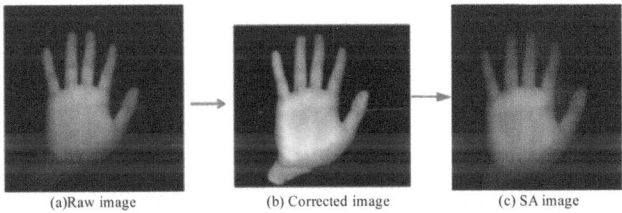

Fig. 6. The process of forging palm vein image.

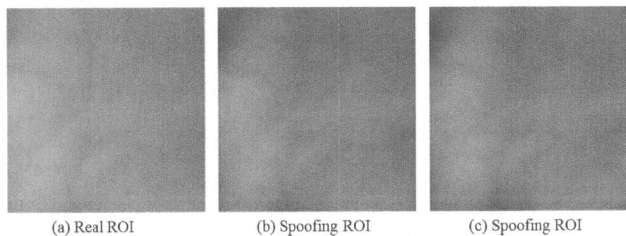

Fig. 7. Realistic spoofing ROI image.

We label Canon, Konica Minolta, and Ricoh printers with the letters C, K, and R respectively. The numbers 1 and 2 signify standard A4 and Munken paper. Accordingly, the six types of SA samples are labeled as C1, C2, K1, K2, R1, and R2. We created two sets of SA images, amassing a collection of 1,500 SA images of the ROI, providing a substantial dataset for our experiments and analysis. The relevant configurations of the dataset are outlined in Table 1.

Table 1. The configurations of SA datasets.

SA dataset		Palm ids	Real PV images	Collection frequency	SA images	
Set 1		100	3	3	900	
Set 2	C1-R2(6 types)	2	5	10	100	600(total)

4.2 Implement Details and Evaluation Metrics

4.2.1 Experiment Setting All experiments are conducted using our self-built real and spoofing datasets. Each sample consists of a grayscale ROI image, which has been uniformly resized to a resolution of 224 × 224 pixels. Typically, the datasets are partitioned into a 50:50 ratio for training and testing, respectively, adhering to the open-set protocol.

MobileNetV2, Adam, and ArcFace are employed as the backbone network, optimizer, and loss function, respectively. We set the batch size to 32, the initial learning rate to 0.0005, and the number of epochs to 500 for network training. Most experimental setting closely adheres to that of the literature [18] except the SAD system B. The final experimental outcomes were obtained from the optimized model.

All deep learning models are implemented using PyTorch, running on the Windows 10 operating system, and leveraged with an NVIDIA RTX 3060 GPU.

4.2.2 Evaluation Metrics Recognition Criteria: The Equal Error Rate (EER) represents the point at which the False Accept Rate (FAR) is equivalent to the False Reject Rate (FRR). EER serves as the metric for the effectiveness of recognition system.

Detection Criteria: Attack Presentation Classification Error Rate (APCER) represents the proportion of attack presentations incorrectly classified as real presentations. APCER serves as the metric for assessing the effectiveness of SAD system.

4.3 Vulnerability Analysis

To validate the significant threat that our meticulously crafted realistic SA samples against the PV recognition system, we trained a PV recognition system. As illustrated in Table 2, the system demonstrates a high recognition accuracy, evidenced by an EER of merely 2.06%.

When using SA samples from set 1 to deceive this system, the APCER alarmingly reaches 87.37%, indicating the recognition system is beset with a critical vulnerability to deception when confronted with this highly realistic SA. Furthermore, when subjected to the SA samples from Set 2, the system's vulnerability is exacerbated, with its risk level potentially reaching as high as 88.83%. Should we intensify our efforts in generating SA samples, there is a strong likelihood that the APCER of the recognition system could surpass the critical threshold of 90%.

Table 2. EER and APCER of the recognition system.

Criteria	PV recognition System
EER	2.06%
APCER (set 1)	87.37%
APCER (set 2)	88.83%

4.4 Performance of SAD Systems

To develop the system's SA detection capabilities, half of the SAs from set 1 and set 2 have been integrated into the training dataset. Two distinct approaches were utilized in training models: SAD system A is implemented in an integrated approach, which groups all SA samples into a single category; SAD system B is implemented in an independent approach, which is essentially a binary classification system to differentiate between real and spoofing palms.

Table 3 demonstrates that systems A and B excel in detecting SAs from set 1, with system B showing exceptional proficiency in detecting this type of SA entirely. However, these systems encounter difficulties with other SA types from set 2. Due to fewer training samples (50 per category) and the integrated approach, system A can't detect $C1 \sim R2$ types completely. Nevertheless, system B significantly outperforms system A, though it exhibits a marginally higher APCER when detecting the K1 and K2 types. It is evident that a standalone SAD system offers superior anti-spoofing capabilities, albeit at the cost of increased system complexity and higher resource consumption.

Table 3. Detection performance of two SAD systems.

SAD system	APCER for two SAD systems (%)						
	Set 1	C1	C2	K1	K2	R1	R2
SAD system A (integrated)	0.7	100	100	100	100	100	100
SAD system B (independent)	0	0	2	24	8	2	0

A SAD system akin to FVRAS-Net [13], which addresses the issue of interclass imbalance in SA samples, is worth investigating.

5 Conclusion

In this study, we observed a noticeable luminance decay during the imaging process. Subsequently, through theoretical modeling and analysis of the imaging process, we concluded that it is feasible to restore a more realistic PV image by devising a correction algorithm. By integrating this algorithm with a bilateral filtering technique, careful selecting printing equipment and paper types, we were able to generate a diverse array of SA samples that are highly realistic. Subsequently, these SA samples were then employed to deceive a deep learning-based recognition system, achieving a significant deception rate of up to 88.83%. The devised algorithm still has ample room for enhancement to generate more realistic SA. In the future, it is entirely feasible to conduct spoofing attacks on more specialized recognition networks, such as StarLKNet [19].

Integrating spoof data into the training process can significantly enhance a system's anti-spoofing ability, especially with ample spoof samples. Experiments show that independent SAD systems offer performance advantages over integrated SAD systems.

Acknowledgments. This work was supported in part by the Natural Science Foundation of Guangdong Province, China (No. 2022A1515010114); in part by the International Science and Technology Cooperation Project of Guangzhou Economic and Technological Development District (No. 2023GH16); in part by the University Student Innovation and Entrepreneurship Training Program of China (No. 202410580008).

References

1. Sun, Z.N., et al.: Overview of biometrics research. J. Image Graph. **26**(06), 1254–1329 (2021)
2. Wu, W., et al.: Review of palm vein recognition. IET Biom. **9**(1), 1–10 (2020)
3. Tome, P., Vanoni, M., Marcel, S.: On the vulnerability of palm vein recognition to spoofing attacks. In: Proceedings of the International Conference on Biometrics (ICB), Phuket, pp. 319–325. IEEE (2015)
4. Tome, P., Vanoni, M., Marcel, S.: On the vulnerability of finger vein recognition to spoofing. In: 2014 International Conference of the Biometrics Special Interest Group (2014)
5. Nguyen, H.H., et al.: Analysis of master vein attacks on finger vein recognition systems. In: 23rd IEEE/CVF Winter Conference on Applications of Computer Vision (WACV), Waikoloa, pp. 1900–1908. IEEE (2023)
6. Shaheed, K., et al.: Recent advancements in finger vein recognition technology: methodology, challenges and opportunities. Inform. Fusion **79**, 84–109 (2022)
7. Qiu, X.W., et al.: Finger vein presentation attack detection using total variation decomposition. IEEE TIFS **13**(2), 465–477 (2018)
8. binti Ashari, N.N., et al.: Multi-scale texture analysis for finger vein anti-spoofing. In: 2021 IEEE International Conference on Artificial Intelligence in Engineering and Technology (IICAIET), Kota Kinabalu, pp. 6–11. IEEE (2021)
9. Schuiki, J., et al.: Confronting a variety of finger vein recognition algorithms with wax presentation attack artefacts. In: 9th International Workshop on Biometrics and Forensics (IWBF), Rome. IEEE (2021)
10. Anjos, A., Tome, P., Marcel, S.: An introduction to vein presentation attacks and detection. In: Marcel, S., Nixon, M.S., Fierrez, J., Evans, N. (eds.) Handbook of Biometric Anti-Spoofing. ACVPR, pp. 419–438. Springer, Cham (2019). https://doi.org/10.1007/978-3-319-92627-8_18
11. Shaheed, K., et al.: Deep learning techniques for biometric security: a systematic review of presentation attack detection systems. Eng. Appl. Artif. Intel. **129**, 1–32 (2024)
12. Qiu, X., Tian, S., Kang, W., Jia, W., Wu, Q.: Finger vein presentation attack detection using convolutional neural networks. In: Zhou, J., et al. (eds.) CCBR 2017. LNCS, vol. 10568, pp. 296–305. Springer, Cham (2017). https://doi.org/10.1007/978-3-319-69923-3_32
13. Yang, W.L., et al.: FVRAS-Net: an embedded finger-vein recognition and Anti-Spoofing system using a unified CNN. IEEE TIM **69**(11), 8690–8701 (2020)
14. Shaheed, K., et al.: Finger-vein presentation attack detection using depthwise separable convolution neural network. Expert Syst. Appl. **198**, 1–16 (2022)
15. Wang, H.X., et al.: Anti-spoofing study on palm biometric features. Expert Syst. Appl. **218**, 1–15 (2023)
16. Ying H., et al.: Multispectral palm image fusion for accurate contact-free palmprint recognition. In: 15th IEEE International Conference on Image Processing, San Diego, pp. 281–284. IEEE (2008)

17. Kang, W.X., Wu, Q.X.: Contactless palm vein recognition using a mutual foreground-based local binary pattern. IEEE TIFS **9**(11), 1974–1985 (2014)
18. Luo, D.C., et al.: Palm vein recognition under unconstrained and weak-cooperative conditions. IEEE TIFS **19**, 4601–4614 (2024)
19. Jin X., et al.: StarLKNet: star Mixup with large kernel networks for palm vein identification. ArXiv preprint, vol. abs/2405.12721

An Image Super-Resolution Based Method for Palmprint Recognition

Zekai Yang[1], Dacan Luo[1], Ming Zeng[1], Hao Wan[1,2(✉)], and Wenxiong Kang[1]

[1] School of Automation Science and Engineering, South China University of Technology, Guangzhou, China
202220117056@mail.scut.edu.cn
[2] Guang Zhou Baiyun International Airport Company Limited, Guangzhou, China

Abstract. Palmprint recognition, noted for its high reliability and privacy has recently aroused wide attention in biometrics. For palmprint recognition, High-quality palmprint images are more effective. However, in real-world scenarios, the quality of palmprint images tends to be low due to limitations in device capabilities and various environmental factors. This study introduced a palmprint recognition method based on image super-resolution (SR), called PPSRNet. The proposed PPSRNet consists of two parallel branches that extract features from SR palmprint images and original images, merging them through score fusion at the final stage. This method employs image SR to enhance image quality and refine the intricate details of palm texture, thereby improving recognition performance. It also utilizes score fusion to address potential negative effects during the image SR process. Experimental results on three popular public palmprint biometric datasets demonstrated the effectiveness of PPSRNet for palmprint recognition.

Keywords: Palmprint Recognition · Image Super-Resolution · Score Fusion

1 Introduction

Biometric recognition has found widespread application in identification systems. Various biometric features, such as the face, fingerprint, palm vein, finger vein, and gait, have been employed across fields like device authentication, financial transactions, and workplace security [1]. Among these, palmprint recognition provides a more user-friendly method that only requires an RGB camera and can even be ported to mobile phones for recognition [2,3]. Furthermore, palmprint recognition is superior in contactless and meeting stringent hygienic standards. However, in practical applications, the quality of palmprint images is often affected by various factors, including imaging hardware, complex environments, varying light intensities, and uneven backgrounds in contactless acquisition scenarios [4]. The impaired quality of palmprint images can hinder the extraction of discriminative biometric features, impacting the identification process. Consequently, improving the quality of palmprint samples plays a critical role and remains a research hotspot for reliable palmprint recognition [5].

Image super-resolution (SR) has demonstrated its promising effectiveness in enhancing image quality by recovering high-resolution (HR) images from their low-resolution (LR) versions. This technique plays a significant role in various fields, including biometric imaging, surveillance, and entertainment, facilitating accurate analysis and detection [5–7]. In face recognition, image SR is utilized as a preprocessing method to enhance recognition performance by creating HR face images [8]. Inspired by that, we tried to introduce image SR as a data enhancement method into palmprint recognition. This endeavor aimed to enhance the quality of palmprint images and boost the model's recognition accuracy.

In this article, we proposed a palmprint recognition network based on image SR, called PPSRNet. As shown in Fig. 1, the proposed PPSRNet consists of two parallel branches. The image SR branch integrates the image SR network (SCNet [9]) with the recognition network in an end-to-end manner. It is essential to note that using the image SR method to enhance original images can improve quality but may inadvertently alter key information. To address this concern, score fusion was implemented. This technique calculates the identity prediction scores of SR images and original images after passing through the recognition network. By utilizing the weighted quasi-arithmetic mean (WQAM) [10] method, the final output scores from both types of images are fused. Compared to solely relying on the SR images, the application of score fusion across multiple benchmark datasets yielded promising results, reducing the Equal Error Rate (EER) and achieving certain performance improvements.

Our contributions can be summarized as follows:

1. We introduce image SR into palmprint recognition and proposed PPSRNet. By using image SR to enhance palmprint images, we refined the texture features and effectively improved the recognition performance of our method.
2. We establish a fusion framework and include a non-SR branch to preserve original image information, effectively improving recognition performance by mitigating potential negative effects of image SR.

2 Related Work

2.1 Palmprint Biometrics

Palmprint recognition methods can be broadly categorized into four groups: subspace-based, statistical-based, coding-based, and deep learning-based. Subspace-based methods, such as Principal Component Analysis (PCA) [11] and Linear Discriminant Analysis (LDA) [12], are utilized to perform dimensionality reduction and feature extraction on palmprint images. Statistical-based methods analyze texture and structural features by statistically summarizing ridge orientations or local patterns. Methods, such as Directional Orientation Histogram (DOH) [13] and Local Binary Patterns (LBP) [14] are commonly employed. Coding-based methods aim to extra discriminative texture features by employing specific encoders to derive directional information from palmprints. Gabor filters are powerful in extracting texture features in palmprint recognition [15].

In recent years, the emergence of deep learning has brought about the development of Convolutional Neural Networks (CNN), which have displayed remarkable capabilities in feature representation and have achieved excellent results in various computer vision tasks. Inspired by these advancements, researchers have proposed deep learning-based approaches in the field of palmprint recognition. Zhong et al. [16] proposed a VGG-16 network based on a siamese architecture with parameter sharing for palmprint feature extraction. Genovese et al. [17] proposed an unsupervised palmprint recognition method called PalmNet, which combined different feature extraction methods, including CNNs, Gabor filters, and PCA. Another method CO3Net [18] integrated Coordinate Attention within the network, enabling dynamic emphasis on salient textures using positional information.

2.2 Palmprint Image Enhancement Methods

In the field of palmprint recognition, image quality is a critical component. While contactless palmprint recognition offers increased safety and convenience, it also introduces problems such as overexposure, blurriness, distortion, and noise. Consequently, researchers have extensively applied image enhancement techniques to improve the accuracy of palmprint recognition. Kusban et al. [4] combined different filtering approaches and coordinated the 3W filter with Gabor orientation scales, matching processes, and dimension reduction methods to improve image quality. Wang et al. [19] developed a palmprint image SR network based on the U-Net architecture, focusing on exploring multi-scale palmprint-specific features to enhance the quality and detail of palmprint images. Subsequent research introduced a hybrid attention mechanism combining CNN and Transformer to extract various palmprint-specific features [5]. Building on this prior work, this study has developed a palmprint recognition network based on image SR. This network directly connects the image SR network with the recognition network, enabling the simultaneous training of both components. This approach is beneficial for refining the textural features of palmprint images and improving image quality.

3 Proposed Method

3.1 Architecture of the Proposed PPSRNet

The model proposed in this article, PPSRNet, is a palmprint recognition network based on image SR. As shown in Fig. 1, PPSRNet consists of two branches, which are utilized to extract the features from SR palmprint images and original images. Subsequently, the features are fused using score fusion.

In our network, we start by inputting a palmprint image $I_{ori} \in \mathbb{R}^{3 \times W \times H}$, and then extract features in parallel through a dual-branch structure. The image SR branch initially enhances I_{ori}, applies SRNet $S(\bullet)$ to perform image SR on it, improves its quality, and obtains a high-quality palmprint image $I_{sr} \in \mathbb{R}^{3 \times W \times H}$,

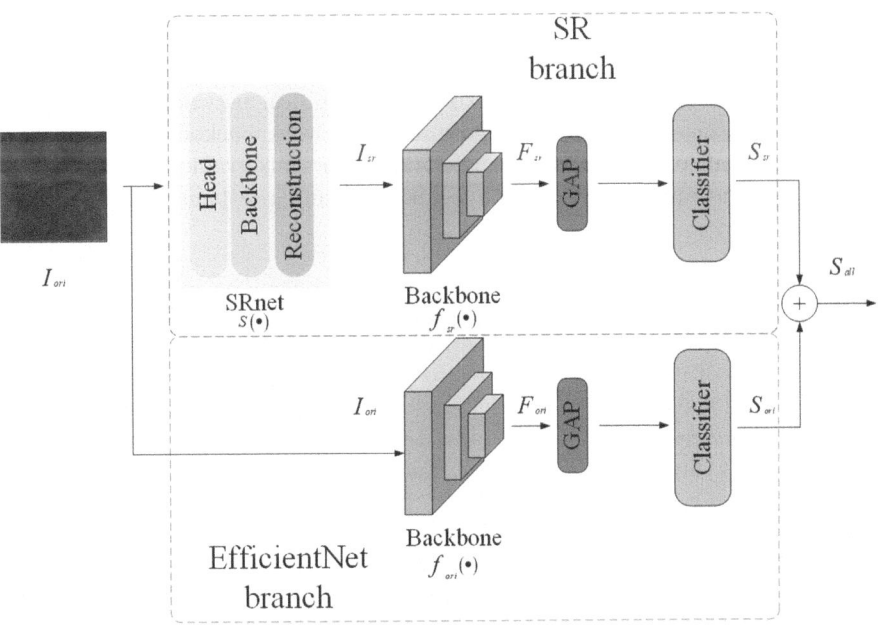

Fig. 1. Architecture of PPSRNet.

which is then fed into the backbone network $f_{sr}(\bullet)$ for feature extraction to obtain a high-quality palmprint feature vector F_{sr}. Finally, after the classification layer, a high-quality palmprint image identity prediction score S_{sr} is obtained. The other branch directly employs the backbone network $f_{ori}(\bullet)$ to extract features and predict identities on the original image I_{ori}, and obtains the original image palmprint feature vector F_{ori} and the identity prediction score S_{ori}. The SR branch score S_{sr} and the original image branch score S_{ori} are fused to obtain the final score.

The image SR branch employs the image SR as a data enhancement method to improve the network recognition performance by refining the texture features of the palmprint image. The other branch inputs the original image into the backbone network $f_{ori}(\bullet)$ for feature extraction. The main reason is that while the quality of the image after image SR is higher, sometimes some key information for recognition is changed because of unclear image SR improvements. To make up for the negative effects of image SR, we added the original image branch and improved the recognition performance through the score fusion.

3.2 Image SR Branch

The image SR branch employs the image SR network as a data enhancement method to improve image quality. To reduce the unclear direction of the quality improvement of palmprint images after image SR, and guide it to a more suitable direction for identity recognition, the SR network is connected end-to-end with the recognition network. We choose the SCNet-T [9] network as the image SRnet for PPSRNet to improve the resolution of palmprint images. We proposed the HR palmprint images as the input to the recognition network. For this, we choose Efficientnet-b1 [20] as the recognition network backbone. To improve model performance, we utilize the network weights pre-trained on ImageNet, provided by the author. We then fine-tune it using the palmprint biometric datasets.

3.3 Score Fusion

It is important to consider that image SR may result in negative effects during the process of upscaling LR images to HR ones. To tackle this problem, we introduce score fusion to promote the interaction between the information contained in SR images and original images. In this article, we utilize score fusion, which combines the matching scores S_{sr} and S_{ori} obtained from SR images and original images after passing through the backbone network and classification layers of the recognition network, respectively. The score fusion methodology employed in this article was derived from the work of Abderrahmane et al. [10], known as WQAM. WQAM uses different trigonometric functions, which contain properties of both weighted mean and quasi-arithmetic mean to reduce the false rejection rate (FRR) and false acceptance rate (FAR).

The score fusion method we utilized is as follows:

$$S_{all} = \frac{2}{\pi} arctan \left(\sum_{k=1}^{n} \frac{1}{n} tan \left(\frac{\pi}{2} s_k \right) \right) \quad (1)$$

where s_k denotes the matching scores and n denotes the number of matching scores to be fused by the operation.

3.4 Loss Function

The Arcface loss [21] and center loss [22] are employed in PPSRNet to improve the discriminability of identity features.

Arcface loss is a loss function based on an improvement of softmax loss:

$$L_{Arc} = -\frac{1}{N} \sum_{i=1}^{N} \log \frac{e^{s[\cos(\theta_{y_i,i}+m)]}}{e^{s[\cos(\theta_{y_i,i}+m)]} + \sum_{j \neq y_i} e^{s[\cos(\theta_{j,i})]}} \quad (2)$$

where N represents the number of samples in each batch, and y_i represents the class of the i-th palmprint image. θ_j is the angle between the weight W_j and feature x_i of the i-th sample. θ_{y_i} is the target optimization angle, and m is the optimization margin.

Center loss aims to enhance the model's robustness to intra-class variations by minimizing the distance between sample features within the same class. The intra-class variance can be expressed as:

$$L_C = \frac{1}{2} \sum_{i=1}^{N} \|x_i - c_{y_i}\|_2^2 \quad (3)$$

where N represents the number of samples, x_i represents the feature vector extracted from the sample i, and $c_{(y_i)}$ represents the average feature of all sample features of the category corresponding to sample i, or the center point of the same type of sample features.

The final loss function for PPSRNet can be expressed as follows:

$$L = L_{Arc} + \lambda L_C \tag{4}$$

where λ is a parameter balancing the ArcFace loss and center loss.

4 Experiments

4.1 Implementation Details

In our experiments, we utilized several widely used publicly available palmprint multimodal datasets, namely IIT-D [23], COEP [24], and Tongji [2] datasets. All images used in this study were resized to dimensions of 224 × 224. We optimized the proposed network using the Adam optimizer with a momentum of 0.9, a learning rate of 0.0001, no weight decay, and a batch size of 4. To train PalmNet, 75% of the data for each palm were used for training. For the other methods, the 1st session data were used for training, while the 2nd session data were used for testing. For computing the EER, we employed the cosine distance metric and iteratively determined the optimal threshold by evaluating the test set. All reported results were generated from models trained for 200 epochs.

4.2 Evaluation of PPSRNet

Table 1. EER (%) of different pipelines on three datasets.

	COEP	IIT-D	Tongji
ResNet18 [25]	0.9459	0.1422	0.0297
ResNet50 [25]	0.1203	0.1907	0.1421
MobileNetV3 [26]	0.7347	0.4492	0.1172
Mobilefacenet [27]	0.5285	0.5387	0.0453
Efficientnet-b1 [20]	0.7759	0.1134	0.0027
PalmNet [17]	\	4.2000	0.0322
CompNet [28]	\	0.5400	0.0250
CO3Net [18]	\	0.4700	0.0050
PPSRNet	**0.3410**	**0.0739**	**0.0001**

To compare the performance of PPSRNet, we selected various classical and state-of-the-art methods, including ResNet18 [25], ResNet50 [25], MobileNetV3

[26], Mobilefacenet [27], Efficientnet [20], PalmNet [17], CompNet [28], CO3Net [18]. Table 1 shows the EERs of PPSRNet compared to these methods on three publicly available palmprint datasets. Experimental results demonstrated the effectiveness of the PPSRNet approach, as it consistently outperforms other methods across all datasets. The EERs of PPSRNet are consistently lower than the other methods across all datasets, demonstrating improved recognition performance. This improvement can be attributed to the enhanced image quality resulting from image SR processing of palmprint images, which allows for more accurate feature extraction and leads to better recognition results. The original image information introduced by the established fusion framework also complements the SR image information well, jointly improving the recognition accuracy.

4.3 Ablation Study

In the following, we conduct a series of ablation experiments to evaluate the effectiveness of our method.

Table 2. EER (%) results of PPSRNet.

	COEP	IIT-D	Tongji
Baseline	0.7759	0.1134	0.0027
+Image SR	0.5446	0.1090	0.0232
+Score Fusion	**0.3410**	**0.0739**	**0.0001**

We enhanced the quality of the palmprint images by applying image SR on the dataset images. The experimental results, displayed in Table 2, demonstrated that image SR is effective for feature extraction in palmprint recognition. Image SR can reconstruct parts of the original image information, thus improving image recognizability. Enhancing palmprint image resolution through image SR preprocessing is feasible and leads to better image quality and improved palmprint recognition performance. Moreover, score fusion significantly improves palmprint recognition performance.

Table 3. Results of EER (%) for different fusion methods.

		COEP	IIT-D	Tongji
Image Fusion	PCA Fusion	1.0440	0.1827	0.0248
	Weight Fusion	0.5925	0.0922	0.0003
	DWT Fusion	0.6249	0.1642	0.0032
Score Fusion		**0.3410**	**0.0739**	**0.0001**

Performing image SR on an image may change certain information. As shown in Table 2, after applying image SR, the performance on Tongji is unsatisfactory. Therefore, it is crucial to include the original image in the feature extraction process of the recognition network, which involves fusing SR images with original images. Image SR can reconstruct the original image information and complement the original image after fusion. The experimental results have indicated score fusion could produce the most optimal results, as shown in Table 2 and Table 3. After applying image SR to the original image, texture features that were not prominent in the original image but possess higher discriminative power may be enhanced, thus improving image recognition. However, the image SR process may alter some texture information of the original image. As demonstrated in Table 3, the fusion of both SR images and original images allows for mutual complementation, resulting in improved performance.

We utilized Grad-CAM++ [29] to highlight the discriminative regions and features for palmprint recognition. The CAM in Fig. 2 demonstrated that PPSR-Net could better locate the palmprint texture after the inclusion of image SR. This indicates that including image SR could effectively refine texture features and enhance the network's recognition function.

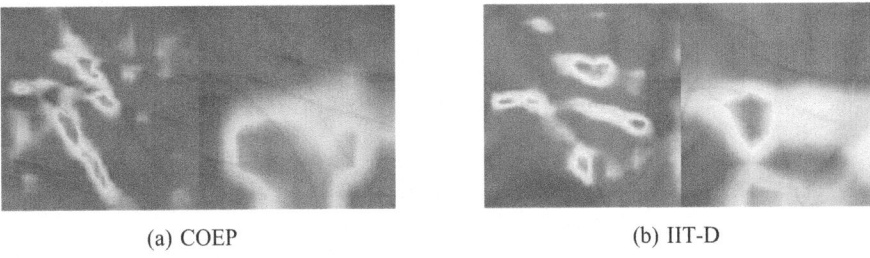

(a) COEP (b) IIT-D

Fig. 2. The Grad CAM++ localization maps of PPSRNet (left) and Efficientnet (right) for predicting a target subject.

5 Conclusion

In this study, we implement image SR technology as a data enhancement tool for palmprint recognition to enhance image quality, consequently improving palmprint recognition performance. Simultaneously, to reduce the potential negative effects of image SR on the original images, we establish a fusion framework that integrates the original image information and employs score fusion to combine the image SR branch with the original image branch. Experimental comparisons conducted on the Tongji, IIT-D, and COEP palmprint datasets demonstrated the effectiveness of our method.

Acknowledgments. This work was supported by the National Natural Science Foundation of China (No. 62376100), the Natural Science Foundation of Guangdong Province, China (No. 2022A1515010114).

References

1. Shakil, S., Arora, D., Zaidi, T.: A study on identification of human using palm vein recognition system. In: Swaroop, A., Kansal, V., Fortino, G., Hassanien, A.E. (eds.) DoSCI 2023. LNNS, vol. 726, pp. 175–183. Springer, Singapore (2023). https://doi.org/10.1007/978-981-99-3716-5_16
2. Zhang, L., Li, L., Yang, A., Shen, Y., Yang, M.: Towards contactless palmprint recognition: a novel device, a new benchmark, and a collaborative representation based identification approach. Pattern Recogn. **69**, 199–212 (2017)
3. Shao, H., Zhong, D., Du, X.: Towards efficient unconstrained palmprint recognition via deep distillation hashing. arXiv preprint arXiv:2004.03303 (2020)
4. Kusban, M., Budiman, A., Purwoto, B.H.: Image enhancement in palmprint recognition: a novel approach for improved biometric authentication. Int. J. Electr. Comput. Eng. (IJECE) **14**(2), 1299–1307 (2024)
5. Wang, Y., et al.: Dense hybrid attention network for palmprint image super-resolution. IEEE Trans. Syst. Man Cybern. Syst. **54**, 2590–2602 (2024)
6. Basak, S., Suresh, S.: Vehicle detection and type classification in low resolution congested traffic scenes using image super resolution. Multimedia Tools Appl. **83**(8), 21825–21847 (2024)
7. Chen, W., Lin, W., Xu, X., Lin, L., Zhao, T.: Face super-resolution quality assessment based on identity and recognizability. IEEE Trans. Biom. Behav. Identity Sci. **6**, 364–373 (2024)
8. Chen, J., Chen, J., Wang, Z., Liang, C., Lin, C.W.: Identity-aware face super-resolution for low-resolution face recognition. IEEE Signal Process. Lett. **27**, 645–649 (2020)
9. Wu, G., Jiang, J., Jiang, K., Liu, X.: Fully 1×1 convolutional network for lightweight image super-resolution. arXiv preprint arXiv:2307.16140 (2023)
10. Abderrahmane, H., Noubeil, G., Lahcene, Z., Akhtar, Z., Dasgupta, D.: Weighted quasi-arithmetic mean based score level fusion for multi-biometric systems. IET Biom. **9**(3), 91–99 (2020)
11. Lu, G., Zhang, D., Wang, K.: Palmprint recognition using eigenpalms features. Pattern Recogn. Lett. **24**(9–10), 1463–1467 (2003)
12. Wu, X.Q., Wang, K.Q., Zhang, D.: Palmprint recognition using Fisher's linear discriminant. In: Proceedings of the 2003 International Conference on Machine Learning and Cybernetics (IEEE Cat. No. 03EX693), vol. 5, pp. 3150–3154. IEEE (2003)
13. Manasa, N., Govardhan, A., Satyanarayana, C.: Touch-less palm print recognition system based on fusion of local and global features. Int. J. Comput. Appl. Technol. **51**(2), 145–154 (2015)
14. Zhang, S., Wang, H., Huang, W., Zhang, C.: Combining modified LBP and weighted SRC for palmprint recognition. In: SIVIP, pp. 1–8 (2018)
15. Fei, L., Zhang, B., Jia, W., Wen, J., Zhang, D.: Feature extraction for 3-d palmprint recognition: a survey. IEEE Trans. Instrum. Meas. **69**(3), 645–656 (2020)
16. Zhong, D., Yang, Y., Du, X.: Palmprint recognition using Siamese network. In: Zhou, J., et al. (eds.) CCBR 2018. LNCS, vol. 10996, pp. 48–55. Springer, Cham (2018). https://doi.org/10.1007/978-3-319-97909-0_6

17. Genovese, A., Piuri, V., Plataniotis, K.N., Scotti, F.: PalmNet: Gabor-PCA convolutional networks for touchless palmprint recognition. IEEE Trans. Inf. Forensics Secur. **14**(12), 3160–3174 (2019)
18. Yang, Z.: Co 3 net: coordinate-aware contrastive competitive neural network for palmprint recognition. IEEE Trans. Instrum. Meas. **72**, 1–14 (2023)
19. Wang, Y., Fei, L., Chai, T., Zhao, S., Kang, P., Jia, W.: U-PISRnet: a Unet-shape palmprint image super-resolution network. In: Jia, W., et al. (eds.) CCBR 2023. LNCS, vol. 14463, pp. 24–33. Springer, Singapore (2023). https://doi.org/10.1007/978-981-99-8565-4_3
20. Tan, M., Le, Q.: EfficientNet: rethinking model scaling for convolutional neural networks. In: International Conference on Machine Learning, pp. 6105–6114. PMLR (2019)
21. Deng, J., Guo, J., Xue, N., Zafeiriou, S.: ArcFace: additive angular margin loss for deep face recognition. In: Proceedings of the IEEE/CVF Conference on Computer Vision and Pattern Recognition, pp. 4690–4699 (2019)
22. Wen, Y., Zhang, K., Li, Z., Qiao, Yu.: A discriminative feature learning approach for deep face recognition. In: Leibe, B., Matas, J., Sebe, N., Welling, M. (eds.) ECCV 2016, Part VII. LNCS, vol. 9911, pp. 499–515. Springer, Cham (2016). https://doi.org/10.1007/978-3-319-46478-7_31
23. Kumar, A., Shekhar, S.: Personal identification using multibiometrics rank-level fusion. IEEE Trans. Syst. Man Cybern. C (Appl. Rev.) **41**(5), 743–752 (2010)
24. College of Engineering, Pune-411005 (An Autonomous Institute of Government of Maharashtra): Palmprint dataset (2020). http://www.coep.org.in/resources/coeppalmprintdatabase
25. He, K., Zhang, X., Ren, S., Sun, J.: Deep residual learning for image recognition. In: Proceedings of the IEEE Conference on Computer Vision and Pattern Recognition, pp. 770–778 (2016)
26. Koonce, B., Koonce, B.: Mobilenetv3. In: Convolutional Neural Networks with Swift for Tensorflow: Image Recognition and Dataset Categorization, pp. 125–144. Apress, Berkeley (2021)
27. Chen, S., Liu, Y., Gao, X., Han, Z.: MobileFaceNets: efficient CNNs for accurate real-time face verification on mobile devices. In: Zhou, J., et al. (eds.) CCBR 2018. LNCS, vol. 10996, pp. 428–438. Springer, Cham (2018). https://doi.org/10.1007/978-3-319-97909-0_46
28. Liang, X., Yang, J., Lu, G., Zhang, D.: CompNet: competitive neural network for palmprint recognition using learnable Gabor kernels. IEEE Signal Process. Lett. **28**, 1739–1743 (2021)
29. Chattopadhay, A., Sarkar, A., Howlader, P., Balasubramanian, V.N.: Grad-CAM++: generalized gradient-based visual explanations for deep convolutional networks. In: 2018 IEEE Winter Conference on Applications of Computer Vision (WACV), pp. 839–847. IEEE (2018)

FCNet: Adaptive Finger Trimodal Feature Crystal Construction and Recognition

Zihao Zhao[1], Ziyun Ye[1], Binmeng Shi[1], Qi Liang[2], Xingzheng Zhu[1(✉)], and Jinfeng Yang[1]

[1] Institute of Applied Artificial Intelligence of the Guangdong-Hong Kong-Macao Greater Bay Area, Shenzhen Polytechnic University, Shenzhen 518055, China
zhuxingzheng@szpu.edu.cn

[2] Tianjin Navigation Instruments Research Institute, Organization, Tianjin 300131, China

Abstract. Finger multimodal recognition methods, which combine fingerprint, finger-knuckle-print, and finger-vein pattern, offer superior accuracy and robustness. However, current research faces significant challenges due to the instability of image acquisition caused by individual differences and feature space mismatches between modalities. This paper proposes a finger trimodal feature recognition model called FCNet. First, three CNNs are used to extract features from the trimodal images, separately. Then, nodes and node-features are generated based on the CNN feature maps. Next, all the nodes are fused into a crystal-shaped graph. Finally, the graph is fed into the GCN model for further optimisation to obtain a feature graph that accurately describes the finger information. Additionally, to improve the robustness of FCNet, we build a contaminated image dataset to train and test the model. The experimental results demonstrate that FCNet exhibits superior recognition performance and robustness in comparison to other models.

Keywords: Finger trimodal biometrics · Crystal graph feature · GCN · Feature extraction · Adaptive model

1 Introduction

Finger multimodal biometric fusion has garnered considerable attention in recent years. Fingers contain unique and rich biometric information, such as fingerprints (FP), finger knuckle prints (FKP), and finger veins (FV), providing higher reliability, effectiveness, and user-friendliness [1]. Especially, the finger vein pattern, which exists underneath the skin, offers excellent advantages such as uniqueness, active liveness detection, and anti-counterfeiting capabilities. Research has shown that finger multimodal biometric recognition improves accuracy and robustness [2], reducing instability caused by uncontrollable factors during image acquisition. Using fused features instead of original images for matching reduces the risk of sensitive information leakage. However, mismatching different feature patterns remains a challenging problem in multimodal feature representation and the exploration of fusion strategies.

Zhang et al. [3] proposed a trimodal fusion recognition method for FP, FV, and FKP based on competitive coding, demonstrating that fusion recognition is superior to unimodal recognition. Li et al. [4] introduced a joint discriminative sparse coding method for fusing FV and FKP features, emphasizing implicit correlations between modalities. Using dominant direction vectors and feature mapping functions, intra-class sample features are made more compact, improving fusion recognition [5]. Traditional methods require manual feature extraction, relying on expert experience and lacking robustness. Convolutional Neural Networks (CNNs) efficiently process high-dimensional data, automatically learn and extract features from raw data, thus capturing biometric nuances and improving recognition accuracy and robustness. Wen et al. [6] proposed an end-to-end CNN-based finger multimodal feature extraction and recognition model, effectively reducing the complexity of the algorithm. Li et al. [7] introduced a multimodal fusion method based on local graph coding strategy combined with CNN, further improving recognition accuracy and stability.

Recent work has focused on fusing coding, graph, and CNN approaches to develop graph network models. In texture images, local texture patterns are often interrelated in complex ways, and graph structure networks can effectively capture these interdependencies. Graph Convolutional Networks (GCNs) are suitable for biometric image recognition tasks due to their flexible representation and powerful feature extraction [8]. Wu et al. [9] proposed a GCN-based FP and FV fusion recognition method to address feature space mismatch. Qu et al. [10] used three GCNs to extract features from all modalities separately and implemented fusion at the feature layer. Zhao et al. [11] converted trimodal images into feature nodes, composed them into a graph, and fed them into a GCN model, achieving good recognition results. Although GCN-based finger trimodal recognition methods have made significant progress in feature extraction and fusion, some challenges remain.

During image acquisition, the quality of FP images can be affected by finger damage or smudges, FV image quality is susceptible to individual differences and low body temperature, and FKP image quality is influenced by external lighting and acquisition posture. Additionally, the inconsistency of trimodal image scales complicates model construction and feature extraction. Feature space mismatch and formulating effective fusion rules are major challenges in the fusion process. To address these issues, this paper proposes the FCNet model. GCN serves as the backbone network. To eliminate image scale differences, the model applies three convolution and pooling operations on the input images to extract high-level features. Each feature map is considered a node, and its content corresponds to the node features, with feature lengths unified using the non-maximum value suppression (NMS) method. These nodes are connected into a crystal-shaped graph by creating edges. The GCN model then learns and extracts features from this graph, outputting a fusion feature that accurately represents finger trimodal information. Simulated contamination is added to the dataset images to improve the model robustness against abnormal samples. Experiments on the finger trimodal dataset demonstrate the effectiveness of this method.

The main contributions of our work are highlighted below: a. A novel finger trimodal feature fusion and recognition method is proposed in this paper. b. Using CNN feature maps as nodes to construct a graph can effectively address the challenges of inconsistent scale in the original image and feature space mismatch problem. c. Our model achieves 98.25% recognition results and is robust to contaminated data.

The rest of this paper is organized as follows: Sect. 2 covers image acquisition and processing. Section 3 details the FCNet model. Section 4 presents experiments and analysis of results. Conclusions are drawn in Sect. 5.

2 Image Acquisition and Processing

Several public finger biometric datasets exist for scientific research. The Fingerprint Verification Competition (FVC) [12] includes FP images from various acquisition conditions. NIST SD-14 [13], provided by the National Institute of Standards and Technology (NIST), is another FP dataset. SDUMLA-HMT [14], provided by Shandong University, is a multimodal biometric dataset that includes FP and FV images. The Hong Kong Polytechnic University offers datasets containing FV and FKP images [15]. However, no dataset captures all three finger modal features.

To further study multimodal fusion recognition, our lab has created an in-house finger trimodal dataset containing FP, FKP, and FV images. The acquisition device is shown in Fig. 1, simultaneously captures trimodal feature images. FP and FKP images are captured in blue visible light, while FV images are captured in near infrared light. ROI localization is completed during image acquisition. We recruit youth-aged volunteers to collect data from six fingers (index, middle, ring) of both hands.

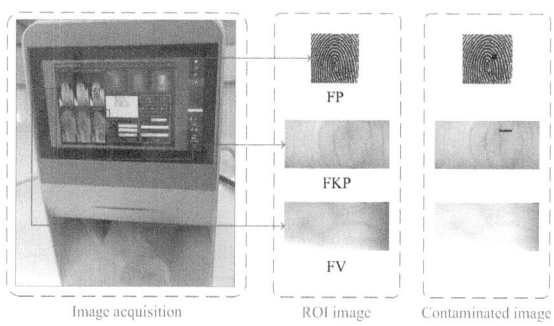

Fig. 1. Finger trimodal image acquisition and processing.

During image acquisition, various factors such as stains or cuts, finger posture, cold weather, bruising, swelling, and congenital defects can affect image quality. These can lead to temporary or permanent defects in acquired biometric images, impacting one or multiple modalities. Low-quality images reduce the accuracy of feature matching and recognition. To improve the model learning ability, we add noise to the dataset images. For FP images, we simulate smudges or cuts by adding noise to randomly selected areas, creating a contaminated image dataset. For FKP images, we generate contaminated images to simulate texture loss due to scratches. For FV images, we simulate blurring caused by cold weather by adjusting pixel values. These contaminated images are added to the dataset to improve and test the model robustness and reduce recognition errors caused by objective factors.

3 The Proposed Model

This paper proposes the FCNet for finger trimodal biometric recognition. The model consists of three modules: the feature extraction module, the crystal graph construction module, and the GCN module. The overall model framework is shown in Fig. 2.

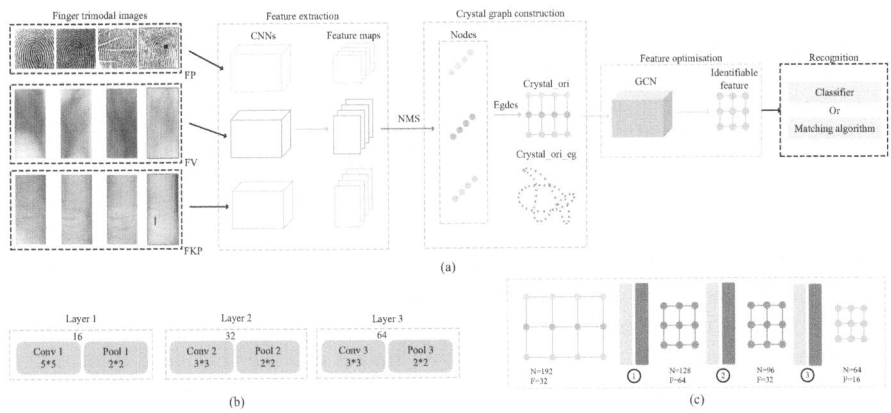

Fig. 2. Architecture of FCNet model. (a) is the whole process, (b) shows the structure of the feature extractor, (c) shows the details of the GCN module, N refers to nodes, and F refers to node features. In addition, we generate a sample crystal-shaped graph based on the adjacency matrix ($Crystal\_ori\_eg$) for the better understanding.

3.1 Feature Extraction

FP, FKP, and FV images contain rich and complex texture information. Traditional graph construction methods generate node and edge sets directly from image texture or by extracting energy points using super-pixel division [16]. These methods can easily destroy original image features and struggle with inconsistent image scale and feature space mismatch. To achieve better feature representation, we use CNN models to extract features from each of the three modal images. The first convolutional layer acts as an edge detector, recognizing local texture patterns. The second layer extracts intermediate-level features, such as intersections and general texture shapes. The third layer detects high-level semantic features, identifying spatial relationships and configurations between feature points. It integrates information from the first two layers to form global features. Constructing a fusion graph based on features from these three convolutional layers effectively addresses issues of image scale and content variability.

The detailed CNN structure for the feature extractor is shown in Fig. 2(b). This CNN has three layers of convolution and pooling. In the first layer, the convolution kernel size is 5×5, with 16 kernels, a stride of 1, and zero padding of 2. In the second layer, the convolution kernel size is 3×3, with 32 kernels, a stride of 1, and zero padding of 1. In the third layer, the convolution kernel size is 3×3, with 64 kernels, a stride of 1, and zero padding of 1. Max pooling is used in all three pooling layers, with a pooling window size of 2×2 and a stride of 2. The ReLU activation function is added to each layer.

3.2 Crystal Graph Construction

Once the model completes CNN-based feature extraction, 64 feature maps are obtained for each modality. Next, nodes and node features are generated based on these feature maps, and the three modalities are fused by constructing an edge set to form a crystal-shaped graph.

We believe that each feature map corresponds to a deep feature, and after three convolutions, the 64 feature maps of different modalities should have more closely matched corresponding features. The model generates nodes based on these feature maps, with each feature map acting as a node, resulting in a total of 64 nodes per modality. Due to the difference in the size of the input images for different modalities, the size of the feature map after three convolutions varies. To ensure the feature length is same for all nodes, we use the NMS method to extract 32 feature points from each feature map. First, the local maxima in the feature map are found using the expansion operation, as follows:

$$\text{dilated}(i,j) = \max_{(m,n)\in \text{kernel}} \text{feature\_map}(i+m, j+n), \qquad (1)$$

where the kernel is usually 3×3 structural elements. Then, local maxima are detected:

$$\text{local\_max}(i,j) = \begin{cases} 1, \text{feature\_map}(i,j) = \text{dilated}(i,j) \\ 0, \text{other} \end{cases}. \qquad (2)$$

Next, the locations and values of the local maxima are identified and sorted. The top 32 local maxima are then selected, and their positions are recorded. These

32 feature points, extracted from each feature map, serve as the node features. Consequently, the three modalities collectively produce 192 nodes, each with a feature length of 32.

To obtain the fused trimodal graph, we construct an adjacency matrix for these nodes. First, the 64 nodes of each modality are connected sequentially within the same modality. Then, nodes of the corresponding order are interconnected between different modalities. The specific adjacency matrix $A_{i,j}$ is as,

$$A_{i,j} = \begin{cases} 1, (i = j - 1) \text{and} (j \div 64 \neq 0) \\ 1, (i = 0, j = 63) \text{or} (i = 64, j = 127) \text{or} (i = 128, j = 191) \\ 1, (i = j - 64) \text{or} (i = j - 128) \\ 0, \text{other} \end{cases}, \quad (3)$$

where i,j are the node numbers, $0 \leq i,j < 192$, and $i < j$. With the nodes, node features, and adjacency matrix, we can construct the graph called trimodal feature crystal graph.

3.3 GCN

FP, FV, and FKP are fused into a crystal graph, which requires further optimization to accurately represent the finger features. This process involves removing unimportant nodes and updating the features of the retained nodes. GCN effectively recognizes various graph structures in classification tasks, aligning perfectly with our requirements. Performing recognition based on the resulting graph not only ensures robust feature characterization but also reduces the risk of privacy leakage.

The model employs three graph convolution layers to update the node features, with output feature lengths of 64, 32, and 16, respectively. Additionally, it uses three pooling layers to identify the most valuable nodes: 128 nodes are retained after the first pooling, 96 nodes after the second pooling, and 64 nodes after the third pooling. The process is illustrated in Fig. 2(c). The model utilizes a custom average pooling method. The final crystal graph has 64 nodes with a feature length of 16. During training, the model is connected to a three-layer classifier for parameter optimization. During testing, the model can be followed by either classifiers or feature matching algorithms, depending on the task. The crystal graphs generated by the trained FCNet serve as carriers for finger trimodal features.

4 Experiments and Analysis of Results

To validate the performance of FCNet, we first conduct comparative experiments based on different model structures and parameters. Next, we compare our model with other state-of-the-art (SOTA) models. Finally, we perform comparative experiments to assess model robustness.

4.1 Datasets and Experimental Conditions

The dataset used for all experiments is a finger trimodal dataset produced in our laboratory. Each modality has 1,000 images, divided into 100 classes with 10 images per class. Additionally, there are 1,000 contaminated samples per modality, also divided into 100 classes. Thus, the dataset comprises 6,000 images. The dataset is split 7:2:1 for training, testing, and validation.

All experiments are conducted on a workstation with an Intel W-2255 CPU at 3.70 GHz, 32 GB of RAM, and the Windows 10 operating system. The graphics card used is an NVIDIA GeForce RTX 3080.

4.2 Evaluation Metrics

Finger feature recognition can be divided into verification and identification. Verification involves a one-to-one comparison resulting in a yes or no outcome. Identification matches finger features in a one-to-many mode, comparing user features with all features in database to identify the user. We test the model performance in identification.

First, we test the overall recognition accuracy of the model. Next, to further understand the model performance, we calculate the False Acceptance Rate (FAR) and False Rejection Rate (FRR) respectively. For class i, FP_i indicates a sample that does not belong to class i is misclassified as class i. TN_i indicates samples that do not belong to class i are correctly classified as other classes. FN_i samples that belong to class i are misclassified as other classes. TP_i indicates a sample that belong to class i is correctly classified as class i. Then, weighted average FAR and FRR are calculated for all classes.

$$FAR = \sum_{i=1}^{C} \frac{N_i}{N} \cdot \frac{FP_i}{FP_i + TN_i}, \quad (4)$$

$$FRR = \sum_{i=1}^{C} \frac{N_i}{N} \cdot \frac{FN_i}{FN_i + TP_i}, \quad (5)$$

where N is the total number of samples from all classes, N_i is the number of samples in class i, C is the total number of classes. Finally, we also compare the computational speed of the models considering the practical application requirements.

4.3 Comparisons with Different Model Structures and Parameters

Both the model structure and the selection of network parameters impact model performance. We determine the best choice through several comparative experiments. We compare model performance based on the feature extractor structure, node feature length, adjacency matrix structure, and the GCN structure (recorded in Table 1). For the feature extractor, the structural choices include the number of convolution layers, the size of the convolution kernels, and the number of convolution kernels. Adjusting the number of convolutional kernels in the feature extractor results in differences in the number of nodes, and consequently, the general structure of the adjacency matrix, although the logic of connecting the nodes remains the same. Finally, differences exist in the number of nodes and the length of features output from each layer in the GCN module.

Table 1. Comparisons with different model structures and parameters.

Module	Structure and parameter	Accuracy
feature extractor	(5,16)(3,32)(3,64)	**98.25%**
	(5,32)(3,64)(3,128)	90.66%
	(3,16)(3,32)(3,64)	97.15%
	(5,16)(5,32)(3,64)(3,128)	85.94%
node feature	32	**98.25%**
	64	95.28%
	16	96.41%
adjacency matrix	192(64 × 3)	**98.25%**
	384(128 × 3)	94.07%
GCN	(128,64)(96,32)(64,16)	**98.25%**
	(128,64)(96,96)(64,64)	96.22%
	(192,64)(96,32)(64,16)	93.58%
	(192,64)(96,96)(64,64)	91.34%

The experimental results in Table 1 show that to achieve optimal model performance, the feature extractor should use 3 layers, with convolution kernel sizes of 5, 3, and 3, and convolution kernel counts of 16, 32, and 64, respectively. The node feature length should be 32, and the adjacency matrix should have a 64 × 3 structure. The number of output nodes per layer of the GCN should be 128, 96, and 64, with node feature lengths of 64, 32, and 16. Then, the FCNet is trained using the Adam optimizer with a learning rate of 0.0005 for 800 epochs, achieving a best recognition rate of 98.25% on the test set.

4.4 Comparisons with Other SOTA Methods

Based on the normal sample image dataset, we compare FCNet with other finger trimodal feature fusion recognition methods through experiments evaluating recognition accuracy, FAR, and FRR metrics. The experimental results are shown in Table 2. The results indicate that FCNet outperforms other methods in terms of accuracy, FAR, and FRR, while the time required to recognize a single image also meets practical requirements.

4.5 Robustness Experiment Results

Many methods achieve good accuracy in finger trimodal feature recognition, highlighting the superiority of multimodal fusion recognition. To understand the robustness differences among these recognition methods, we conduct comparative experiments using contaminated images. In the first test, only one modal

Table 2. Comparisons with other SOTA methods.

Method	Acc	FAR	FRR	Time
SAGPool-pro [11]	94.50%	1.03%	4.82%	0.0736 s
Eigenvector fusion [10]	96.75%	2.46%	1.02%	0.0482 s
Graph fusion [3]	97.25%	1.53%	1.39%	0.0194 s
Coding fusion [17]	97.75%	1.14%	1.09%	0.0058 s
Local coding [18]	98.00%	1.36%	0.83%	0.0039 s
FCNet	98.25%	0.51%	1.27%	0.0295 s

image is contaminated; in the second test, two modal images are contaminated; and in the third test, all three modal images are contaminated. The recognition accuracy results from these experiments are recorded in Table 3. The results indicate that FCNet exhibits the best robustness for contaminated images. In practical applications, even if the acquired images have quality problems, FCNet can still achieve accurate recognition.

Table 3. Comparisons for robustness with other SOTA methods.

Method	Acc	Acc-1	Acc-2	Acc-3
SAGPool-pro [11]	94.50%	93.75%	91.75%	90.00%
Eigenvector fusion [10]	96.75%	94.25%	93.00%	90.25%
Graph fusion [3]	97.25%	94.50%	92.75%	89.75%
Coding fusion [17]	97.75%	96.00%	93.50%	91.50%
Local coding [18]	98.00%	96.25%	92.75%	90.50%
FCNet	98.25%	98.00%	97.50%	96.75%

5 Conclusions

In finger trimodal feature fusion recognition, input image scale differences and feature space mismatches are significant challenges. To solve these problems, this paper proposed a FCNet-based method. During graph construction, nodes and node features were generated from feature maps extracted by the CNN feature extractor, and the GCN model updated the graph features to accurately represent the finger trimodal fusion information. Additionally, three classes of contaminated images were generated to improve model adaptivity and reduce the possible negative effects of quality defects in image acquisition. Comparative experimental results showed that FCNet achieved better and more robust recognition performance to other SOTA models.

Acknowledgements. This work was supported by the National Natural Science Foundation of China (62076166), the Scientific Research Startup Fund for Shenzhen High-Caliber Personnel of SZPU (602333000*K), the Research Projects of Department of Education of Guangdong Province (2023ZDZX1081, 2023KCXTD077), the

University-Enterprise Joint Research and Development Center (602431007PQ), the Smart Agriculture Innovation Application University-Enterprise Joint Research and Development Center (602431001PQ).

References

1. Shen, J., et al.: Finger vein recognition algorithm based on lightweight deep convolutional neural network. IEEE Trans. Instrum. Meas. **71**, 1–13 (2022)
2. Guo, Z., Ma, H., Liu, J.: NLNet: a narrow-channel lightweight network for finger multimodal recognition. Digit. Signal Process. **150**, 104517 (2024)
3. Zhang, H., Li, S., Shi, Y., Yang, J.: Graph fusion for finger multimodal biometrics. IEEE Access **7**, 28607–28615 (2019)
4. Li, S., Zhang, B.: Joint discriminative sparse coding for robust hand-based multimodal recognition. IEEE Trans. Inf. Forensics Secur. **16**, 3186–3198 (2021)
5. Li, S., Zhang, B., Fei, L., Zhao, S.: Joint discriminative feature learning for multimodal finger recognition. Pattern Recognit. **111**, 107704 (2021)
6. Wen, M., Zhang, H., Yang, J.: End-to-end finger trimodal features fusion and recognition model based on CNN. In: Feng, J., Zhang, J., Liu, M., Fang, Y. (eds.) CCBR 2021. LNCS, vol. 12878, pp. 39–48. Springer, Cham (2021). https://doi.org/10.1007/978-3-030-86608-2_5
7. Li, S., Zhang, H., Yang, J.: Finger vein recognition based on local graph structural coding and CNN. In: Tenth International Conference on Graphics and Image Processing (ICGIP), vol. 11069, p. 110693I (2019)
8. Zhang, M., Cui, Z., Neumann, M., Chen, Y.: An end-to-end deep learning architecture for graph classification. In: Thirty-Second Conference on Artificial Intelligence, (AAAI), New Orleans, Louisiana, USA, 2–7 February 2018, pp. 4438–4445 (2018)
9. Wu, Z., Qu, H., Zhang, H., Yang, J.: Robust graph fusion and recognition framework for fingerprint and finger-vein. IET Biom. **12**(1), 13–24 (2023)
10. Qu, H., Zhang, H., Yang, J., Wu, Z., He, L.: A generalized graph features fusion framework for finger biometric recognition. In: Feng, J., Zhang, J., Liu, M., Fang, Y. (eds.) CCBR 2021. LNCS, vol. 12878, pp. 267–276. Springer, Cham (2021). https://doi.org/10.1007/978-3-030-86608-2_30
11. Zhao, Z., Ye, Z., Yang, J., Zhang, H.: Finger crystal feature recognition based on graph convolutional network. In: Feng, J., Zhang, J., Liu, M., Fang, Y. (eds.) CCBR 2021. LNCS, vol. 12878, pp. 203–212. Springer, Cham (2021). https://doi.org/10.1007/978-3-030-86608-2_23
12. Maio, D., Maltoni, D., Cappelli, R., Wayman, J., Jain, A.: FVC 2000: fingerprint verification competition. IEEE Trans. Pattern Anal. Mach. Intell. **24**(3), 402–412 (2002)
13. Cao, K., Jain, A.K.: Fingerprint indexing and matching: an integrated approach. In: 2017 IEEE International Joint Conference on Biometrics (IJCB), pp. 437–445 (2017)
14. Yin, Y., Liu, L., Sun, X.: SDUMLA-HMT: a multimodal biometric database. In: Sun, Z., Lai, J., Chen, X., Tan, T. (eds.) CCBR 2011. LNCS, vol. 7098, pp. 260–268. Springer, Heidelberg (2011). https://doi.org/10.1007/978-3-642-25449-9_33
15. Zhang, L., Zhang, L., Zhang, D., Zhu, H.: Online finger-knuckle-print verification for personal authentication. Pattern Recogn. **43**(7), 2560–2571 (2010)

16. Ye, Z., Zhao, Z., Wen, M., Yang, J.: Weighted graph based feature representation for finger-vein recognition. In: Yu, S., et al. (eds.) PRCV 2022. LNCS, vol. 13535, pp. 467–478. Springer, Cham (2022). https://doi.org/10.1007/978-3-031-18910-4_38
17. Wen, M., Ye, Z., Yang, J.: Finger trimodal features coding fusion method. In: Deng, W., et al. (eds.) CCBR 2022. LNCS, vol. 13628, pp. 466–474. Springer, Cham (2022). https://doi.org/10.1007/978-3-031-20233-9_47
18. Li, S., Zhang, H., Shi, Y., Yang, J.: Novel local coding algorithm for finger multimodal feature description and recognition. Sensors **19**(9), 2213 (2019)

Unsupervised Fingerprint Registration: A Reinforcement Learning Approach

Jing Xing, Yuwei Jia, Zhe Cui[✉], and Fei Su

Beijing Key Laboratory of Network System and Network Culture, Beijing University
of Posts and Telecommunications, Beijing, China
cuizhe@bupt.edu.cn

Abstract. Fingerprint recognition is a crucial biometric authentication technology, known for its uniqueness and stability. Despite recent advancements in fingerprint matching, fingerprint distortions still pose significant challenges to fingerprint matching algorithms. To address this, fingerprint registration techniques have been developed. While supervised dense registration shows promise, it is hindered by speed, accuracy, and data annotation challenges. Unsupervised methods offer a solution to the lack of labeled data to deal with incorrect matches and weak regularization. Inspired by reinforcement learning (RL), this paper introduces an RL-based approach for fingerprint registration, decomposing the process into manageable steps and leveraging the Normalized Cross-Correlation (NCC) reward for unsupervised learning. By decomposing the registration process into incremental steps, our method effectively balances the trade-off between accuracy and the need for extensive data annotation. Experimental results on the FVC2004 dataset demonstrate improved performance, adaptability, and reduced reliance on labeled data. This study enhances the efficiency of fingerprint registration, presenting a robust approach for handling complex deformation fields.

Keywords: Fingerprint Registration · Reinforcement Learning · Unsupervised Learning · Recursive Registration

1 Introduction

Fingerprint recognition, as one of the most widely used biometric authentication technologies today, plays a crucial role in the fields of security and personal identification due to its uniqueness and stability. Despite the development of fingerprint recognition algorithms, distortions in fingerprint images present significant challenges to these tasks, severely impacting the performance of fingerprint matching algorithms. Based on this premise, fingerprint registration has been introduced to mitigate the effects of fingerprint deformations [1].

In recent years, supervised dense fingerprint registration algorithms have been proposed that align fingerprints by estimating elastic skin deformations [2–6]. Among these, Cui et al. [3] developed a phase-based fingerprint registration algorithm that achieved high matching scores, though its speed and accuracy need further improvement. Deep learning-based methods offer faster computational speeds, but supervised algorithms inevitably face challenges related to dataset annotation and often lack sufficiently varied training data, which can affect registration outcomes and matching scores.

To address these issues, unsupervised image registration algorithms have been introduced [7]. Although the performance of unsupervised methods may not surpass that of supervised methods, they are still of significant interest and value as they can solve the problem of lacking extensive manually labeled data.

However, these methods often do not account for incorrect matches, applying these methods may attempt to align incorrect matchers with true matchers to achieve higher scores, and they generally exhibit weak regularization strength in predicting deformation fields, leading to broken ridges and distortions in fingerprint images. To improve upon these issues, Jia et al. [8] proposed an unsupervised dense fingerprint registration algorithm that resolves previous challenges in balancing speed, matching scores, and accuracy, achieving state-of-the-art performance. However, in fingerprint registration tasks involving deformable transformations, directly predicting complex, dense deformation fields is a challenging task for most deep learning (DL)-based approaches.

To address this issue, incremental image registration methods have been proposed [9], which align images by applying a series of local or global deformations, showing great potential in deformable image registration (DIR) tasks. Inspired by this, methods based on reinforcement learning (RL) have been introduced for image registration [10–17], capitalizing on RLs emphasis on the continuity in processes and the sequentiality of decision steps. RL-based approaches adjust the deformation field progressively, optimizing it step-by-step towards optimal alignment.

Building on RL in image registration, this paper extends the application to the domain of fingerprint registration, decomposing the overall learning process of DIR into small steps. To address the learning challenges in high-dimensional continuous action spaces, the decision process is divided into two steps: state to low-dimensional plan, and plan to deformation field action. The plan guides the action, and the critic evaluates the plan to learn effective fingerprint registration strategies. In the registration environment, the Normalized Cross-Correlation (NCC) reward is calculated in an unsupervised manner, eliminating the need for extensive manually annotated data required by supervised methods. Experimental results on the FVC2004 dataset demonstrate promising performance, with continuous improvements across iterations. This innovative approach not only enhances the adaptability and efficiency of fingerprint registration but also reduces the reliance on extensive labeled training data.

The organization of this paper is structured as follows: Sect. 2 offers an overview of related work in fingerprint registration and reinforcement learning, as well as the specific modules utilized in this research. Section 3 delineates the design and implementation of the proposed method. Section 4 provides experimental results within the targeted application area. Section 5 concludes by summarizing our findings and outlining the contributions of this study.

2 Related Work

2.1 Finperprint Registration

The three-dimensional flexibility of fingers naturally introduces deformations when using conventional contact-based fingerprint collection techniques, making it difficult to comprehensively capture fingerprint information in one go. Such deformations pose significant challenges for fingerprint recognition and fingerprint stitching processes. In fingerprint recognition, fingerprint registration technology is typically employed first to align the fingerprint to be compared with those in the database before calculating the matching score.

In the realm of fingerprint registration, Si et al. [2] addressed the issue of dense fingerprint registration, introducing a correlation-based method that significantly enhances matching accuracy. Subsequently, Cui et al. [3] leveraged the phase characteristics of fingerprints to further improve matching accuracy. However, the registration speed of their methods is slow, which may pose limitations for applications requiring rapid response. Jia et al. [6] employed deep learning techniques to develop an unsupervised dense fingerprint registration algorithm that offers considerable improvements in speed, matching scores, and accuracy.

Overall, dense fingerprint registration is an exceptionally challenging task that not only requires robust training data support but also involves complex estimations of high-dimensional deformation fields while addressing issues of true and false matches, distinguishing it from general image registration tasks.

2.2 Reinforcement Learing

Compared to rigid image registration, DIR involves vast and continuous state and action spaces. Directly learning to predict accurate deformation fields is challenging. Therefore, RL agent-based methods have been introduced to address the registration problem.

The first attempt to use agent-based methods for registration was proposed by Liao et al. [10]. Unlike standard methods that focus on optimizing matching metrics, this agent-based approach seeks to find the optimal sequence of actions to align images for registration. Krebs et al. [11] proposed an RL-based DIR method, but their approach relies on supervised learning with ground truth deformation fields, which is impractical for most DIR tasks. Moreover, using traditional statistical deformation models to reduce and discretize the action space results in poor performance in complex deformation registration. Subsequently, Luo et al. [17] introduced a new RL architecture called the Stochastic Planner-Actor-Critic (SPAC), which handles high-dimensional continuous state and action spaces with notable performance.

Currently, most RL-based image registration work is applied in the field of medical imaging, and there are no methods applied to fingerprint registration.

We hope to bring new insights and advancements to the field of fingerprint registration.

3 Methods

Directly learning such high-dimensional actions poses a significant challenge for RL. Our approach transforms the learning of high-dimensional continuous action spaces into learning a low-dimensional representation vector, which is then expanded back into the high-dimensional space. This reduces the complexity of the learning task, making it more manageable for RL algorithms while preserving the ability to capture the required transformations.

The detailed implementation process is illustrated in Fig. 1. First, a pair of fingerprint images is inputted into the planner to obtain a low-dimensional vector, called the *plan*, containing dense deformation field information. This plan is then passed to the actor, which restores it into the required high-dimensional dense deformation field. Meanwhile, the critic evaluates the quality of the plan, providing guidance for policy optimization to ensure more stable and efficient updates.

3.1 Architecture of Network

Our method is grounded in the SPAC [17], which is articulated through three core modules: the Planner, the Actor, and the Critic, each controlled by the parameters $\psi, \phi, and\ \theta$, respectively.

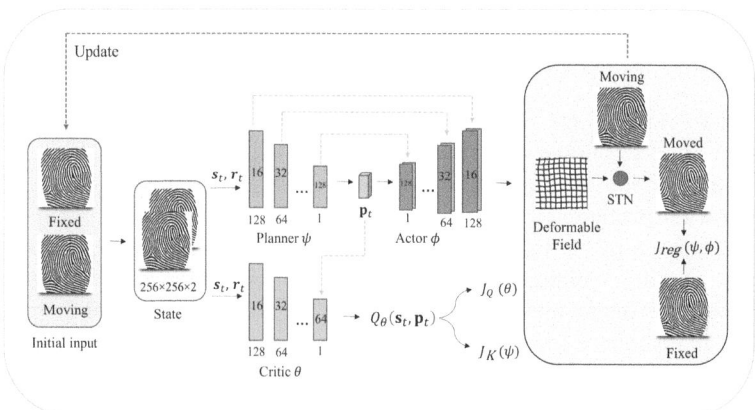

Fig. 1. The Structure of Networks. The rectangle represents a 2D image (or feature map), the number of channels is shown inside the rectangle, and the responding resolution is shown underneath.

The primary function of the Planner is to generate high-level policy guidance within a low-dimensional latent space. Then the policies are then passed on to the Actor, who crafts semi-high-dimensional actions based on them. Concurrently, the Critic evaluates these strategies. The semi-high-dimensional actions restored by the Actor are converted into a dense, smooth deformation field. The deformation field, along with the moving image, is input into the STN module to produce the registered image. The similarity score between the registered and fixed images is used to supervise and learn the parameters $\psi, \phi, and\ \theta$ of the Planner, Actor, and Critic, ultimately mastering the strategy to accomplish complex fingerprint registration tasks.

3.2 Registration Steps

In the implementation of fingerprint registration, we decompose the complex registration task into T steps. Initially, when a pair of fingerprint images is read, we calculate the intersection of the initial fixed image and the initial moving image to create a mask. Then, both images, overlaid with this mask, are provided to the planner. This approach helps to avoid unnecessary deformation processes that can arise from large discrepancies between the two images.

At time step t, the current fixed image and the intermediate moving image (256×256) are input into the Planner κ_ψ, resulting in a low-dimensional plan $\mathbf{p}_t$. In practice, $\mathbf{p}_t$ is not obtained directly and explicitly by the planner. Instead, the planner initially determines a Gaussian probability distribution, which models a subspace influencing subsequent actions of $\mathbf{p}_t$, broadening the action space for more robust strategies. During training, $\mathbf{p}_t$ is sampled from this distribution. With a parameterized planner κ_ψ and actor π_ϕ, we have $\mathbf{p}_t \sim \kappa_\psi(\mathbf{p}_t \mid \mathbf{s}_t)$, after which the low-dimensional plan $\mathbf{p}_t$ is restored by the Actor π_ϕ into a semi-high-dimensional sparse deformation field, and then converted into a high-dimensional dense deformation field.

Under this setup, our aim is to maximize the entropy of $\mathbf{p}_t$ to enhance exploration and robustness. The augmented objective function is defined as:

$$\max_{\psi,\phi} \sum_{t=1}^{T} \mathbb{E}_{(\mathbf{s}_t,\mathbf{p}_t,\mathbf{a}_t)\sim\rho_{(\kappa,\pi)}} \left[r_t\left(\mathbf{s}_t, \mathbf{p}_t, \mathbf{a}_t\right) + \alpha \mathcal{H}\left(\kappa_\psi\left(\cdot \mid \mathbf{s}_t\right)\right) \right] \quad (1)$$

where α is a temperature parameter, and $\rho_{(\kappa,\pi)}$ represents the trajectory distribution under $\kappa_\psi(\mathbf{p}_t|\mathbf{s}_t)$ and $\pi_\phi(\mathbf{a}_t|\mathbf{p}_t)$.

It is essential to clarify that the high-dimensional dense deformation field $\Omega_{\psi,\phi}^t$ is not directly obtained from $\mathbf{a}_t$. Instead, it is recursively produced by the effects of at applied to the deformation field from $t-1$. This iterative approach to transformation ensures a gradual and controlled adaptation of the deformation field, allowing for more precise and reliable alignment of fingerprint images through successive steps. This method not only provides fine control over the deformation process but also significantly enhances the fidelity and accuracy of the final moved image, ensuring effective adaptation to the complex nature of fingerprint registration tasks.

$$\Omega_{\psi,\phi}^t = \begin{cases} 0 & \text{if } t = 0, \\ \mathcal{C}(\mathbf{a}_t, \Omega_{\psi,\phi}^{t-1}) & \text{otherwise} \end{cases} \quad (2)$$

where
$$\mathcal{C}(\mathbf{a_t}, \Omega_{\psi,\phi}^{t-1}) = \Omega_{\psi,\phi}^{t-1} + (\mathbf{a_t} \circ \Omega_{\psi,\phi}^{t-1}). \tag{3}$$

After obtaining the deformation field at time t, a new moving image ($I_M \circ \Omega_{\psi,\phi}^t$) is produced. In the process of recursive registration, the aim is for the new moving image to continually approximate and ultimately align with the fixed image. Thus, this registration process can be described as a minimization problem based on an energy function:

$$\min_{\psi,\phi} E(\psi,\phi) := \frac{1}{T}\sum_{t=1}^{T} G\left(I_F, I_{M_t} \circ \Omega_{\psi,\phi}^t\right) + \lambda R\left(\Omega_{\psi,\phi}^t\right) \tag{4}$$

where $G(\cdot)$ quantifies the measure of similarity between the fixed image and the deformed image, $R(\cdot)$ represents the regularization of the deformation field, and λ is a hyperparameter balancing these two terms.

3.3 Reinforcement Learning

Unlike traditional reinforcement learning algorithms, the critic Q_θ in our framework evaluates the plan $\mathbf{p}_t$ instead of the action $\mathbf{a}_t$. Specifically, the low-dimensional plan $\mathbf{p}_t$ sampled is connected with the critic and together with the state at the time t, inputs into and outputs the soft Q function $Q_\theta(\mathbf{s}_t, \mathbf{p}_t)$. This function assesses the current state and plan, where both the soft Q values and the rewards collectively guide the learning and refinement of the stochastic policy. During evaluation, the network learns the planning strategy κ_ψ, and by minimizing the soft Bellman residual, it fits the parameterized Q function $Q_\theta(\mathbf{s}_t, \mathbf{p}_t)$ (the critic) using transitions sampled from the replay pool $\mathcal{D}$:

$$J_Q(\theta) = \mathbb{E}_{(\mathbf{s}_t,\mathbf{p}_t)\sim\mathcal{D}}\left[\frac{1}{2}\left(Q_\theta(\mathbf{s}_t,\mathbf{p}_t) - \left(r_t + \gamma \mathbb{E}_{\mathbf{s}_{t+1}}[V_{\bar\theta}(\mathbf{s}_{t+1})]\right)\right)^2\right] \tag{5}$$

where
$$V_{\bar\theta}(\mathbf{s}_t) = \mathbb{E}_{\mathbf{p}_t \sim \kappa_\psi}[Q_{\bar\theta}(\mathbf{s}_t,\mathbf{p}_t) - \alpha\log\kappa_\psi(\mathbf{p}_t \mid \mathbf{s}_t)] \tag{6}$$

To stabilize training, a target network $Q_{\bar\theta}$ for the critic is employed, whose parameters θ are obtained through an exponential moving average of the critic network parameters: $\bar\theta \to \tau\theta + (1-\tau)\bar\theta$. The hyperparameter $\tau \in [0,1]$ manages the update rate.decisions.

For updating planner, we minimize the KL divergence between the policy induced by the Q-function and the Boltzmann distribution:

$$J_\kappa(\psi) = \mathbb{E}_{\mathbf{s}_t\sim\mathcal{D}}\left[\mathbb{E}_{\mathbf{p}_t\sim\kappa_\psi}\left[\alpha\log\left(\kappa_\psi(\mathbf{p}_t \mid \mathbf{s}_t)\right) - Q_\theta(\mathbf{s}_t,\mathbf{p}_t)\right]\right] \tag{7}$$

where $\mathbf{p}_t$ is modeled as a sample from a stochastic policy. The hyperparameter α, which controls the trade-off between entropy and reward, can also be adaptively tuned to optimize policy performance.

Through these mechanisms, our approach effectively balances exploration and exploitation, enabling the system to adapt and improve in complex decision-making environments, particularly in tasks requiring careful sequential planning and execution such as dynamic image registration.

During the registration process, to align the moving fingerprint with the fixed fingerprint, we employ NCC as a metric to learn the appearance similarity between the fixed fingerprint and the warped fingerprint: $G(I_F, I_{M_t}) = NCC\left(I_F, I_M \circ \Omega^t_{\psi,\phi}\right)$.

To generate realistic warped fingerprints, we use a total variation regularizer to smooth the spatial gradients of the deformation field: $R(\Omega_\psi, \phi^t) = \left\|\nabla \Omega^t_{\psi,\phi}\right\|^2_2$

The final registration loss J_{reg} is defined as:

$$J_{\text{reg}}(\psi,\phi) = \mathbb{E}_{s_t \sim \mathcal{D}}\left[-NCC\left(I_F, I_M \circ \Omega^t_{\psi,\phi}\right) + \lambda \left\|\nabla \Omega^t_{\psi,\phi}(\mathbf{s}_t)\right\|^2_2\right] \quad (8)$$

In experiments, the optimization of all parameters of SPAC is based on samples from the replay pool.

This formulation integrates both the fidelity of the alignment, as assessed by the NCC, and the smoothness of the deformation field, enforced by the total variation regularizer. The hyperparameter λ balances these two aspects, ensuring that the deformation does not introduce unrealistic changes to the moving image while still achieving a high degree of similarity with the fixed image. This approach effectively guides the learning process in a manner that enhances the plausibility and accuracy of the image registration task.

4 Experiment

4.1 Implementation Details

The experiments were conducted on an Intel(R) Core(TM) i9-9900K CPU and two NVIDIA GeForce 2080Ti GPUs with 11 GB memory. We used the Adam optimizer, where the learning rates for the alpha and actor were 4×10^{-5}, and the learning rates for the planner and critic were 8×10^{-6}, with $(\beta_1, \beta_2) = (0.5, 0.9)$. During training, we set 3,000 global epochs, each containing 20 registration iteration substeps. During parameter updates, the planner and actor were updated every 8 and 4 substeps, respectively. All parameters were optimized based on samples from the replay pool D, with a sample size of 8 each time. The training data used was the same as in [5], and the data augmentation methods were also consistent with [5].

4.2 Experiment Result

We conducted tests on the FVC2004 DB1_A dataset. The key idea of our proposed method is to decompose the overall registration process into multiple steps

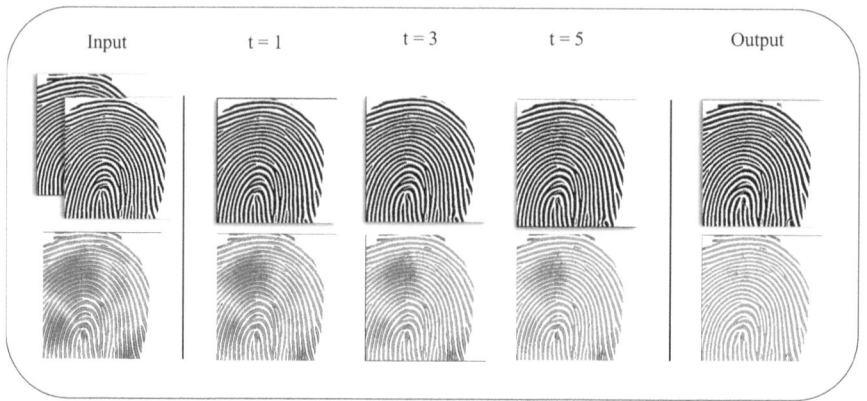

Fig. 2. A step-wise registration example of our method

and progressively improve the registration results. Figure 2 illustrates an example of the stepwise registration process.

In the experiments, we observed that the correlation scores for non-matching fingerprint pairs could also be elevated to a certain extent during the fingerprint registration process, which can potentially affect and confuse the distinction between genuine and impostor matches. To address this issue, we adopted the following strategy when calculating the matching scores for fingerprint pairs:

$$Score_{\text{matching}}(I_F, I_M) = NCC(I_F, I_M) - c\left\|\nabla\Omega\right\|_2^2 \tag{9}$$

where c is a weighting coefficient that balances the contribution of the NCC score and the smoothness of the resulting deformation field Ω.

We considered not only the NCC scores between the images but also the smoothness of the resulting deformation field. Although we applied a regularization term to enforce the smoothness of the deformation field during the learning process, the deformation fields obtained for non-matching fingerprint pairs are still significantly larger than those for genuine pairs. Therefore, considering the smoothness of the deformation field can help better distinguish between genuine and impostor fingerprint pairs. The DET curve of the image correlator on FVC2004 DB1_A is shown in Fig. 3. The matching accuracy of the image correlator on FVC2004 DB1_A is shown in Table 1.

Although there is a gap between our method and the state-of-the-art in terms of matching accuracy, we achieve the highest image correlation, as shown in Fig. 3.(b). The average matching scores of methods [1–4,8] on 2800 real pairs in FVC2004 DB1_A are 0.7662, 0.8473, 0.7979, 0.7778, and 0.8597 respectively, while our method achieves the highest score of 0.9130.

This suggests that the method prioritizes aligning the fingerprint images to maximize the correlation score, inadvertently boosting the scores of false matches—a problem that can be addressed in future research and work.

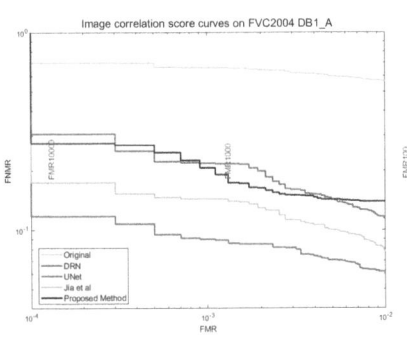
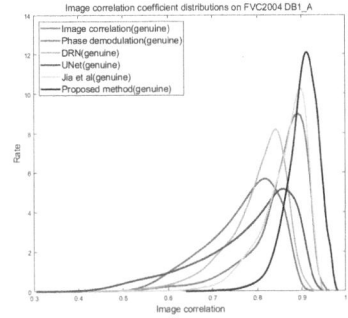

(a) DET curves of image correlator

(b) Genuine Image pairs correlation distributions

Fig. 3. DET curves and Genuine image pairs correlation distributions on FVC2004 DB1_A

Table 1. Matching accuracy of different dense registration algorithms for processing fingerprints in FVC2004 DB1_A.

Method	EER	FNMR@FMR = 0	FNMR@FMR = 10^{-2}
Image Correlation [2]	0.073	0.436	0.151
Phase Demodulation [3]	0.041	0.166	0.065
DRN [4]	0.058	0.306	0.114
UNet Registration [5]	0.045	0.117	0.061
Jia et al. [8]	0.045	0.173	0.078
Ours	0.069	0.275	0.099

5 Conclusion

This paper introduces a novel reinforcement learning-based approach for fingerprint registration to address complex deformations in fingerprint images. By decomposing the registration process into multiple steps, our method effectively balances accuracy and data annotation requirements. Although our method has not yet surpassed the state-of-the-art methods in matching performance, it has exhibited a refined learning capability, indicating its potential to achieve high image correlation scores while maintaining robust structural integrity. Future work will focus on optimizing the model and exploring advanced initial registration methods to further enhance accuracy.

Acknowledgments. This work was supported by the National Natural Science Foundation of China 62206026.

References

1. Maltoni, D., Maio, D., Jain, A.K., Prabhakar, S., Feng J.: Handbook of Fingerprint Recognition. Springer, Cham (2022). https://doi.org/10.1007/978-3-030-83624-5
2. Si, X., Feng, J., Yuan, B., Zhou, J.: Dense registration of fingerprints. Pattern Recognit. **63**, 87–101 (2017)
3. Cui, Z., Feng, J., Li, S., Lu, J., Zhou, J.: 2-D phase demodulation for deformable fingerprint registration. IEEE Trans. Inf. Forensics Secur. **13**(12), 3153–3165 (2018)
4. Cui, Z., Feng, J., Zhou, J.: Dense fingerprint registration via displacement regression network. In: 2019 International Conference on Biometrics (ICB), pp. 1–8. IEEE (2019)
5. Cui, Z., Feng, J., Zhou, J.: Dense registration and mosaicking of fingerprints by training an end-to-end network. IEEE Trans. Inf. Forensics Secur. **99**, 1 (2020)
6. Yu, Y., Wang, H., Zhang, Y., Chen, P.: A STN-based self-supervised network for dense fingerprint registration. In: Feng, J., Zhang, J., Liu, M., Fang, Y. (eds.) CCBR 2021. LNCS, vol. 12878, pp. 277–286. Springer, Cham (2021). https://doi.org/10.1007/978-3-030-86608-2_31
7. Balakrishnan, G., Zhao, A., Sabuncu, M.R., Guttag, J., Dalca, A.V.: VoxelMorph: a learning framework for deformable medical image registration. IEEE Trans. Med. Imaging **38**(8), 1788–1800 (2019)
8. Jia, Y., Cui, Z., Su, F.: Unsupervised fingerprint dense registration. In: Jia, W., et al. (eds.) CCBR 2023. LNCS, vol. 14463, pp. 3–12. Springer, Singapore (2023). https://doi.org/10.1007/978-981-99-8565-4_1
9. Zhao, S., Dong, Y., Chang, E. I., Xu, Y.: Recursive cascaded networks for unsupervised medical image registration. In: 2019 IEEE International Conference on Computer Vision (ICCV), pp. 10600–10610 (2019)
10. Liao, R., et al.: An artificial agent for robust image registration. In: AAAI Conference on Artificial Intelligence (2017)
11. Ma, K., et al.: Multimodal image registration with deep context reinforcement learning. In: Descoteaux, M., Maier-Hein, L., Franz, A., Jannin, P., Collins, D.L., Duchesne, S. (eds.) MICCAI 2017. LNCS, vol. 10433, pp. 240–248. Springer, Cham (2017). https://doi.org/10.1007/978-3-319-66182-7_28
12. Miao, S., Liao, R.: Agent-based methods for medical image registration. In: Lu, L., Wang, X., Carneiro, G., Yang, L. (eds.) Deep Learning and Convolutional Neural Networks for Medical Imaging and Clinical Informatics. ACVPR, pp. 323–345. Springer, Cham (2019). https://doi.org/10.1007/978-3-030-13969-8_16
13. Sun, S., et al.: Robust multimodal image registration using deep recurrent reinforcement learning. In: Jawahar, C., Li, H., Mori, G., Schindler, K. (eds.) ACCV 2018. LCNS, vol. 11362, pp. 511–526. Springer, Cham (2019). https://doi.org/10.1007/978-3-030-20890-5_33
14. Hu, J., et al.: End-to-end multimodal image registration via reinforcement learning. Med. Image Anal. **68**, 101878 (2021). https://doi.org/10.1016/j.media.2020.101878
15. Luo, Z., et al.: A spatiotemporal agent for robust multimodal registration. IEEE Access **8**, 75347–75358 (2020). https://doi.org/10.1016/ACCESS.2020.2989150
16. Krebs, J., et al.: Robust non-rigid registration through agent-based action learning. In: Descoteaux, M., Maier-Hein, L., Franz, A., Jannin, P., Collins, D.L., Duchesne, S. (eds.) MICCAI 2017. LNCS, vol. 10433, pp. 344–352. Springer, Cham (2017). https://doi.org/10.1007/978-3-319-66182-7_40
17. Luo, Z., et al.: Stochastic planner-actor-critic for unsupervised deformable image registration. In: AAAI, vol. 36, no. 2, pp. 1917–1925 (2022)

Region of Interest Extraction for Palm in the Wild

Haoheng Lin, Junqin Huang, Dacan Luo, Ming Zeng, and Wenxiong Kang[✉]

School of Automation Science and Engineering, South China University of Technology, Guangzhou, China
auwxkang@scut.edu.cn

Abstract. Most current contactless palm vein (PV) recognition systems are designed for indoor scenes. However, in the wild, the performance of traditional region of interest (ROI) extraction methods can be significantly degraded or even fail. To tackle the challenges above, in this paper, we propose a method for extracting ROI specifically designed for PV in the wild. A top-down keypoint classification network (KCNet) for PV ROI extraction is designed. To verify the validity of our model, we annotate five keypoint datasets of SCUT_PV_v1, CASIA, TJ_PV and VERA, and for the first time, construct a PV dataset for wild scenes called SCUT_PV_Wild. Extensive experiments demonstrate that our method can achieve stable and efficient ROI extraction and get remarkable results on five annotated datasets.

Keywords: ROI Extraction · Wild Scenes · Keypoint Detection · Coordinate Classification

1 Introduction

Biometrics is becoming the mainstream method for identifying individuals due to its convenience. The commonly studied biometric traits include face, gaits, palm vein (PV), fingerprint, finger vein, and so on [1]. Among them, PV authentication has gained popularity due to its user-friendliness, high level of security, and resistance to spoofing attacks [2]; hence, an increasing number of researchers and engineers have dedicated themselves to this booming biometric method. However, PV authentication still needs to improve regarding on-the-fly and in-the-wild scenes: the current design of contactless PV recognition systems is susceptible to strong ambient illumination disturbances. The performance of traditional region of interest (ROI) extraction methods can be significantly degraded or even fail in the wild.

In order to extract features from PV, it is necessary to process the raw PV images, remove identity-unrelated background areas, and retain the palm area related to identity information. PV ROI extraction is crucial for a PV recognition system. If there is a deviation in the extracted ROI area for the same palm, it will ultimately affect the recognition system's performance. Traditional

ROI extraction mainly includes palm edge contour extraction, palm keypoint localization, and ROI localization. Traditional ROI extraction requires the palm background to be as clean as possible; otherwise, there will be positioning errors in the process of palm edge contour extraction and keypoint localization, which ultimately affects the recognition system's performance. Therefore, traditional ROI extraction cannot extract the PV ROI in wild scenes due to the complex background and intense light, as shown in Fig. 1.

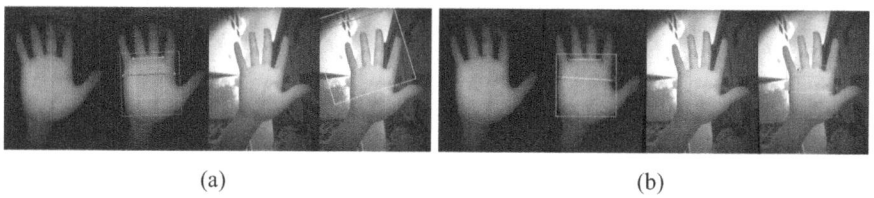

Fig. 1. Comparison of traditional ROI extraction method with the proposed method, (a) Traditional ROI extraction method, (b) our method. Our method works well in the wild scene compared with the traditional method.

To solve the challenges and factors above, we propose a method for extracting PV ROI designed especially for such wild scenes, which is a top-down keypoint detection network based on coordinate classification (KCNet) for PV ROI extraction. Figure 2 shows the basic framework of the proposed KCNet. KCNet predicts keypoints using a SimCC-based [3] algorithm that treats keypoint localization as a classification task. To verify the validity of our model, we annotate five keypoint datasets of SCUT_PV_v1, CASIA, TJ_PV and VERA, and, for the first time, construct a PV dataset for wild scenes called SCUT_PV_Wild. Extensive experiments demonstrate that our method can achieve stable and efficient PV ROI extraction and get state of the art (SOTA) results on five annotated datasets.

The main contributions of this work can be summarized as follows:

- We propose a keypoint detection network for extracting PV ROI designed especially for wild scenes called KCNet.
- We annotate five keypoint datasets for PV keypoint detection and for the first time, construct a PV dataset for wild scenes called SCUT_PV_Wild.
- We achieve SOTA results on five annotated datasets. Through extensive experiments, our method can obtain stable and efficient PV ROI extraction models and solve the problem of in-the-wild PV ROI extraction.

The remainder of this paper is organized as follows. Section 2 introduces related works about PV ROI extraction and keypoint detection. Section 3 describes the novel KCNet method. Section 4 describes the idea behind the construction of the four public datasets and especially the self-build dataset. Comparative experiments on five annotated datasets are presented in Sect. 5. Finally, the conclusion is given in Sect. 6.

2 Related Works

2.1 ROI Extraction

Traditional ROI Extraction. Typically, the PV images captured by imaging devices include the fingers, wrist, and background outside the palm area. However, only the palm region containing abundant vein structures needs to be handled during palm vein image processing, and this area is referred to as ROI. Several methods have been proposed to address palm pose variations by extracting ROI at the pre-processing stage. Michael et al. [4] propose a novel competitive hand valley detection (CHVD) algorithm to locate the ROI of the palm. Kauba et al. [5] appropriated finger valleys and centre of mass-selected and rotationally aligned hand image with maximum possible ROI fitted. Shao et al. [6] established a novel database with more than 30,000 palm images and manually labelled 14 keypoints on each image for ROI extraction.

Deep ROI Extraction. Although the above traditional methods are famous and widely used, they depend on the gaps between the fingers as reference points to determine the coordinate system, which means that all fingers must be spread. The hand should be facing toward the camera, resulting in limited effectiveness in scenarios with complex backgrounds and hand poses. Izadpanahkakhk et al. [7] first extracted palmprint ROI by convolutional neural networks. Liu et al. [8] proposed to use R-CNN to detect ROI and trained a palm ROI detector through R-CNN. Chen et al. [9] focused on the research of ROI extraction algorithm for palm vein recognition to achieve multiple tasks such as palm classification, ROI localization, and gesture correction.

2.2 Top-Down Keypoint Detection

Top-down keypoint detection algorithms use off-the-shelf detectors to provide bounding boxes and crop the human to a uniform scale for pose estimation. The term "top-down" refers to the hierarchical nature of the process, where the algorithm first identifies the person at a higher level and then estimates the detailed pose information at a lower level. This approach contrasts with bottom-up pose estimation, where keypoints are detected first and then grouped into individual persons [10]. For PV authentication, since the datasets are all single-hand, the detector can be ignored, and the training of the estimator can be carried out directly.

Previous pose estimation approaches usually regard keypoint localization as either coordinate regression or heatmap regression [10]. SimCC [3] introduced a new scheme that reformulated human pose estimation as two classification tasks for horizontal and vertical coordinates, which treats keypoint localization as a classification task. SimCC can omit additional refinement post-processing and exclude upsampling layers under specific settings, resulting in a more straightforward and effective human pose estimation pipeline. Inspired by SimCC, Jiang [11] et al. proposed a real-time multi-person pose estimation (RTMPose) with a more lightweight SimCC head and achieved state-of-the-art in popular benchmarks.

3 Proposed Method

3.1 Model Overview

The proposed KCNet consists of a backbone, a feature interaction (FI) block, a feature aggregation (FA) block, and a Gated Attention Unit (GAU) [12] to refine four keypoint representations for ROI extraction. Specifically, we leverage the output features of the last three stages of the backbone S_3, S_4, S_5 and make the S_5 as the input to the FI block. The FA block transforms multi-scale features into a sequence of image features S_4, S_5. Finally, a SimCC-based head is used to predict the horizontal and vertical location of keypoints. The overview of the model architecture is illustrated in Fig. 2.

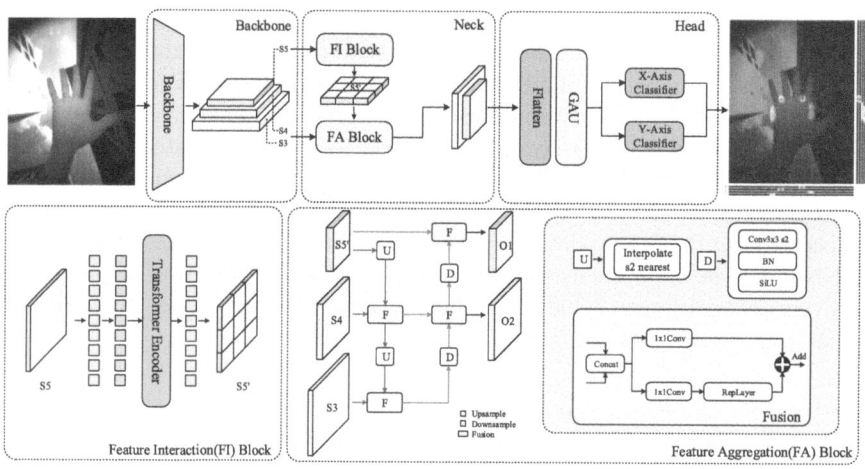

Fig. 2. The overall architecture of KCNet, which consists of CSPNeXt as the backbone, a feature interaction (FI) block and a feature aggregation (FA) block and a Gated Attention Unit (GAU) to refine four keypoint representations for ROI extraction. Along with the blocks mentioned above, the 2D keypoint detection is regarded as two classification tasks for x-axis and y-axis coordinates. KCNet predicts keypoints using a SimCC-based head to predict the horizontal and vertical location of keypoints.

3.2 Feature Interaction Block

As shown in Fig. 2, the FI block performs intra-scale interaction on S_5 regarding that the high-level feature contains the low-level feature. We split the feature map S_5 into fixed-size patches, linearly embed each of them, add position embeddings, and feed the resulting sequence of vectors to a standard transformer encoder. Then we reconstruct the features processed by the transformer encoder into a new feature with the same scale. We can formulate this process as follows:

$$Q = K = V = Flatten(S_5)$$
$$S_5' = Reshape(Attn(Q, K, V)) \quad (1)$$
$$Out = FI(S_5)$$

3.3 Feature Aggregation Block

As shown in Fig. 2, FA block performs cross-scale interaction on S_3, S_4, S_5'. FA block consists of a Feature Pyramid Network (FPN) and a Path Aggregation Network (PAN). The top-down FPN starts with the highest-resolution feature map and iteratively merges itself with lower-resolution maps, gradually reducing dimensionality with lateral convolutions and upsampling. The bottom-up PAN is reversed, starting with the highest-resolution inner output and merging it with lower-resolution maps. These merged features are processed to produce final output feature maps. Together, these operations integrate features from different scales to enhance the model's ability to capture hierarchical information. We can formulate this process as follows:

$$Out = \{O_1, O_2\} = FA(\{S_3, S_4, S_5'\}) \quad (2)$$

3.4 Gated Attention Unit

To further exploit the global and local spatial information, we refine the keypoint representations with a self-attention module, and then the Gated Attention Unit (GAU) is adapted. GAU is a simpler yet more performant layer than Transformers. The key idea is to formulate attention and GLU [12] as a unified layer and to share their computation as much as possible. This not only results in higher param/compute efficiency but also naturally enables a powerful attentive gating mechanism. We can formulate this process as follows:

$$\begin{aligned} U &= \phi_u(XW_u) \\ V &= \phi_v(XW_v) \\ O &= (U \odot AV)W_o \end{aligned} \quad (3)$$

where $\odot$ is the pairwise multiplication and ϕ is the activation function. A contains token-token attention weights.

3.5 Loss Function

The KLDiscretLoss [3] is designed to compute the Discrete Kullback-Leibler (KL) Divergence loss for SimCC-based head. This loss function is often used in tasks like semantic segmentation or object detection, where the network output needs to be compared against discrete target distributions. The loss encourages the predicted distribution to match the target distribution, thus improving the model's accuracy. The mathematical formulation of the KL Discrete Loss can be expressed as follows:

$$\text{KLDiscretLoss}(P||Q) = \frac{1}{N} \sum_{i=1}^{N} P(i) \log \left(\frac{P(i)}{Q(i)} \right) \qquad (4)$$

where P represents the predicted distribution produced by the model, Q represents the ground truth labels, N is the total number of the classes or categories, $P(i)$ and $Q(i)$ are the probabilities of occurrence for class i in distributions P and Q respectively. The goal is to minimize this difference during training, effectively aligning the model's predictions with the ground truth labels.

4 Dataset Construction

To better evaluate the performance of KCNet we annotate five keypoint datasets including four public datasets with simple background and our self-build dataset in the wild. We manually annotate four keypoints on each image for ROI extraction and for the first time, construct a PV dataset for wild scenes called SCUT_PV_Wild. The following list is a brief description of each of these five PV datasets, all of which are annotated with four keypoints as shown in Fig. 3 (a-e).

(1) **Public Datasets**:
   (a) SCUT_PV_v1 [13]: It is a large-scale database with 11,000 PV images from 550 individuals with each palm captured 10 times. We annotated 834 palms of it, yielding a total of 8,340 PV images.
   (b) TJ_PV [14]: This dataset contains images of 600 palms, with each palm captured 10 times with 2 sessions, yielding a total of 12,000 PV images. It's worth noting that this dataset involves two sessions, and all sessions are used for the experiments.
   (c) CASIA [15]: A sub-dataset of 1,200 palm images acquired at 850 nm is selected, and six images of the same palm acquired in two cycles are considered as one category.
   (d) VERA [16]: VERA Palm vein consists of 2,200 images depicting human palm vein patterns. Palm vein images were acquired from 110 volunteers for both left and right hands. For each subject, images were obtained in two sessions of five pictures each per hand.
(2) **Self-build Dataset**:
   (e) SCUT_PV_Wild: This dataset contains a total of 3,140 PV images captured indoor and we implemented the construction of the wild dataset using a pre-background fusion approach, in brief, we segmented the palm of the original dataset and then fused it with the wild scene in multiple scenes, yielding a total of 6,280 PV images. This dataset simulates PV images with complex backgrounds and strong illumination in the wild.

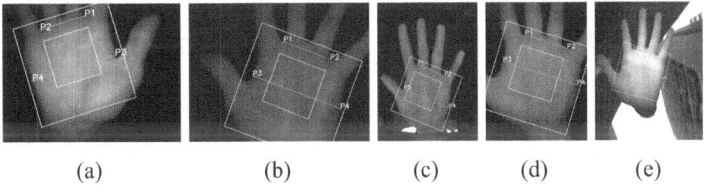

Fig. 3. The details of keypoint annotation. Green lines represent the connections between annotated points, while yellow boxes indicate ROI. (a) SCUT_PV_v1, (b) TJ_PV, (c) CASIA, (d) VERA, (e) SCUT_PV_Wild. (Color figure online)

5 Experiment

In order to verify the effectiveness of the proposed method, we perform a series of experiments using five datasets. The first set of experiments involve comparing the proposed KCNet with SOTA pose estimation methods. This comparison is intended to evaluate the effectiveness and priority of the KCNet. The second set of experiments, ablation experiments, is designed to demonstrate the effectiveness of each component in the KCNet. The last experiment is the feature visualization, which demonstrates the localization performance of KCNet on five PV datasets indoors as well as outdoors.

5.1 Experimental Settings

In the experiment, the learning rate is set to 0.001 and the randomness is 21. AdamW is used as the optimizer, and stochastic gradient descent method is used to update the weights of the model. The input size of the raw palm vein is resized as 256×256; the maximum of training epoches is set to 200; the batchsize is set to 32. The experiments are conducted using the PyTorch framework, and the training and testing run on the NVIDIA GTX 3090 GPU.

The Area Under the Curve (AUC) and Endpoint Error (EPE) are used as the main evaluation metrics for performance evaluation. AUC metric is used to evaluate the model's ability to distinguish between correct and incorrect pose predictions across different threshold values. A higher AUC value indicates better performance. EPE calculates the average distance between corresponding keypoints across all examples in the dataset, providing a quantitative measure of the model's overall performance. A lower EPE value indicates better accuracy, as it signifies that the predicted keypoints are closer to their ground truth counterparts.

5.2 Comparison with Other Keypoint Detection Methods

To compare the performance of our method on the task of PV ROI extraction, the comparison experiments between our proposed KCNet method and the current SOTA keypoint detection methods are conducted, including Deeppose [17],

HRNet [18], LiteHRNet [19], SimCC [3] and RTMPose [11]. The experimental results are shown in the Table 1, where bold font indicates an optimal value and the underlined type indicates the sub-optimal results. Experimental results show that our method has the best performance in PV ROI extraction due to the three main components and the effective SimCC-based classification header.

Table 1. Comparison with SOTA Methods on five datasets. *AUC ↑, EPE ↓.

Method	SCUT_PV		Tongji_PV		CASIA_PV		VERA_PV		SCUT_PVWild	
	AUC	EPE	AUC	EPE	AUC	EPE	AUC	EPE	AUC	EPE
Deeppose	0.789	5.649	0.747	7.180	0.671	10.354	0.660	13.422	0.645	11.844
HRNet	0.793	5.514	0.740	7.598	0.705	9.330	0.769	9.829	0.601	13.173
LiteHRNet	0.771	6.147	0.734	7.641	0.726	8.568	0.762	10.589	0.621	12.602
SimCC	<u>0.832</u>	<u>4.331</u>	0.788	6.140	<u>0.735</u>	8.319	<u>0.808</u>	<u>8.661</u>	0.714	9.720
RTMPose	0.824	4.600	<u>0.805</u>	<u>5.483</u>	<u>0.735</u>	<u>8.272</u>	0.778	10.922	<u>0.716</u>	<u>9.588</u>
Ours	**0.841**	**4.141**	**0.816**	**5.281**	**0.761**	**7.556**	**0.824**	**7.988**	**0.733**	**9.139**

5.3 Ablation Experiment

To further verify the effectiveness and contributions of each component of our proposed KCNet, ablation experiments are demonstrated in this section and seven ablation models are built as Table 2 shown. The experimental results are shown in Table 2. The experimental results show that when the model ablates any of the components of KCNet, it cannot achieve the best performance. Based on these results, we can draw a conclusion that each component of KCNet works effectively because the ablation of any component leads to a degradation of performance.

Table 2. Ablation experiment on five datasets. *AUC ↑, EPE ↓.

Components			SCUT_PV		Tongji_PV		CASIA_PV		VERA_PV		SCUT_PVWild	
FI	FA	GAU	AUC	EPE	AUC	EPE	AUC	EPE	AUC	EPE	AUC	EPE
✓			0.817	4.799	0.806	5.610	0.757	7.773	0.808	9.100	0.718	9.564
	✓		0.830	4.473	0.800	5.793	0.753	7.906	<u>0.822</u>	9.147	0.722	9.550
		✓	<u>0.834</u>	<u>4.301</u>	<u>0.815</u>	<u>5.294</u>	0.758	7.698	0.815	8.812	0.725	9.383
✓	✓		0.831	4.432	0.806	5.644	0.751	8.015	**0.824**	<u>8.621</u>	0.721	9.528
✓		✓	0.830	4.407	<u>0.815</u>	5.321	0.760	<u>7.624</u>	0.812	9.152	<u>0.731</u>	<u>9.147</u>
	✓	✓	0.831	4.425	0.803	5.688	**0.762**	**7.556**	<u>0.822</u>	8.694	0.722	9.517
✓	✓	✓	**0.841**	**4.141**	**0.816**	**5.281**	<u>0.761</u>	**7.556**	**0.824**	**7.988**	**0.733**	**9.139**

5.4 Visualization

The detected heatmaps of the test datasets indoors and outdoors inferenced by above SOTA methods were visualized and compared in this section. The corresponding visualization results are shown in Fig. 4. In addition to the obvious improvement in the experimental metrics, the heatmap visualization shows that the proposed KCNet exhibits improved precision and more focus on the keypoint, further improving the performance of PV ROI extraction.

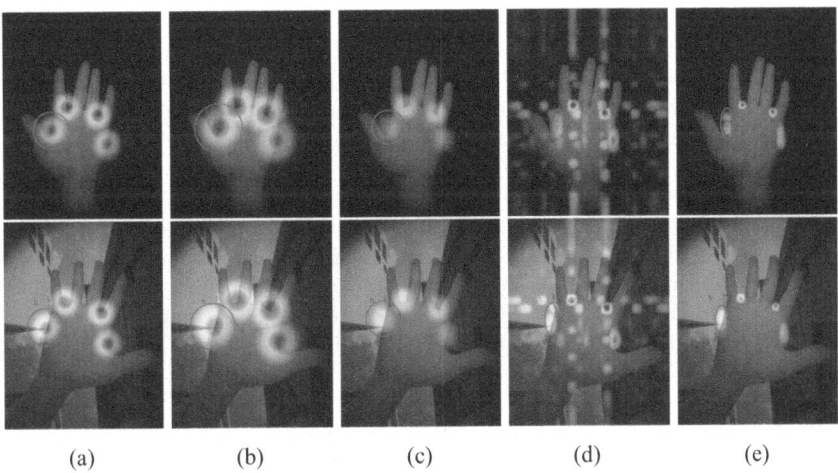

Fig. 4. Comparison results. (a)–(d) is the result with the code given by [18] [19] [3] and [11] respectively, (e) is the result by our method. The red circled areas in the figures indicate the attention of keypoint for each method. (Color figure online)

6 Conclusions and Future Works

In this paper, we explore deep ROI extraction in PV images in wild secens and for the first time, construct a PV dataset for wild scenes called SCUT_PV_Wild. A top-down keypoint classification network for PV ROI extraction (KCNet) is proposed, which consists of efficient and lightweight blocks. Extensive experiments demonstrate that our method can obtain stable and efficient PV ROI extraction models and achieve SOTA results on five annotated datasets. We hope the proposed KCNet can meet some of the demands for applicable PV authentication in the industry in multiple scenes. This will be a key focus of our future work.

Acknowledgment. This work was supported by the Natural Science Foundation of Guangdong Province, China (No. 2022A1515010114).

References

1. Sun, Z.N., et al.: Overview of biometrics research. J. Image Graph. **26**(6), 1254–1329 (2021)
2. Wu, W., Elliott, S.J., Lin, S., Sun, S., Tang, Y.: Review of palm vein recognition. IET Biometrics **9**(1), 1–10 (2020)
3. Li, Y.: SimCC: a simple coordinate classification perspective for human pose estimation. In: Avidan, S., Brostow, G., Cissé, M., Farinella, G.M., Hassner, T. (eds.) ECCV 2022. LNCS, vol. 13666, pp. 89–106. Springer, Cham (2022). https://doi.org/10.1007/978-3-031-20068-7_6
4. Michael, G.K.O., Connie, T., Teoh, A.B.J.: Touch-less palm print biometrics: novel design and implementation. Image Vis. Comput. **26**(12), 1551–1560 (2008)
5. Kauba, C., Prommegger, B., Uhl, A.: Combined fully contactless finger and hand vein capturing device with a corresponding dataset. Sensors **19**(22), 5014 (2019)
6. Shao, H., Zhong, D., Du, X.: Efficient deep palmprint recognition via distilled hashing coding. In: Proceedings of the IEEE/CVF Conference on Computer Vision and Pattern Recognition Workshops (2019)
7. Izadpanahkakhk, M., Razavi, S.M., Taghipour-Gorjikolaie, M., Zahiri, S.H., Uncini, A.: Deep region of interest and feature extraction models for palmprint verification using convolutional neural networks transfer learning. Appl. Sci. **8**(7), 1210 (2018)
8. Liu, Y., Kumar, A.: A deep learning based framework to detect and recognize humans using contactless palmprints in the wild. arXiv preprint arXiv:1812.11319 (2018)
9. Chen, X., Genke, Y.: Research on accurate ROI localization algorithm for omni-directional palm vein recognition based on improved SSD model. In: Jia, W., et al. (eds.) CCBR 2023. LNCS, vol. 14463, pp. 13–23, Springer, Singapore (2023). https://doi.org/10.1007/978-981-99-8565-4_2
10. Doosti, B.: Hand pose estimation: a survey. arXiv preprint arXiv:1903.01013 (2019)
11. Jiang, T., et al.: RTMPose: real-time multi-person pose estimation based on MMPose. arXiv preprint arXiv:2303.07399 (2023)
12. Hua, W., Dai, Z., Liu, H., Le, Q.: Transformer quality in linear time. In: International Conference on Machine Learning, pp. 9099–9117. PMLR (2022)
13. Luo, D., Qiao, Y., Xie, D., Zhang, S., Kang, W.: Palm vein recognition under unconstrained and weak-cooperative conditions. IEEE Trans. Inf. Forensics Secur. (2024)
14. Hao, Y., Sun, Z., Tan, T., Ren, C.: Multispectral palm image fusion for accurate contact-free palmprint recognition. In: 2008 15th IEEE International Conference on Image Processing, pp. 281–284. IEEE (2008)
15. Zhang, L., Cheng, Z., Shen, Y., Wang, D.: Palmprint and palmvein recognition based on DCNN and a new large-scale contactless palmvein dataset. Symmetry **10**(4), 78 (2018)
16. Tome, P., Marcel, S.: Palm vein database and experimental framework for reproducible research. In: 2015 International Conference of the Biometrics Special Interest Group (BIOSIG), pp. 1–7. IEEE (2015)
17. Toshev, A., Szegedy, C.: DeepPose: human pose estimation via deep neural networks. In: Proceedings of the IEEE Conference on Computer Vision and Pattern Recognition, pp. 1653–1660 (2014)

18. Sun, K., Xiao, B., Liu, D., Wang, J.: Deep high-resolution representation learning for human pose estimation. In: Proceedings of the IEEE/CVF Conference on Computer Vision and Pattern Recognition, pp. 5693–5703 (2019)
19. Yu, C., et al.: Lite-HRNet: a lightweight high-resolution network. In: Proceedings of the IEEE/CVF Conference on Computer Vision and Pattern Recognition, pp. 10440–10450 (2021)

A GAN-Based Data Augmentation Method for Palm Vein Authentication

Junqin Huang, Jiyi Huang, Haoheng Lin, Dacan Luo, and Wenxiong Kang(✉)

School of Automation Science and Engineering, South China University of Technology, Guangzhou 510630, China
auwxkang@scut.edu.cn

Abstract. Generative Adversarial Network (GAN) has drawn increasing attention to augment training data to improve palm vein authentication performance. However, existing GAN-based data augmentation methods focus on generating only intra-class or inter-class samples. In this paper, we propose generating intra-class and inter-class samples by the same GAN, leading to an inter-intra collaborative data augmentation method for palm vein authentication. Furthermore, to effectively exploit the generative data for training, we design a domain adaption network to alleviate the domain discrepancy between the real data and synthetic data. Experiments conducted on the SCUT_PV_V1, PolyU_NIR, and CASIA-MS-PalmprintV1 databases have demonstrated the effectiveness of our method that performs competitive performance for palm vein authentication tasks.

Keywords: Palm Vein Authentication · Data Augmentation · Generative Adversarial Network · Domain Adaption

1 Introduction

Significant progress has been witnessed in palm vein authentication in the deep learning era. As an effective way to inefficient data training, and improve performance, data augmentation has been an essential research in this field [1–6]. Among them, the generative adversarial networks, unlike geometric transformations or color adjustments that augment only intra-class data [1,6], augment either intra-class data [3] or inter-class data [2,5] by generating new palm vein images. However, there are still some limitations. With no inter-class sample augmentation and limited subjects, more synthetic intra-class samples would be suspected of overfitting [3]. While there is always only one image for a generated new inter-class subject makes palm vein authentication a one-shot learning task which is much more challenging [5]. Moreover, with the learned real data distribution, it is still challenging for the generator to generate data without distribution discrepancy to real data, hindering the synthetic data for effective model training. Some studies propose to address this problem by transfer learning [7] and adversarial learning [4]. However, the domain shift caused by the distribution discrepancy has not been discussed in palm vein authentication.

To address the above limitations, as shown in Fig. 1, we propose a GAN-based inter-intra collaborative data augmentation method to generate both discriminative inter-class and intra-class samples. Meanwhile, we design a domain adaption framework to train the backbone for palm vein authentication by both real data and synthetic data. Specifically, instead of generating the inter-class samples, we propose a style latent code selection strategy that consists of a pre-trained generator and a pre-trained feature extractor to select serial inter-class style latent code from random style latent code. After that, several intra-class samples are generated from one inter-class style latent code with noise by the same generator in the previous step. Furthermore, we regard the real data and synthetic data to be the source domain and target domain, respectively. Real data and synthetic data are then fed to two branches for feature extraction which are optimized individually. The Multi-Kernel Maximum Mean Discrepancies (MK-MMD) loss [8] is introduced to reduce the domain shift between the source domain and target domain, thereby effectively utilizing the synthetic data for model training. Finally, this trained feature extractor can be adopted for palm vein authentication tasks. To demonstrate the effectiveness of our method, we have conducted experiments on three public palm vein databases. The experimental results and analysis indicate that both the synthetic inter-class and intra-class can boost the performance of the feature extractor, resulting in a competitive palm vein authentication performance compared to State-of-The-Art (SOTA) methods. In summary, the main contributions of this paper are as follows:

- We propose a new GAN-based inter-intra collaborative data augmentation method for simultaneously generating both discriminative inter-class and intra-class palm vein samples to address inefficient training data.
- We propose to reduce the domain shift caused by the data distribution discrepancy between the real data and synthetic data for effective synthetic palm vein sample utilization.

2 Related Works

2.1 Data Augmentation in Palm Vein Authentication

In recent years, deep learning-based models have demonstrated exceptional generalization and robustness. Data augmentation plays a crucial role in this process. It increases the diversity of data and improves the generalization of the model [9,10]. Due to their ability to generate new synthetic samples, GAN-based augmentation methods have received considerable attention from researchers. Huang et al. [11] proposed a motion transfer (MT) model for finger vein image data augmentation that facilitates the generation of finger vein images in various poses. [12] proposed a hierarchical GAN network to obtain more intra-class samples. Qin et al. [4] proposed an Adversarial vein automatic augmentation approach that generates challenging samples to train a more robust vein classifier for palm-vein identification by alternatively optimizing the vein classifier and a set of latent variables. All of the above methods focus on sample augmentation with existing identities and are unable to generate entirely new inter-class samples, resulting in limited performance gains. Ou et al. [5] employed contrastive learning to pre-train on the synthetically augmented dataset and subsequently fine-tune on the real dataset, but not accurate enough. Our proposed method is a collaborative intra-class inter-class enhancement that can further improve the diversity of training data.

2.2 Domain Adaptation

In [13], transfer learning was proposed to solve the domain shift problem, which is also called domain adaptation. The aim was to reduce the differences between the two domains and align the data distributions. Tzeng et al. [14] proposed the deep domain confusion (DDC) method, which calculated the maximum mean discrepancy (MMD) [15] loss in the embedding layer of an AlexNet between the source and target domains to extract the features that had a similar distribution. Long et al. [8] improved the DDC method and proposed a deep adaptation network (DAN); it used the MK-MMD to measure the distribution more accurately than the MMD. They also proposed JMMD [16], a modified MMD for joint distributions.

Domain adaptation is also widely used in the field of hand authentication. Shao et al. [17] proposed firstly to design an autoencoder and discriminator to pull in the distance between source and target domains in the field of palmprint recognition. Zhang et al. [18] used domain adaptive loss to reduce the difference in the distribution of two domains under different illumination and proposed a light-invariant feature extractor.

3 Methodology

In this section, we introduce our proposed method in detail. First, we describe the pre-training process for the generator and feature extractor. To select the latent codes that generate inter-class samples, we design a specific criterion for inter-class style latent codes. Next, we apply intra-class variation in the synthetic inter-class samples to achieve collaborative enhancement. Finally, we present our proposed training framework and overall loss function.

3.1 The Pretraining of Generator and Feature Extractor

The style-based generation has become a prominent approach for GAN in the field of image generation. In this paper, we use a pre-trained StyleGAN2 [19] on a real dataset to generate synthetic images of palm veins. Formally, the training loss function is denoted as follows:

$$L = minmaxV(D,G) + \mathbb{E}_{\mathbf{w},\mathbf{y} \sim \mathcal{N}(0,\mathbf{I})} \left(\left\| \mathbf{J}_{\mathbf{w}}^T \mathbf{y} \right\|_2 - a \right)^2 + R_1 \quad (1)$$

where $minmaxV$ is the loss function of the original GAN, y is the synthetic image corresponding to w, $\mathcal{J}_{\mathbf{w}} = \partial G(\mathbf{w})/\partial \mathbf{w}$ is the Jacobi matrix of the generator output over w, and a is the moving average of x, which will be dynamically

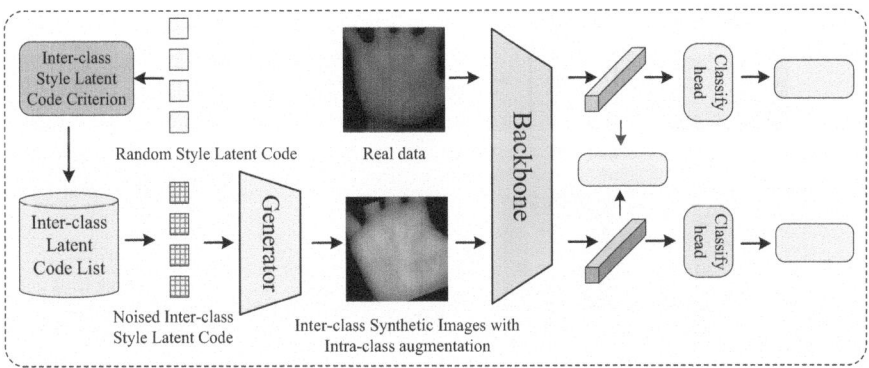

Fig. 1. The overall architecture.

adjusted during the training process. R_1 is the regularity term, which is intended to prevent the gradient from vanishing or exploding by limiting its gradient to 1.

We pre-train a feature extractor on the real dataset to extract the feature vectors of the real and synthetic samples. Specifically, the feature extractor consists of a stem layer and four bottleneck modules [20], with a max pooling layer between each layer for downsampling, and finally a global average pooling. The stem layer includes a 3×3 convolution and a max pooling layer. Margin-based loss function has shown excellent performance in the field of palm vein recognition [21]. Therefore, we utilize CosFace [22] as the loss function. We apply traditional data enhancements on real data, including a brightness dithering in the region of 0.7–1.3, an affine transformation with a rotation angle of 5, and a translation interval of (0.001,0.005).

3.2 The Inter-class Style Latent Code Criterion

In order to select a series of style latent codes to generate inter-class samples from random style latent code, we design an inter-class style latent code criterion shown in Fig. 2.

We first extract feature vectors of the samples in the real dataset by the pre-trained feature extractor and save them as a list. Next, the pre-trained feature extractor is used to extract feature vectors from the synthetic images. Our inter-class criterion involves calculating the similarity between the feature vectors of synthetic data and those of the real data. Samples are considered valid if their minimum similarity exceeds the threshold while maintaining the input style latent for generating this synthetic image. In order to visually compare the improvement in model performance with synthetic data, the hyperparameter threshold is set to the value corresponding to the best EER (Equal Error Rate) reported by the feature extractor in the pre-training phase in our manuscript. In CASIA, POLYU, and SCUT_PV_V1, respectively, are 0.42, 0.65, 0.65.

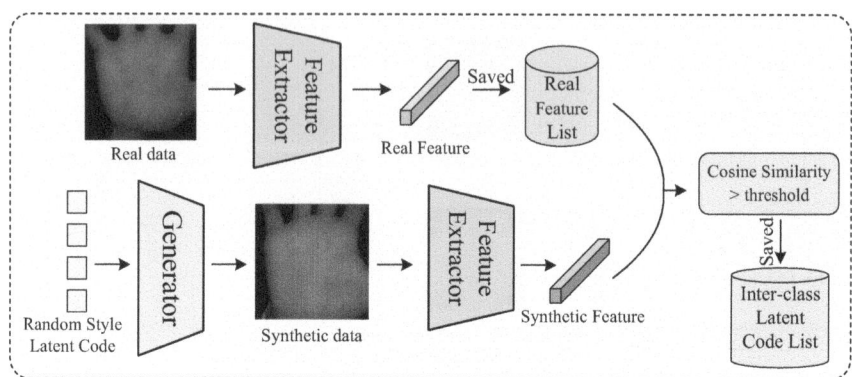

Fig. 2. The inter-class sample criterion.

3.3 GAN-Based Intra and Inter-class Data Augmentation

In Sect. 4.2, inter-class style latent code sampled from the list is fed into the generator, which can generate inter-class samples, but there is only one sample for each category, turning authentication into a one-hot learning task. Hence, we add noise to the style latent code w, so that the synthesized image does not change the identity semantic information on the premise of changing the style variables, such as light, vein thickness, depth, etc., to achieve the intra-class augmentation. We can formulate this process as follows:

$$w' = w + \text{noise} \cdot \text{scale} \tag{2}$$

where w is a style latent code, scale is a noise scale factor that controls the size of the noise, and is set to 0.2 in our manuscript.

3.4 The Training Framework and Loss Function

There are differences in data distribution between synthetic and real data [23], and simply joint training can hinder the inefficient utilization of synthetic data and even impair model performance. Hence, We design a two-branch training framework as shown in Fig. 1. Real and synthetic data are considered as source and target domains respectively and we calculate the MK-MMD loss between them. This loss helps to align the feature spatial distribution of both domains, thereby mitigating the domain shift caused by the different datasets.

Totally, the loss function comprises three components: the classification loss on the real dataset, the classification loss on the synthetic data, and the MK-MMD loss, which is denoted as $\mathcal{L}_{cls\_real}$, $\mathcal{L}_{cls\_gen}$ and $\mathcal{L}_{mk-mmd}$. We compute the MK-MMD loss at the feature layer for both the real and synthetic data. For individual sub-branches, we compute the same loss as the feature extractor in Sect. 3.1 after the classification head. The overall final loss function is denoted as:

$$\mathcal{L} = \alpha \cdot \mathcal{L}_{cls\_real} + \mathcal{L}_{cls\_gen} + \lambda \cdot \mathcal{L}_{mk-mmd} \tag{3}$$

where α and λ are hyperparameters that regulate the weights of the synthetic data classification loss and the domain adaptive loss, respectively. In our manuscript, α is set to 0.5 with the same classification loss contribution for synthetic and real data, and λ is set to 1.

To visually compare the effectiveness of our methods, the backbone structure adopts the same structure as the feature extractor in Sect. 3.1, but the feature extractor only takes the real data as input, while the backbone is a two-branch model with shared parameters. Furthermore, we apply the same data augmentation on the real branch image as we did when pre-training the feature extractor. In summary, the generator generates inter-class synthetic data. For each class, we sample 10 images, each subjected to intra-class augmentation. During the inference phase, the feature vectors extracted by the backbone are adopted for palm vein authentication task.

4 Experiments

In this section, we conduct a series of experiments on CASIA-MS-PalmprintV1 [24], PolyU_NIR [25] and SCUT Palm Vein Database version 1 [6], referred to as CASIA, POLYU and SCUT_PV_V1 respectively throughout the manuscript. CASIA is a multispectral palmprint database, we only use images with the wavelength of 850 nm. First, we detail the experimental setup and evaluation protocol. Second, we compare the model performance under varying numbers of synthetic inter-class samples. Additionally, we conduct ablation experiments to demonstrate the effectiveness of each proposed component. Finally, we show a comparison with SOTA palm vein authentication methods.

4.1 The Details of Training and Evaluation Protocol

The experiments are conducted using the PyTorch framework, and the training and testing run on the NVIDIA RTX 3090 GPU. The input noise and style latent code dimensions of 512. The optimizer is Adam [26], where the learning rate of the generator is 1.6×10^{-3} with beta of $(0, 0.99^{0.8})$ and that of the discriminator is 1.88×10^{-3} with beta of $(0, 0.99^{0.94})$. Training is conducted for a total of 100,000 iterations, with a data batch size of 32 for each iteration. For palm vein images, we follow the method proposed [6] and use the region of interest (ROI) of size 256×256 with a scale factor of 1.6.

The backbone set the number of epochs to 800 for the network training and used the Adam optimizer with a momentum of 0.9. The initial learning rate is 0.001, and we employ the cosine annealing schedule as the learning rate change scheduler. The maximum number of iterations and the minimum learning rate are 150 and $1e^{-9}$, respectively and the batch size is set to 50. For palm vein images, We use the same roi as the training generator, but scaled to 224×224.

For evaluation protocol and metrics, we are consistent with that in [6]. EER and TAR@FAR = 0.01 are also employed as the main evaluation metrics in our experiments.

4.2 Experiments of Different Numbers of Synthetic Inter-class Samples

We conduct comparative experiments on three publicly available datasets by generating different numbers of inter-class sample. We take the feature extractor pre-trained on real data as a benchmark and report its test results in the second column of Table 1. In addition, we report the computational costs of generating different classes. In our manuscript, we adopt the quantities of random style latent codes and the runtime on a single 3090 GPU to measure.

Specifically, we generate 400, 800, 1200, and 1600 classes, and keep the real branch the same as the baseline. The experimental results, presented in Table 1, indicate that model performance improves with an increasing number of inter-class samples in synthetic data. This demonstrates that the model learns more semantic representations from the synthetic datasets, thereby enhancing its generalization capability. Computational costs increases with the number of synthetic inter-class samples.

Interestingly, we find that the model reaches the best trade-off between performance and computational costs at class 1200. The model performance saturates, and at the same time, generating inter-class samples becomes more difficult and the runtime increases severely. We attribute this to the fact that GAN captures less diversity compared to likelihood-based models [27]. Although more classes of data are generated, the semantic features are similar and do not allow the model to learn more representational information.

Table 1. EER(%) WITH DIFFERENT NUMBER OF INTER-CLASS SAMPLE

Database	Categories of quantities												
	Baseline	400			800			1200			1600		
		EER(%)	Quantity	Time(s)	EER(%)	Quantity	Time(s)	EER(%)	Quantity	Time(s)	EER(%)	Quantity	Time(s)
SCUT_PV_V1	0.65	0.50	1377	81.53	0.30	5461	254.25	0.42	12684	662.46	0.43	48556	1647.94
POLYU	2.15	0.90	2938	289.88	0.69	10566	370.36	0.64	24707	857.59	0.71	28078	3265.41
CASIA	3.03	2.87	7474	612.87	2.80	23811	631.97	2.43	78587	2093.59	2.23	170125	4523.64

4.3 Compared with SOTA Method

Table 2 presents the experimental results across three public datasets, our experimental results is competitive, and achieves SOTA on the SCUT_PV_V1 datasets. While on the CASIA and POLYU datasets, there is still a gap between our method and the SOTA method. We analyze that SCUT_PV_V1 is a non-contact dataset, the user has no fixed posture during the acquisition, and the data contains more information about posture and light changes, and CASIA and POLYU belong to fixed contact acquisition. Generators trained on SCUT_PV_V1 can learn more variations of real scenarios. In other words, the synthetic data from the SCUT_PV_V1 underwent data augmentation, whereas the CASIA and

POLYU were used without any augmentation. [6,28] proposed data augmentation method for palm vein authentication can well simulate the change of the hand in free posture, improves the generalization of the model, and achieves better results on the CASIA and POLYU.

Table 2. SUMMARY OF EER WITH THE PALM AUTHENTICATION METHOD

Model	Year	Protocol		Databases		
		Cross-validation	Split Ratio	CASIA	POLYU	SCUT_PV_V1
M-Densenet-161 [29]	2021	T-V-T Split	4:1:5	2.42	-	-
MPSNet [30]	2022	K-Fold	k = 5	1.52	0.47	-
FCPVN [28]	2023	T-T Split	5:5	2.44	**0.28**	
AMPVNet [6]	2024	T-T Split	5:5	**1.80**	0.57	0.51
Ours	2024	T-T Split	5:5	2.43	0.64	**0.42**

4.4 Ablation Experiments

In this section, we design four sets of ablation models on three publicly available datasets to validate the effectiveness of our proposed key modules. We use the 1200 class of experiments in Sect. 4.2 as a baseline. The results of the ablation experiments are shown in Table 3. Notice that only inter-class enhancement negatively affects the model performance on the CASIA and SCUT_PV_V1 datasets, verifying that single inter-class sample augmentation makes authentication a one-hot learning task. Whereas, our proposed inter-class and intra-class collaborative augmentation significantly improves the performance of the model. MK-MMD narrows down the domain discrepancy between the real and the synthetic data, making our proposed method reach the optimization.

Table 3. RESULTS OF ABLATION EXPERIMENTS(%)

Components			Database					
Inter-class	Intra-class	MK-MMD	SCUT_PV_V1		POLYU		CASIA	
			EER ↓	TAR@FAR = 0.01 ↑	EER ↓	TAR@FAR = 0.01 ↑	EER ↓	TAR@FAR = 0.01 ↑
✗	✗	✗	0.65	99.47	2.15	96.27	3.03	89.33
✓	✗	✓	0.66	99.40	1.02	98.89	3.17	93.17
✓	✓	✗	0.57	99.49	1.02	98.89	2.60	94.13
✓	✓	✓	**0.42**	**99.70**	**0.64**	**99.39**	2.43	**95.60**

5 Conclusions and Future Works

In this paper, we present a GAN-based inter-intra collaborative data augmentation to simultaneously generate both discriminative inter-class and intra-class samples for addressing inefficient training data in palm vein authentication. By reducing the domain discrepancy between the real data and synthetic data, the synthetic palm vein samples are effectively utilized and the feature extraction performance of the model is boosted. Experimental results have demonstrated the effectiveness of our method which performs competitive performance for authentication tasks compared to SOTA methods.

For future works, We will extend our method to other hand biometrics to explore its effectiveness and generalization.

Acknowledgment. This work was supported by the Natural Science Foundation of Guangdong Province, China (No. 2022A1515010114).

References

1. Hassan, N.F., Abdulrazzaq, H.I.: Pose invariant palm vein identification system using convolutional neural network. Baghdad Sci. J. (2018)
2. Ou, W.F., Po, L.M., Zhou, C., Xian, P.F., Xiong, J.J.: Gan-based inter-class sample generation for contrastive learning of vein image representations. IEEE Trans. Biometrics Behav. Identity Sci. **4**(2), 249–262 (2022)
3. Qin, H., El-Yacoubi, M.A., Li, Y., Liu, C.: Multi-scale and multi-direction GAN for CNN-based single palm-vein identification. IEEE Trans. Inf. Forensics Secur. **16**, 2652–2666 (2021)
4. Qin, H., Xi, H., Li, Y., El-Yacoubi, M.A., Wang, J., Gao, X.: Adversarial learning-based data augmentation for palm-vein identification. IEEE Trans. Circuits Syst. Video Technol. (2023)
5. Ou, W.F., Po, L.M., Huang, X.F., Yu, W.Y., Zhao, Y.Z.: GSCL: generative self-supervised contrastive learning for vein-based biometric verification. IEEE Trans. Biometrics Behav. Identity Sci. (2024)
6. Luo, D., Qiao, Y., Xie, D., Zhang, S., Kang, W.: Palm vein recognition under unconstrained and weak-cooperative conditions. IEEE Trans. Inf. Forensics Secur. (2024)
7. Hernández-García, R., Salazar-Jurado, E.H., Barrientos, R.J., Castro, F.M., Ramos-Cózar, J., Guil, N.: From synthetic data to real palm vein identification: a fine-tuning approach. In: 2023 IEEE 13th International Conference on Pattern Recognition Systems (ICPRS), pp. 1–7. IEEE (2023)
8. Long, M., Cao, Y., Wang, J., Jordan, M.: Learning transferable features with deep adaptation networks. In: International Conference on Machine Learning, pp. 97–105. PMLR (2015)
9. Liu, Z., Mao, H., Wu, C.Y., Feichtenhofer, C., Darrell, T., Xie, S.: A convnet for the 2020s. In: Proceedings of the IEEE/CVF Conference on Computer Vision and Pattern Recognition, pp. 11976–11986 (2022)
10. Touvron, H., Cord, M., Douze, M., Massa, F., Sablayrolles, A., Jégou, H.: Training data-efficient image transformers & distillation through attention. In: International Conference on Machine Learning, pp. 10347–10357. PMLR (2021)

11. Huang, X.F., Po, L.M., Ou, W.F.: Motion transfer-driven intra-class data augmentation for finger vein recognition. In: ICASSP 2024-2024 IEEE International Conference on Acoustics, Speech and Signal Processing (ICASSP), pp. 4585–4589. IEEE (2024)
12. Wang, G., Sun, C., Sowmya, A.: Learning a compact vein discrimination model with ganerated samples. IEEE Trans. Inf. Forensics Secur. **15**, 635–650 (2019)
13. Ribani, R., Marengoni, M.: A survey of transfer learning for convolutional neural networks. In: 2019 32nd SIBGRAPI Conference on Graphics, Patterns and Images Tutorials (SIBGRAPI-T), pp. 47–57. IEEE (2019)
14. Tzeng, E., Hoffman, J., Darrell, T., Saenko, K.: Simultaneous deep transfer across domains and tasks. In: Proceedings of the IEEE International Conference on Computer Vision, pp. 4068–4076 (2015)
15. Borgwardt, K.M., Gretton, A., Rasch, M.J., Kriegel, H.P., Schölkopf, B., Smola, A.J.: Integrating structured biological data by kernel maximum mean discrepancy. Bioinformatics **22**(14), e49–e57 (2006)
16. Long, M., Zhu, H., Wang, J., Jordan, M.I.: Deep transfer learning with joint adaptation networks. In: International Conference on Machine Learning, pp. 2208–2217. PMLR (2017)
17. Shao, H., Zhong, D., Du, X.: Cross-domain palmprint recognition based on transfer convolutional autoencoder. In: 2019 IEEE International Conference on Image Processing (ICIP), pp. 1153–1157. IEEE (2019)
18. Zhang, Z., Zhong, F., Kang, W.: Study on reflection-based imaging finger vein recognition. IEEE Trans. Inf. Forensics Secur. **17**, 2298–2310 (2021)
19. Karras, T., Laine, S., Aittala, M., Hellsten, J., Lehtinen, J., Aila, T.: Analyzing and improving the image quality of StyleGAN. In: Proceedings of the IEEE/CVF Conference on Computer Vision and Pattern Recognition, pp. 8110–8119 (2020)
20. Sandler, M., Howard, A., Zhu, M., Zhmoginov, A., Chen, L.C.: MobileNetV2: inverted residuals and linear bottlenecks. In: Proceedings of the IEEE Conference on Computer Vision and Pattern Recognition, pp. 4510–4520 (2018)
21. Kuzu, R.S., Maiorana, E., Campisi, P.: Loss functions for CNN-based biometric vein recognition. In: 2020 28th European Signal Processing Conference (EUSIPCO), pp. 750–754. IEEE (2021)
22. Wang, H., et al.: CosFace: large margin cosine loss for deep face recognition. In: Proceedings of the IEEE Conference on Computer Vision and Pattern Recognition, pp. 5265–5274 (2018)
23. Gulrajani, I., Ahmed, F., Arjovsky, M., Dumoulin, V., Courville, A.C.: Improved training of wasserstein GANs. In: Advances in Neural Information Processing Systems, vol. 30 (2017)
24. Hao, Y., Sun, Z., Tan, T., Ren, C.: Multispectral palm image fusion for accurate contact-free palmprint recognition. In: 2008 15th IEEE International Conference on Image Processing, pp. 281–284. IEEE (2008)
25. Zhang, D., Guo, Z., Lu, G., Zhang, L., Zuo, W.: An online system of multispectral palmprint verification. IEEE Trans. Instrum. Meas. **59**(2), 480–490 (2009)
26. Loshchilov, I., Hutter, F.: Decoupled weight decay regularization. arXiv preprint arXiv:1711.05101 (2017)
27. Dhariwal, P., Nichol, A.: Diffusion models beat GANs on image synthesis. In: Advances in Neural Information Processing Systems, vol. 34, pp. 8780–8794 (2021)
28. Ma, Y., Huang, H., Luo, D., Zhang, S., Kang, W., Xie, D.: Focal contrastive learning for palm vein authentication. IEEE Trans. Instrum. Meas. (2023)

29. Kuzu, R.S., Maiorana, E., Campisi, P.: Vein-based biometric verification using transfer learning. In: 2020 43rd International Conference on Telecommunications and Signal Processing (TSP), pp. 403–409. IEEE (2020)
30. Horng, S.J., Vu, D.T., Nguyen, T.V., Zhou, W., Lin, C.T.: Recognizing palm vein in smartphones using RGB images. IEEE Trans. Industr. Inf. **18**(9), 5992–6002 (2021)

3D Palmprint MCI Synthesis for 2D-3D Heterogeneous Palmprint Recognition

Le Su[1], Lunke Fei[1(✉)], Shuping Zhao[1], Shuyi Li[2], and Jia Wei[3]

[1] School of Computer Science and Technology, Guangdong University of Technology, Guangzhou, China
flksxm@126.com
[2] Faculty of Information Technology, Beijing University of Technology, Beijing, China
[3] School of Computer and Information, Hefei University of Technology, Hefei, China

Abstract. Cross-2D-to-3D (2D-3D) heterogeneous palmprint recognition aims to matching a 2D palmprint probe with the 3D palmprint galleries, which shows great potential for biometric applications due to rich information of 3D images and the low-cost of 2D image acquisition. However, the large structural discrepancy between 2D and 3D palmprint images makes it hard to directly conduct matching between 2D-3D heterogeneous palmprint images. In this paper, we propose a palmprint image generative adversarial network (PIGAN) to convert 2D palmprint images into 3D domain for 2D-3D heterogeneous palmprint recognition. We first calculate the mean curvature images (MCIs) to present the 3D palm surface measurements of 3D palmprint images. Then, we employ an image-to-image generation backbone to transform 2D palmprint images into 3D MCI representations. To make the fake MCIs realistic, we impose both adversarial and identity-aware learning losses to protect the discriminative information of MCIs, and further introduce a visual-recovery loss to restore the visual-specific texture characteristics of palmprints. By this way, high-quality 3D palmprint MCI can be synthesized with high similarity as the real ones at both feature and visual levels, such that the pixel-level gap between 2D and 3D palmprint images can be effectively reduced for 2D-3D heterogeneous palmprint recognition. Extensive experimental results on the widely-used PolyU 2D-3D palmprint database clearly show the effectiveness of the proposed PIGAN in improving the performance of 2D-3D heterogeneous palmprint recognition.

Keywords: Biometrics · Heterogeneous palmprint recognition · 3D palmprint MCI · Image generation

1 Introduction

Biometric recognition aims to identify a human by using one's biological or behavioral traits, which has shown great potential for "anywhere" and "anytime" personal authentication, such as identity confirmation of mobile payment and long-distance business. In recent years, palmprint has become one of the most attractive biometric traits due to its rich reliable features, less invasiveness and high user-friendliness [1]. In addition, human can conveniently control the acquisition of palmprint images. For example, palmprint images can be easily captured with one's agreement and are difficult to be collected without one's permission. For these reasons, palmprint recognition has become a hot topic in not only academic [1] but also the industrial communities, such as the palmprint-payment systems of "Amazon One" and "Tencent WePalm".

Over the past decades, there have been a number of methods proposed for palmprint recognition, and most of them focus on 2D palmprint images, including the handcraft-based [2–4], subspace learning-based [5,6] and deep learning-based [7] palmprint descriptors. For example, Fei et al. [3] proposed a double-orientation encoding method to represent different direction feature of palmprint. In addition, Fei et al. [5] learned a subspace of compact discriminative direction for palmprint recognition, and Shao et al. [7] developed a deep distillation hashing network to generate a palmprint binary feature descriptor. With the development of depth cameras, there have also been some studies on 3D palmprint recognition by capturing 3D palmprint images, which convey one more dimension of depth information than 2D palmprint images with excellent robustness to illumination changes [8]. For instance, Li et al. [9] extracted both line and orientation features from the mean curvatures of 3D palmprint images for feature representation and recognition, and Fei et al. [10] further proposed a complete binary representation by extracting compact surface types of 3D palmprint images for 3D palmprint recognition.

While 3D palmprint images contain more robust features than 2D counterparts, it is usually expensive and time-consuming to capture 3D palmprint images due to the special requirement of 3D imaging, hindering the development of 3D palmprint recognition in practical applications. By contrast, 2D palmprint images can be easily captured by using various common 2D cameras with less time cost. This motivates us to collect 3D palmprint images offline as galleries, and capture 2D palmprint images as probes in real-time, as 2D-3D heterogeneous face recognition [11]. In this way, 2D-3D heterogeneous palmprint recognition becomes an interesting and meaningful solution for reliable palmprint recognition with rich features of 3D gallery set and low-time cost of probing 2D palmprint images. However, due to large structural discrepancy between 2D and 3D images, 2D-3D heterogeneous palmprint recognition poses a serious challenge beyond the homogeneous palmprint recognition with the same dimension of palmprint images. To the best of our knowledge, there is still no work to study this topic of 2D-3D heterogeneous palmprint recognition.

In this paper, we propose a 3D palmprint image generative adversarial network (PIGAN), which aims to convert 2D palmprint images into 3D domain for 2D-3D heterogeneous palmprint recognition. Specifically, we first convert the 3D palmprint images into MCIs to represent the 3D surface structural measurements. After that, we design a palmprint-specific image generation network to convert 2D palmprint images into 3D palmprint MCI representations. To make the fake MCIs more similar to their real counterparts, we develop both adversarial and identity-aware losses to extensively preserve the discriminative features in the synthetic palmprint images. Moreover, we enforce a visual-recovery loss to make the fake images more visually similar to the real ones. By doing so, we can generate high-quality MCIs from 2D palmprint images with small intra-class features and visual gaps from the real 3D palmprint images. Lastly, we conduct 2D-3D heterogeneous palmprint recognition experiments on the PolyU 2D-3D palmprint database to demonstrate the effectiveness of the proposed PIGAN on 3D palmprint MCI generation.

The main contributions of this paper can be summarized as follows: (1) We propose a 2D to 3D palmprint image generation network, i.e., PIGAN, to solve the matching problem of 2D and 3D heterogeneous palmprint images with large structural feature discrepancies. To the best of our knowledge, this is the first work with an attempt to study 2D-3D heterogeneous palmprint recognition. (2) We develop both identity-aware and visual-recovery losses to guide the image generation of the proposed method, which can generate high-quality MCIs from 2D palmprint images with preserving both the discriminative features and the visual characteristics. (3) We conduct extensive experiments on the PolyU 2D-3D palmprint database to evaluate the proposed method, and the experimental results clearly show that high-quality 3D palmprint MCIs can be generated by our proposed PIGAN with significantly improving the performance of 2D-3D heterogeneous palmprint recognition.

2 Proposed Method

3D palmprint images generally describe the depth information of palm surfaces, which depicts highly different characteristics from their 2D counterparts. To achieve the matching goal of crossing 2D to 3D palmprint images, our proposed PIGAN aims to convert a 2D palmprint image into its 3D representation. In this section, we elaborate on our proposed PIGAN for 2D to 3D palmprint image generation.

2.1 Overview of the PIGAN

3D palmprint image is essentially the structural measurement of a palmprint surface with diverse convex and concave shapes, which can be effectively characterized by using mean curvature information. For this reason, we employ the widely-used MCI as the 3D palmprint image measure, which can be easily obtained by convolving the 3D palmprint image with pre-defined templates [10]. Then, we develop a 3D palmprint-specific generator with the aim of converting a 2D palmprint image into its MCI counterpart. Figure 1 shows the basic architecture of PIGAN, which mainly consists of an image-to-image generation backbone and three learning guidance losses for 3D palmprint-specific image generation. To be more specific, we employ the powerful image transformation network, i.e., ITNet [12], as the image generation backbone, which aims to synthesize the basic 3D palmprint MCI information. Moreover, to make the fake MCI closer to its real 3D palmprint counterparts, we enforce three learning constraints on the palmprint generator, including discriminative feature preservation, identity-aware consistency and visual recovery.

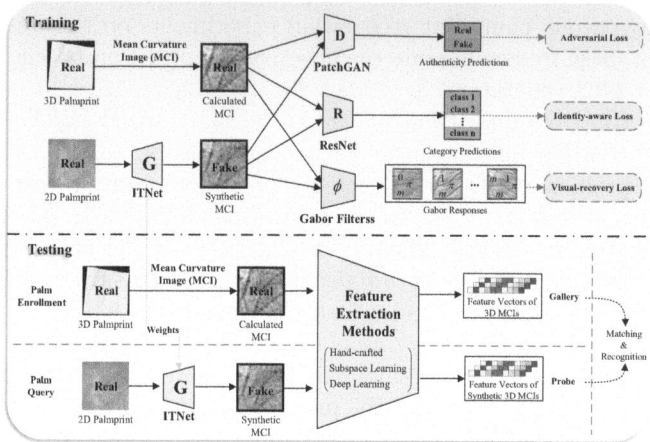

Fig. 1. The basic architecture of the proposed PIGAN. We first calculate the MCIs of the 3D palmprint images to characterize the structural features of 3D palmprint surfaces. Then, we employ an image-to-image generator to convert the 2D palmprint images into fake MCIs. Moreover, we develop three learning principles to guide the generator to synthesize high-quality 3D palmprint MCIs.

2.2 Discriminative Features Preservation

To make the generated MCI hard to be distinguished from the real one, we employ the widely-used adversarial generation training [13] to guide the MCI generator to extensively preserve the 3D palmprint-specific characteristics in the fake 3D palmprint MCI. Specifically, we employ the widely-used PatchGAN [13] as the authenticity discriminator to distinguish the synthetic MCI from real MCI, which can function as follows:

$$L_{adv} = \min_G \max_D E_{y \sim p_{data}(y)} [\log D(y)] + E_{x \sim p_{data}(x)} [\log (1 - D(G(x)))], \quad (1)$$

where x and y denote the 2D palmprint image and its corresponding 3D MCI, respectively. G denotes the MCI generator (i.e., ITNet) and D represents the authenticity discriminator (i.e., PatchGAN). L_{adv} represents the adversarial loss, which can enhance the recognition ability of the discriminator D to distinguish fake palmprint MCI, and meanwhile promote the generator G to generate more realistic MCI to fool the discriminator D. Having obtained a balance, G can generate a faithful 3D palmprint MCI with preserving more characteristics as the real counterpart.

2.3 Identity-Aware Consistency

To achieve reliable 2D to 3D palmprint recognition, we have an aim that the identity information of the palmprint can remain unchanged during fake MCI generation. To achieve this, we utilize the ResNet [14] as the recognizer to learn the identity information of synthetic MCI, and further define the following identity-aware loss to maintain identity consistency between intra-class real and fake MCIs:

$$L_{id} = \min_{G} E_{\substack{x \sim p_{data}(x) \\ y \sim p_{data}(y)}} [\|R(y) - R(G(x))\|_1] + \min_{R} E_{y \sim p_{data}(y)} [\gamma(R(y))], \quad (2)$$

where $\gamma(\cdot)$ is the cross-entropy loss function [14] and $\|\cdot\|_1$ represents the L_1-norm. R represents the palmprint recognizer (i.e., ResNet) to predict the identities of palmprint MCIs. L_{id} denotes the identity-aware loss, in which the first term aims to guarantee the identity by minimizing the class-level difference between real and fake MCIs, and the second one aims to enhance the prediction ability of the recognizer R by fine-tuning it on the real palmprint MCIs (i.e., y) via cross-entropy loss [14].

2.4 Visual Recovery

Having achieved the identity consistency, we further recover more visual characteristics in the generated 2D palmprint MCIs. It is well known that palmprint images comprise of various textures such as line and ridge patterns, which form the main visual characteristics of palmprints. In addition, existing studies have shown that the Gabor filter [1] can effectively characterize the texture features of palmprint images. Motivated by this, we employ a bank of Gabor filters with different orientations to recover various texture characteristics of palmprint images, making the generated MCIs highly similar to the real ones at visual level. To be more specific, we first define m groups of Gabor filters with the orientations of $(i-1)\pi/m$ $(i = 1, 2, ..., m)$, referred to as ϕ_i. Then, we calculate the Gabor responses of real and fake MCIs on different orientations, and make the Gabor response difference between them as small as possible, as follows:

$$L_{vis} = \min_{G} E_{\substack{x \sim p_{data}(x) \\ y \sim p_{data}(y)}} \left[\frac{1}{m} \sum_{i=1}^{m} \|\phi_i(y) - \phi_i(G(x))\|_1\right], \quad (3)$$

where $\phi_i(\cdot)$ represents the Gabor response of a palmprint image on the i-th orientation. L_{vis} denotes the visual-aware loss, which aims to minimize the Gabor responses between real and false MCIs. By doing this, the generated MCIs can obtain similar Gabor-based texture features as the real 3D palmprint MCI, such that more visual similarity can be preserved during MCI generation. In this study, we empirically set m to 6, and set the hyperparameters of the Gabor filters following to [7].

2.5 Overall Loss Function

By combining adversarial learning, identity-aware consistency and visual-aware recovery, our proposed generator G follows an overall loss function as the following:

$$L_{all} = L_{adv} + \alpha \cdot L_{id} + \beta \cdot L_{vis}, \tag{4}$$

where α and β are two balance parameters, which control the importance of the identity-aware and the visual-recovery losses, respectively.

3 Experiments

In this section, we conduct 2D-3D heterogeneous palmprint recognition experiments to evaluate the synthetic samples generated by our proposed method on the widely-used PolyU 2D-3D palmprint database [8]. All the experiments were conducted based on the PyTorch V2.0.0 framework running on the Ubuntu18.04 system, and the NVIDIA GPU RTX3060Ti with 8G RAM memory and 12-core Intel CPU i7-12700F.

3.1 PolyU 2D-3D Palmprint Database

The PolyU 2D-3D palmprint database [8] contains 8,000 3D palmprint images with palm surface measurements collected from the two hands of 200 volunteers, and each hand provided 20 samples. Moreover, 8,000 2D palmprint images were also simultaneously collected during 3D image capture in the PolyU database. To the best of our knowledge, the PolyU database is the only publicly available palmprint database with 2D-3D heterogeneous palmprint images so far. In this experiment, all 2D and 3D palmprint samples are cropped into ROIs and resized to the sizes of 128 × 128 pixels. Figure 2 shows the typical 2D and 3D palmprint samples randomly selected from the PolyU 2D-3D palmprint database.

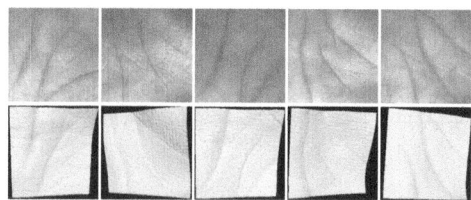

Fig. 2. The typical 2D palmprint images (first row) and the corresponding 3D palmprint images (second row) randomly selected from the PolyU 2D-3D palmprint database.

3.2 2D-3D Heterogeneous Palmprint Recognition Results

In this section, we use the PIGAN to generate 3D palmprint MCIs from PolyU 2D palmprint images for 2D to 3D palmprint recognition, and compare the proposed method with state-of-the-art image-to-image GANs, including the CycleGAN [15] and Pix2Pix [13]. Specifically, we randomly select 25% subjects of samples from the PolyU database as the training set, and use the rest as the testing set. For a fair comparison, all comparison GANs are uniformly trained for 100 epochs with a batch size of 2 and use the Adam optimizer with a learning rate of 0.0002. After that, we employ the widely-used palmprint recognition methods to conduct cross-2D-to-3D palmprint identification (the real 3D images are used as the galleries and the synthetic 3D samples are used as the probes), including four hand-crafted palmprint descriptors such as CompCode [2], DOC [3] and LDDBP [4], two feature learning-based methods such as LCMFC [5] and LSIR [6], and few typical deep learning networks such as ResNet [14], ConvNeXt [16] and EfficientViT [17]. Among them, the two deep learning-based networks are uniformly trained for 30 epochs with a batch size of 32 and use the Adam optimizer with a learning rate of 0.0002. In the feature matching stage, the Euclidean distance is employed as the similarity metric and the nearest neighbor classifier is used for feature identification.

Table 1. The 2D-3D heterogeneous palmprint identification accuracies achieved by different palmprint descriptors based on the synthetic 3D palmprint MCIs generated by different GANs.

Palmprint Recognition methods	2D-3D Palmprint GANs			
	GAN-free	CycleGAN	Pix2Pix	PIGAN (ours)
CompCode	57.95	86.44	93.15	**97.75**
DOC	85.59	89.59	93.35	**95.38**
LDDBP	78.37	81.71	86.02	**90.16**
LCMFC	54.54	81.26	93.24	**98.43**
LSIR	84.33	86.56	94.12	**98.85**
ResNet	27.60	67.00	86.10	**92.75**
ConvNeXt	60.60	74.30	89.15	**94.90**
EfficientViT	20.05	74.05	89.30	**96.75**

Table 1 tabulates the rank-one 2D-3D heterogeneous palmprint identification accuracies of different palmprint descriptors based on the synthetic 3D samples generated by different GANs. For a better comparison, the recognition results based on the original 2D and 3D palmprint images are also presented in the table (referred to as "GAN-free"). It can be seen that the 2D-3D heterogeneous palmprint identification accuracies can be significantly improved with the synthetic 3D MCIs generated by our proposed method compared with GAN-free. This is because our method can project the 2D palmprint images into the 3D palmprint domain with specially preserving identity-aware features, such that the pixel-level feature gaps between the 2D and 3D palmprint images can be significantly narrowed and higher recognition accuracy can be obtained. Moreover, our proposed PIGAN is superior to the CycleGAN and Pix2Pix with obviously higher recognition accuracies on the synthetic samples generated by the PIGAN. This is because our proposed PIGAN preserves diverse discriminative features as much as possible via both adversarial and identity-aware learning strategies. As a result, with the generated MCI samples by our proposed method, most palmprint methods can extract specific discriminative features via different schemes, such that higher recognition accuracies are obtained.

Moreover, as shown in Fig. 3, we present some typical synthetic 3D palmprint MCIs generated by our proposed PIGAN in comparison with the CycleGAN and Pix2Pix methods. It can be observed that our proposed PIGAN can generate clearer 3D palmprint MCI with high-quality texture characteristics than that obtained by the CycleGAN and Pix2Pix methods. This is beneficial to the proposed visual-aware recovery strategy. This ensures that more visual texture characteristics can be restored in the synthetic MCI, such that high-quality MCI can be obtained.

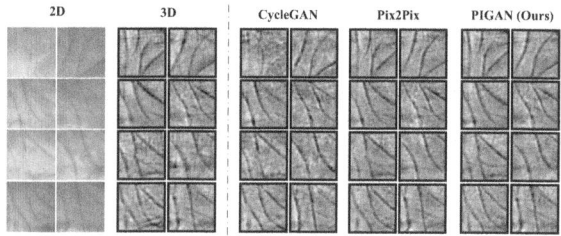

Fig. 3. Some synthetic 3D palmprint MCIs generated by using different GANs, where the first two columns show the original 2D palmprint images and the corresponding 3D palmprint MCIs, respectively.

3.3 Hyperparameter Analysis

Our proposed PIGAN aims to achieve 2D to 3D palmprint transformation under the guidance of adversarial loss, identity-aware and visual-recovery strategies balanced by two parameters, i.e., α and β. In addition, m groups of Gabor filters are designed during the visual texture feature learning. To the best of our knowledge, there is no efficient way to directly find the optimal values for these hyperparameters. In this study, we employ a simple yet effective way to find the approximate optimal values of these hyperparameters by traversing a parameter with fixing others in advance. Specifically, we first set the hyperparameter m to the values ranging in $\{2, 4, 6, 8, 10, 12, 14, 16\}$ while fixing the α and β to 1. Then, we calculate the rank-one 2D-to-3D palmprint identification accuracies via ResNet based on the synthetic 3D palmprint MCIs generated by our proposed

Table 2. The identification accuracies of the proposed method with ResNet versus different values of m.

m	2	4	6	8	10	12	14	16
Accuracy	90.20	88.25	**92.75**	91.35	91.65	92.60	92.10	88.80

PIGAN, as reported in Table 2. We can observe that the PIGAN obtains the best recognition performances when m is set to 6.

After that, by fixing the value of m to 6, we set the two balance parameters α and β to different values ranging in $\{0.001, 0.01, 0.1, 1, 10, 100\}$ and calculate the identification results on the PolyU 2D-3D palmprint database. Figure 4 shows the identification accuracy versus different values of α and β. We can see that the proposed PIGAN with recognition network ResNet usually achieves obvious higher accuracies when $\alpha \geq 1$ and $\beta \leq 1$ than that with other parameter settings, and the identification accuracy achieves the best when $\alpha = 1$ and $\beta = 1$. As a result, we empirically set both α and β to 1, and set m to 6 for our proposed PIGAN method.

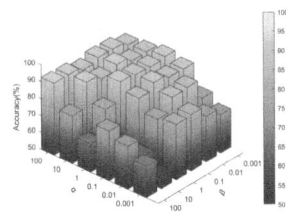

Fig. 4. The identification accuracies of the proposed PIGAN with recognition network ResNet versus different values of α and β on the PolyU 2D-3D palmprint database.

4 Conclusion

In this paper, we proposed a new palmprint image-to-image generative adversarial network, i.e., PIGAN, to transform a 2D palmprint image into 3D MCI descriptor for 2D-3D heterogeneous palmprint recognition. The proposed method first converts 2D palmprint images into fake 3D MCIs via an ITNet-based image generation backbone, and then enforces three learning strategies, including adversarial learning, identity-aware consistency and visual recovery, to guarantee the high-quality of the fake 3D MCIs, with extensive preserving the discriminative features and visual similarity. By this way, the pixel-level discrepancy between 2D and 3D heterogeneous palmprint images can be narrowed, making it feasible to recognize palmprint images crossing 2D to 3D spaces. Extensive experimental results on the PolyU 2D-3D palmprint database clearly show the effectiveness of the proposed PIGAN for 2D-3D heterogeneous palmprint recognition. For future work, it seems to be an interesting direction to extend our proposed method to other heterogeneous palmprint recognition tasks such as cross visible to near-infrared palmprint image matching.

Acknowledgments. This work was supported in part by the National Natural Science Foundation of China under Grant 62176066, and in part by the Natural Science Foundation of Guangdong Province under Grant 2023A1515012717.

References

1. Fei, L., Lu, G., Jia, W., Teng, S., Zhang, D.: Feature extraction methods for palmprint recognition: a survey and evaluation. IEEE Trans. Syst. Man Cybern. Syst. **49**(2), 346–363 (2018)
2. Kong, A.K., Zhang, D.: Competitive coding scheme for palmprint verification. In: Proceedings of the 17th International Conference on Pattern Recognition, ICPR 2004, vol. 1, pp. 520–523. IEEE (2004)
3. Fei, L., Xu, Y., Tang, W., Zhang, D.: Double-orientation code and nonlinear matching scheme for palmprint recognition. Pattern Recogn. **49**, 89–101 (2016)
4. Fei, L., Zhang, B., Xu, Y., Huang, D., Jia, W., Wen, J.: Local discriminant direction binary pattern for palmprint representation and recognition. IEEE Trans. Circuits Syst. Video Technol. **30**(2), 468–481 (2019)
5. Fei, L., Zhang, B., Zhang, L., Jia, W., Wen, J., Wu, J.: Learning compact multifeature codes for palmprint recognition from a single training image per palm. IEEE Trans. Multimedia **23**, 2930–2942 (2020)
6. Fei, L., Wong, W.K., Zhao, S., Wen, J., Zhu, J., Xu, Y.: Learning spectrum-invariance representation for cross-spectral palmprint recognition. IEEE Trans. Syst. Man Cybern. Syst. (2023)
7. Shao, H., Zhong, D., Du, X.: Deep distillation hashing for unconstrained palmprint recognition. IEEE Trans. Instrum. Meas. **70**, 1–13 (2021)
8. Zhang, D., Lu, G., Li, W., Zhang, L., Luo, N.: Three dimensional palmprint recognition using structured light imaging. In: 2008 IEEE Second International Conference on Biometrics: Theory, Applications and Systems, pp. 1–6. IEEE (2008)
9. Li, W., Zhang, D., Zhang, L., Lu, G., Yan, J.: 3-D palmprint recognition with joint line and orientation features. IEEE Trans. Syst. Man Cybern. Part C (Appl. Rev.) **41**(2), 274–279 (2010)
10. Fei, L., Lu, G., Jia, W., Wen, J., Zhang, D.: Complete binary representation for 3-D palmprint recognition. IEEE Trans. Instrum. Meas. **67**(12), 2761–2771 (2018)
11. Ouyang, S., Hospedales, T., Song, Y.Z., Li, X., Loy, C.C., Wang, X.: A survey on heterogeneous face recognition: sketch, infra-red, 3D and low-resolution. Image Vis. Comput. **56**, 28–48 (2016)
12. Johnson, J., Alahi, A., Fei-Fei, L.: Perceptual losses for real-time style transfer and super-resolution. In: Leibe, B., Matas, J., Sebe, N., Welling, M. (eds.) ECCV 2016. LNCS, vol. 9906, pp. 694–711. Springer, Cham (2016). https://doi.org/10.1007/978-3-319-46475-6_43
13. Isola, P., Zhu, J.Y., Zhou, T., Efros, A.A.: Image-to-image translation with conditional adversarial networks. In: Proceedings of the IEEE Conference on Computer Vision and Pattern Recognition, pp. 1125–1134 (2017)
14. He, K., Zhang, X., Ren, S., Sun, J.: Deep residual learning for image recognition. In: Proceedings of the IEEE Conference on Computer Vision and Pattern Recognition, pp. 770–778 (2016)
15. Zhu, J.Y., Park, T., Isola, P., Efros, A.A.: Unpaired image-to-image translation using cycle-consistent adversarial networks. In: Proceedings of the IEEE International Conference on Computer Vision, pp. 2223–2232 (2017)

16. Liu, Z., Mao, H., Wu, C.Y., Feichtenhofer, C., Darrell, T., Xie, S.: A convnet for the 2020s. In: Proceedings of the IEEE/CVF Conference on Computer Vision and Pattern Recognition, pp. 11976–11986 (2022)
17. Liu, X., Peng, H., Zheng, N., Yang, Y., Hu, H., Yuan, Y.: EfficientViT: memory efficient vision transformer with cascaded group attention. In: Proceedings of the IEEE/CVF Conference on Computer Vision and Pattern Recognition, pp. 14420–14430 (2023)

Palmprint Recognition Method Based on Orientation Features: A Survey

Hao Lu, Cunyu Sheng$^{(\boxtimes)}$, and Wei Jia

Hefei University of Technology, No. 485 Danxia Road, Hefei, Anhui, China
2024110481@mail.hfut.edu.cn

Abstract. Palmprint recognition technology is an emerging and effective biometric technology, with palmprint images containing various unique features that can be utilized for individual identity verification, including principal lines, wrinkles, ridges, and so forth. Various palmprint recognition methods based on different feature types have been developed, encompassing line-based approaches, orientation-based methods, texture-based techniques, subspace learning-based strategies, and deep learning-based approaches. This paper reviews and introduces the orientation-based methods, with a particular focus on the feature extraction and feature matching stages in palmprint recognition, which are of paramount importance.

Keywords: Biometrics · palmprint recognition · orientation features

1 Introduction

Biometric recognition technology refers to the identification of an individual's identity information based on their physiological or behavioral characteristics, known as biometric features [1]. Because many physiological or behavioral characteristics are unique to each individual, biometric-based personal identification is considered a highly reliable method of identification [2]. Any physiological or behavioral attribute is eligible to be a biometric feature. Ideally, a biometric feature should be universal, possessed by all individuals; unique, distinctive and easily distinguishable for each person; persistent, not subject to change over an extended period; and collectible, able to be gathered by sensors. Additionally, there are other influencing factors, such as acceptability, whether the population accepts the collection of the feature; spoofability, whether features can be easily stolen or counterfeited; and so on [3].

The palm is the inner surface of the hand between the wrist and fingers, while palmprint refers to the principal lines, wrinkles, and ridges on the palm. Palmprint contains abundant characteristic information. These features are considered to be unique and long-term stable biometric identifiers possessed by everyone. With high acceptability and user-friendliness, palmprint recognition is regarded as a non-invasive biometric technology. Therefore, palmprint recognition is believed to have the potential for high accuracy and reliable performance in achieving personal verification and identification [4,5].

Numerous unique features present in palmprint images can be utilized for personal identification. The surface of the palm typically comprises three types of creases: flexion creases, secondary creases, and ridges. [6] Among them, flexion creases, also known as principal lines, and secondary creases, referred to as wrinkles, are considered reliable and stable characteristics that can distinguish one individual from another. In addition to these, minutiae points, singular points, and textures are also included as useful features for palmprint recognition [7]. Figure 1 gives an example of these features.

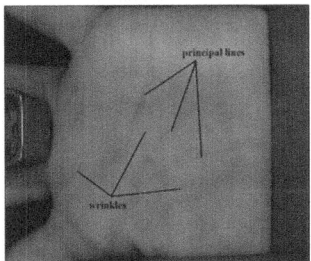

Fig. 1. Characteristics of palm lines.

In palmprint images with varying resolutions, features at different levels of detail can be observed. The study of palmprint images employs both high-resolution (>400 dpi) and low-resolution (<100 dpi) images [2]. For high-resolution palmprint images, it is possible to extract features that fold many singularities and details similar to those found in fingerprints. In contrast, while these detailed features may not be discernible in low-resolution palmprint images, primary features such as principal lines and wrinkles can still be extracted from them.

Initially, palmprint research focused primarily on high-resolution images, but now the majority of research efforts have shifted towards low-resolution images [8]. Currently, among the palmprint recognition methods, the most commonly used approaches include: line-based methods, orientation-based methods, texture-based methods, subspace-based methods, and deep learning-based methods. The aforementioned classification is dependent on the type of features employed for palmprint representation.

Line-based methods focus on extracting the principal lines and local lines within palmprint images, enabling them to capture the inherent features of palmprint lines. Orientation-based methods emphasize on extracting the intrinsic orientation information from palmprint images and encoding this information into a compact and informative representation. Texture-based methods, on the other hand, leverage the fine-grained texture characteristics present in palmprint images. Subspace-based methods are dedicated to extracting key features in a compact form from palmprint images via latent subspaces. Lastly, deep learning-based methods primarily utilize deep learning techniques such as neural networks for feature extraction and classification.

Among these methods, orientation-based methods are considered one of the mainstream methods. This is attributed to the fact that palmprint lines, as the most prominent and fundamental features in low-resolution palmprint images, possess abundant orientation characteristics. Furthermore, orientation features exhibit robustness against variations in illumination [2].

In this paper, our main contributions can be briefly summarized as follows:

We provide a concise introduction to the relevant principles and methods of palmprint recognition, with a particular focus on reviewing the orientation-based palmprint recognition approaches. A brief introduction and summary of the algorithms are presented.

By examining the evolution of orientation-based palmprint recognition algorithms, we aim to guide and inspire emerging scholars in this field to delve deeper into related content.

2 Orientation-Based Methods

As shown in Fig. 2, a classic palmprint recognition process consists of five sections: palmprint image acquisition, preprocessing, feature extraction, feature matching, and database [9].

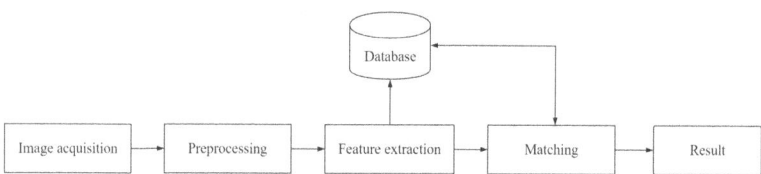

Fig. 2. A classic palmprint recognition process.

For palmprint image acquisition, a camera is used to capture palm images and palmprint images with different resolutions are captured as a source for feature extraction. For preprocessing, the region of interest (ROI) is extracted from the palmprint image and pre-processed to improve the image quality. For feature extraction, a specific algorithm is utilized on the preprocessed image to extract the unique feature information of the palmprint. For feature matching, the extracted feature information is compared with the information in the database for matching or identification. For database, palmprint templates with known identity information are saved. In the context of orientation-based methods, the most distinctive aspects compared to other palmprint recognition approaches lie in the feature extraction and feature matching phases. Several research works have been carried out on orientation-based methods, which can be subdivided into two subcategories: coding-based methods, and histogram-based methods.

2.1 Coding-Based Methods

Coding-based methods use different coding methods to encode the features into feature vectors and use different matching strategies for palm print recognition. Table 1 shows a summary of these methods.

Table 1. Summary of coding-based methods.

Year	Method name	Filter type	Filter number	Scale	Direction levels	Coding strategy	Matching strategy	Ref
2003	PalmCode	zero DC Gabor filter	1	1	1	One direction filtering	Hamming distance	[2]
2004	CompCode	real part of Gabor filter	6	1	1	Winner-take-all	Angular distance	[10]
2005	OrdinalCode	Gaussian filter	3 pairs	1	3 pairs	Ordinal measure	Hamming distance	[11]
2005	POC	Directional	4	1	1	Winner-take-all	Hamming distance	[12]
2006	FusionCode	elliptical Gabor filter	2	1	1	Winner-take-all, phase coding	Hamming distance	[13]
2008	RLOC	MFRAT	6	1	1	Winner-take-all	Pixel-to-area matching	[14]
2008	MCC	real part of Log-Gabor filter	12	2	1	Winner-take-all	Combined angular distance	[15]
2009	BOCV	real part of Gabor filter	6	1	6	Six direction filtering	Hamming distance	[16]
2010	SMCC	sDoG	18	3	1	Sparse code, Winner-take-all	Angular distance	[17]
2010	ICP	4th order steerable filter of Gaussian	8	1	1	Winner-take-all	Angular distance	[18]
2011	ContourCode	non-subsampled bandpass pyramidal filter, non-subsampled directional filter	8	1	1	Winner-take-all	Binary ContourCode matching	[19]
2012	E-BOCV	real part of Gabor filter	6	1	6	Six direction filtering	Hamming distance	[20]
2013	XOR_SUM	Gabor filter	4	1	1	XOR-SUM	Angular distance	[21]
2016	DOC	real part of revised Gabor filter	6	1	2	Responses'sorting	Nonlinear angular distance	[22]
2016	DHOC	Half-Gabor filter	12	1	2	Winner-take-all	Hamming distance	[23]
2016	Fast_CompCode	real part of Gabor filter	1 pair	1	1 pair	Winner-take-all	Hamming distance	[24]
2016	COC	Banana filter	3 pairs	1	1 pair	Winner-take-all	Hamming distance	[25]
2016	NDI	real part of Gabor filter	6	1	1	Neighboring direction	Hamming distance	[26]
2017	SeqC	Gabor filter	5	1	1	Sequency	Angular distance	[27]
2018	DRCC	real part of Gabor filter	6	1	2	Winner-take-all, side code	Angular distance	[28]
2019	DLLDR	real part of Gabor filter / MFRAT	12	1	2/12	Responses' sorting, $(2D)^2LDA$	Euclidean distance	[29]
2020	DBM	Overlapping block	2	1	2	Two direction filtering	Hamming distance	[30]
2022	ODTC	Fabor filter	18	3	1	MBCC, Winner-take-all	Hamming distance	[31]
2023	CDCI	CAGF	3	1	1	zero crossing	Hamming distance	[32]
2024	ROC	real part of Gabor filter	8	1	2	Responses'sorting	Bitwise Similarity	[8]

Zhang et al. (2003) [2] pioneered the development of PalmCode for palmprint recognition in low-resolution images. This approach utilizes a Gabor filter and encodes the phase features from the convolution results, ultimately calculating the Hamming distance for matching. Kong et al. (2004) [10] subsequently introduced CompCode, which extracts directional information using Gabor filters of various orientations. They devised the Winner-take-all rule, where the orientation of the filter with the maximum response is considered the dominant orientation for each sample point. Matching is performed by calculating the angular distance between these dominant orientations. These two works laid a solid conceptual foundation for coding-based methods.

To extract orientation features more efficiently, Wu et al. (2005) [12] proposed palmprint orientation code (POC), designing novel rectangular orientation templates. Zhang et al. (2006) [13] proposed FusionCode, which utilizes both magnitude and phase information for encoding. Jia et al. (2008) [14] proposed robust line orientation code (RLOC) scheme, extracting palmprint orientation features through the modified finite Radon transform (MFRAT). Yue et al. (2010) [18] proposed the ICP method, employing high order steerable filters to simultaneously extract positional and orientation features of principal line. Khan et al. (2011) [19] proposed ContourCode based on the Nonsubsampled Contourlet Transform (NSCT), obtaining dominant directional subband through a two stage filtering. Tamrakar et al. (2013) [21] proposed XOR-SUM code leveraging the imaginary part information of Gabor filters. Zheng et al. (2016) [24] theoretically analyzed the advantages of binary feature representation in palmprint recognition, leading to the proposal of Fast-CompCode, a more efficient and rapid palmprint recognition method. Tabejamaat et al. (2016) [25] studied the positive and negative concavity of palm curves, proposing Concavity Orientation Coding (COC) scheme, using two Banana filters for concavity to extract orientation features. Fei et al. (2016) [26] proposed the neighboring direction indicator (NDI) method, pointing out the direction of dominant orientations. Dubey et al. (2017) [27] proposed Sequency code (SeqC), extracting 1-0 or 0-1 bit transition information across different directions. Van et al. (2019) [29] combined two-directional two-dimensional linear discriminant analysis ($2D^2LDA$) to reduce the dimensionality of features and proposed Discriminant local line Directional Representation (DLLDR). Almaghtuf et al. (2020) [30] proposed a method based on the Difference of Block Means (DBM), utilizing only basic operations, resulting in low computational cost. Dubey et al. (2023) [32] proposed Combined Differential Concavity and Infirmity (CDCI) code, calculating features through curvi-linear anisotropic Gaussian filters (CAGF).

Considering the multiscale nature of palm lines, where the principal lines manifest at higher scales while wrinkles appear at lower scales, Zuo et al. (2008) [15] proposed a multiscale competitive code (MCC) method, separately extracting the dominant orientation at each scale for matching. Later, Zuo et al. (2010) [17] introduced the sparse multiscale competitive code (SMCC), deriving the multiscale orientation field through l1-norm sparse coding. Dubey et al. (2022) [31] put forward optimal directional texture code (ODTC) based on multiscale filtering, computing bit transitions across multiple scales for each orientation.

In real-world scenarios, a single point on palm lines may exhibit multiple dominant orientations. Sun et al. (2005) [11] proposed the ordinal relationship among neighborhood image pixels or regions to propose Ordinalcode, which uses orthogonal Gaussian filters to extract the sequential relationship of palmprint directions. Guo et al. (2009) [16] proposed binary orientation co-occurrence vector (BOCV) for multiple directions, preserving orientation information from all six directions for matching. Zhang et al. (2012) [20] further enhanced BOCV by introducing the concept of fragile bits, extending BOCV to E-BOCV. Fei et al. (2016) [22] proposed double-orientation code (DOC), selecting the top two directions with the highest responses as orientation features. They also proposed double half-orientation code (DHOC) [23], utilizing two types of half-Gabor filters to extract two directional information from curves. Xu et al. (2018) [28] proposed discriminative and robust competitive code (DRCC), extracting both the dominant orientation code and the side code of the dominant orientation code from palm images. Fan et al. (2024) [8] proposed rich orientation code (ROC), extracting intersecting lines' orientation information and relative widths based on local minima of responses.

Regarding matching methods, Jia et al. (2008) [14], in their proposed robust line orientation code (RLOC), designed a pixel-to-area comparison-based matching approach to improve the robustness of matching.

2.2 Histogram-Based Methods

After extracting the directional features of palmprints, histogram-based methods segment the palmprint image into blocks. The histograms of all the blocks are then concatenated to form a single feature vector. The feature vector distance is calculated to perform palmprint recognition. Table 2 shows a summary of these methods.

Jia et al. (2014) [33] proposed histogram of oriented lines (HOL) method based on histogram of oriented gradients (HOG) used for solving pedestrian detection, which lets the gradient be replaced by line features. The dominant orientation is extracted using a Gabor filter or MFRAT, the histogram of feature vectors is computed and connected in chunks, and matched using Euclidean distance. After this, researchers have made continuous innovations in histogram based palmprint recognition methods.

For the extraction of directional features, Luo et al. (2016) [34] proposed a LBP-like descriptor called local line directional patterns (LLDP), which encodes the local neighborhood structure in three different ways using Gabor filters or MFRAT. Fei et al. (2019) [37] combine the apparent and latent direction features, proposing the combined apparent and latent direction code (ALDC). Furthermore, Fei et al. (2019) [38] proposed a discriminant direction binary code (DDBC) method, which learns an objective function to obtain feature vectors. Fei et al. (2020) [40] proposed learn compact multifeature code (LCMFC), which combines texture and orientation features to learn an objective function in order to derive compact feature vectors.

Table 2. Summary of histogram-based methods.

Year	Method name	Filter type	Filter number	Scale	Direction levels	Coding strategy	Matching strategy	Ref
2014	HOL	real part of Gabor filter	12	1	1	Winner-take-all	Euclidean distance	[33]
2016	LLDP	real part of Gabor filter	12	1	2/12	Responses' sorting	Chi-square distance / Manhattan distance	[34]
2016	LMDP	real part of Gabor filter	12	1	1/2	Neighboring direction	Chi-square distance	[35]
2017	CR_CompCode	real part of elliptical Gabor filter	6	1	1	Winner-take-all	CRC_RLS	[36]
2019	ALDC	Gabor filter	6	1	1	Winner-take-all	Chi-square distance	[37]
2019	DDBC	real part of Gabor filter	12	1	1	Neighboring direction, hash learning	Chi-square distance	[38]
2020	LDDBP	real part of Gabor filter	12	1	2	Neighboring direction	Chi-square distance	[37]
2020	OSC	real part of Gabor filter	6	1	2	Responses' sorting	MTPSR	[39]
2020	LCMFC	Gabor filter	12	1	12	Binary Learning	Chi-square distance	[40]
2023	MSMDB	Gabor filter	60	5	1	DAV, Binary Learning	Cchi-square distance	[41]
2024	FFLOC	real part of Gabor filter, Log-Gabor filter, MFRAT	12 pairs	1	2/12	Responses' sorting	Chi-square distance / Manhattan distance	[42]

Addressing multi-directionality and multi-scale information, Fei et al. (2016) [35] proposed a local multiple directional pattern (LMDP), which detects the position and number of bit transitions, reflecting the number, position, and confidence of dominant orientations. Subsequently, Fei et al. (2020) [37] proposed a local discriminant direction binary pattern (LDDBP), calculating 0-1 bit transitions to obtain several dominant orientations. Ma et al. (2023) [41] proposed a multiscale multidirection binary (MSMDB) pattern, defining an optimization objective function to learn the collaborative representation of multi-scale and multi-direction feature codes. Wang et al. (2024) [42] proposed feature Fusion coding schemes of Local Order Code (FFLOC), utilizing different directional information encodings and employing a dimension control factor to reduce feature dimensionality.

Researchers have also sought faster and more efficient classification approaches. Zhang et al. (2017) [36] built upon CompCode to propose CR_CompCode, utilizing collaborative representation based classification with regularized least square (CRC_RLS) for classification. Liang et al. (2020) proposed a orientation-space code (OSC) scheme to represent the orientation space feature of palmprint and designed a multi-feature two-phase sparse representation (MTPSR) scheme for feature matching.

In general, orientation-based methods mainly consider how to be able to extract the directional features of palmprint images more accurately, while at the same time, they are also developing towards multi-direction and multi-scale, and using different classification methods to classify palmprints more quickly and efficiently.

3 Conclusion

This paper briefly introduces the relevant principles and methods of palmprint recognition, with a particular focus on reviewing the orientation-based methods. We provides a concise overview and summary of the methods, further analyzing the motivations and theories behind these methods, encompassing both coding-based methods and histogram-based methods. The most notable area of interest is the feature extraction and feature matching phases in palmprint recognition.

In summary, in recent years, research on palmprint recognition based on orientation features has aimed to extract more accurate and robust orientation feature information from palmprint images, while retaining as much valuable information as possible and representing the orientation features more compactly. Consequently, researchers have proposed various methods for extraction, encoding, and dimensionality reduction, and palmprint recognition is evolving towards multi-scale and multi-orientation trends.

Looking ahead, potential research directions for palmprint recognition may encompass the utilization of feature-level fusion methods, integrating multiple types of feature information to enhance the effectiveness and uniqueness of the extracted features. Incorporating 3D information is also noteworthy, as the majority of current based methods primarily focus on 2D palmprint images. The lack of depth information in two-dimensional representations often compromises accuracy.

References

1. Jain, A., Hong, L., Pankanti, S.: Biometric identification. Commun. ACM **43**(2), 90–98 (2000)
2. Zhang, D., Kong, W.K., You, J., Wong, M.: Online palmprint identification. IEEE Trans. Pattern Anal. Mach. Intell. **25**(9), 1041–1050 (2003)
3. Jain, A., Ross, A., Prabhakar, S.: An introduction to biometric recognition. IEEE Trans. Circuits Syst. Video Technol. **14**(1), 4–20 (2004)
4. You, J., Li, W., Zhang, D.: Hierarchical palmprint identification via multiple feature extraction. Pattern Recogn. **35**(4), 847–859 (2002)
5. Fei, L., Lu, G., Jia, W., Teng, S., Zhang, D.: Feature extraction methods for palmprint recognition: a survey and evaluation. IEEE Trans. Syst. Man Cybern. Syst. **49**(2), 346–363 (2018)
6. Kong, A., Zhang, D., Kamel, M.: A survey of palmprint recognition. Pattern Recogn. **42**(7) 1408–1418 (2009)
7. Unar, J., Seng, W.C., Abbasi, A.: A review of biometric technology along with trends and prospects. Pattern Recogn. **47**(8), 2673–2688 (2014)
8. Fan, D., Liang, X., Jia, W., Zhang, D.: Toward large-scale palmprint image analysis by a rich orientation code. IEEE Trans. Syst. Man Cybern. Syst. (2024)
9. Zhong, D., Du, X., Zhong, K.: Decade progress of palmprint recognition: a brief survey. Neurocomputing **328**, 16–28 (2019)
10. Kong, A.K., Zhang, D.: Competitive coding scheme for palmprint verification. In: Proceedings of the 17th International Conference on Pattern Recognition, ICPR 2004, vol. 1, pp. 520–523. IEEE (2004)

11. Sun, Z., Tan, T., Wang, Y., Li, S.Z.: Ordinal palmprint represention for personal identification [representation read representation]. In: 2005 IEEE Computer Society Conference on Computer Vision and Pattern Recognition (CVPR 2005), vol. 1, pp. 279–284. IEEE (2005)
12. Wu, X., Wang, K., Zhang, D.: Palmprint authentication based on orientation code matching. In: Kanade, T., Jain, A., Ratha, N.K. (eds.) AVBPA 2005. LNCS, vol. 3546, pp. 555–562. Springer, Heidelberg (2005). https://doi.org/10.1007/11527923_57
13. Kong, A., Zhang, D., Kamel, M.: Palmprint identification using feature-level fusion. Pattern Recogn. **39**(3), 478–487 (2006)
14. Jia, W., Huang, D.S., Zhang, D.: Palmprint verification based on robust line orientation code. Pattern Recogn. **41**(5), 1504–1513 (2008)
15. Zuo, W., Yue, F., Wang, K., Zhang, D.: Multiscale competitive code for efficient palmprint recognition. In: 2008 19th International Conference on Pattern Recognition, pp. 1–4. IEEE (2008)
16. Guo, Z., Zhang, D., Zhang, L., Zuo, W.: Palmprint verification using binary orientation co-occurrence vector. Pattern Recogn. Lett. **30**(13), 1219–1227 (2009)
17. Zuo, W., Lin, Z., Guo, Z., Zhang, D.: The multiscale competitive code via sparse representation for palmprint verification. In: 2010 IEEE Computer Society Conference on Computer Vision and Pattern Recognition, pp. 2265–2272. IEEE (2010)
18. Yue, F., Zuo, W., Zhang, D.: ICP registration using principal line and orientation features for palmprint alignment. In: 2010 IEEE International Conference on Image Processing, pp. 3069–3072. IEEE (2010)
19. Khan, Z., Mian, A., Hu, Y.: Contour code: robust and efficient multispectral palmprint encoding for human recognition. In: 2011 International Conference on Computer Vision, pp. 1935–1942. IEEE (2011)
20. Zhang, L., Li, H., Niu, J.: Fragile bits in palmprint recognition. IEEE Signal Process. Lett. **19**(10), 663–666 (2012)
21. Tamrakar, D., Khanna, P.: Palmprint verification with XOR-SUM code. SIViP **9**(3), 535–542 (2015)
22. Fei, L., Xu, Y., Tang, W., Zhang, D.: Double-orientation code and nonlinear matching scheme for palmprint recognition. Pattern Recogn. **49**, 89–101 (2016)
23. Fei, L., Xu, Y., Zhang, D.: Half-orientation extraction of palmprint features. Pattern Recogn. Lett. **69**, 35–41 (2016)
24. Zheng, Q., Kumar, A., Pan, G.: Suspecting less and doing better: new insights on palmprint identification for faster and more accurate matching. IEEE Trans. Inf. Forensics Secur. **11**(3), 633–641 (2015)
25. Tabejamaat, M., Mousavi, A.: Concavity-orientation coding for palmprint recognition. Multimedia Tools Appl. **76**, 9387–9403 (2017)
26. Fei, L., Zhang, B., Xu, Y., Yan, L.: Palmprint recognition using neighboring direction indicator. IEEE Trans. Hum.-Mach. Syst. **46**(6), 787–798 (2016)
27. Dubey, P., Kanumuri, T., Vyas, R.: Sequency codes for palmprint recognition. SIViP **12**, 677–684 (2018)
28. Xu, Y., Fei, L., Wen, J., Zhang, D.: Discriminative and robust competitive code for palmprint recognition. IEEE Trans. Syst. Man Cybern. Syst. **48**(2), 232–241 (2016)
29. Van, H.T., Hung, K.D., Van, G.V., Thi, Q.P., Le, T.H.: Palmprint recognition using discriminant local line directional representation. In: Le Thi, H.A., Le, H.M., Pham Dinh, T., Nguyen, N.T. (eds.) ICCSAMA 2019. AISC, vol. 1121, pp. 208–217. Springer, Cham (2020). https://doi.org/10.1007/978-3-030-38364-0_19

30. Almaghtuf, J., Khelifi, F., Bouridane, A.: Fast and efficient difference of block means code for palmprint recognition. Mach. Vis. Appl. **31**(6), 1–10 (2020). https://doi.org/10.1007/s00138-020-01103-3
31. Dubey, P., Kanumuri, T., Vyas, R.: Optimal directional texture codes using multi-scale bit crossover count planes for palmprint recognition. Multimedia Tools Appl. **81**(14), 20291–20310 (2022)
32. Dubey, P., Kanumuri, T., Vyas, R., Murthy, K.V.S.R., Choubey, C.K., Nandan, D.: Enhanced palmprint recognition via curvi-linear anisotropic gaussian filter-based combined differential concavity and infirmity codes. Traitement du Signal **40**(4) (2023)
33. Jia, W., Hu, R.X., Lei, Y.K., Zhao, Y., Gui, J.: Histogram of oriented lines for palmprint recognition. IEEE Trans. Syst. Man Cybern. Syst. **44**(3), 385–395 (2013)
34. Luo, Y.T., et al.: Local line directional pattern for palmprint recognition. Pattern Recogn. **50**, 26–44 (2016)
35. Fei, L., Wen, J., Zhang, Z., Yan, K., Zhong, Z.: Local multiple directional pattern of palmprint image. In: 2016 23rd International Conference on Pattern Recognition (ICPR), pp. 3013–3018. IEEE (2016)
36. Zhang, L., Li, L., Yang, A., Shen, Y., Yang, M.: Towards contactless palmprint recognition: a novel device, a new benchmark, and a collaborative representation based identification approach. Pattern Recogn. **69**, 199–212 (2017)
37. Fei, L., Zhang, B., Zhang, W., Teng, S.: Local apparent and latent direction extraction for palmprint recognition. Inf. Sci. **473**, 59–72 (2019)
38. Fei, L., Zhang, B., Xu, Y., Guo, Z., Wen, J., Jia, W.: Learning discriminant direction binary palmprint descriptor. IEEE Trans. Image Process. **28**(8), 3808–3820 (2019)
39. Liang, L., Chen, T., Fei, L.: Orientation space code and multi-feature two-phase sparse representation for palmprint recognition. Int. J. Mach. Learn. Cybern. **11**, 1453–1461 (2020)
40. Fei, L., Zhang, B., Zhang, L., Jia, W., Wen, J., Wu, J.: Learning compact multifeature codes for palmprint recognition from a single training image per palm. IEEE Trans. Multimedia **23**, 2930–2942 (2020)
41. Ma, S., Hu, Q., Zhao, S., Wu, W., Wu, J.: Multiscale multidirection binary pattern learning for discriminant palmprint identification. IEEE Trans. Instrum. Meas. **72**, 1–12 (2023)
42. Wang, H., Mariano, V.Y.: Fast local ordinal code for small sample palmprint recognition. IEEE Access (2024)

Arm Vein Recognition Based on Multi-hop Graph Convolutional Networks

Siyu Huang, Chaoying Tang(✉), and Yuren Sun

College of Automation Engineering, Nanjing University of Aeronautics and Astronautics, Jiangsu 211106, China
cytang@nuaa.edu.cn

Abstract. Currently, vein recognition technology is mainly limited to the hand (finger, dorsal, and palm). In comparison, the arm region has more vein textures and richer feature information. It shows a broader application potential. Traditional vein feature matching techniques have poor robustness. While the method based on convolutional neural networks (CNNs) can take into account the global features of the image, it is easy to ignore the structural relationship between vein features. Recognition accuracy is especially low in some small-sample datasets. In this study, we propose an arm vein recognition method based on multi-hop graph convolutional networks (GCNs). The endpoints and bifurcation points of veins are chosen as nodes, and the vein vessels between nodes are edges. In order to overcome the over-smoothing problem and enhance the feature differentiation performance, a multi-hop graph mechanism is introduced to construct a multi-branch GCN. Meanwhile, an adaptive feature fusion module (AFFM) is introduced to adaptively fuse the node embeddings learned from multiple branches. An Arcface multi-classifier is adopted for the final recognition. Experimental results show that the proposed arm vein recognition method outperforms other matching recognition techniques and effectively handles the small sample problem. The ablation studies further confirm the effectiveness of the multi-hop graphs and the Arcface multi-classifier.

Keywords: Arm vein recognition · Convolution neural network · Graph convolution neural network · Biometric graph · Multi-hop graph

1 Introduction

In certain criminal scenes, suspects intentionally cover their faces and avoid leaving their fingerprints [1]. However, they tend to be less cautious with body parts such as arms and legs, which are more readily exposed in skin images. These skin images can be utilized to extract vein texture features for identification. Thus, the extraction and recognition of vein texture features are of significant value.

Current biometric classification and recognition methods based on GCN still face several problems: (1) In some studies, the simple linear iterative clustering (SLIC) method is typically employed to construct a graph structure by treating local regions of the image as nodes [2]. This approach is incapable of representing the vein pattern accurately as the filters are not sensitive to endings and junctions, which are common in a vein pattern, resulting in potential information loss. (2) Current GCN methods often take a 1-hop graph as input to the network. The problem of over-smoothing arises when attempting to deepen the network to access more profound information for recognition.

To solve these problems, this paper proposes an effective method for constructing graph structures. Meanwhile, a multi-hop GCN model is introduced to extract more comprehensive information and enhance recognition performance. The main contributions of this paper are summarized as follows:

- We propose a graph structure extraction method that includes more vein features. Endpoints and bifurcation points are obtained as nodes by accumulating the pixel values in the eight neighborhoods of each point on the pre-processed image. The seed filling algorithm is employed to get the edges. It represents global features of the vein patterns, concurrently delineating the interrelations among local features effectively.
- We propose an arm vein recognition method based on multi-hop GCN. With integrating the multi-hop mechanism and the AFFM module, deeper features in the graph structure can be learned, thereby enhancing recognition accuracy and circumventing the issue of over-smoothing.
- We introduce the Arcface loss function in multi-classification. In arm vein recognition, the Acrface loss facilitates a larger angular distance among the vein feature vectors from different individuals, which contributes to improving the recognition performance of the model.

2 Related Work

2.1 Vein Recognition

Numerous algorithms have been proposed for vein recognition, which can be categorized into two main groups: (1) Methods of vein recognition based on classical feature extraction. Ladoux et al. [3] introduced a method for extracting feature points of palm veins by scale-invariant feature transform (SIFT). Lu et al. [4] proposed a method for palm vein recognition utilizing local binary pattern (LBP) orientation information. Studies employing this approach have yielded promising recognition results. However, these results heavily rely on manually designed feature extraction algorithms. Furthermore, the robustness of this method is poor when there are changes in lighting conditions or the background environment of the vein images. (2) Vein recognition methods based on deep learning. Processing vein images using convolutional neural networks (CNNs) can avoid the limitations imposed by manual design. Current research mainly concentrates on finger, palm, and dorsal vein recognition. Yang et al. [5] introduced a lightweight CNN that outputs both vein recognition and anti-spoofing results. Thapar et al. [6] proposed a palm vein recognition model, employing an end-to-end CNN to match biometric features with limited training samples. Wang et al. [7] proposed a network that brings together a constrained CNN and CycleGAN for dorsal vein recognition.

2.2 Graph Convolutional Neural Network

Deep learning on graphs is an emerging technique for applying deep learning models to graph data [8]. One of the most representative works is GCN. Some tasks, such as node prediction and graph classification, can be accomplished using the features learned from graph structure data. GCNs are divided into spatial and spectral domains by graph convolution methods. Spatial convolution aggregates feature information from the neighborhood, such as GraphSAGE [9], graph attention networks (GAT) [10], and graph isomorphism network (GIN) [11]. The current GCNs suffer from the problem of over-smoothing. With the increase of network layers and iterations, the representations of each node will converge to the same value, which can significantly impact the recognition results. To solve this problem, Wang et al. [20] proposed a direct multi-hop attention based graph neural network (DAGN). It extended the attention score from adjacent nodes to multi-hop neighboring nodes to increase the receptive field of each message passing layer.

3 Methodology

3.1 Image Pre-processing

The database employed in this paper consists of the Near-Infrared (NIR) images of the arms captured from 150 individuals. Two images were gathered from each individual over a two-week interval, amounting to 300. A JAI-ADC080CL NIR camera served as the acquisition device, and some example images from this database are shown in Fig. 1.

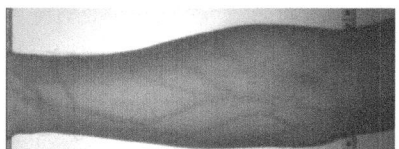
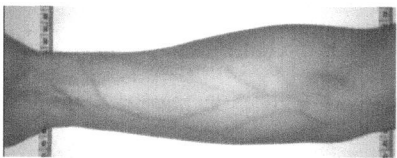

Fig. 1. Images collected by the same experimenter at two-week intervals

To transform vein features from arm NIR images into graph structures. First, the contrast of the original images is augmented using the contrast-limited adaptive histogram equalization (CLAHE) method. Then, 16 Gabor filters of varying orientations and scales are employed to extract the veins. The results of the Gabor filters are shown in the first row of Fig. 2. The Otsu algorithm combined with the morphological skeleton extraction algorithm is utilized to acquire the binary single-pixel line image. Burr trimming is applied to eliminate the noisy curves that are shorter and do not impact the comprehensive pattern of the vein. The second row of Fig. 2 shows the extracted vein lines and the result after burr trimming.

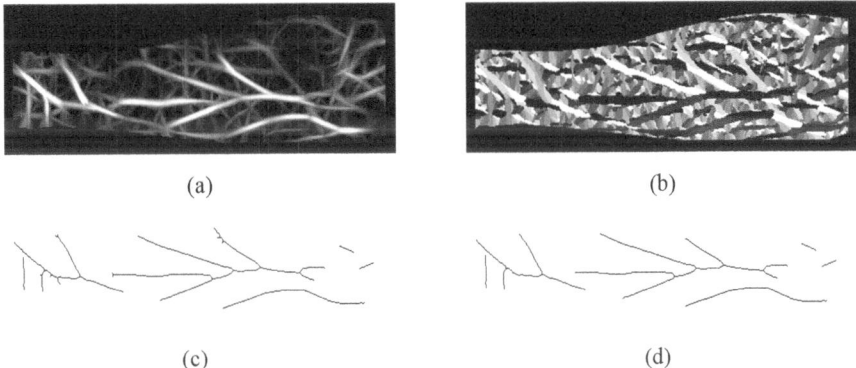

Fig. 2. The results of arm vein image pre-processing. (a) is the enhanced Gabor energy image, (b) is the enhanced Gabor orientation image, (c) is the binary single-pixel line image, and (d) is the result after burr trimming of (c).

3.2 Construction of Graphs

The pre-processed vein binary single-pixel line image is well-suited as a graph structure to reflect the global features of vein patterns. In addition, the relationship amid local features can also be aptly described by using the connection between veins. A vein biometric graph includes a node set and an edge set. An example is shown in Fig. 3. To facilitate visualization, edges within the biometric graph are represented as straight lines signifying the shortest distance between two nodes.

Node Set Construction. The SLIC method is often employed for constructing the graph structure, utilizing local regions of the image as nodes. This approach does not adequately characterize graph structures such as vein images. Consequently, this leads to a loss of information, impacting recognition accuracy. To solve this problem, we select endpoints and bifurcation points of veins as nodes. They are obtained by calculating the accumulation of points with a pixel value of 1 in each point's 8-neighborhood on the binary single-pixel line image. If the aggregated sum of the pixel values in the 8-neighborhood of a point equals 1, this signifies the point as an endpoint. Similarly, if the aggregate sum of pixel values within a point's 8-neighborhood is three or more, the point is identified as a bifurcation point.

In a graph, the nodes contain important feature information. Single-pixel vein line binary images lack grayscale information. In order to increase the feature information of each node, we utilize orientation and energy distribution features derived from the Gabor filter.

Edge Set Construction. A vein connecting two nodes, v_i and v_j, is regarded as an edge (v_i, v_j). In the vein line images, edges are identified by employing the seed filling algorithm. An endpoint or bifurcation point is randomly selected as the starting seed point, followed by a scan of its 8*8 neighborhood. If there is only one unmarked point with a pixel value of 1, this point is recorded and subsequently utilized as the new seed point for further exploration. The process ceases upon encountering a new endpoint or bifurcation point. In this way, the edge set is obtained.

To further enhance the expressiveness of the biometric graph structure, we determine the weight of an edge with the similarity in orientation and energy between neighboring nodes:

$$w(i,j) = \begin{cases} e^{-\sum_{d=1}^{D}(f_i(d)-f_j(d))^2/2\sigma^2}, & A_{i,j} = 1 \\ 0, & \text{otherwise} \end{cases} \quad (1)$$

where f_i and f_j are the feature vectors composed of the orientation and energy of different nodes v_i and v_j. D represents the length of the feature vector.

Fig. 3. The result of the construction of the vein biometric graph.

3.3 The Proposed Network

We adopt a multi-hop graph mechanism to construct a multi-branch GCN to overcome the over-smoothing problem while enhancing the feature differentiation performance. The data of k-hop within the graph structure serve as input to the graph convolution group of different branches. Successive layers learn features of graph convolutions. The adaptive feature fusion module (AFFM) is applied to fuse the node embeddings learned from multiple branches. Subsequently, these features are integrated via fully connected layers. Finally, the attribution of these graph structures to respective categories is determined by the Arcface multi-classifier. The graph convolution group comprises three sequential GCN Layers employing ReLU as the activation function. The proposed model is shown in Fig. 4.

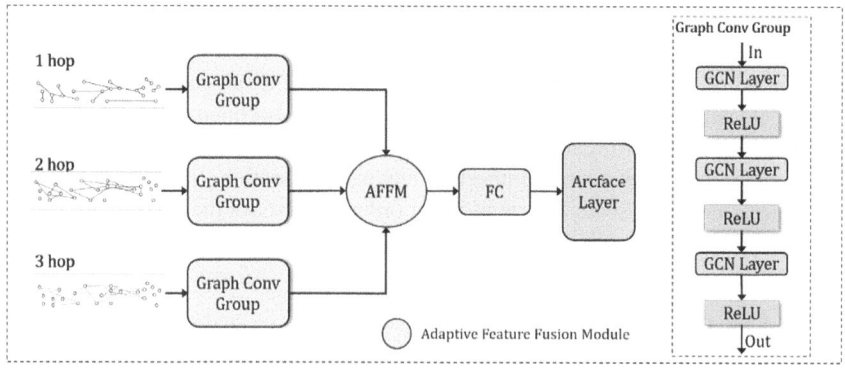

Fig. 4. The overview of the proposed multi-hop GCN model.

In this paper, we take the adjacency matrix $A^{(ik)}$ and the feature matrix $F^{(ik)}$ of graph $G = \{V_{ik}, E_{ik}\}$ as inputs to the graph convolution group, where k represents the order of hops. The process is as follows:

$$F^{(i)} = h_i\left(A^{(ik)}, \alpha_{i-1}\left(F^{(i-1)k}\right)\right) \tag{2}$$

where h_i and α_i correspond to the ith convolutional and activation layer, respectively ($i = 1, \cdots, n$). Moreover, α_i represents the application of the ReLU function to suppress the nonlinearity of the GCN model, enhancing the fit to the trained data.

Multi-hop Graph Mechanism. Current GCN methods usually utilize a 1-hop graph as the input to the network. Features within this framework are extracted via multiple GCN layers. At times, the node feature information extracted by graph convolution proves insufficient. To acquire deeper information necessitates an increase in the number of layers. This approach is constrained by the Laplacian matrix in the convolution kernel, resulting in over-smoothed learned node features that lack discriminative power. To solve this problem, we employ multi-hop graphs in constructing GCNs, thus enhancing the discriminative capability of the features. This is undertaken to capture the graph structure across different hops. For every node v within the graph, a depth-first search (DFS) algorithm is initially applied to enumerate each node v_k and the corresponding paths extending k hops from v. Then, the adjacency matrix for different hops is derived using the edge weight matrix W:

$$A_k(v, v_k) = \frac{1}{k}(W(v, v_1) + W(v_1, v_2) + \cdots + W(v_{k-1}, v_k)) \tag{3}$$

where $v_1, v_2, \ldots, v_{k-1}$ denote the intermediate nodes between v and v_k For multiple paths connecting two nodes, the path exhibiting the maximum weight is retained.

Adaptive Feature Fusion Module. We propose an adaptive feature fusion module to fuse the node features learned from different branches. The node feature matrix $F^{(ok)}$ acquired at different hops is employed as the input. The weight coefficients w_k corresponding to the node feature matrices at different hops are computed through a single-layer feed-forward neural network:

$$w_k = \frac{\exp(\tanh(F^{ok}\alpha))}{\sum_{ok=1}^{3}\exp(\tanh(F^{ok}\alpha))} \tag{4}$$

where $\alpha \in \mathbb{R}^D$ is the weight vector. The final feature is:

$$F_{out} = \sum_{ok=1}^{3} w_k F^{ok} \tag{5}$$

Arcface Loss Function. The Arcface loss is devised as an augmentation to the Softmax loss function, introducing an additional angular margin. An inverse cosine function is used to calculate the angle between the extant feature vector and the weight vector. Then, an additional angle margin m is incorporated into this angle. Recalculating the backpropagation process of logistic regression via the cosine function. The Arcface loss can be expressed as:

$$L = -\frac{1}{N}\sum_{i=1}^{N} \log \frac{e^{s\cos(\theta_{y_i}+m)}}{e^{s\cos(\theta_{y_i}+m)} + \sum_{j=1,j\neq y_i}^{n} e^{s\cos\theta_j}} \tag{6}$$

where $cos(\theta_{y_i} + m)$ denotes the target logical value. s and y_i represent the normalized feature vector and class label, respectively, of the ith sample. N is the batch size and n is the total number of classes.

4 Experimental Results and Analysis

4.1 Database and Experimental Details

We evaluated the proposed model on the database comprising 300 vein images obtained from 150 individuals, as mentioned in Sect. 3.1. For each individual, one image was selected as the training set and the other as the test set. The training set was augmented using techniques including random light alteration, random rotation, and horizontal and vertical flipping.

All experiments were conducted on a single NVIDIA GeForce RTX 3090 GPU, utilizing the PyTorch deep learning framework. As for the model training parameters, the batch size was 8, with the training epoch set to 300 and the initial learning rate of 0.012. Meanwhile, we employed Adam to optimize the model with a weight decay of 0.0001. The cumulative matching characteristic (CMC) curve was adopted to evaluate the matching performance.

4.2 Comparison with the State-Of-The-Art Methods

In this section, we compared the proposed model with the state-of-the-art methods. Firstly, we compared it with the traditional vein feature matching recognition methods, including the graph matching method, coherent point drift (CPD) algorithm [12], grid-based motion statistics (GMS) [13], and the feature matching method based on SURF [14]. The CMC curves are shown in Fig. 5(a), and the Rank-1% accuracies are listed in Table 1. It can be seen that the recognition performance of the proposed model surpasses other methods, achieving a Rank-1% recognition rate of up to 94.8%.

Considering the limited sample size of the arm vein dataset, some deep learning methods designed for small sample problems have been employed for comparative analysis. Including the DenseNet-121 [15], GCN [16], Siamese CNN [17], Transfer Learning [18], and SGRN [19]. The models based on deep learning demonstrated superior performance compared to traditional methods. The proposed model achieved the best recognition results compared to these deep learning methods. The CMC curves are shown in Fig. 5(b), with the Rank-1% accuracies listed in Table 2. Experimental results indicate that the proposed arm vein recognition method outperforms other matching recognition techniques and effectively handles the small sample problem.

Table 1. Rank-1% accuracies of traditional methods and our proposed.

Methods	Graph matching	CPD	GMS	SURF	Ours
Rank-1%	74.6%	74.0%	55.6%	32.7%	**94.8%**

Table 2. Rank-1% accuracies of deep learning methods and our proposed.

Methods	DenseNet-161	GCN	Siamese CNN	Transfer Learning	SGRN	Ours
Rank-1%	94.6%	85.7%	83.8%	80.2%	87.3%	**94.8%**

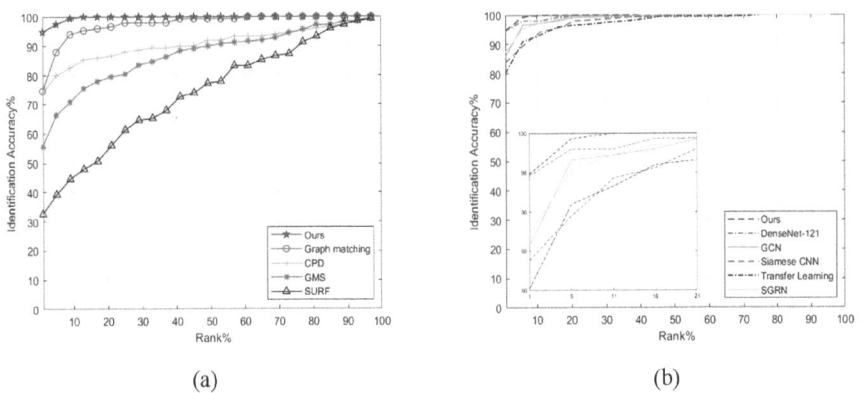

Fig. 5. The CMC curves of our proposed compared with the SOTA method

4.3 Ablation Experiment

This section analyzes the contributions of different components in the proposed model, including the multi-hop mechanism, AFFM, and Arcface loss. To evaluate the multi-hop mechanism and the AFFM module, we first experimented with a 1-hop graph structure, which is the original graph structure data input to the network, and then we changed the number of k hops. Table 3 shows that the proposed method can achieve a better recognition rate. The AFFM layer facilitates extracting local and global structural information from 1 to k-hop neighbors. It can be seen that the multi-hop mechanism and the AFFM module can significantly improve the recognition performance, achieving an accuracy rate up to 94.8%.

Then, we verified the contribution of Arcface loss to vein recognition compared with Softmax loss, Center loss, and Cosface loss. The results are shown in Table 4. With Arcface loss, the proposed model could effectively deal with subtle variations in veins between individuals. This refinement led to improved classification accuracy in individual recognition.

Table 3. Comparison of the accuracy of different input branches.

1-hop	2-hop	3-hop	AFFM	Accuracy%
√	-	-	-	90.7%
-	√	-	-	84.0%
-	-	√	-	75.3%
√	√	-	√	93.4%
√	-	√	√	92.0%
√	√	√	√	**94.8%**

Table 4. Comparison of the accuracy of different loss functions.

Loss function	Softmax loss	Center loss	Cosface loss	Arcface loss
Accuracy%	92.7%	78.6%	69.3%	**94.8%**

5 Conclusion

In this paper, we propose an arm vein recognition model based on multi-hop GCNs, designed to enhance recognition performance and effectively tackle the small sample challenge. By suitable pre-processing of NIR arm vein images, binary single-pixel line images amenable to graph structure representation are attained. The endpoints and bifurcation points of veins serve as nodes, while the veins between nodes are designated as edges. The multi-hop mechanism is introduced to expand the receptive field, extracting deeper features inherent to the graph structure. The proposed AFFM can adaptively fuse node features learned from different branches. In addition, Arcface loss is integrated, facilitating the model in effectively distinguishing vein patterns of distinct individuals. Experimental results demonstrated that the model has superior performance compared to state-of-the-art methods. In future work, we will further optimize the network structure and improve recognition accuracy.

References

1. Liu, Y., Zhang, Y., She, J., Wang, F., Lim, K.: Review of new face occlusion inpainting technology research. J. Front. Comput. Sci. Technol. **15**(10), 1773–1794 (2021)
2. Fabijanska, A.: Graph convolutional networks for semi-supervised image segmentation. IEEE Access **10**, 104144–104155 (2022)
3. Ladoux, P.O., Rosenberger, C., Dorizzi, B.: Palm Vein Verification System Based on SIFT Matching. In: Tistarelli, M., Nixon, M.S. (eds) Advances in Biometrics: Third International Conference, ICB 2009, vol. 5558, pp. 1290–1298. Springer, Berlin Heidelberg (2009)
4. Lu, W., Li, M., Zhang, L.: Palm vein recognition using directional features derived from local binary patterns. Int. J. Sig. Process. Image Process. Pattern Recogn. **9**(5), 87–98 (2016)

5. Yang, W., Luo, W., Kang, W., Huang, Z., Wu, Q.: FVRAS-Net: an embedded finger-vein recognition and antispoofing system using a unified CNN. IEEE Trans. Instrum. Meas. **69**(11), 8690–8701 (2020)
6. Thapar, D., Jaswal, G., Nigam, A., Kanhangad, V.: PVSNet: Palm vein authentication siamese network trained using triplet loss and adaptive hard mining by learning enforced domain specific features. In: 2019 IEEE 5th international conference on identity, security, and behavior analysis (ISBA), pp. 1–8. IEEE (2019)
7. Wang, G., Sun, C., Sowmya, A.: Learning a compact vein discrimination model with GANerated samples. IEEE Trans. Inf. Forensics Secur. **15**, 635–650 (2019)
8. Zhou, J., et al.: Graph neural networks: A review of methods and applications. AI open. **1**, 57–81 (2020)
9. Hamilton, W., Ying, Z., Leskovec, J.: Inductive representation learning on large graphs. In: Proceedings of the 31st International Conference on Neural Information Processing Systems, pp. 1025–1035 (2017)
10. Veličković, P., Cucurull, G., Casanova, A., Romero, A., Lio, P., Bengio, Y.: Graph attention networks. arXiv preprint arXiv:1710.10903 (2017)
11. Xu, K., Hu, W., Leskovec, J., Jegelka, S.: How powerful are graph neural networks?. arXiv preprint arXiv:1810.00826 (2018)
12. Myronenko, A., Song, X.: Point set registration: Coherent point drift. IEEE Trans. Pattern Anal. Mach. Intell. **32**(12), 2262–2275 (2010)
13. Bian, J., Lin, W.Y., Matsushita, Y., Yeung, S.K., Nguyen, T.D., Cheng, M.M.: GMS: grid-based motion statistics for fast, ultra-robust feature correspondence. In: Proceedings of the IEEE Conference on Computer Vision and Pattern Recognition, pp. 4181–4190 (2017)
14. Agrawal, P., Sharma, T., Verma, N.K.: Supervised approach for object identification using speeded up robust features. Int. J. Adv. Intell. Paradigms **15**(2), 165–182 (2020)
15. Zhang, Y.F.: Research on feature extraction and matching method of low quality vein images. M.A. thesis, Nanjing University of Aeronautics and Astronautics, Nanjing, China (2022)
16. Qiu, H.Y., Zhang, H.G., Yang, J.F.: Finger-vein recognition based on graph convolutional networks. J. Signal Process. **36**(3), 389–396 (2020)
17. Tang, S., Zhou, S., Kang, W., Wu, Q., Deng, F.: Finger vein verification using a Siamese CNN. IET biometrics. **8**(5), 306–315 (2019)
18. Kuzu, R.S., Maiorana, E., Campisi, P.: Vein-based biometric verification using transfer learning. In: 2020 43rd International Conference on Telecommunications and Signal Processing (TSP), pp. 403–409. IEEE (2020)
19. Yao, Q., Chen, C., Song, D., Xu, X., Li, W.: A novel finger vein verification framework based on Siamese network and Gabor residual block. Mathematics **11**(14), 3190 (2023)
20. Wang, G., Ying, R., Huang, J., Leskovec, J.: Direct multi-hop attention based graph neural network. arXiv preprint arXiv:2009.14332, 137 (2020)

Face Detection, Recognition and Tracking

Deepfake Video Detection Guided by Identity and Temporal Inconsistency

Yufei Zhang[1,2], Bo Peng[2], Jing Dong[2(✉)], Weike You[1], and Wei Wang[2]

[1] School of Cyberspace Security, Beijing University of Posts and Telecommunications, Beijing, China
zhangyufei@bupt.edu.cn
[2] New Laboratory of Pattern Recognition (NLPR), Institute of Automation, Chinese Academy of Sciences, Beijing, China
jdong@nlpr.ia.ac.cn

Abstract. With the rapid development of deepfake technology, the need for detecting deepfake videos has become increasingly important. Current deepfake detection methods mainly rely on specific low-level texture clues present in deepfake videos. However, as the generation technology continues to improve, deepfakes are becoming more and more realistic, with fewer low-level artifacts, making detection more challenging. To address this challenge, we introduce the Identity Comparison Network (ICN), which leverages high-level semantic information to identify deepfakes by analyzing facial ID inconsistencies. The Spatial Comparison Network (SCN) extracts traditional image artifact information to enhance the detection process. Additionally, we introduce the Frames Comparison Network (FCN) to identify inconsistencies between frames within a video, leveraging the weaknesses inherent in frame-by-frame forgeries. We propose a new method that fuses the above information to detect forgeries at both the intra-frame and inter-frame level. Through experimental evaluation on FF++ and Celeb-DF, we have demonstrated the effectiveness and generalization ability of our method in detecting deepfake videos.

Keywords: DeepFake Detection · Video Analysis · Identity Inconsistency · Temporal Inconsistency

1 Introduction

The misuse of deepfake technology has raised public concern due to its potential to harm social security, enabling malicious activities like disinformation, political incitement, and telecom fraud. Effective detection methods are needed to identify fake videos.

Some existing methods [1–4] leverage low-level image artifacts for detection. For instance, they utilize RGB information [1], auxiliary masks [2], and blending boundary information [3]. Artifacts are also used in AIGC detection [4]. However, these methods rely on artifacts and datasets. As the quality of forged images continues to improve, methods that depend on low-level textures of generation artifacts struggle to maintain their effectiveness.

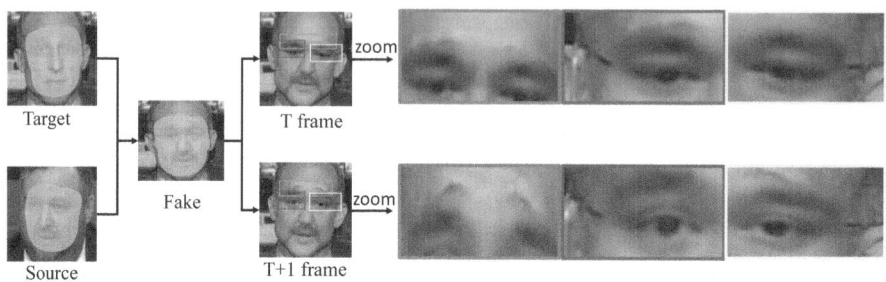

Fig. 1. During the face forgery stage, the gray areas are replaced. When comparing frame T and T+1, temporal inconsistencies are observed, such as duplicated eyebrows and eyeglasses without lenses. (Color figure online)

As shown in Fig. 1, forged images retain some target identity features outside the face-swap region (gray contour), leading to inconsistencies between the deepfake's source and target identities-an issue current face-swap techniques overlook. Inspired by previous ID-based detection methods [5–7], we hypothesize that real faces have continuous ID information, while deepfakes exhibit hybrid and discontinuous IDs.

Although sophisticated forgery methods create realistic components, the videos are synthesized by forging frames, causing temporal inconsistencies, particularly in facial areas between frames, as shown in Fig. 1. Intra-frame detection methods fail to capture these temporal features. While models like C3D [8] and I3D [9] are used for deepfake detection, they are computationally intensive and not optimized for this task, leading to suboptimal performance.

Drawing from these observations, we introduce the Identity Comparison Network (ICN), a method designed to extract identity (ID) information from individual video frames. This ID information, indicative of personal identity traits, is then integrated with spatial feature extracted by the SCN, to expose spatial inconsistencies. The FCN employs an ingeniously crafted 1D CNN architecture, offering an alternative paradigm to traditional approaches. By compressing the video to reduce dimensionality and slicing it along the temporal dimension. It captures differences between adjacent frames, thereby obtaining temporal inconsistency information. Utilizing the temporal dimension effectively, our model significantly reduces the number of parameters without compromising classification accuracy. By integrating spatial and temporal inconsistency information, our model performs binary classification to discern between authentic and forged videos. The proposed method is designed to detect deepfake videos by leveraging the vulnerabilities inherent in the forgery methods themselves and utilizes high-level semantic information from both intra-frame and inter-frame perspectives. We summarize the contributions of this paper as follows:

- We introduce a novel deepfake detection approach that exploits identity and temporal inconsistencies within deepfake videos, utilizing integrated spatial and temporal features for detection. This provides a new and effective model for deepfake detection.
- Incorporating facial information as high-level semantic information into the detection of spatial inconsistencies enhances the generalization ability and interpretability of deepfake detection.
- The FCN compresses the video to reduce dimensionality and slices it along the temporal dimension, effectively capturing differences between frames to obtain temporal inconsistency information. Compared to traditional 2D CNNs and 3D CNNs, it reduces the number of network parameters.

2 Related Work

2.1 Identity Inconsistency Based Detection

Texture-based methods such as XceptionNet [10] and EfficientNet [11] detect subtle forgery in deepfakes. Despite their effectiveness, they rely on basic image cues, which may limit their robustness. To enhance detection stability and reliability, identity (ID) inconsistency-based methods have been introduced. Dong et al. [5] use a Transformer network to analyze inconsistencies between inner and outer face. Huang et al. [6] discuss the presence of explicit and implicit identities in deepfakes. Cozzolino et al. [7] highlight the potential of facial identity information in detection. Liu et al. [12] extract facial features for a temporal-classification network, showing the robustness of facial information under image degradation. However, these methods struggle with precise delineation of inner and outer facial regions. Our approach integrates identity as high-level semantic information, directly extracting complete ID information for comprehensive judgment.

2.2 Temporal Inconsistency Based Detection

In video classification, C3D [8] and I3D [9] traditionally use 3D convolutions, but at a computational expense. To streamline this, 2D CNN methods such as TSM [13], TEINet [14], and TDN [15] efficiently capture temporal cues. For deepfake detection, methods like the CNN-RNN combination [16] and the time-aware strategy [17] have been introduced to detect inconsistencies. Gu et al. [18] proposes a method to horizontally and vertically slice videos separately to compare temporal inconsistencies. Our approach leverages 1D CNNs to compress and analyze videos, effectively reducing computational demands while maintaining detection precision, providing an efficient deepfake detection technique.

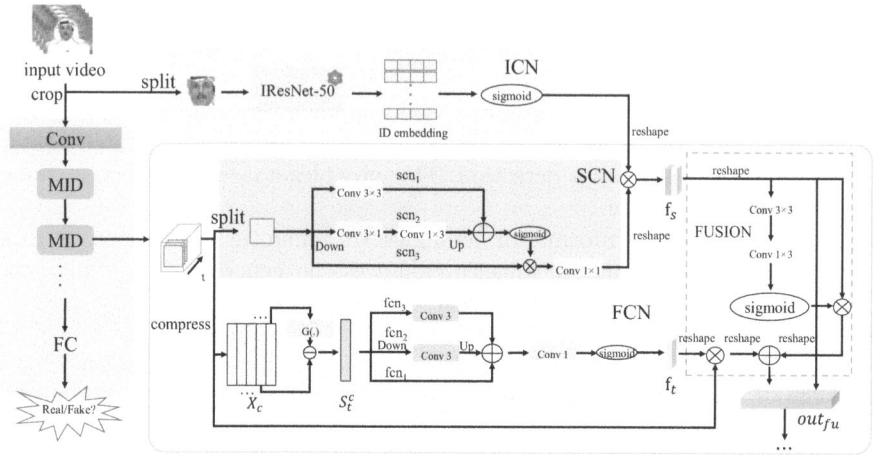

Fig. 2. Our proposed method. In ICN, an ID extractor extracts identity-related inconsistent features. SCN extracts other spatial inconsistency information in the images for supplement. FCN focuses on extracting temporal inconsistencies.

3 Proposed Method

We propose a multi-branch architecture specifically designed for deepfake detection, treating it as a binary classification problem based on inconsistencies in space and time. Our method integrates Multidimensional Inconsistency Detection (MID) blocks into the ResNet-50 framework, as shown in Fig. 2. The ICN extracts identity features from individual video frames, while the SCN captures additional spatial forgeries. The features from ICN and SCN are combined. Additionally, FCN branch is designed to detect temporal inconsistencies caused by manipulations across consecutive video frames. These inconsistencies are identified by first compressing the video features and then applying differential operations to the compressed features, revealing unique characteristics that highlight the temporal differences typical of deepfakes. This combination of spatial and temporal feature extraction across the network branches gives our model strong capabilities in identifying deepfake artifacts, providing a detailed and comprehensive approach to deepfake detection.

3.1 Identity Comparison Network (ICN)

The ICN is an ID extractor that utilizes a frozen pre-trained iResNet network [19]. iResNet is a widely used model in facial recognition tasks and has been employed for extracting ID information in deepfake detection tasks [12]. Consequently, iResNet can effectively extract facial ID information from both real and forgery images. In forged video frames, there are discontinuous ID information areas in the facial region, whereas a real face contains only a single, continuous piece of ID information. Due to the differences between the ID information of real and forged facial images, we can detect the authenticity of faces based on ID information. We directly extract the complete facial ID information and train a model using supervised learning to detect the consistency of the entire facial ID information. This method avoids issues related to the segmentation of facial regions and the separation of ID information between inconsistency areas of the face. The process begins with the segmentation of video embeddings to obtain discrete frame embeddings F_{emb}. Each frame is then processed by iResNet to extract identity information F_{id}. It processes input of size $H \times W \times C$ and outputs an embedding F_{id} for each frame:

$$F_{\text{id}}[t] = \text{IRN}(F_{\text{emb}}[t]), \tag{1}$$

where $F_{\text{emb}}[t]$ is the t-th frame feature in the video. IRN is used to extract facial information with IResNet.

3.2 Spatial Comparison Network (SCN)

The second part is the SCN network. Facial images may contain perceptible artifacts after forgery [20,21]. Therefore, we design the SCN to extract spatially inconsistent information. Inspired by some detection methods [18,22], the SCN introduces multiple branches to capture spatial inconsistencies. These branches perform convolution operations at different receptive fields to capture features at different scales. As shown in Fig. 2, The first branch network scn_1, uses 3×3 convolutions to extract relatively broad spatial features. The second branch network, scn_2, performs downsampling on the input using avgpool, and then employs 3×1 and 1×3 convolutions to extract local detailed features. These two convolutional operations can respectively extract feature details along the horizontal and vertical directions, and the multi-directional convolutional operations are more helpful in identifying potential forgery traces. Subsequently, it utilizes interpolation for upsampling to restore the original size. The third branch scn_3 utilizes the original feature vectors. It preserves the raw, unaltered information, capturing subtle details and nuances that may be lost during the process of feature transformation. This helps to enhance the model's ability to learn complex patterns and improve overall performance. Finally, the embeddings from these three branches are fused using the following formula:

$$\text{out}_{\text{scn}}(x_t) = \sigma(\text{scn}_1(x_t) + \text{scn}_2(x_t)) \times \text{scn}_3(x_t), \quad 1 \leq t \leq T \tag{2}$$

where X is the input vector to the MID block, and x_t belongs to $X^{T \times C \times H \times W}$ representing the corresponding vector for each frame, where T, C, H, W respectively denote the number of frames, the number of image channels, the height of the image, and the width of the image. σ is the sigmoid function. The fused features $out_{\text{scn}}(x_t)$ contain both global and local spatially inconsistent information, providing a comprehensive representation of the spatial inconsistency information.

3.3 Frames Comparison Network(FCN)

We designed FCN to extract temporal inconsistencies with 1D CNN. FCN first compresses the input X to obtain the compressed embedding X_c. X_c is then frame-processed to get x_t^c. The difference embedding S_t for each frame is obtained by performing a difference operation on x_t^c. S_t is used to extract features through a multi-branch network.

As shown in Fig. 2, by reducing the dimension of X, FCN compresses the video vector of size $C \times T \times H \times W$ along both horizontal and vertical directions simultaneously, thereby producing a feature vector X_c of size $HW \times C \times T$. Compressing the embedding along both horizontal and vertical directions allows the model to effectively capture spatial artifacts in video frames.

$$S_t = G(x_{t+1}^c) - x_t^c \quad \text{for } x_t^c \in X_c, \quad 1 \leq t \leq T \tag{3}$$

where S_t represents the final difference vector obtained, shaped as $HW \times C$. The function $G(\cdot)$ denotes a 1D convolution with a kernel size of 3 and padding of 1, which is utilized to extract information from adjacent frames effectively. x_t^c is the frame information taken from the compressed video vector X_c.

We use an iterative method to obtain frame information along the temporal dimension within the video vector X_c. We obtain the difference information between each frame and the subsequent frame. In this way, temporal inconsistencies can be effectively detected both horizontally and vertically with FCN.

Subsequently, we adopt a multi-branch approach to process the temporal feature S_t. We employed a three-branch network structure to process S_t, where distinct convolutional operations are utilized to effectively extract both local and global information from the feature maps:

$$\begin{aligned} out'_{fcn} &= \sum_{t=1}^{T} fcn_1(S_t) + fcn_2(S_t) + fcn_3(S_t) \\ out_{fcn} &= \sigma(conv_1(out'_{fcn})) \end{aligned} \tag{4}$$

where fcn_1 branch returns the unprocessed S_t vector, which helps to preserve the original information of the image. The fcn_2 employs pooling downsampling operations, followed by convolution with a kernel size of 3, and finally uses interpolation for upsampling. This increases the receptive field of the network, allowing it to receive a wide range of contextual information. The fcn_3 utilizes convolution with a kernel size of 3. The $conv_1$ is a convolutional operation with a kernel size of 1, and the final output is denoted as out_{fcn}.

3.4 Fusion

In the fusion part, we employ a multi-branch network for integration:

$$f_s = \sum_{t=1}^{T} F_{\text{id}}[t] + out_{scn}(x_t) \tag{5}$$

$$f_s^{'} = (H_{fu}(f_s)) \times (f_s)) \tag{6}$$

where f_s represents the video feature that integrate ID information and spatial inconsistency information. $H_{fu}(\cdot)$ is a branch processing structure composed of a 3×3 convolution and a 1×3 convolution followed by a sigmoid function. The role of $H_{fu}(\cdot)$ is to enhance the fusion of two types of spatial information, ultimately yielding the processed spatial information $f_s^{'}$.

$$out_{fu}^{'} = (f_t \times X) + f_s^{'} \tag{7}$$

$$out_{fu} = concat(out_{fu}^{'}, f_s) \tag{8}$$

The video temporal inconsistency information extracted using FCN (denoted as f_t) is obtained from the combination of S_t, which is then integrated with the input video information X. To ensure compatibility for subsequent operations, f_t and the transformed spatial information f_s' are both reshaped to match the dimensions of X. We then perform element-wise multiplication between f_t and X to emphasize temporal changes within the spatial context of each frame. Additionally, f_s' is fused with the result of this multiplication to form $out_{fu}^{'}$, which integrates spatial and temporal cues. Finally, $out_{fu}^{'}$ is concatenated with f_s to output out_{fu}.

4 Experiments

4.1 Experimental Datasets

In our experiments, we utilize two datasets: FaceForensics++(FF++) [31] and Celeb-DF [32]. The FF++ dataset is a widely used deepfake detection dataset, which consists of three categories: raw (original quality), c23 (low compression), and c40 (high compression). It employs four methods to create fake videos: DeepFakes (DF), Face2Face (F2F), FaceSwap (FS), and NeuralTextures (NT). Later on, the FaceShifter (FST) method was also added for generating forgeries. The Celeb-DF dataset comprises 5639 high-quality manipulated videos and 590 real videos. These manipulated videos are generated by an improved synthesis method.

Table 1. Results of Different Models on 5 Methods in FF++ Dataset with ACC(%). The best performance is indicated in bold. * denotes the reproduction of the method.

Methods	DF	F2F	FST	FS	NT
C3D [8]	89.29	82.86	-	87.86	87.14
I3D [9]	91.07	86.43	-	91.43	78.57
Rahmouni [23]	73.25	62.33	-	67.08	62.59
SPSL [24]	92.65	87.12	90.23	92.14	75.68
MesoNet [25]	89.52	84.44	-	83.56	75.74
Xception [10]	94.28	89.56	90.22	92.70	77.10
STIL [18]*	94.21	92.36	93.54	96.89	90.14
Ours	**99.64**	**94.29**	**95.93**	**98.21**	**92.36**

Table 2. Methods are trained on the FF++ dataset and tested on both the FF++ dataset and the Celeb-DF dataset. Our final results are reported in terms of AUC (%). The best performance is indicated in bold.

Method	FF++	Celeb-DF
Multi-task [26]	76.30	54.30
Capsule [27]	96.60	57.50
Two-branch [28]	93.20	73.40
MesoInception4 [25]	83.00	53.60
Xception [10]	95.50	65.50
SPSL [24]	96.91	76.88
F^3-Net [29]	97.97	65.17
M2TR [30]	95.31	68.20
STIL [18]*	97.12	75.58
Ours	**98.17**	**78.59**

4.2 Implementation Details

We integrate the MID block into the ResNet-50 network, replacing the original Bottleneck block, with input image sizes of 224 × 224 pixels. We utilize the Adam optimizer and binary cross-entropy loss. The model is trained for 30 epochs with a batch size of 16. The initial learning rate is set to 0.0002, and it decays by a factor of 10 every 10 epochs. Training and testing are conducted on the FF++ c40 training and test sets, respectively, and testing is also performed on the Celeb-DF test set for cross-dataset experiment. We use MTCNN [33] to detect facial regions and input them into the model. For training, 8 consecutive video frames are extracted from each video, and 16 frames for testing. We use the Area Under the Receiver Operating Characteristic Curve (AUC) and Accuracy (ACC) as evaluation metrics.

4.3 Intra-dataset Performance Comparison

Table 1 shows that our proposed method achieves good performance on all five methods in FF++. Furthermore, the comparison with other methods demonstrates that our approach outperforms a majority of existing methods with significant improvements. SPSL [24] is a method specifically designed for detection using low-level texture. The superior performance of our method over SPSL indicates that identity features (high-level semantic information) exhibit strong generalization capabilities. Low-level texture features are dependent on image quality. Detection methods that utilize low-level texture features tend to perform relatively poorly. Additionally, our approach integrates temporal information from videos and detects forgery clues in the temporal dimension. Compared with traditional video methods that use 3D CNN networks, such as C3D [8] and I3D [9], it can be observed that we have employed a purposefully designed 1D CNN network in the temporal branch, which has achieved better results than traditional video classification methods. Our method has surpassed STIL, demonstrating the effectiveness of spatial inconsistency information with ID cues and the designed temporal inconsistency information in our approach.

4.4 Cross Dataset Performance Comparision

To validate the generalizability of our approach, we conduct a comparative analysis of various deepfake detection methods across different datasets. As demonstrated in Table 2, Xception [10] is a detection method based on single-frame analysis, while STIL [18] focuses on extracting spatial and temporal inconsistencies. Upon comparison, our approach has achieved the best results, demonstrating that the integration of identity information and the inconsistencies in time and space can lead to superior generalization capabilities.

4.5 Analysis

To evaluate the effectiveness of our proposed method, we conduct ablation experiments on the FF++ datasets by assessing the efficacy of three components: ICN, SCN and FCN. Table 3 displays the results of the experiments. It is evident that the most effective method incorporates all three components, demonstrating the necessity of integrating temporal spatial and ID information. We also conduct experiments on temporal extraction methods. Specifically, we employ the FCN(STIL) + ICN + SCN approach which transfer the temporal inconsistency extraction method used in STIL to FCN for experiment. Experiment shows that our method achieve improvement compare to the original method. The experiments prove that the absence of any one of ID cues, spatial information or temporal information leads to a decrease in performance, further confirming the rationality of our design scheme.

As shown in Table 4, we compare the parameter count of our proposed method with several video classification models. Compared to traditional methods based on 3D CNN [8,9,34] and 2D CNN detection method [18], our method has the fewest parameters and performs the best.

Table 3. We evaluate the components according to the following experimental schemes and represented the results in terms of AUC (%).

variants	FF++
w/o ICN	94.36
w/o SCN	80.54
w/o FCN	92.48
FCN(STIL [18])+ICN+SCN	95.61
ours	98.17

As shown in Fig. 3, we employ the Grad-CAM method [35] to visualize the decision-making process of our method. It can be observed that our method primarily focuses on the areas where two identities are joined in the face replacement methods DF and FS, such as the eyes, eyebrows, and forehead. This observation confirms that our model utilizes the merged ID information to discern forged images based on discontinuous ID areas, and also locates forged areas in other methods. It verifies that our method has achieved its intended design goal, and the judgment based on discontinuous ID areas is highly interpretable.

Table 4. We quantified the parameter count for various methods and compared their experimental results presented by ACC(%).

Method	Params	FF++
I3D [9]	25M	88.43
C3D [8]	79M	87.47
3D-Fused [34]	39M	-
STIL [18]	22.68M	94.81
ours	21.45M	96.08

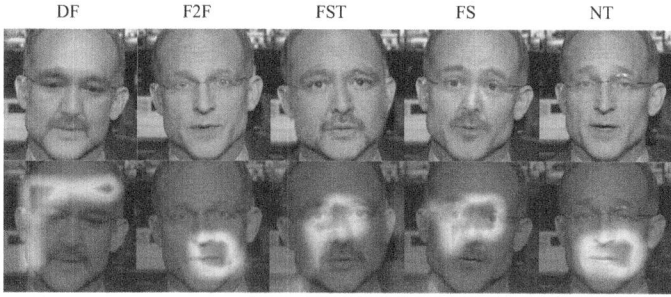

Fig. 3. Our method's Grad-CAM outputs for images processed by five different manipulations demonstrate the interpretability of our approach. The first row consists of forged images, while the second row displays the corresponding CAM images.

5 Conclusion

Our method proposed in this paper utilizes ID information as high-level semantic information, enhancing interpretability and generalization ability. It achieves good results by complementing other spatial information. Additionally, we employ a tailored 1D CNN network to capitalize on the temporal discrepancies between adjacent frames in forgery videos for detection. Compared to traditional video classification models, this approach reduces the parameter count and yields satisfactory experimental outcomes. By detecting clues from multiple dimensions, extensive experiments have demonstrated the effectiveness of the proposed method.

Acknowledgments. This work is supported by the National Key Research and Development Program of China under Grant No. 2021YFC3320103, the National Natural Science Foundation of China (NSFC) under Grant No. 62272460 and No.62172053, Beijing Natural Science Foundation under Grant No. 4232037, Shanghai Key Laboratory of Forensic Medicine and Key Laboratory of Forensic Science, Ministry of Justice (KF202420).

References

1. Dong, F., Zou, X., Wang, J., Liu, X.: Contrastive learning-based general deepfake detection with multi-scale RGB frequency clues. J. King Saud Univ.-Comput. Inf. Sci. **35**(4), 90–99 (2023)
2. Chen, Z., Xie, L., Pang, S., He, Y., Zhang, B.: MagDR: mask-guided detection and reconstruction for defending deepfakes. In: Proceedings of the IEEE/CVF Conference on Computer Vision and Pattern Recognition, pp. 9014–9023 (2021)
3. Shiohara, K., Yamasaki, T.: Detecting deepfakes with self-blended images. In: Proceedings of the IEEE/CVF Conference on Computer Vision and Pattern Recognition, pp. 18720–18729 (2022)
4. Meng, Z., Peng, B., Dong, J., Tan, T., Cheng, H.: Artifact feature purification for cross-domain detection of AI-generated images. Comput. Vis. Image Underst. **247**, 104078 (2024)
5. Dong, X., et al.: Protecting celebrities from deepfake with identity consistency transformer. In: Proceedings of the IEEE/CVF Conference on Computer Vision and Pattern Recognition, pp. 9468–9478 (2022)
6. Huang, B., et al.: Implicit identity driven deepfake face swapping detection. In: Proceedings of the IEEE/CVF Conference on Computer Vision and Pattern Recognition, pp. 4490–4499 (2023)
7. Cozzolino, D., Rössler, A., Thies, J., Nießner, M., Verdoliva, L.: ID-Reveal: identity-aware deepfake video detection. In: Proceedings of the IEEE/CVF International Conference on Computer Vision, pp. 15108–15117 (2021)
8. Tran, D., Bourdev, L.D., Fergus, R., Torresani, L., Paluri, M.: C3D: generic features for video analysis. arXiv preprint arXiv:1412.0767 (2014)
9. Carreira, J., Zisserman, A.: Quo Vadis, action recognition? A new model and the kinetics dataset. In: Proceedings of the IEEE Conference on Computer Vision and Pattern Recognition, pp. 6299–6308 (2017)

10. Chollet, F.: Xception: deep learning with DepthWise separable convolutions. In: Proceedings of the IEEE Conference on Computer Vision and Pattern Recognition, pp. 1251–1258 (2017)
11. Tan, M., Le, Q.: EfficientNet: rethinking model scaling for convolutional neural networks. In: International Conference on Machine Learning, pp. 6105–6114. PMLR (2019)
12. Liu, H., et al.: It wasn't me: irregular identity in deepfake videos. In: 2023 IEEE International Conference on Image Processing (ICIP), pp. 2770–2774. IEEE (2023)
13. Lin, J., Gan, C., Han, S.: TSM: temporal shift module for efficient video understanding. In: Proceedings of the IEEE/CVF International Conference on Computer Vision, pp. 7083–7093 (2019)
14. Liu, Z., et al.: TEINet: towards an efficient architecture for video recognition. Proc. AAAI Conf. Artif. Intell. **34**, 11669–11676 (2020)
15. Wang, L., Tong, Z., Ji, B., Wu, G.: TDN: temporal difference networks for efficient action recognition. In: Proceedings of the IEEE/CVF Conference on Computer Vision and Pattern Recognition, pp. 1895–1904 (2021)
16. Sabir, E., Cheng, J., Jaiswal, A., AbdAlmageed, W., Masi, I., Natarajan, P.: Recurrent convolutional strategies for face manipulation detection in videos. Interfaces (GUI) **3**(1), 80–87 (2019)
17. Li, X., et al.: Sharp multiple instance learning for deepfake video detection. In: Proceedings of the 28th ACM International Conference on Multimedia, pp. 1864–1872 (2020)
18. Gu, Z., et al.: Spatiotemporal inconsistency learning for deepfake video detection. In: Proceedings of the 29th ACM International Conference on Multimedia, pp. 3473–3481 (2021)
19. Duta, I.C., Liu, L., Zhu, F., Shao, L.: Improved residual networks for image and video recognition. In: 2020 25th International Conference on Pattern Recognition (ICPR), pp. 9415–9422. IEEE (2021)
20. Li, L., et al.: Face X-ray for more general face forgery detection. In: Proceedings of the IEEE/CVF Conference on Computer Vision and Pattern Recognition, pp. 5001–5010 (2020)
21. Zhao, H., Zhou, W., Chen, D., Wei, T., Zhang, W., Yu, N.: Multi-attentional deepfake detection. In: Proceedings of the IEEE/CVF Conference on Computer Vision and Pattern Recognition, pp. 2185–2194 (2021)
22. Luo, C., Yuille, A.L.: Grouped spatial-temporal aggregation for efficient action recognition. In: Proceedings of the IEEE/CVF International Conference on Computer Vision, pp. 5512–5521 (2019)
23. Rahmouni, N., Nozick, V., Yamagishi, J., Echizen, I.: Distinguishing computer graphics from natural images using convolution neural networks. In: IEEE Workshop on Information Forensics and Security (WIFS), pp. 1–6. IEEE (2017)
24. Liu, H., et al.: Spatial-phase shallow learning: rethinking face forgery detection in frequency domain. In: Proceedings of the IEEE/CVF Conference on Computer Vision and Pattern Recognition, pp. 772–781 (2021)
25. Afchar, D., Nozick, V., Yamagishi, J., Echizen, I.: Mesonet: a compact facial video forgery detection network. In: IEEE International Workshop on Information Forensics and Security (WIFS), pp. 1–7. IEEE (2018)
26. Nguyen, H.H., Fang, F., Yamagishi, J., Echizen, I.: Multi-task learning for detecting and segmenting manipulated facial images and videos. In: IEEE 10th International Conference on Biometrics Theory, Applications and Systems (BTAS), pp. 1–8. IEEE (2019)

27. Nguyen, H.H., Yamagishi, J., Echizen, I.: Capsule-forensics: using capsule networks to detect forged images and videos. In: ICASSP 2019-2019 IEEE International Conference on Acoustics, Speech and Signal Processing (ICASSP), pp. 2307–2311. IEEE (2019)
28. Masi, I., Killekar, A., Mascarenhas, R.M., Gurudatt, S.P., AbdAlmageed, W.: Two-branch recurrent network for isolating deepfakes in videos. In: Computer Vision–ECCV 2020: 16th European Conference, Glasgow, UK, August 23–28, 2020, Proceedings, Part VII 16, pp. 667–684. Springer (2020)
29. Qian, Y., Yin, G., Sheng, L., Chen, Z., Shao, J.: Thinking in frequency: face forgery detection by mining frequency-aware clues. In: European Conference on Computer Vision, pp. 86–103. Springer (2020)
30. Wang, J., et al.: M2TR: multi-modal multi-scale transformers for deepfake detection. In: Proceedings of the 2022 International Conference on Multimedia Retrieval, pp. 615–623 (2022)
31. Rossler, A., Cozzolino, D., Verdoliva, L., Riess, C., Thies, J., Nießner, M.: Faceforensics++: learning to detect manipulated facial images. In: Proceedings of the IEEE/CVF International Conference on Computer Vision, pp. 1–11 (2019)
32. Li, Y., Yang, X., Sun, P., Qi, H., Lyu, S.: Celeb-DF: a large-scale challenging dataset for deepfake forensics. In: Proceedings of the IEEE/CVF Conference on Computer Vision and Pattern Recognition, pp. 3207–3216 (2020)
33. Zhang, K., Zhang, Z., Li, Z., Qiao, Y.: Joint face detection and alignment using multitask cascaded convolutional networks. IEEE Sig. Process. Lett. **23**(10), 1499–1503 (2016)
34. Feichtenhofer, C., Pinz, A., Zisserman, A.: Convolutional two-stream network fusion for video action recognition. In: Proceedings of the IEEE Conference on Computer Vision and Pattern Recognition, pp. 1933–1941 (2016)
35. Selvaraju, R.R., Cogswell, M., Das, A., Vedantam, R., Parikh, D., Batra, D.: Grad-CAM: visual explanations from deep networks via gradient-based localization. In: Proceedings of the IEEE International Conference on Computer Vision, pp. 618–626 (2017)

Reflectance Recovery Guided Learning of Illumination-Invariant Features for Person Re-Identification

Xianbiao Chen[1,2,3] and Xiaohua Xie[1,2,3(✉)]

[1] School of Computer Science and Engineering, Sun Yat-sen University, Guangzhou, China
chenxb66@mail2.sysu.edu.cn,xiexiaoh6@mail.sysu.edu.cn
[2] Guangdong Province Key Laboratory of Information Security Technology, Guangzhou, China
[3] Key Laboratory of Machine Intelligence and Advanced Computing, Ministry of Education, Guangzhou, China

Abstract. In real-world scenarios, the changes of illumination are noticeable and can significantly impact the performance of re-identification (ReID) algorithms. However, the existing person ReID methods predominantly concentrate on tackling challenges in scenarios with minimal illumination fluctuations. The key to tackling this issue is to extract illumination-invariant features. So we propose a joint learning framework which combines the recovery of reflectance map and extraction of illumination-invariant feature. By sharing parameters, the proposed module, which can be seamlessly detached during the inference phase, contributes to a reduction in inference computation time. We also introduce an adversarial learning mechanism, utilizing illumination category and person identity to facilitate the extraction of features that are invariant to illumination. Besides, due to the lack of person ReID dataset containing images under diverse lighting conditions, we construct a real-world dataset called ICReID in which images have drastic illumination changes. Extensive experiments demonstrate the effectiveness of the proposed method, which achieves significant performance on both synthetic and real datasets.

Keywords: Person re-identification · Illumination-adaptive · Image decomposition

1 Introduction

Person re-identification (ReID) is a crucial research area in the field of computer vision, aiming to address the challenge of tracking pedestrians across multiple cameras in surveillance systems. In recent years, significant progress [2,7,11,13,14] has been made in person re-identification, due to the powerful representation learning capabilities of deep Convolutional Neural Networks. To tackle challenges posed by variations in viewpoints [15], clothing changes [3], and occlusions [24], existing methods generally focus on extracting and matching local features of pedestrians. However, these methods overlook the impact of changes in illumination conditions.

In the real world, we often obtain person images with various illuminations in various scenarios. For instance, in low light environment, we may acquire low light images which contains color shifts, low contrast, and noise. The illumination greatly affects the performance of ReID model. We need to develop the *Illumination-Adaptive Person Re-identification* (IA-ReID) [20].

To overcome the influence of lighting conditions on ReID, some researchers explore methods for transforming images with different lighting conditions to a common lighting condition. Wang et al. [19] learned a feature projection matrix to project image features from one camera into the feature space of another camera. Zhang et al. [21] proposed an Illumination Restore and Reconstruct Network, which can transform images to a common illumination. Another approach to address this issue is to extract illumination-invariant features from the images. Kviatkovsky et al. employed a structured color distribution as an invariant feature extractor. Zeng et al. [20] proposed an Illumination-Identity Disentanglement network, which separates illumination information from identity information. Huang et al. [6] leveraged the illumination-invariant properties of reflection maps and designed a bottom-up attention network to extract illumination-invariant features.

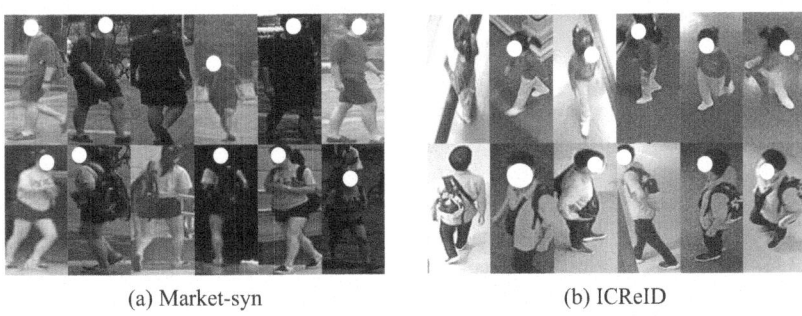

(a) Market-syn   (b) ICReID

Fig. 1. Examples of the images in Market-syn and ICReID datasets. Each row shows images of the same identity.

The aforementioned methods can address the issues in IA-ReID to some extent. However, most of these approaches [1,6,21] introduce a large number of additional computation. There is one major challenge we are trying to solve: eliminating the influence of illumination without introducing additional computation. So, we propose a joint learning approach, combining the recovery of reflectance maps and feature extraction by sharing parameters. Additionally, we introduce an adversarial learning method based on the collaboration between illumination and identity, enforcing the backbone to extract illumination-invariant features.

Current person ReID datasets are typically collected under different cameras in a short time span, such as Market-1501 [23], where illumination changes are minimal. Due to the absence of publicly available datasets specific to IA-ReID, we construct an illumination-changing dataset named ICReID, shown in Fig. 1(b). In this newly constructed dataset, each identity's images exhibit noticeable illumination differences.

Our contributions can be summarized as follows:

- A joint learning framework is proposed that combines the recovery of reflectance maps and feature extraction.
- We present an adversarial learning method based on the collaboration between illumination and identity.
- We construct a dataset called ICReID for IA-ReID research. Our proposed method achieves significant performance on both real and synthetic datasets.

2 Related Work

Illumination-Adaptive Re-identification. In recent years, several research methods addressing IA-ReID have achieved great success [1,8,20,21]. Kviatkovsky et al. [8] proposed an invariant feature extraction method using color distribution structures based on different body parts. Bhuiyan et al. [1] learned a robust illuminance transfer function to mitigate illumination variations from one camera to another. Zeng et al. [20] proposed an Illumination-Identity Disentanglement network, which separates illumination information from identity information. In this paper, we concentrate on complex scenes with diverse illumination changes, utilizing reflectance maps and proposing a multi-positive class adversarial loss to decouple the illumination-invariant features of person images.

Adversarial Learning. Adversarial learning, initially introduced to compel models to generate realistic images, now has widespread applications. Wang et al. [18] proposed PAR which enforces model focus on discriminative global information by penalizing the predictive ability of local features. In [3], Gu et al. introduce CAL, presenting an adversarial loss based on clothing to decouple features unrelated to clothing. Inspired by these approaches, this paper introduces a multi-positive class adversarial loss based on illumination labels to extract illumination-invariant features, drawing motivation from the successes of PAR and CAL in focusing on specific aspects of information.

3 The Proposed Method

Fig. 2 illustrates the overall architecture of our method. In this section, we first introduce the image Decomposition&Restoration Network, which is employed to extract reflectance maps as a prior guidance. Subsequently, we propose a joint learning framework based on the reflectance maps to extract illumination-invariant features. Meanwhile, we employ an adversarial learning mechanism to address complex lighting challenges.

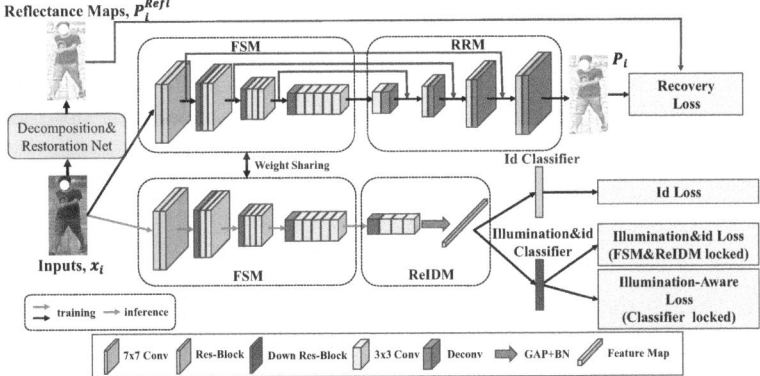

Fig. 2. Overview of the proposed network, which consists of reflectance map recovery branch, ReID branch and a pretrained Decomposition&Restoration Net. Decomposition&Restoration Net is employed to extract reflectance maps as a prior guidance. Recovery branch and ReID branch share the Feature Sharing Module. Besides, an Illumination&id classifier is added at the end of the ReID branch. The Illumination&id loss and the Illumination-Aware loss engage in a mutual adversarial relationship, guiding the backbone to learn illumination-invariant features.

3.1 Image Decomposition&Restoration Network

The retinex theory assumes that an image I is the product of reflectance map R and illumination map L, which can be expressed as:

$$I = R \odot L \quad (1)$$

where $\odot$ represents element-wise multiplication. A perfect decomposition enables us to obtain a reflectance map representing the intrinsic colors and textures of a scene, and notably, this reflectance map is illumination-invariant.

In order to obtain reflectance map of the input image effectively, we employ the framework introduced by Zhang et al. [22]. First, the input image is decomposed into a reflectance map and an illumination map by a decomposition network. Subsequently, a restoration network is used to eliminate noise on the reflectance map which will be used for subsequent joint learning.

3.2 Joint Learning Based on Decoupling

As shown in Fig. 2, the proposed joint learning framework consists of two branches: the ReID branch and the reflectance map recovery branch. During the training phase, both two branches share a feature sharing module (FSM). The output of FSM is simultaneously fed into the reflectance map recovery module (RRM) and the ReID module (ReIDM). During the inference phase, we only need to use FSM and ReIDM to extract features. With such a joint learning architecture, we not only avoid increasing the computational burden but also improve the performance of network under complex lighting conditions.

ReID Branch. In ReID branch, we use ResNet50 as our backbone. The embedding features generated by ReIDM are fed to Id classifier and Illumination&id classifier separately. The architecture of both classifiers is a fully connected layer with one layer. The Id classifier is used for calculating the widely used identity loss. Identity loss is as follows:

$$\mathcal{L}_{id} = -\frac{1}{N}\sum_{i=1}^{N}\log\frac{e^{\sigma_i^{y_i}}}{\sum_{j=1}^{N_{id}}e^{\sigma_i^j}} \quad (2)$$

where N denotes the batch size, σ_i^j represents the output of Id classifier with class j based on i^{th} input image. N_{id} represents the total number of id class. y_i is the ground truth id class.

The output dimension of the Illumination&id classifier aligns with the number of Illumination&id class, and it is used for computing the Illumination-Aware Loss (IAL). We will elaborate on the specific details in the next subsection.

Reflectance Map Recovery Branch. The structure of this branch comprises FSM and RRM. The RRM consists of four upsampling modules. After each upsampling step, the output is fused and concatenated with the corresponding feature map from FSM. Finally, it outputs an image with the same resolution as input. Through this branch, the recovery of reflectance map enables FSM to extract features that are invariant to illumination. The loss function of this branch can be expressed as follows:

$$\mathcal{L}_{RRB} = \sum_{i=1}^{N}\left\|P_i - P_i^{Refl}\right\|_1 \quad (3)$$

where P_i and P_i^{Refl} represent the predicted reflectance map and the corresponding reflectance map obtained through the Decomposition&Restoration Network.

3.3 Adversarial Learning for Feature Disentanglement

Inspired by the decoupling of specific information capabilities in [3,18], we propose an adversarial learning method to extract illumination-invariant information. An Illumination&id classifier is introduced at the end of the ReID branch. The training process involves two iterative steps. In the first step, backbone's parameters are frozen, and we optimize the parameters of the Illumination&id classifier using cross-entropy loss. The loss function is defined as follows:

$$\mathcal{L}_{Iid} = -\sum_{i=1}^{N}\log\frac{e^{f_i\cdot\xi_{y_i^D}}}{\sum_{j=1}^{N_{Iid}}e^{f_i\cdot\xi_j}} \quad (4)$$

where ξ_j represent the weight of jth Illumination&id classifier, N_{Iid} is the number of Illumination&id class in the training set, f_i denotes the embedding vector obtained by passing x_i through the ReIDM, y_i^D is the ground truth Illumination&id class of x_i. This loss enables the Illumination&id classifier to learn the ability to distinguish pedestrians with different illuminations for the same id.

In the second step, we lock the parameters of Illumination&id classifier and penalize classifier for its ability to distinguish lighting conditions. It compels the model's backbone to learn illumination-invariant features. Our objective is making the trained Illumination&id classifier cannot distinguish samples with the same identity and different illuminations. Since pedestrians with the same id under different illuminations are each other's positive class, we introduce an Illumination-Aware loss (IAL) which is a multi-positive class classification loss. The loss function is defined as follows:

$$\mathcal{L}_{IAL} = -\sum_{i=1}^{N}\sum_{c=1}^{N_{Iid}} p(c) \log \frac{e^{(f_i \cdot \xi_c / \tau)}}{\sum_{j \in S_i^*} e^{(f_i \cdot \xi_j / \tau)} + e^{(f_i \cdot \xi_c / \tau)}} \quad (5)$$

$$p(c) = \begin{cases} \alpha & \text{, if } c = y_i^D \\ \frac{1-\alpha}{N_{S_i^+}} & \text{, if } c \in S_i^+ \\ 0 & \text{, otherwise} \end{cases} \quad (6)$$

where $S_i^+(S_i^*)$ denotes the set of classes with the same identity but different illuminations (different identities but the same illumination) as x_i, $N_{S_i^+}$ is the size of S_i^+, and $p(c)$ is the weight of loss for c^{th} Illumination&id class. α is used to adjust the weights between the positive class with the same illumination and positive classes with different illuminations, τ is a temperature parameter. Generally, the positive class with the same illumination has a bigger weight than the positive classes with different illuminations. We analyse the influence of α and τ in the ablation study.

During the optimization of IAL, the Id classifier is concurrently refined through $\mathcal{L}_{id}$, $\mathcal{L}_{id}$ enables the model to learn easy samples, while $\mathcal{L}_{IAL}$ compels the model to distinguish challenging samples (different identities, same illumination). Two losses work together to improve the overall performance. The total loss of our approach is as follows:

$$\mathcal{L}_{Total} = \mathcal{L}_{RRB} + \mathcal{L}_{id} + \mathcal{L}_{Iid} + \mathcal{L}_{IAL} \quad (7)$$

4 Experiments

4.1 Datasets

Real-world Dataset. Due to the lack of public person ReID datasets for IA-ReID, we construct a dataset called ICReID. In ICReID, images are captured by 31 cameras in exhibition halls with significant light changing. For each image in ICReID, we provide an identity label and an illumination label. The identity labels are manually annotated, while the illumination labels are divided into two brightness categories by considering the brightness of the image. Through the identity label and the illumination label, we can easily obtain the fine-grained Illumination&id label of the image. Examples and detailed composition of this

Table 1. The constitution of Market-syn and ICReID datasets. (#IDs/#Images)

Dataset	Train	Query	Gallery
Market-syn	751/12185	750/3368	751/15913
ICReID	493/11550	105/857	105/1687

dataset are illustrated in Fig. 1 and summarized in Table 1. The proposed ICReID dataset will be released soon.

Synthetic Dataset. For the synthetic dataset, we create a synthetic dataset called Market-syn based on the Market-1501 dataset. To emulate variations in illumination, we apply gamma correction with gamma value randomly selected from 1,2,3,4 to the images. Additionally, we add gaussian noise with a variance of 5 to each image. The illumination labels of the synthetic dataset have a total of four categories depending on the selected gamma values. Examples and detailed composition of this dataset are presented in Fig. 1 and Table 1.

4.2 Implementation Details

Image Decomposition and Restoration Network Training. To train the Image Decomposition& Restoration Network, we synthesize a large dataset of normal light-low light image pairs based on the PASCAL VOC image dataset. The synthesis method is consistent with the Market-syn mentioned above. Specifically, we utilize the Adam optimizer with a learning rate of 10^{-4}, set batch size to 16, randomly crop images from the dataset to sizes of 256×128, and employ data augmentation techniques such as random horizontal flipping and cropping.

Joint Training. In this stage, we employ the image Decomposition&Restoration Network trained in the first phase to process input images, obtaining corresponding reflectance maps. These maps serve as the ground truth for the reflectance map recovery branch, and the parameters of pretrained network are frozen. The parameters of both ReID branch and the reflectance map recovery branch are trained using ReID loss and Recovery loss. We use Adam optimizer, setting the initial learning rate to $3.5e^{-4}$, and reduce the learning rate by a factor of 3 every 10 epochs. The batch size is set to 64, and input images are resized to 256×128, with additional data augmentation such as random horizontal flipping and random cropping. The hyper parameter τ is set to $1/12$ and α is set to 0.8.

4.3 Comparison with State-of-the-Art Methods

Due to the fact that methods [1,6,20] specifically designed for IA-ReID have not open-sourced their code, we compare our results with other existing CNN-based ReID methods. Besides, we respectively employ some image enhancement methods as pre-processing and integrate them with BOT into two-stage approachs. It can be observed that in IA-ReID task, only LIME improves the performance of ReID model, while other methods weaken the performance. Moreover, these

Table 2. Comparison with the State-of-The-Art Methods on ICReID and Market-syn datasets. We show best scores in bold and the second scores underline.

Method	Pre-enhanced	ICReID		Market-syn	
		top-1	mAP	top-1	mAP
MGN [17]		95.1	87.1	86.5	70.8
BOT [11]		95.3	87.3	86.4	70.6
GCP [7]		94.9	87.1	85.9	70.6
CDN [10]		94.8	87.2	86.5	70.7
LUPnl [2]		<u>95.4</u>	<u>87.5</u>	<u>87.0</u>	70.9
BOT-LIME [4]	✓	95.3	87.2	86.8	<u>71.0</u>
BOT-zeroDCE++ [9]	✓	94.2	85.8	85.9	68.7
BOT-SCI [12]	✓	94.5	85.5	86.9	70.7
Ours		**96.1**	**88.4**	**88.6**	**72.3**

Table 3. Effectiveness of the proposed Joint Learning (JL) and IAL on ICReID and Market-syn datasets. 'JL*' represents Joint Learning using normal light images.

Method	ICReID		Market-syn	
	top-1	mAP	top-1	mAP
Baseline	94.6	85.0	83.8	64.4
Baseline+JL*	-	-	84.4	64.8
Baseline+JL	95.7	87.8	85.3	67.4
Baseline+IAL	95.9	88.2	87.8	71.3
Baseline+JL+IAL	**96.1**	**88.4**	**88.6**	**72.3**

two-stage approach incur expensive computational costs. As shown in Table II, compared to the current state-of-the-art CNN-based method LUPnl, our model achieves an improvement by 0.9%/0.7% on mAP/top-1 metrics in ICReID and by 1.4%/1.6% on mAP/top-1 metrics in Market-syn.

4.4 Ablation Study

Component Ablation. We conduct an ablation study to evaluate the individual components of our method. Table 3 demonstrate the effectiveness of both joint learning and adversarial learning mechanism. Furthermore, in the Market-syn dataset, we have images under normal light condition, allowing us to compare two joint learning approaches: recovering normal light images and recovering reflectance maps. The second and third rows shows that recovering reflectance maps proves to better enable the model to learn illumination-invariant features.

We also compare our IAL with various metric losses. As shown in Table 4, all the considered losses outperform using ID loss alone, but IAL stands out as

Table 4. Comparison with other metric losses on ICReID and Market-syn datasets.

Method	ICReID		Market-syn	
	top-1	mAP	top-1	mAP
ID loss	94.6	85.0	83.9	64.4
ID loss+Circle loss [16]	94.9	84.8	84.6	66.2
ID loss+Contrast loss [5]	94.5	84.5	85.7	69.1
ID loss+Triplet loss [11]	95.3	87.3	86.4	70.7
ID loss+IAL(Ours)	**95.9**	**88.2**	**87.8**	**71.3**

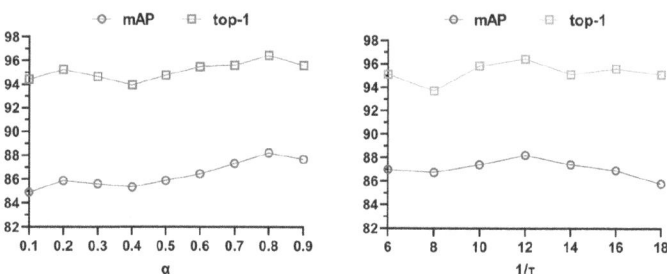

Fig. 3. The mAP and top-1 of our method with different α and τ on ICReID datasets.

superior to other losses. This comparison illustrates that IAL is capable of better assisting the model in mining illumination-invariant features.

Influence of α and τ in IAL. We analyze the influence of τ in Equation (5). We show the results with varying τ on ICReID in Fig. 3. The best performance is achieved when $\tau = 1/12$. Besides, by varying α in Equation (6), as shown in Fig. 3, we get the best result when $\alpha = 0.8$.

5 Conclusion

In this paper, we focus on the problem of IA-ReID. To better extract illumination-invariant features, a joint learning framework and an adversarial learning method are introduced, enabling backbone to learn illumination-invariant features. Compared to other methods, our proposed module, which can be seamlessly detached during the inference phase, contributes to a reduction in inference computation time. Besides, due to the lack of dataset specific to this problem, we contribute a real-world person ReID dataset called ICReID, which contains noticeable light changes. Extensive experiments demonstrate the effectiveness of our method on both real and synthetic datasets, achieving significant performance.

Acknowledgements. This work was supported in part by the National Natural Science Foundation of China (U22A2095, 62072482), and the Key-Area Research and Development Program of Guangzhou (202206030003).

References

1. Bhuiyan, A., Perina, A., Murino, V.: Exploiting multiple detections to learn robust brightness transfer functions in re-identification systems. In: ICIP, pp. 2329–2333 (2015)
2. Fu, D., et al.: Large-scale pre-training for person re-identification with noisy labels. In: CVPR, pp. 01–11 (2022)
3. Gu, X., Chang, H., Ma, B., Bai, S., Shan, S., Chen, X.: Clothes-changing person re-identification with RGB modality only. In: CVPR, pp. 1060–1069 (2022)
4. Guo, X., Li, Y., Ling, H.: Lime: low-light image enhancement via illumination map estimation. TIP **26**(2), 982–993 (2016)
5. Hadsell, R., Chopra, S., LeCun, Y.: Dimensionality reduction by learning an invariant mapping. In: CVPR, pp. 1735–1742 (2006)
6. Huang, Y., Zha, Z.J., Fu, X., Zhang, W.: Illumination-invariant person re-identification. In: ACMMM, pp. 365–373 (2019)
7. Hyunjong, P., Bumsub, H.: Relation network for person re-identification. In: AAAI, vol. 34, pp. 11839–11847 (2020)
8. Kviatkovsky, I., Adam, A., Rivlin, E.: Color invariants for person reidentification. TPAMI **35**(7), 1622–1634 (2012)
9. Li, C., Guo, C., Loy, C.C.: Learning to enhance low-light image via zero-reference deep curve estimation. TPAMI **44**(8), 4225–4238 (2021)
10. Li, H., Wu, G., Zheng, W.S.: Combined depth space based architecture search for person re-identification. In: CVPR, pp. 6729–6738 (2021)
11. Luo, H., Gu, Y., Liao, X., Lai, S., Jiang, W.: Bag of tricks and a strong baseline for deep person re-identification. In: CVPR Workshops (2019)
12. Ma, L., Ma, T., Liu, R., Fan, X., Luo, Z.: Toward fast, flexible, and robust low-light image enhancement. In: CVPR, pp. 5637–5646 (2022)
13. Shen, F., Du, X., Zhang, L., Tang, J.: Triplet contrastive learning for unsupervised vehicle re-identification. arXiv preprint (2023)
14. Shen, F., Shu, X., Du, X., Tang, J.: Pedestrian-specific bipartite-aware similarity learning for text-based person retrieval. In: ACMMM, pp. 8922–8931 (2023)
15. Shen, F., Ye, H., Zhang, J., Wang, C., Han, X., Wei, Y.: Advancing pose-guided image synthesis with progressive conditional diffusion models. In: ICLR (2023)
16. Sun, Y., et al.: Circle loss: a unified perspective of pair similarity optimization. In: CVPR, pp. 6398–6407 (2020)
17. Wang, G., Yuan, Y., Chen, X., Li, J., Zhou, X.: Learning discriminative features with multiple granularities for person re-identification. In: ACMMM, pp. 274–282 (2018)
18. Wang, H., Ge, S., Lipton, Z., Xing, E.P.: Learning robust global representations by penalizing local predictive power. NeurIPS **32** (2019)
19. Wang, Y., Hu, R., Liang, C., Zhang, C., Leng, Q.: Camera compensation using feature projection matrix for person re-identification. In: ICME, pp. 1–6 (2013)
20. Zeng, Z., Wang, Z., Wang, Z., Zheng, Y., Chuang, Y.Y., Satoh, S.: Illumination-adaptive person re-identification. TMM **22**(12), 3064–3074 (2020)
21. Zhang, G., Luo, Z., Chen, Y., Zheng, Y., Lin, W.: Illumination unification for person re-identification. TCSVT **32**(10), 6766–6777 (2022)
22. Zhang, Y., Zhang, J., Guo, X.: Kindling the darkness: a practical low-light image enhancer. In: ACMMM, pp. 1632–1640 (2019)
23. Zheng, L., Shen, L., Tian, L., Wang, S., Wang, J., Tian, Q.: Scalable person re-identification: a benchmark. In: ICCV, pp. 1116–1124 (2015)
24. Zhuo, J., Chen, Z., Lai, J., Wang, G.: Occluded person re-identification. In: ICME, pp. 1–6. IEEE (2018)

Exposing Deepfakes with Noise-Based Clues

Shaocong Yang[1], Xiaolong Qi[1], Huiling Wang[1], Jian Wang[3], and Yunlian Sun[2(✉)]

[1] Yili Normal University, 448 Jiefang Road, Yining, Xinjiang, China
yangshaocong2023@163.com
[2] Nanjing University of Science and Technology, 200 Xiaolingwei Street, Nanjing, Jiangsu, China
[3] Nanjing University of Posts and Telecommunications, 9 Wenyuan Road, Nanjing, Jiangsu, China

Abstract. Current deepfake detection methods focus on learning specific forged traces, but they struggle with unknown forgery types. To address this issue, we propose a noise feature consistency-based approach. We utilize both spatial and noise features in face images, as noise features effectively capture forged traces. To achieve robust feature representations, we design a cross-attention module to interact between noise and spatial features. Additionally, we design a comprehensive consistency guidance module to consider both intra- and inter-instance feature consistency. Experiments prove that our proposed method has good robustness and generalization.

Keywords: deepfakes · deepfake detection · noise feature

1 Introduction

With the rapid development of deepfake technology, deepfakes are becoming harder to identify, posing potential security threats to people's daily lives and social stability. Hence, deepfake detection is being extensively studied. Many detectors [1–5] learn specific forgery traces, performing well within domains but struggling with unknown forgery types.

To address the above challenges, some researchers have proposed utilizing information from the image transformation domain for forged face detection [1,4,6,7]. Similarly, We find forgery traces in the noise domain can also be utilized. As shown in Fig. 1, the noise in the real face image is relatively uniform and consistent, while there are obvious areas of inconsistent noise in these forged face images. Therefore, we propose a deepfake detection method which utilizes both the spatial and noise features of the images. We also design a cross-attention

---

Supported by National Natural Science Foundation of China under Grant 62076131, Program of Yili Normal University under Grant 2023YSYB027 and Postdoctoral Fellowship Program of CPSF under Grant Number GZC20240743.

Fig. 1. Face images and their corresponding noise images. The forged images are enclosed in red boxes, while the real images are enclosed in green boxes. (Color figure online)

module(CAM) to enhance the information interaction between two branches, further improving each branch's ability to capture anomalous information. In addition, to better detect forgery traces and strengthen the model's focus on feature consistency, the proposed method designs a consistency guidance module(CGM) that directs the model to attend to intra-instance and inter-instance feature consistency. This enables the model to have excellent detection capabilities for different forgery methods, enhancing its attention to local details and improving the generalization ability of the method.

2 Related Work

In this section, we introduce the spatial-based and noise-based deepfake detection methods. The main principle of deepfake detection methods lies in the fact that, during the forgery process, usually the internal regions of the source image's face are tampered with. This leads to inconsistency in the forged image [8–13].

Spatial-Based Deepfake Detection. Zhou et al. [8] introduces a two-branch network for deepfake detection based on steganographic features, but it's not end-to-end. Zhao et al. [9] proposes an end-to-end method to detect forged faces by measuring the consistency of image source features. Miao et al. [14] utilizes Transformers to focus on local facial patch features and encode their relationships, achieving good robustness. Nirkin et al. [10] introduces a method comparing the consistency of manipulated facial regions with their context for forgery detection. However, these methods only utilize spatial domain information and lack robustness when faced with unknown forgery methods.

Noise-Based Deepfake Detection. Cozzolino et al. [11] utilizes noise to calculate local features from the collinearity of image residuals, effectively distinguishing the authentic regions from the tampered regions in tampered images. Rao et al. [15] initializes a convolutional neural network using noise features to improve detection accuracy. However, most of these methods are only effective against specific forgery techniques, such as copy-move, and perform poorly against most deepfake methods.

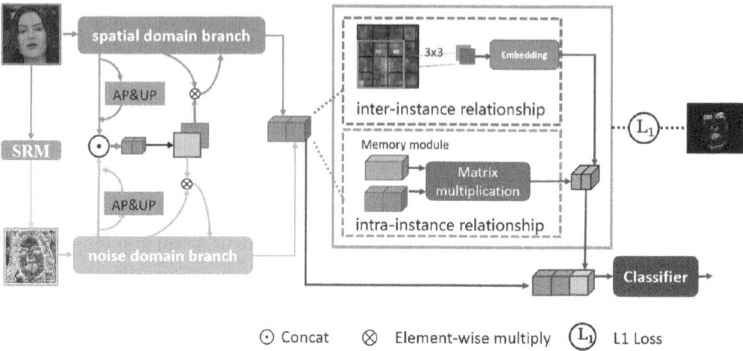

Fig. 2. The overview framework of our proposed method.

3 Methods

Architecture. To enhance the extraction and utilization of noise features, we employ the SRM filter [12] to generate a noise image. Furthermore, we design two modules: CAM and CGM. The comprehensive network architecture incorporating these modules is illustrated in Fig. 2.

Cross-Attention Module: For a feature map F, our cross-attention module first performs downsampling using average pooling (AP), then upsamples the features to their original size using nearest neighbor interpolation. Finally, we subtract the upsampled features from the original feature map F. This process not only magnifies the details of texture features in the spatial domain but also highlights the abnormal regions in the noise domain. The above process can be expressed mathematically as:

$$F^e = F - Up(AP(F)), \tag{1}$$

where Up represents upsampling, and F^e stands for the feature map after feature enhancement. After completing the feature enhancement, the interaction of information between two features is conducted. Specifically, the features from two image transformation domains are first concatenated, and then two attention maps are generated through two sets of 1×1 convolutions and sigmoid function. Subsequently, the original feature map is multiplied with the attention maps using an element-wise multiplication operation, and the multiplied features are added to the original feature. The cross-attention module is placed after the 7th module of Xception [16].

Consistency Guidance Module: As observed in Fig. 3, forgery traces become more apparent through comparative analysis. Comparing features of different areas detects inconsistent traces in Fig. 3(a) and Fig. 3(b). However, intra-instance regional comparisons alone may be insufficient. In Fig. 3(c), the overall

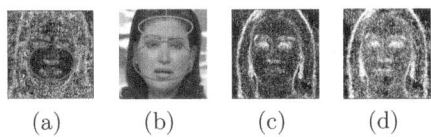

(a) (b) (c) (d)

Fig. 3. The comparative analysis of forgery traces. (a)Noise image of a forged face with inconsistent regional noise features. (b)Forged face image with inconsistent regional spatial features. (c)Noise map of a forged face with relatively consistent regional noise features. (d)The noise image of a real face image

noise pattern is uniform, but differences are clear when compared to a real face in Fig. 3(d).

Therefore, we design CGM (Fig. 4) to model intra- and inter-instance feature consistency. For intra-instance consistency, local features and their regional context are modeled using a 3×3 convolution on feature F. These are concatenated, and relationship mapping is conducted. For inter-instance consistency, we utilize a global memory module M to obtain the instance consistency, and a 1×1 convolution to perform relationship mapping. Both relations are concatenated to generate a total consistency map.

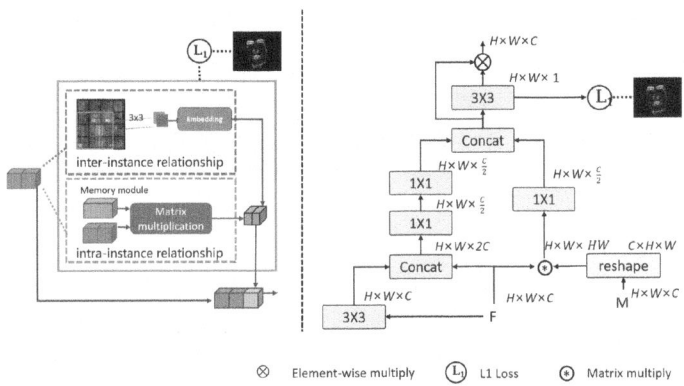

Fig. 4. The consistency guidance module.

Loss Function: For the classification loss, We adopt Focal Loss [17] as the classification loss for the network, which prioritizes difficult samples by amplifying their loss contribution, while minimizing the impact from easily classified samples. specifically:

$$L_c = -\alpha y(1-p)^\gamma log(p) - (1-\alpha)(1-y)p^\gamma log(1-p) \qquad (2)$$

where p is the final classification probability, y is the image label (1 for real, 0 for fake). $(1-p)^\gamma$ and $(1-y)p^\gamma$ adjust for classification difficulty, while α balances categories. In the experiment, we set the value of α to 0.7 and γ to 2. In addition, for the relationship-guided loss, we calculate the L1 loss between the SSIM map and the relationship map output by CGM, specifically as follows:

$$L_r = ||M_r - M_f||_1 \tag{3}$$

Therefore, the total loss function is

$$L = L_c + L_r \tag{4}$$

4 Experiments

4.1 Settings

Datasets: We use Face Forensics++ (FF++) [3] and Celeb-DF [18] to conduct experiments. FF++ is a widely used large-scale deepfake dataset, consisting of 5000 videos. The fake videos are generated by four forgery methods: Deepfakes(DF), NeuraTextures(NT), Face2Face(F2F), and FaceSwap(FS). Additionally, FF++ dataset contains three types of videos with different compression qualities: raw videos (RAW), high-quality videos (HQ) with slight compression, and low-quality videos (LQ) with heavy compression. The Celeb-DF dataset contains 6529 videos, including 890 real videos and 5639 fake videos.

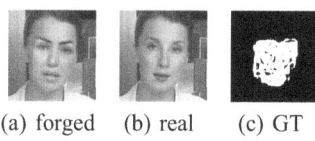

(a) forged   (b) real   (c) GT

Fig. 5. The face image structural similarity map.

Generation of Facial Image Structural Similarity Map: The structural similarity(SSIM) algorithm [19] is employed to ultimately obtain the similarity degree between the forged face image and its corresponding real face image. This serves as the ground truth(GT) map to guide the model in learning the consistency. Specifically, it can be seen in Fig. 5.

4.2 Quantitative Analysis

To verify effectiveness, in-domain and cross-domain experiments are conducted on FF++ and Celeb-DF datasets. "*" in tables indicates that the model is retrained using the official code under unified experimental settings. Table 1 presents quantitative results on FF++ dataset with high quality and low quality settings. We can observe that the proposed method achieves the best performance in terms of various detection metrics for both low-quality and high-quality videos compared to the current state-of-the-art methods. In particular, it achieves excellent performance in detecting face forgery in low-quality videos, with an AUC improvement of 2.13% and an ACC improvement of 1.16% compared to Multi-attentional method. This is attributed to focusing on spatial and noise features, and CGM.

Table 1. Quantitative results (ACC (%) and AUC (%)) on FF++ dataset.

Methods	Low quality		High quality	
	ACC	AUC	ACC	AUC
LD-CNN [20]	58.69	-	78.45	-
MesoNet [21]*	79.95	54.35	79.99	52.23
Face X-ray [22]	-	61.60	-	87.40
Xception-ELA [23]*	80.53	73.06	88.14	92.22
Two Branch [24]	-	86.59	-	98.70
Xception [16]*	86.04	87.78	95.71	98.74
Multi-attentional [5]*	86.41	88.46	96.14	98.90
SPSL [25]	81.57	82.82	91.50	95.32
Ours	**87.57**	**90.59**	**96.27**	**99.03**

To further verify the generalization ability of our proposed method, we conduct cross-dataset generalization experiments, where we train the model on the DF dataset of FF++ and test it on the Celeb-DF dataset. The results of the generalization experiments for all comparison methods are shown in Table 2. As can be seen from Table 2, our method still exhibits excellent detection capabilities for completely unknown forgery techniques. We suspect the main reason is that CGM can effectively guide the model to identify anomalous features within instances and compare them among instance features, thus discovering inconsistent features between instances, which further enhances the model's generalization ability.

To validate the generalization capability of our proposed method on video datasets of varying qualities, we conduct two sets of video quality generalization experiments, training on one video quality (HQ or LQ) of the FF++ dataset and testing on the other (LQ or HQ). The experimental results are presented in Table 3. We can observe that our method demonstrates robust detection capabilities when the quality of the forgery images differs from the quality of the training face images. This indicates that the features extracted and modules used in our method remain highly effective for data of varying qualities, achieving significant improvements compared to the backbone method.

Table 2. Cross-database evaluation from FF++ to others (AUC (%)).

Methods	FF++(DF)	Celeb-DF
Two-stream [1]	70.10	53.80
MesoNet [21]*	71.75	53.99
Multi-task [26]	76.30	54.30
Xception [16]*	99.85	66.89
F3-net [4]	98.10	65.17
Multi-attentional [5]*	99.86	67.89
Two Branch [24]	93.18	73.44
CFFs [27]	-	74.2
Zhuang et al. [28]	-	72.77
Ours	99.88	**75.22**

Table 3. Cross-quality evaluation(AUC (%)).

Methods	Setting	Testing Set			
		DF	F2F	FS	NT
Xception [16]*	train on FF++(HQ)	74.61	65.64	74.01	65.68
Ours	test on Testing Set(LQ)	**86.97**	**75.36**	**90.97**	**67.35**
Xception [16]*	train on FF++(LQ)	86.89	85.17	83.67	81.66
Ours	test on Testing Set(HQ)	**95.34**	**93.88**	**88.47**	**85.19**

4.3 Qualitative Analysis

To visually demonstrate the feature activation maps of the proposed method, we chose face image structural similarity maps, input images of the spatial domain branch and their corresponding output feature activation maps, as well as input images of the noise domain branch and their corresponding output feature activation maps. As shown in Fig. 6, the activation maps of spatial domain features can better describe the forged regions in the images. The activation regions of the output features of the noise domain branch are more consistent with the local abnormal regions in the input noise images. Overall, we find that the spatial domain and noise domain feature activation maps both describe the forged regions well and can complement each other effectively.

4.4 Ablation Study

To demonstrate the benefit of each module, we evaluate the proposed model and its variants on the FF++(LQ) database. As shown in Table 4, when only the spatial domain branch is used, the model achieves an AUC of 87.78%. As we gradually introduce the noise branch, CAM, and CGM, the AUC of the model progressively improves. Additionally, the significance of intra-instance and inter-instance relations is also validated. When either of these relations is incorporated

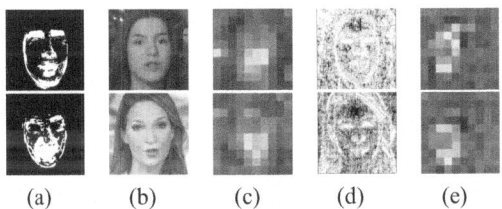

Fig. 6. The visualization of the feature maps extracted by spatial and noise branch. (a)GT. (b)Spatial branch inputs. (c)Spatial branch feature maps. (d)Noise branch inputs. (e)Noise branch feature maps.

independently, the AUC of the model is enhanced. However, when both relations are fully included, the performance is optimal.

Table 4. Ablation study on FF++(LQ)(AUC(%)).

Spatial Branch	Noise Branch	CAM	CGM		AUC
			intra	inter	
✓	-	-	-		87.78
✓	✓	-	-		89.22
✓	✓	✓	-		89.77
✓	✓	✓	✓		**90.59**
✓	✓	✓	✓	-	90.15
✓	✓	✓	-	✓	90.10
✓	✓	✓	✓	✓	**90.59**

5 Conclusion

In this paper, we proposed a deepfake method based on noise feature consistency. It utilized a dual-branch network to extract spatial and noise features. CAM enhanced and facilitated interaction between these features, while CGM improved the generalization capabilities. Experiments conducted on the Celeb-DF and FF++ datasets confirmed its effectiveness, robustness, and excellent generalization. Ablation experiments further verified the effectiveness of each module.

References

1. Zhou, P., Han, X., Morariu, V.I., Davis, L.S.: Two-stream neural networks for tampered face detection. arXiv preprint arXiv:1803.11276 (2018)
2. Li, Y., Lyu, S.: Exposing deepfake videos by detecting face warping artifacts. In: IEEE Conference on Computer Vision and Pattern Recognition Workshops, CVPR Workshops 2019, Long Beach, CA, USA, June 16-20, 2019, Computer Vision Foundation / IEEE, pp. 46–52 (2019)

3. Rössler, A., Cozzolino, D., Verdoliva, L., Riess, C., Thies, J., Nießner, M.: Faceforensics++: learning to detect manipulated facial images. In: 2019 IEEE/CVF International Conference on Computer Vision, ICCV 2019, Seoul, South Korea, October 27 - November 2, 2019, pp. 1–11. IEEE (2019)
4. Qian, Y., Yin, G., Sheng, L., Chen, Z., Shao, J.: Thinking in frequency: face forgery detection by mining frequency-aware clues. In: Vedaldi, A., Bischof, H., Brox, T., Frahm, J. (eds.) Computer Vision - ECCV 2020 - 16th European Conference, Glasgow, UK, August 23-28, 2020, Proceedings, Part XII. LNCS, vol. 12357, pp. 86–103. Springer (2020)
5. Zhao, H., Zhou, W., Chen, D., Wei, T., Zhang, W., Yu, N.: Multi-attentional deepfake detection. In: IEEE Conference on Computer Vision and Pattern Recognition, CVPR 2021, Virtual, June 19-25, 2021, Computer Vision Foundation / IEEE, pp. 2185–2194 (2021)
6. Masi, I., Killekar, A., Mascarenhas, R.M., Gurudatt, S.P., AbdAlmageed, W.: Twobranch recurrent network for isolating deepfakes in videos. In Vedaldi, A., Bischof, H., Brox, T., Frahm, J., eds.: Computer Vision - ECCV 2020 - 16th European Conference, Glasgow, UK, August 23-28, 2020, Proceedings, Part VII. LNCS, vol. 12352, pp. 667–684. Springer (2020)
7. Wang, J., Sun, Y., Tang, J.: Lisiam: localization invariance Siamese network for deepfake detection. IEEE Trans. Inf. Forensics Secur. **17**, 2425–2436 (2022)
8. Zhou, P., Han, X., Morariu, V.I., Davis, L.S.: Two-stream neural networks for tampered face detection. In: 2017 IEEE Conference on Computer Vision and Pattern Recognition Workshops, CVPR Workshops 2017, Honolulu, HI, USA, July 21-26, 2017, pp. 1831–1839. IEEE Computer Society (2017)
9. Zhao, T., Xu, X., Xu, M., Ding, H., Xiong, Y., Xia, W.: Learning self-consistency for deepfake detection. In: 2021 IEEE/CVF International Conference on Computer Vision, ICCV 2021, Montreal, QC, Canada, October 10-17, 2021, pp. 15003–15013. IEEE (2021)
10. Nirkin, Y., Wolf, L., Keller, Y., Hassner, T.: Deepfake detection based on discrepancies between faces and their context. IEEE Trans. Pattern Anal. Mach. Intell. **44**(10), 6111–6121 (2022)
11. Cozzolino, D., Poggi, G., Verdoliva, L.: Splicebuster: A new blind image splicing detector. In: 2015 IEEE International Workshop on Information Forensics and Security, WIFS 2015, Roma, Italy, November 16-19, 2015, pp. 1–6. IEEE (2015)
12. Zhou, P., Han, X., Morariu, V.I., Davis, L.S.: Learning rich features for image manipulation detection. In: 2018 IEEE Conference on Computer Vision and Pattern Recognition, CVPR 2018, Salt Lake City, UT, USA, June 18-22, 2018, pp. 1053–1061. Computer Vision Foundation / IEEE Computer Society (2018)
13. Wang, J., Du, X., Cheng, Y., Sun, Y., Tang, J.: SI-Net: spatial interaction network for deepfake detection. Multim. Syst. **29**(5), 3139–3150 (2023)
14. Miao, C., Chu, Q., Li, W., Gong, T., Zhuang, W., Yu, N.: Towards generalizable and robust face manipulation detection via bag-of-local-feature. arXiv preprint arXiv:2103.07915 (2021)
15. Rao, Y., Ni, J.: A deep learning approach to detection of splicing and copy-move forgeries in images. In: IEEE International Workshop on Information Forensics and Security, WIFS 2016, Abu Dhabi, United Arab Emirates, December 4-7, 2016, pp. 1–6. IEEE (2016)
16. Chollet, F.: Xception: deep learning with DepthWise separable convolutions. In: 2017 IEEE Conference on Computer Vision and Pattern Recognition, CVPR 2017, Honolulu, HI, USA, July 21-26, 2017, pp. 1800–1807. IEEE Computer Society (2017)

17. Li, X., Lv, C., Wang, W., Li, G., Yang, L., Yang, J.: Generalized focal loss: towards efficient representation learning for dense object detection. IEEE Trans. Pattern Anal. Mach. Intell. **45**(3), 3139–3153 (2023)
18. Li, Y., Yang, X., Sun, P., Qi, H., Lyu, S.: Celeb-DF: a large-scale challenging dataset for deepfake forensics. In: 2020 IEEE/CVF Conference on Computer Vision and Pattern Recognition, CVPR 2020, Seattle, WA, USA, June 13-19, 2020, pp. 3204–3213. Computer Vision Foundation / IEEE (2020)
19. Wang, Z., Bovik, A.C., Sheikh, H.R., Simoncelli, E.P.: Image quality assessment: from error visibility to structural similarity. IEEE Trans. Image Process. **13**(4), 600–612 (2004)
20. Cozzolino, D., Poggi, G., Verdoliva, L.: Recasting residual-based local descriptors as convolutional neural networks: an application to image forgery detection. In: Stamm, M.C., Kirchner, M., Voloshynovskiy, S. (eds.) Proceedings of the 5th ACM Workshop on Information Hiding and Multimedia Security, IH&MMSec 2017, Philadelphia, PA, USA, June 20-22, 2017, pp. 159–164. ACM (2017)
21. Afchar, D., Nozick, V., Yamagishi, J., Echizen, I.: Mesonet: a compact facial video forgery detection network. In: 2018 IEEE International Workshop on Information Forensics and Security, WIFS 2018, Hong Kong, China, December 11-13, 2018, pp. 1–7. IEEE (2018)
22. Li, L., et al.: Face X-ray for more general face forgery detection. In: 2020 IEEE/CVF Conference on Computer Vision and Pattern Recognition, CVPR 2020, Seattle, WA, USA, June 13-19, 2020, pp. 5000–5009. Computer Vision Foundation / IEEE (2020)
23. Gunawan, T.S., Hanafiah, S.A.M., Kartiwi, M., Ismail, N., Nordin, A.N.: Development of photo forensics algorithm by detecting photoshop manipulation using error level analysis. Indonesian J. Electr. Eng. Comput. Sci. **7**(1), 131–137 (2017)
24. Chen, S., Yao, T., Chen, Y., Ding, S., Li, J., Ji, R.: Local relation learning for face forgery detection. In: Thirty-Fifth AAAI Conference on Artificial Intelligence, AAAI 2021, Thirty-Third Conference on Innovative Applications of Artificial Intelligence, IAAI 2021, The Eleventh Symposium on Educational Advances in Artificial Intelligence, EAAI 2021, Virtual Event, February 2-9, 2021, pp. 1081–1088. AAAI Press (2021)
25. Liu, H., et al.: Spatial-phase shallow learning: rethinking face forgery detection in frequency domain. In: IEEE Conference on Computer Vision and Pattern Recognition, CVPR 2021, Virtual, June 19-25, 2021, pp. 772–781. Computer Vision Foundation / IEEE (2021)
26. Nguyen, H.H., Fang, F., Yamagishi, J., Echizen, I.: Multi-task learning for detecting and segmenting manipulated facial images and videos. In: 10th IEEE International Conference on Biometrics Theory, Applications and Systems, BTAS 2019, Tampa, FL, USA, September 23-26, 2019, pp. 1–8. IEEE (2019)
27. Yu, P., Fei, J., Xia, Z., Zhou, Z., Weng, J.: Improving generalization by commonality learning in face forgery detection. IEEE Trans. Inf. Forensics Secur. **17**, 547–558 (2022)
28. Zhuang, W., Chu, Q., Yuan, H., Miao, C., Liu, B., Yu, N.: Towards intrinsic common discriminative features learning for face forgery detection using adversarial learning. In: IEEE International Conference on Multimedia and Expo, ICME 2022, Taipei, Taiwan, July 18-22, 2022, pp. 1–6. IEEE (2022)

Adaptive Multi-modal Fusion Based Face Anti-spoofing with RGB-D Images

Zhan Teng[1], Wei Fang[1(✉)], Zhanli Liu[2], and Lixi Chen[1]

[1] School of Intelligent Engineering and Automation, Beijing University of Posts and Telecommunications, Beijing, China
fangwei@bupt.edu.cn
[2] Megahunt Technologies Inc., Beijing, China

Abstract. The rapid advancement of face recognition technology has underscored the importance of face anti-spoofing techniques to ensure the security of these systems. While numerous deep learning-based face anti-spoofing methods have been proposed, including single classifier approaches using RGB or depth data, those based on multimodal data (RGB, depth, and infrared) have demonstrated superior performance. However, the fusion strategy for multimodal information at the score level remains underexplored. To address this gap, we present a comprehensive workflow for face anti-spoofing detection and introduce an adaptive fusion strategy for RGB and depth scores considering image quality. This approach effectively mitigates the limitations of individual RGB and depth models, enhancing their robustness against various attack types in diverse environments. We validate our method's efficacy through tests on the CASIA-SURF, and 3DMAD datasets, comparing it with other methods. Furthermore, we demonstrate the system's performance in real-world scenarios by testing in a realistic environment.

Keywords: face anti-spoofing · adaptive fusion · RGB-D · multimodal

1 Introduction

Face recognition technology is extensively utilized in diverse sectors, including security, online payments, and access control systems, owing to its convenience, universality, and non-contact nature. However, the current face recognition systems are not without security vulnerabilities. The escalating volume of face-bound information and the ease with which faces can be used as biometric spoofing samples have led to increased attacks on these systems. Common forms of attack include high-definition photo printing of faces, tablet videos [1], 3D face masks [2], and head molds made from various materials [3]. Consequently, enhancing the ability of face recognition systems to recognize and resist different forms of attack is crucial for ensuring their security.

Numerous anti-spoofing methods have been proposed to enhance the security of face recognition systems. In computer vision, data-driven deep learning techniques typically outperform manual feature-based methods. Deep learning in face anti-spoofing has emerged as a significant area of research. Practical applications of live detection algorithms can be broadly divided into action live detection algorithms [4] and silent live detection algorithms [5]. Action live detection primarily relies on the active behavior of the detected individual, such as blinking, mouth movement, head shaking, etc. However, this method is often hampered by user interference and low detection efficiency. Some users may not be able or willing to perform the required actions, necessitating additional time for user cooperation. Silent live detection, on the other hand, utilizes machine learning and deep learning algorithms to analyze facial biometrics from a single or multiple images for comprehensive judgment. Unlike action live detection, silent live detection does not require user cooperation or specific actions, eliminating the need for additional operations or commands. It simply captures facial information for detection. Silent live detection offers higher security and faster recognition speeds, making it particularly suitable for areas such as finance, border control, and access control. Consequently, this paper primarily focuses on research in silent live detection.

2 Related Work

2.1 Face Anti-spoofing on RGB-D Images

Traditional single-modal anti-face spoofing methods typically involve manually extracting features from RGB images, and identifying the discrepancies between live and attack images to determine whether the current image feature is live or not. Maatta et al. [6] proposed a feature extraction method based on multiple LBPs and utilized a classifier to distinguish between live and fake bodies. Boulkenafet et al. [7] analyzed the dataset through color texture analysis, determining whether the images were live or not, examining different color space information, and integrating the features of color texture as the feature information for classification. Recently, deep learning-based face anti-spoofing methods have surpassed traditional methods in performance. Given that real faces possess three-dimensional structural information, depth data can be employed to identify the majority of face attacks, including printed faces and video playback. Liang et al. [8] introduced a ternary network, comprising a depth prediction network and a ternary feature map area network. This design allows the depth prediction to effectively highlight disparities between a real individual and an attacking face, particularly about lighting inconsistencies, discontinuities, and blurring. George et al. [9] proposed a cross-modal focal loss to modulate the contribution of each modality to the loss function, aiding in capturing complementary information among modalities and mitigating overfitting. Yu et al. [10] developed a cross-attention fusion module, integrated with ResNet, to construct a three-channel FAS model for RGB, depth, and infrared. Multimodal face anti-spoofing techniques leverage depth and other supplementary data to significantly enhance model accuracy. However, these methods often fail to adequately integrate the features across different data types and neglect to fully exploit the potential of multimodal data in countering various attack modalities.

2.2 Multimodal Information Fusion

In the field of multimodal anti-spoofing, with the recent expansion of datasets, this field has begun to gain attention. Presently, mainstream multimodal fusion live detection methods can be categorized into feature level fusion and score level fusion methods. Zhang et al. [11] proposed the use of ResNet-18 as the backbone for a fusion network that processes three distinct data streams: RGB, depth, and IR. Each stream is tasked with extracting features from its respective data type, which are subsequently merged and directed to the final two residual blocks. Li et al. [12] employed the Swin-Transformer to generate local features and constructive depth features, subsequently proposing a detection method that integrates both local texture and constructive structure depth information from RGB images. Deng et al. [13] introduced a dual-stream learning framework grounded in a multichannel comparative learning strategy. In this framework, the first stream extracts primary features from sensors using a baseline network, while the second stream acquires auxiliary features from an additional deployed sensor. A master-slave fusion module (MSMF) is designed, utilizing a cross-channel spatial attention mechanism, to effectively amalgamate the primary features with the auxiliary information. Current multimodal fusion techniques leverage the complementary information inherent in multimodal data to enhance resilience against various attack types and ensure robust performance in face anti-spoofing tasks. However, these strategies often overlook the influence of environmental factors on image quality. Consequently, they fail to adapt effectively based on the predicted scores of image quality impact when employing multiple classifiers for face anti-spoofing tasks.

3 Proposed Method

Numerous researchers have conducted fusion at the score level to facilitate multimodal live detection, but the study of score adaptive fusion methods remains insufficient. To enhance the accuracy and robustness of deep learning-based multimodal data face anti-spoofing, this paper proposes a method that optimizes the fusion of scores. The proposed method primarily integrates the scores of RGB images and depth images. These scores are calculated by applying weighted factors, which are determined by image quality. This adaptive adjustment of score weights between the two modalities yields the final facial spoofing prediction results. The fusion scores are used to determine face spoofing prediction results.

3.1 Complete Workflow for Face Anti-spoofing

Our proposed methodology comprises four distinct steps, as illustrated in Fig. 1. Initially, the target's RGB image (Fig. 1(b)) and depth image (Fig. 1(c)) are captured using a RealSense D435i camera. Subsequently, the face detection network localizes the face, aligns it, and crops it based on the standard facial five points (eyes, nose, and mouth corners). This process yields the channel-aligned RGB and depth images (Fig. 1(d), (e)). The face segmentation network then segments the facial part to create a face mask (Fig. 1 (f)). This mask separates the facial region in both the RGB and depth images from the background region. The resulting RGB and depth images (Fig. 1(g), (h)) serve as the final input for the live detection network. These images are subsequently processed by the RGB and depth models to derive the respective face spoofing scores for each image. Finally, an adaptive weighting of the RGB and depth scores is performed based on image quality to produce the final score, from which prediction results are derived.

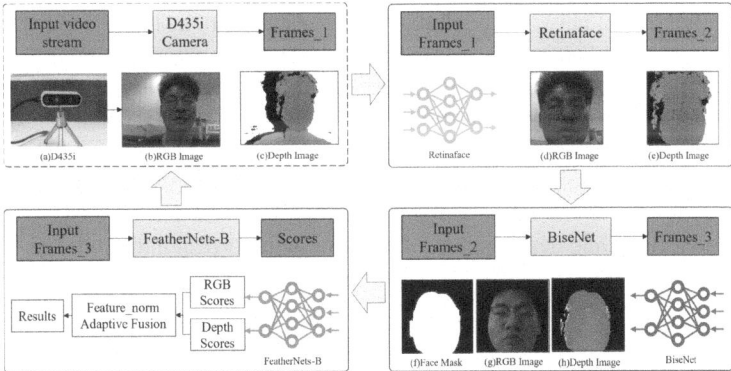

Fig. 1. A complete face anti spoofing process based on RGB-D adaptive fusion score based on image quality

3.2 RGB-D Scores Adaptive Fusion

Numerous methods and concepts exist for the fusion of RGB and depth image features. RGB images are adept at capturing nuanced color variations in a face, including skin tone, shadows, and highlights. These images also encompass texture and detailed information about the face, which is crucial in face anti-counterfeiting as this data is challenging to replicate. However, RGB images only provide planar information about the face and are sensitive to lighting conditions. The quality of RGB images is also influenced by external factors such as weather and noise, which can lead to blurring, distortion, or noise in the image, thereby affecting the accuracy of vivisection. In contrast, depth images offer information about the three-dimensional shape and structure of objects in a scene. In the context of face anti-counterfeiting, depth images can capture details about the 3D shape of the face, including facial undulations, nose height, and eye depth. While traditional 2D RGB images are susceptible to deception by photos and videos, depth images possess the capability to detect the three-dimensional shape of an object, thereby facilitating accurate recognition barring flat prosthetic attacks. Furthermore, depth images exhibit less dependence on lighting variations and surface textures, maintaining their utility even under suboptimal lighting conditions. In comparison to RGB images, depth images demonstrate superior resilience when confronted with accessories such as eyeglasses, masks, and hats that obscure or alter facial features. Given these considerations, RGB and depth images can synergistically enhance each other's capabilities in preventing face spoofing, thereby improving the accuracy and robustness of live detection models against a variety of attacks including photos, videos, 3D masks, and head models.

Given the unique characteristics of various data types and the influence of image quality on prediction outcomes, we employ feature norm to adaptively fuse RGB image and depth image scores. Face anti-spoofing can be conceptualized as a binary classification challenge, where all test types except for real-person tests are considered to attack faces. Utilizing the FeatherNetB [14] network as a foundation, the feature norm of the images is computed during the forward propagation of the network. Both RGB and depth data are employed to train two distinct model classifiers. As depicted in Fig. 2, batches of images are fed into the neural network to yield a feature vector with a shape of (1,1024). This data undergoes normalization via the BatchNorm function before its two-dimensional paradigm is computed, serving as the feature paradigm in this study, as represented by Eq. (1). The feature norm represents the image's quality without necessitating additional computations. The refined RGB and depth images are then inputted into their respective models—the RGB model and the depth model—both trained using FeatherNetB as a framework. The network model subsequently provides the true and spoofed probabilities for each paired RGB and depth image, along with their corresponding feature norm.

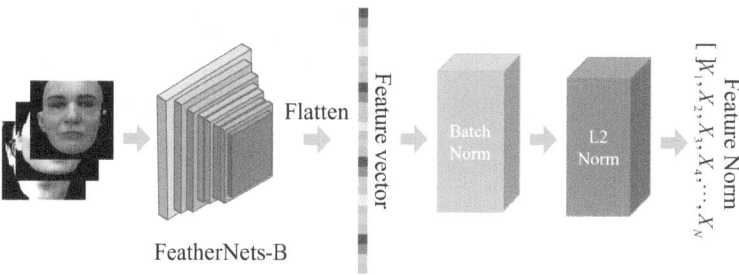

Fig. 2. Image feature norm calculation process based on FeatherNets extraction

In Eq. (1), X_F represents the feature norm, where $x_1, x_2, \cdots x_n$ is the 1024 elements in the normalized feature vector.

$$X_F = \sqrt{x_1^2 + x_2^2 + \cdots + x_n^2}. \tag{1}$$

The final weighted score for face anti-spoofing prediction can be calculated by integrating the true probability, deception probability, and image feature norm derived from both RGB and depth images. The computation process is outlined in Eq. (2).

$$S_{Ff} = \frac{e^{x_i}}{e^{x_i} + e^{x_j}} S_{if} + \frac{e^{x_j}}{e^{x_i} + e^{x_j}} S_{jf}, S_{Fr} = \frac{e^{x_i}}{e^{x_i} + e^{x_j}} S_{ir} + \frac{e^{x_j}}{e^{x_i} + e^{x_j}} S_{jr}. \tag{2}$$

In Eq. (2), S_{Ff} represents the final score predicted by the model indicative of a spoofing attack, while S_{if} and S_{jf} represent the scores predicted by the RGB and depth models respectively, indicating that the image is a spoofing attack. Similarly, in Eq. (2), S_{Fr} denote the final score predicted by the model as a real face, and the scores S_{if}, S_{jf} predicted by the RGB and depth models respectively, indicating that the image is a real face. The x_i, x_j represents the image quality indicator, with its calculation process detailed in Eq. (3).

$$x_i, x_j = \frac{h(X_F - \mu_x)}{\sigma_x}. \tag{3}$$

In Eq. (3), the feature norm X_F computed above are normalized by batch statistics μ_x and σ_x. In particular, μ_x and σ_x are the mean and standard deviation of a batch of feature norm, respectively. To make most values fall in the interval $[-1, 1]$, the parameter h, is introduced and empirically set to 0.33.

In this study, the issue of face anti-spoofing is conceptualized as a binary classification problem. The final predicted real score S_{Fr} and attack score S_{Ff} are derived from the RGB image score and the depth image score. The magnitude of these two scores is then compared. If $S_{Fr} \geq S_{Ff}$, the test subject is identified as a real person. Conversely, if $S_{Fr} < S_{Ff}$, the test subject is classified as an attacking face.

4 Experiments

Datasets: Two publicly available datasets are utilized: CASIA-SURF and 3DMAD. The CASIA-SURF dataset comprises 21,000 videos of attacks on printed faces across three modalities (RGB, Depth, and IR), which contain real individuals and six different types of printed faces. The 3DMAD dataset contains 76,500 images of 17 individuals with real individuals and 3D mask attack data.

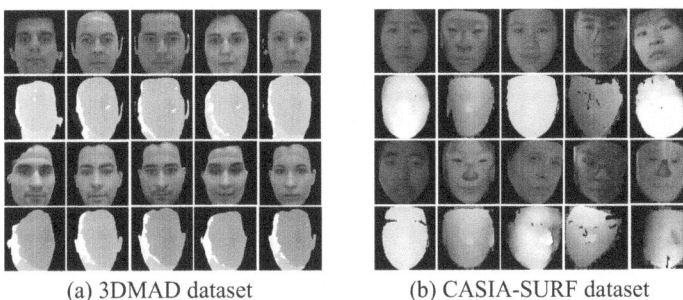

(a) 3DMAD dataset   (b) CASIA-SURF dataset

Fig. 3. Typical Examples of public datasets. The first and third lines are preprocessed faces. The second and fourth lines are their corresponding facial depth maps.

Data Processing: The 3DMAD dataset aligns and normalizes the images using Retinaface, unifying all image dimensions to 112×112 pixels. A face mask is subsequently generated via the BiseNet segmentation model, which delineates the facial and background regions within the images. The images containing facial data are then enhanced to create a 3DMAD dataset comprising 44,370 RGB images and depth images, 70% of the images were set as the training set, with the live target label as 0 and all other labels set to 1. The remaining 30% was used as the test set for our experiments. Some examples of the dataset's images are presented in Fig. 3 (a). CASIA-SURF was used with the dataset that has been processed and released by the original authors for use and is displayed in Fig. 3 (b).

Deployment Details: The FeatherNetB network structure was used to train the model using the Adam optimizer with an initial learning rate of 0.01 and an empirical learning rate decay strategy with a decay factor of 0.6 per generation. The training process was continued for 300 iterations to achieve convergence. The algorithm was implemented in PyTorch 1.12.0 on Windows and trained on a Nvidia 3090 GPU with a batch size of 32.

4.1 Comparisons with the State-of-the-Art

To evaluate the performance of the proposed adaptive fusion multi-modal scoring method based on image quality, the method is compared with several representative multi-modal live detection methods. Firstly, the RGB model and depth model are trained with the same dataset (3DMAD and CASIA-SURF) respectively and perform model evaluation using their test sets for each. The three methods (RGB-based method, depth-based method, and the multi-model score adaptive fusion scoring method) are tested independently. Following this, several important measures such as TPR (True Positive Rate), BPCER (Live Attack Classification Error Rate), APCER (Artifact Attack Classification Error Rate), and ACER (Average Attack Error Rate) are recorded, as well as the comparison results of our proposed method with other methods on different datasets are shown in Table 1 and Table 2.

Table 1. Comparison of our other methods on the CASIA-SURF dataset. All four methods except ours are fusions of RGB, Depth, and IR modal data.

Method	TPR (%)		APCER (%)	BPCER (%)	ACER (%)
	@FPR = 10^{-2}	@FPR = 10^{-3}			
NHF fusion (2019) [11]	89.1	33.6	5.6	3.8	4.7
Single-Scale SE fusion (2019) [11]	96.7	81.8	3.8	1	2.4
Multi-Scale SE fusion (2020) [15]	99.8	98.4	1.6	0.08	0.8
PSMM-Net (2021) [16]	99.9	99.3	0.5	0.02	0.2
Ours	99.93	98.7	0.9	0.04	0.47

The proposed method is tested on the CASIA-SURF dataset and also compared with the existing well-performing methods. As illustrated in Table 1, the maximum value of 99.93% is achieved by our method at TPR@FPR = 10–2 and only drops 0.6% from the SOTA at TPR@FPR = 10–3. Although the APCER, BPCER, and ACER are slightly lower than SOTA, our method only uses RGB and depth images (compared with three modalities of information in SOTA), and the network structure used is FeatherNetsB, which is a very lightweight network with only 0.35M parameters. This facilitates the deployment of face anti-spoofing algorithms on embedded devices.

As demonstrated in Table 2, the proposed method performs the best on the 3DMAD dataset compared to the other methods in various measures. in addition, the TPR reaches 100% at FPR = 10–2 as well as at FPR = 10–3.

Furthermore, the RGB dataset and Depth dataset of CASIA-SURF and 3DMAD are used for the training of the FeatherNetB model, respectively, and the performance of

Table 2. Comparison with other methods on the 3DMAD dataset

Method	TPR (%)		APCER (%)	BPCER (%)	ACER (%)
	@FPR = 10^{-2}	@FPR = 10^{-3}			
TransFAS (2023) [17]	-	-	5	17.5	11.2
AttackNet (2024) [18]	1	1	-	-	-
Ours	1	1	0	1.86	0.93

the three methods is compared. As illustrated in Table 3, we can find it can be seen that the RGB model performs well on the 3DMAD dataset but poorly on the CASIA-SURF dataset. On the contrary, the Depth-based method performs better on the CASIA-SURF dataset than the 3DMAD dataset. It is worth pointing out that based on the integration of depth information with RGB information, our method not only improves the robustness of the model to different types of attacks, but also performs better on both datasets, and our method achieves 100% TPR on the 3DMAD dataset.

Table 3. Performance of our method on the dataset

Modality	CASIA-SURF			3DMAD		
	TPR (%)		ACER (%)	TPR (%)		ACER (%)
	FPR = 10^{-2}	FPR = 10^{-3}		FPR = 10^{-2}	FPR = 10^{-3}	
RGB	70.45	36.14	23.99	99.57	98.78	2.94
Depth	99.66	94.96	0.58	72.28	69.77	14.5
Ours (RGB + Depth)	99.93	98.7	0.47	1	1	0.93

4.2 Live Testing in Actual Scene

For real-world testing, our dataset was collected with 8 real people, 6 different printed masks, and 12 3D silicone head molds. The attack types encompassed real individuals wearing various printed faces and 3D silicone head molds. The dataset was procured using a D435i camera, with 100 pairs of high-quality RGB and depth images collected for each distinct object. Each pair of images underwent sequential detection, localization, and cropping for faces, which were then input into the BiseNet segmentation model to generate a face mask, thereby preserving only facial information. Subsequently, the images of facial information were augmented by flipping and rotating, resulting in a dataset comprising 39,990 pairs of RGB and depth images, as depicted in Fig. 4.

To verify the feasibility of our method in practical applications, we developed a user interface (UI) based on PyQt and conducted real-world PC-based detection experiments.

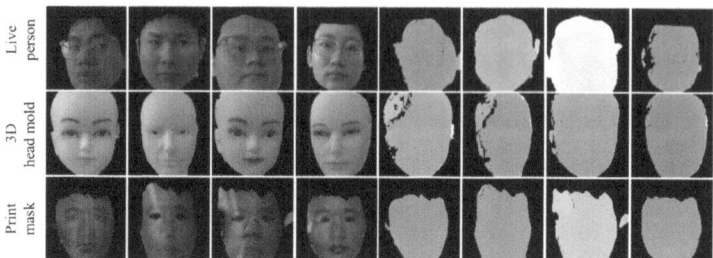

Fig. 4. Dataset collected by D435i camera in real scenarios

The experiment included four attack modes (real person, printed mask, 3D silicone head model, and flat-screen playback). Each mode was tested 100 times, including 50 frontal and 50 small-angle head turns in posture, for a total of 400 times. The number of successes and failures of each attack mode were counted to calculate the accuracy.

As demonstrated in Table 4, Target RGB and depth data are gathered by the D435i camera and fed into the neural network model for detection. Under attacks from real humans, printed masks, and flat-panel playback video, the accuracy of our methodology is 100%. In addition, the system also achieved 100% accuracy in detecting frontal poses in the face of more challenging 3D head model attacks. The face anti-spoofing system can achieve heightened security if the test subject is confined to a frontal stance.

Table 4. Test results for different attack types in real-world environments

	Live People		Print Mask		Pad Video		Head Mold	
	Front	Turn Head	Front	Turn Head	Front	Turn Head	Front	Turn Head
Test Times	50	50	50	50	50	50	50	50
Right Times	50	50	50	50	50	50	50	48
Accuracy (%)	100	100	100	100	100	100	100	96

5 Conclusion

In the field of face anti-spoofing tasks utilizing multimodal data, numerous studies have focused on fusion at both the score level and feature level. However, there is a notable absence of research on adaptive fusion at the score level. In this paper, a strategy for adaptively fusing RGB image scores with depth image scores is introduced, taking into account image quality. Initially, RGB and depth models are trained by using the Feather-NetB network, subsequently obtaining a pair of RGB and depth image scores by inputting corresponding image pairs. Then a method is introduced to compute a feature paradigm that characterizes image quality based on this paradigm, which is determined during network forward propagation. Finally, a method based on feature norm adaptive fusion of RGB and depth scores is proposed to obtain the final results. Extensive experiments are conducted to compare our method with other approaches across various datasets and to test different attack types in a real-world setting. The comprehensive experimental results underscore the effectiveness of our proposed method. However, the method in this paper will be affected by the environmental exposure, and the feature level adaptive fusion is not designed in this paper. How to adaptively fuse image features according to the image quality is also the focus of our subsequent research.

Acknowledgement. This work was supported by the National Natural Science Foundation of China (No. 52105505).

References

1. Lu, J., Liong, V.E., Wang, G., et al.: Joint feature learning for face recognition. IEEE Trans. Inf. Forensics Secur. **10**(7), 1371–1383 (2015)
2. Liu, A., Zhao, C., Yu, Z., et al.: Contrastive context-aware learning for 3d high-fidelity mask face presentation attack detection. IEEE Trans. Inf. Forensics Secur. **17**, 2497–2507 (2022)
3. George, A., Mostaani, Z., Geissenbuhler, D., et al.: Biometric face presentation attack detection with multi-channel convolutional neural network. IEEE Trans. Inf. Forensics Secur. **15**, 42–55 (2019)
4. Ng, E.S., Chia, A.Y.S.: Face verification using temporal affective cues. In: Proceedings of the 21st International Conference on Pattern Recognition, pp. 1249–1252 (2012)
5. Yang, X., Luo, W., Bao, L., et al.: Face anti-spoofing: model matters, so does data. In: Proceedings of the IEEE/CVF Conference on Computer Vision and Pattern Recognition, pp. 3507–3516 (2019)
6. Maatta, J., Hadid, A., Pietikainen, M.: Face spoofing detection from single images using micro-texture analysis. In: Proceedings of International Joint Conference on Biometrics, pp. 1–7 (2011)
7. Boulkenafet, Z., Komulainen, J., Hadid, A.: Face spoofing detection using colour texture analysis. IEEE Trans. Inf. Forensics Secur. **11**(8), 1818–1830 (2016)
8. Liang, B., Wang, Z., Huang, B., et al.: Depth map guided triplet network for deepfake face detection. Neural Netw. **159**, 34–42 (2023)
9. George, A., Marcel, S.: Cross modal focal loss for RGBD face anti-spoofing. In: Proceedings of the IEEE/CVF Conference on Computer Vision and Pattern Recognition, pp. 7882–7891 (2021)
10. Yu, Z., Liu, A., Zhao, C., et al.: Flexible-modal face anti-spoofing: a benchmark. In: Proceedings of the IEEE/CVF Conference on Computer Vision and Pattern Recognition, pp. 6345–6350 (2023)
11. Zhang, S., Wang, X., Liu, A., et al.: A dataset and benchmark for large-scale multi-modal face anti-spoofing. In: Proceedings of the IEEE/CVF Conference on Computer Vision and Pattern Recognition, pp. 919–928 (2019)
12. Li, L., Yao, Z., Gao, S., et al.: Face anti-spoofing via jointly modeling local texture and constructed depth. Eng. Appl. Artif. Intell. **133**, 108345 (2024)
13. Deng, P., Ge, C., Wei, H., et al.: Multimodal contrastive learning for face anti-spoofing. Eng. Appl. Artif. Intell. **129**, 107600 (2024)

14. Zhang, P., Zou, F., Wu, Z., et al.: FeatherNets: convolutional neural networks as light as feather for face anti-spoofing. In: Proceedings of the IEEE/CVF Conference on Computer Vision and Pattern Recognition Workshops (2019)
15. Zhang, S., Liu, A., Wan, J., et al.: Casia-surf: A large-scale multi-modal benchmark for face anti-spoofing. IEEE Trans. Biom. Behav. Identity Sci. **2**(2), 182–193 (2020)
16. Liu, A., Tan, Z., Wan, J., et al.: CASIA-SURF CeFA: a benchmark for multi-modal cross-ethnicity face anti-spoofing. In: Proceedings of the IEEE/CVF Winter Conference on Applications of Computer Vision, pp. 1179–1187 (2021)
17. Chaudhry, D., Goel, H., Verma, B.: TransFAS: transformer-based network for face anti-spoofing using token guided inspection. In: 2023 IEEE 8th International Conference for Convergence in Technology (I2CT), pp. 1–7. IEEE (2023)
18. Kuznetsov, O., Zakharov, D., Frontoni, E., et al.: AttackNet: enhancing biometric security via tailored convolutional neural network architectures for liveness detection. Comput. Secur. **141**, 103828 (2024)

Enhancing Deepfake Detection via Adversarial Generative Learning

Zengqiang Chen, Xudong Wang, and Yuezun Li[✉]

School of Computer science and Technology, Ocean University of China, Qingdao, China
`liyuezun@outlook.com`

Abstract. Deepfake technology generates highly realistic videos effortlessly, raising serious concerns about privacy violations, misinformation, and financial fraud. Detecting Deepfakes is the most effective solution to address these issues. While existing detection methods perform well on standard protocols, they struggle with real-world scenarios due to constantly emerging unknown forgery types. To enhance detection generalization, recent methods augment training images by synthesizing diverse forged faces (pseudo-fake faces) and identifying common forgery features. In this paper, we describe a new augmentation-based method to further improve the detection generalization. Our method leverages adversarial generative learning, which adaptively synthesizes effective pseudo-fake faces based on a generator network, a face synthesizer, a face reconstruction, and a discriminator. Extensive experiments on several public datasets demonstrate the efficacy of our method.

Keywords: Deepfake Detection · Adversarial Training

1 Introduction

Deepfake technology has garnered widespread attention because it generates high-realistic videos effortlessly, leading to serious concerns, such as violating personal privacy, spreading misinformation, causing large-scale financial fraud, etc. [2,3,16,23]. Therefore, detecting Deepfakes is important in mitigating these security concerns. Many efforts have been proposed to detect Deepfakes [5,6,21,26,32], determining whether the input face is authentic or not. These methods have shown promising performance on standard evaluation protocols, where the training and testing set are from the same dataset. However, such evaluation protocols are not applicable in real-world scenarios, as the evaluated videos are often crafted by unknown Deepfake technology, resulting in a severe distribution discrepancy with the training data. Such discrepancy poses a significant challenge for practical Deepfake detection

To address this concern, several recent methods have concentrated on enhancing detection generalization, *i.e.*, detecting unknown Deepfakes. Works such as [19,43] attempt to increase training diversity by synthesizing new forged faces (pseudo-fake faces) through empirically designed augmentation techniques. However, the choices of these augmentation strategies are limited, restricting data diversity. Other methods uncover the common forgery features like detail discrepancies [25] and frequency characteristics [24,32], but these features are often subtle and easily disrupted by simple image processing operations (*e.g.*, JPEG compression). The work [9] improves data augmentation with an adversarial training strategy, using a generator to create manipulation configurations and a discriminator to verify if the synthesized faces can be detected. While it shows promising results, the diversity of pseudo-fake faces can be further improved.

In this paper, we follow the spirit of [9] and describe a new augmentation-based method for generalizable Deepfake detection. Our method contains four major components: a generator network for creating augmentation types, a face synthesizer for blending two faces based on the created augmentation types, a decoder network for face reconstruction, and a discriminator for enhancing the quality of reconstructed faces. **Compared to [9], our method features three key improvements:** 1) The generator network not only creates manipulation types but also extracts the identity features, to make the generator more aware of the input context. 2) We introduce a decoder network to reconstruct the synthesized faces based on the features from the generator network, to explicitly incorporate the identity information into the augmented faces. 3) The discriminator is designed to distinguish the manipulation types as well as the identity information. It also performs a binary classification to determine whether the input image is real or fake. Extensive experiments on FF++[33], DFDC [1], CelebDF [23], and DeeperForensics-1.0 [16] datasets demonstrate the efficacy of our method, outperforming most advanced detectors.

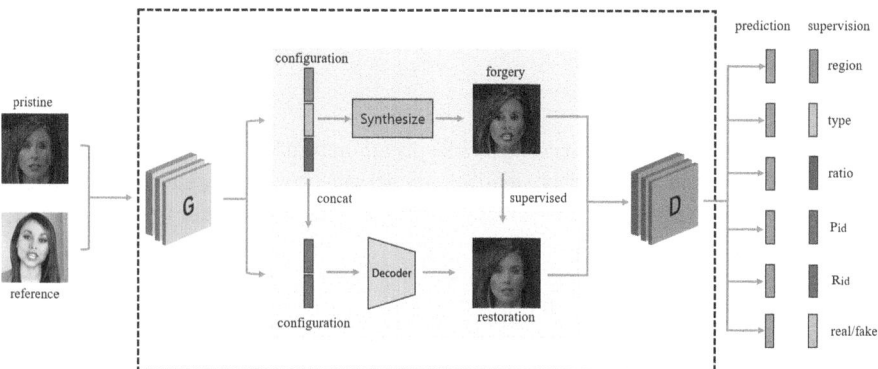

Fig. 1. Overview of the proposed method., illustrating the process of synthesizing a forgery from a pristine image using the generator (G) and restoring the pristine image using the decoder, followed by predictions and supervisions for various tasks such as region, type, ratio, P_{id}, R_{id}, and real/fake detection by the discriminator (D)

2 Related Works

In recent years, Deepfake technology has achieved significant advancement, creating fake videos with highly realistic. While it holds positive potential for applications in entertainment and virtual reality, its misuse has led to serious risks [11,22]. To counter these negative impacts, extensive studies have been proposed to detect Deepfake [5–7,12,14,18,19,21,24–26,30–34,37]. These methods typically employ Deep Neural Networks (DNNs) to learn the detectable forgery features, including the physiological signals [21,30,34], the artifacts in image and frequency domains [6,18,24], and the holistic data-driven strategies [5,12,19]. Although these methods have shown promising results in public datasets, they are ineffective in detecting unknown forgery videos, limiting their practical application in real-world scenarios.

Recently, several methods have been proposed to detect unknown forgery videos, e.g., [5,6,9,12,19,26,43]. These approaches focus on improving the detection performance by leveraging various techniques such as locality-aware autoencoders [12], face X-ray methods [19], and two-branch recurrent networks [26]. However, how to effectively enhance the generalization of Deepfake detection remains an open and hot problem.

3 Proposed Method

3.1 Overview

We introduce an adversarial generative learning strategy to synthesize effective pseudo-fake faces, to enhance the generalization ability of Deepfake detectors. Figure 1 shows the overview of our method. Our method contains four components: a generator network, a face synthesizer, a face reconstructor, and a discriminator, respectively.

In the training stage, we take two face images as input. One is a pristine image and the other is a randomly selected reference image. These two images are concatenated and fed into the generator network (G) to generate manipulation configurations and identity information corresponding to the two images. Based on these manipulation configurations, a face synthesizer (S) is designed to create pseudo-fake faces. Then we describe a face reconstructor (R), which takes the identity information as input and reconstructs the pseudo-fake faces created by the face synthesizer S. The discriminator (D) is developed to extract the manipulation configurations and the identity information, as well as the authentic prediction (real or fake). Once training is complete, we only employ the discriminator D is used to detect Deepfakes.

3.2 Framework

Generator Network. Inspired by [9], we design a generator to create the manipulation configurations. In addition, we extract the identity information of the paired input images as the important feature for augmentation. Specifically,

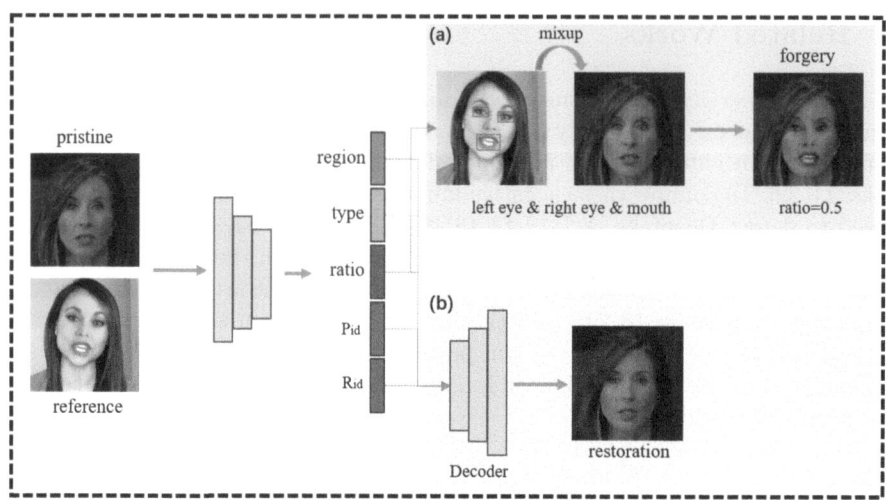

Fig. 2. This image illustrates an image processing pipeline, consisting of the forgery part and the decoder part (i.e. (a) and (b)). In the forgery part (a), we select the left eye, right eye, and mouth regions from the reference image and apply the mixup method to blend them with the pristine image, setting the ratio to 0.5, thus generating a forged image. In the decoder part (b), the decoder reconstructs the input image to produce the final restored image. The entire process is visually detailed in the diagram

the generator network G_θ takes a raw image $I_p \in \mathbb{R}^{H \times W \times 3}$ and a reference image $I_f \in \mathbb{R}^{H \times W \times 3}$ as input and outputs five types of configuration information: 1) The fake region reference index R_g: specifies the regions of the facial image to be synthesized; 2) The mix type reference index T_g: represents the blending techniques applied; 3) The mix ratio A_g: denotes the blending ratios used to combine the original and synthesized images; 4) The real identity information P_{id}: indicates the identity information of the real image; 5) The fake identity information R_{id}: represents the identity information of the forged image.

Face Synthesizer. Given the generated configuration parameters R_g, T_g, and A_g, we can create pseudo-fake faces by the face synthesizer. Concretely, we first utilize R_g to determine the regions of the face to be manipulated. Then T_g is applied to blend the original and reference images according to the specified technique. Finally, A_g determines the blending ratio between the original and reference images, ensuring a realistic integration of facial features, as shown in Fig. 2.

Face Reconstructor. We reconstruct the pseudo-fake faces using the manipulation configuration and identity information extracted by the generator network, as shown in Fig. 2. Since identity swapping is the critical step in creating pseudo-fake faces, we extract identity information in the generator, which instructs the face reconstructor to learn the face blending process adaptively. It receives a vector concatenated by five configuration parameters: P_{id}, R_{id}, R_g, T_g, and A_g.

The reconstruction process is supervised by the pseudo-fake faces created by the face synthesizer.

Discriminator. The discriminator network is designed to differentiate between real and fake images and predict five types of configuration information. Through adversarial training, the discriminator learns to identify the reconstructed faces with detailed feedback, which, in turn, forces the face reconstructor to create more realistic fake faces.

3.3 Objectives and Training

We adopt a multi-task learning strategy, enabling the model to simultaneously learn the main task and a series of auxiliary self-supervised tasks. Each task and its corresponding loss function are described in detail below.

Main Task Loss $\mathcal{L}_m$. The main task is a binary classification task of predicting whether a given input image is real or fake. Following previous work [9,25], we adopt the AM-Softmax Loss[38] as the main task loss function. Compared to conventional cross-entropy loss, this loss effectively reduces intra-class variation and increases inter-class differences.

Self-Supervised Loss $\mathcal{L}_s$. Our method is improved based on [9], which introduces five loss terms: the reconstruction loss $\mathcal{L}_r$, the identity consistency loss $\mathcal{L}_{id}$, the forgery region loss $\mathcal{L}_f$, the blending type loss $\mathcal{L}_{bt}$, and the blending ratio loss $\mathcal{L}_{br}$.

- **Reconstruction Loss** $\mathcal{L}_r$. We apply Mean Square Error (MSE) loss to measure the difference between the reconstructed face and the synthesized face.
- **Identity Consistency Loss** $\mathcal{L}_{id}$. For each predicted identity information from the discriminator, we compute the cosine similarity with its corresponding identity information from the generator. Thus this loss can be defined as

$$\mathcal{L}_{id} = -\cos(P'_{id}, P_{id}) - \cos(R'_{id}, R_{id}), \tag{1}$$

where P'_{id} and R'_{id} represent the predicted identity information by discriminator and P'_{id} and R'_{id} represent the extracted identity information from generator.
- **Forgery Region Loss** $\mathcal{L}_f$. This loss corresponds to predicting the forgery mask using an additional head attached to the discriminator. Denote M as the forgery mask represented by the configuration R_g and M' as the predicted mask recovered from the discriminator. Specifically, if the input image is forged, M is the mask provided by the dataset; if the image is real and has not undergone any forgery process, M is a matrix of zeros; when forgery is applied to a real image, M represents the mask generated by the synthesizer. We employ the ℓ_1 norm to measure the error as

$$\mathcal{L}_f = \|M - M'\|_1, \tag{2}$$

- **Blending Type Loss** $\mathcal{L}_{bt}$. This task aims to predict the blending method used in the input image. The ground-truth blending type T depends on the input data category: newly forged images, real images, and original forged images from the training dataset. The value of T ranges from $\{0, 1, 2, 3\}$, corresponding to different blending methods: alpha, Poisson[13], mixup and do-nothing. To evaluate this, the task uses AM-Softmax Loss[38] to compute $\mathcal{L}_{bt}$.
- **Blending Ratio Loss** $\mathcal{L}_{br}$. This task estimates the blending ratio A' used during forgery synthesis, relevant only when mixup blending is applied. A represents the ground truth blending ratio and is a continuous value in the range $[0, 1]$. The ℓ_1 norm is used to calculate $\mathcal{L}_{br}$:

$$\mathcal{L}_{br} = \tau \times \|A - A'\|_1, \tag{3}$$

where τ ensures that $\mathcal{L}_{br}$ is active only for mixup blending scenarios.

Overall Objectives. To better utilize the forgery enhancement space, we use adversarial training to dynamically construct the most challenging auxiliary tasks. Specifically, we use the synthesizer network $G(\cdot, \theta)$ as the generator and adversarially train it to maximize the training loss of the target discriminator (i.e., the detector network $D(\cdot, \cdot)$). In this process, the decoder receives the output from the generator and generates forged images to challenge the detector's discrimination ability. The optimization process can be expressed as:

$$\min_w \max_\theta \mathcal{L}, \text{ s.t. } \mathcal{L}(\theta, w) = \mathcal{L}_m + \alpha \mathcal{L}_f + \mu \mathcal{L}_{bt} + \gamma \mathcal{L}_{br} + \beta \mathcal{L}_r + \delta \mathcal{L}_{id} + \eta \mathcal{L}_s, \tag{4}$$

where α, μ, γ, β, δ, and η are weight hyperparameters. Note that θ represents all parameters in the generation process. According to the standard adversarial training strategy, we can approximate the solution to the above optimization problem by iteratively updating the discriminator (D) and the generator (G).

Reinforcement Learning Based Optimization. First, let's describe the learning mechanism of the discriminator. Equation((4)) represents the minimization problem with respect to w. While keeping the current generator parameters θ fixed, we set the learning rate to η and the batch size to N, and perform gradient descent updates:

$$w^{t+1} = w^t - \frac{\eta}{N} \sum_{n=1}^{N} \nabla_{w^t} \mathcal{L}_n(\theta^t, w^t), \tag{5}$$

where $\mathcal{L}_n$ denotes the loss for the n-th sample in the mini-batch. The generator aims to increase the discriminator's training loss by synthesizing more challenging samples, thereby encouraging the discriminator to learn more general features in a zero-sum adversarial framework. It uses the decoder to produce realistic reconstructed images and supervises them against forged images from a forgery configuration pool. This promotes diverse and challenging outputs to enhance performance. Mathematically, this can be expressed as a maximization problem according to Eq.((4)).

$$\theta^{t+1} = \arg\max_{\theta^t} \mathcal{L}(w^{t+1}, \theta^t), \tag{6}$$

Since the sampling operation in adversarial training is non-differentiable, directly solving Eq.((6)) to update the generator parameters θ is challenging. To address this issue, we use the REINFORCE[39] algorithm to approximate the gradient calculation for θ:

$$\theta^{t+1} = \theta^t + \epsilon \nabla_{\theta^t} \mathcal{L}_b \approx \theta^t + \epsilon \frac{1}{M} \sum_{m=1}^{M} \mathcal{L}_b \nabla_{\theta^t} \log p_m, \tag{7}$$

where $\mathcal{L}_b = \frac{1}{N}\sum_{n=1}^{N}\mathcal{L}_n(w^{t+1},\theta^t)$ is the average loss over the batch, M denotes the number of configuration sequences selected in the batch, and p_m represents the probability of generating R_g and T_g, which are estimated by the synthesizer network $G(\cdot,\theta)$.

4 Experiments

4.1 Settings

Training Datasets. This study draws on the latest deepfake detection methods[8,9,15,18,19,24,25,32,37,40] and trains models on the Faceforensics++ (FF++) dataset.[33] The dataset contains 1,000 original videos, with 720 used for training, 140 for testing, and the remainder for validation. All videos are forged using four advanced deepfake techniques: Deepfake (DF)[2], Face2Face (F2F)[36], FaceSwap (FS)[3], and NeuralTextures (NT)[35], and are produced with varying compression levels: RAW, high quality (HQ), and low quality (LQ). In the experiments, we evaluate using HQ and LQ versions, with the HQ version serving as the default training set.

Testing Datasets. To evaluate the generalization of our method, we selected the following three benchmark datasets for experiments: CelebDF[23], which includes 408 real videos and 795 fake videos synthesized using improved deepfake techniques; Deepfake Detection Challenge (DFDC)[1], which contains over 1,000 real videos and over 4,000 fake videos manipulated by Deepfake, GAN, and non-learning methods; and DeeperForensics-1.0 (DF1.0)[16], which was generated using the DFVAE[16] method and contains over 11,000 fake videos.

Implementation Details. We built the synthesizer and detector networks based on the Xception[10] network pre-trained on ImageNet, and used the Adam[17] optimizer for training. The learning rates for the synthesizer and detector networks are set to 2×10^{-4} and 5×10^{-5}, respectively, with a fixed batch size of 32. In the loss function, the hyperparameters are set as follows: $\alpha = 0.1$, $\mu = 0.05$, $\gamma = 0.1$, $\beta = 0.05$, $\delta = 0.05$, and $\eta = 0.1$.

4.2 Generalizability Comparisons

To comprehensively evaluate the generalization of our method, we compared it with several state-of-the-art methods, including Xception[33], Face X-ray[19], F3Net[32], RFM[37], SRM[25], SLADD[9], and UCF[40]. To ensure a fair comparison, we used the official implementations of these methods: Xception[33], RFM[37], SRM[25], and SLADD[9] provided their code.

Generalizations Under Different Datasets. We conducted challenging experiments to evaluate the generalization of our method. We trained all comparative models using the four forgery methods from the FF++ dataset[33] and evaluated them on benchmark datasets such as CelebDF[23], DFDC[1], and DF1.0[16]. This setup effectively tests the model's ability to generalize to different forgery techniques and datasets, as the original and forged images in the test datasets were not present in the training set.

We used the AUC metric to compare the performance of different methods, as shown in Table 1. Our method outperforms others, demonstrating its effectiveness. SRM[25] and F3Net[32] rely on high-frequency image components to detect forgeries, but their generalization performance is inferior to ours. This could be due to their dependency on specific dataset characteristics like those in FF++[33]. RFM[37] enhances generalization by using multiple facial regions, but still suffers from data source bias. Face X-ray[19] uses mixed artifacts for generalization, but struggles when these artifacts vary across datasets. Xception[33], without any enhancements, shows significant performance decline on new forgeries. SLADD[9] and UCF[40] perform well in certain tests but lack comprehensive adversarial augmentation and self-supervised tasks, limiting their generalization.

Generalizations Under Different Compression Levels. Given that forged images may undergo various post-processing steps such as compression, deployed deepfake detectors must be capable of defending against these unknown processing steps. To evaluate the model's generalization capability across different

Table 1. Performance comparison of different methods. The first row shows the training data, and the second row shows the corresponding test datasets. Our method outperforms the compared models in terms of AUC across multiple test datasets

Method	DF			F2F			FS			NT		
	DFDC	Celeb	DF1.0	DFDC	Celeb	DF1.0	DFDC	Celeb	DF1.0	DFDC	Celeb	DF1.0
Xception[33]	0.654	0.681	0.617	0.708	0.598	0.745	0.708	0.601	0.605	0.646	0.625	0.838
Face X-ray[19]	0.609	0.554	0.668	0.633	0.684	0.766	0.646	0.697	0.795	0.613	0.703	0.866
F3Net[32]	0.682	0.664	0.658	0.679	0.654	0.761	0.679	0.636	0.651	0.672	0.689	0.932
RFM[37]	0.758	0.723	0.717	0.736	0.663	0.732	0.714	0.591	0.714	0.726	0.600	0.846
SRM[25]	0.679	0.650	0.720	0.687	0.693	0.775	0.671	0.643	0.771	0.656	0.651	0.936
SLADD[9]	0.772	0.730	0.742	0.787	0.781	0.786	**0.742**	**0.800**	0.695	0.741	0.759	0.889
UCF[40]	0.767	**0.749**	0.870	0.765	0.782	0.908	0.711	**0.800**	0.943	**0.800**	**0.808**	0.943
Ours	**0.785**	0.734	**0.873**	**0.792**	**0.789**	**0.916**	0.728	0.742	**0.960**	0.760	0.764	**0.955**

Table 2. AUC comparison across different compression levels shows our method performs comparably to existing methods

Training set	Method	Testing set			
		LQ		HQ	
		DF	FS	DF	FS
NT	Xception [33]	0.587	0.517	0.770	0.718
	Face X-ray [19]	0.571	0.510	0.585	0.779
	F3Net [32]	0.583	0.519	0.805	0.612
	RFM[37]	0.558	0.516	0.798	0.639
	SRM[25]	0.555	0.529	0.838	**0.795**
	SLADD [9]	0.628	0.568	0.846	0.721
	Ours	**0.652**	**0.591**	**0.886**	0.721

Table 3. Performance comparison of various methods on F2F and FS datasets

Training set	Method	Testing set	
		F2F	FS
F2F	LAE[12]	0.909	0.632
	ClassNSeg [28]	0.928	0.541
	Forensic-Trans [11]	0.945	0.726
	SLADD[9]	0.960	**0.848**
	Ours	**0.977**	0.727

processing methods, we trained on the NT dataset and tested on DF and FS datasets with different compression levels.

Table 2 shows the AUC values for the evaluations. The results demonstrate that models[9,19,25,32,33,37] perform well with the same compression level for training and testing data. However, models that rely on subtle image patterns perform poorly on unknown LQ data due to compression-induced distortion of low-level visual features, as also noted by RFM[37]. Exploring more facial areas does not ensure good generalization across different compression levels. Our proposed method, which uses generic forgery configurations and a decoder module, outperforms other models and is less affected by compression levels. The improvements seen in models similar to Xception[33] are due to the adversarial self-supervision frameworks.

4.3 State-of-the-Art Comparisons

Comparison to Multi-Task Learning Detectors. Previous research, such as LAE[12], ClassNSeg[28], Forensic-Trans[11], and SLADD[9], adopted multi-task learning strategies for deepfake detection, recommending simultaneous classification and localization of fake regions. Unlike these methods, our approach is more comprehensive, improving detection accuracy and robustness. As shown in Table 3, while our method outperforms most others, it performs slightly worse on the FS[3] dataset compared to SLADD. This may be because SLADD focuses on identifying fake regions and utilizes multiple facial areas for feature extraction, capturing subtle changes introduced by FS techniques more effectively. Although

Table 5. To demonstrate the effectiveness of the proposed self-supervised auxiliary tasks, we use the AUC metric. We evaluate their impact by assigning zero weight to the corresponding loss functions, effectively disabling the self-supervised tasks

$\mathcal{L}_s$	$\mathcal{L}_{id}$	$\mathcal{L}_f$	$\mathcal{L}_{bt}$	$\mathcal{L}_{br}$	DF			F2F			FS			NT		
					DFDC	Celeb	DF1.0	DFDC	Celeb	DF1.0	DFDC	Celeb	DF1.0	DFDC	Celeb	DF1.0
-	-	-	-	-	0.717	0.703	0.674	0.739	0.778	0.735	0.737	0.644	0.602	0.662	0.722	0.794
-	-	✓	✓	✓	0.772	0.730	0.742	0.787	0.781	0.786	**0.742**	**0.800**	0.695	0.741	0.759	0.889
-	✓	✓	✓	✓	0.774	0.725	0.797	0.782	0.783	0.806	0.713	0.725	0.816	0.737	0.748	0.827
✓	-	✓	✓	✓	0.783	**0.740**	0.844	0.789	0.776	0.855	0.721	0.736	0.858	0.751	0.753	0.919
✓	✓	✓	✓	✓	**0.785**	0.734	**0.873**	**0.792**	**0.789**	**0.916**	0.728	0.742	**0.960**	**0.760**	**0.764**	**0.955**

our method enhances generalization, it also increases complexity, which may reduce precision in handling FS-specific detail changes.

Comparison to Other State-of-the-Art Detectors. To comprehensively evaluate our method, we compared it with several advanced models, including Two-stream[44], MesoNet[4], Headpose [41], FWA[22], VA-MLP[27], Capsule[29], SMIL[20], Two-branch[26], SPSL[24], MADD[42], SLADD[9], UCF[40], IID[15], and ETD[8]. We trained these models on the FF++ dataset[33] and tested them on both the FF++ and CelebDF[23] datasets. As shown in Table 4, our method performed exceptionally well on both datasets, achieving the best results on the CelebDF dataset, further demonstrating the effectiveness and superior generalization capability of our approach.

4.4 Ablation Study

We aimed to enhance the model's generalization capability by integrating auxiliary self-supervised tasks. An ablation study was conducted by setting each task's weight to zero to evaluate their impact. The auxiliary tasks include: Fake Region Estimation (L_R), Mixed Type Estimation (L_T), Mixed Ratio Estimation (L_A), and Identity Vector Estimation (L_{ID}). All models were trained on the FF++ dataset[33] and evaluated on benchmark

Table 4. The results of extensive evaluations in terms of AUC for several state-of-the-art models trained on the FF++ dataset are presented

Method	FF++	CelebDF
Two-stream[44]	0.701	0.538
Meso4[4]	0.847	0.548
MesoInception4[4]	0.830	0.536
FWA[22]	0.801	0.569
DSP-FWA[22]	0.930	0.646
Xception[17]	0.997	0.653
VA-MLP[27]	0.664	0.550
Headpose[41]	0.473	0.546
Capsule[29]	0.966	0.575
SMIL[20]	0.968	0.563
Two-branch[26]	0.932	0.734
SPSL[24]	0.969	0.724
MADD[42]	**0.998**	0.674
SLADD[9]	0.984	0.797
UCF[40]	0.981	0.802
IID[15]	0.994	0.783
ETD[8]	0.983	0.807
Ours	0.989	**0.809**

datasets using the same settings. Table 5 shows that each auxiliary task is crucial. The best performance is achieved when all tasks are integrated. Omitting any task leads to decreased performance, with significant drops when only L_R, L_T, and L_A are used. This validates the effectiveness of our self-supervised tasks.

5 Conclusions

This paper introduces an adversarial generative learning framework that can synthesize effective pseudo-fake faces to enhance detection generalization across different scenarios. Specifically, our method contains four key components: a generator to create manipulation configurations and identity information, a face synthesizer to generate pseudo-fake faces using configurations, a face reconstructor to synthesize pseudo-fake faces based on identity information and a discriminator to inspect the face authenticity. Experimental results demonstrate the superiority of our method on detecting both known and unknown Deepfakes.

Acknowledgement. This work was supported in part by the National Natural Science Foundation of China under Grant No.62402464, China Postdoctoral Science Foundation under Grant No.2021TQ0314 and Grant No.2021M703036.

References

1. Deepfake detection challenge. www.kaggle.com/c/deepfake-detection-challenge. Accessed 24 April 2021
2. Deepfakes. https://www.github.com/deepfakes/faceswap. Accessed 24 April 2021
3. Faceswap. https://www.github.com/MarekKowalski/FaceSwap. Accessed 24 April 2021
4. Afchar, D., Nozick, V., Yamagishi, J., Echizen, I.: Mesonet: a compact facial video forgery detection network. In: 2018 IEEE International Workshop on Information Forensics and Security (WIFS), pp. 1–7. IEEE (2018)
5. Agarwal, S., Farid, H., Gu, Y., He, M., Nagano, K., Li, H.: Protecting world leaders against deep fakes. In: CVPR Workshops, vol. 1, pp. 38 (2019)
6. Amerini, I., Galteri. L., Caldelli, R., Bimbo, A.D.: Deepfake video detection through optical flow based CNN. In: Proceedings of the IEEE/CVF International Conference on Computer Vision Workshops (2019)
7. Asnani, V., Yin, X., Hassner, T., Liu. X.: Reverse engineering of generative models: inferring model hyperparameters from generated images. IEEE Trans. Pattern Analy. Mach. Intell. (2023)
8. Ba, Z., et al.: Exposing the deception: uncovering more forgery clues for deepfake detection. In: Proceedings of the AAAI Conference on Artificial Intelligence, vol. 38, pp. 719–728 (2024)
9. Chen, L., Zhang, Y., Song, Y., Liu, L., Wang, J.: Self-supervised learning of adversarial example: towards good generalizations for deepfake detection. In: Proceedings of the IEEE/CVF Conference on Computer Vision and Pattern Recognition, pp. 18710–18719 (2022)
10. Chollet, F.: Xception: deep learning with depthwise separable convolutions. In: Proceedings of the IEEE Conference on Computer Vision and Pattern Recognition, pp. 1251–1258 (2017)

11. Cozzolino, D., Thies, J., Rössler, A., Riess, C., Nießner, M., Verdoliva, L.: Forensictransfer: weakly-supervised domain adaptation for forgery detection. arXiv preprint arXiv:1812.02510 (2018)
12. Du, M., Pentyala, S., Li, Y., Hu, X.: Towards generalizable deepfake detection with locality-aware autoencoder. In: Proceedings of the 29th ACM International Conference on Information & Knowledge Management, pp. 325–334 (2020)
13. Gangnet, M., Blake, A., et al.: Poisson image editing. In: ACM SIGGRAPH, pp. 313–318 (2003)
14. Haliassos, A., Vougioukas, K., Petridis, S., Pantic, M.: Lips don't lie: a generalisable and robust approach to face forgery detection. In: Proceedings of the IEEE/CVF Conference on Computer Vision and Pattern Recognition, pp. 5039–5049 (2021)
15. Huang, B., et al.: Implicit identity driven deepfake face swapping detection. In: Proceedings of the IEEE/CVF Conference on Computer Vision and Pattern Recognition, pp. 4490–4499 (2023)
16. Jiang, L., Li, R., Wu, W., Qian, C., Loy, C.C.: Deeperforensics-1.0: a large-scale dataset for real-world face forgery detection. In: Proceedings of the IEEE/CVF Conference on Computer Vision and Pattern Recognition, pp. 2889–2898 (2020)
17. Kingma, D.P., Ba, J:. Adam: a method for stochastic optimization. arXiv preprint arXiv:1412.6980 (2014)
18. Li, J., Xie, H., Li, J., Wang, Z., Zhang, Y.: Frequency-aware discriminative feature learning supervised by single-center loss for face forgery detection. In: Proceedings of the IEEE/CVF Conference on Computer Vision and Pattern Recognition, pp. 6458–6467 (2021)
19. Li, L., et al.: Face X-ray for more general face forgery detection. In: Proceedings of the IEEE/CVF Conference on Computer Vision and Pattern Recognition, pp. 5001–5010 (2020)
20. Li, X., et al.: Sharp multiple instance learning for deepfake video detection. In: Proceedings of the 28th ACM International Conference on Multimedia, pp. 1864–1872 (2020)
21. Li, Y., Chang, M.C., Lyu, S.: In Ictu Oculi: exposing AI created fake videos by detecting eye blinking. In: 2018 IEEE International Workshop on Information Forensics and Security (WIFS), pp. 1–7. IEEE (2018)
22. Li, Y., Lyu, S.: Exposing deepfake videos by detecting face warping artifacts. arXiv preprint arXiv:1811.00656 (2018)
23. Li, Y., Yang, X., Sun, P., Qi, H., Lyu, S.: Celeb-DF: a large-scale challenging dataset for deepfake forensics. In: Proceedings of the IEEE/CVF Conference on Computer Vision and Pattern Recognition, pp. 3207–3216 (2020)
24. Liu, H., et al.: Spatial-phase shallow learning: rethinking face forgery detection in frequency domain. In: Proceedings of the IEEE/CVF Conference on Computer Vision and Pattern Recognition, pp. 772–781 (2021)
25. Luo, Y., Zhang, Y., Yan, J., Liu, W.: Generalizing face forgery detection with high-frequency features. In: Proceedings of the IEEE/CVF Conference on Computer Vision and Pattern Recognition, pp. 16317–16326 (2021)
26. Masi, I., Killekar, A., Mascarenhas, R.M., Gurudatt, S.P., AbdAlmageed, W.: Two-branch recurrent network for isolating deepfakes in videos. In: Vedaldi, A., Bischof, H., Brox, T., Frahm, J.-M. (eds.) ECCV 2020. LNCS, vol. 12352, pp. 667–684. Springer, Cham (2020). https://doi.org/10.1007/978-3-030-58571-6_39
27. Matern, F., Riess, C., Stamminger, M.: Exploiting visual artifacts to expose deep-fakes and face manipulations. In: 2019 IEEE Winter Applications of Computer Vision Workshops (WACVW), pp. 83–92. IEEE (2019)

28. Nguyen, H.H., Fang, F., Yamagishi, J., Echizen, I.: Multi-task learning for detecting and segmenting manipulated facial images and videos. In: 2019 IEEE 10th International Conference on Biometrics Theory, Applications and Systems (BTAS), pp. 1–8. IEEE (2019)
29. Nguyen, H.H., Fang, F., Yamagishi, J., Echizen, I.: Capsule-forensics: Using capsule networks to detect forged images and videos. In: ICASSP 2019-2019 IEEE International Conference on Acoustics, Speech and Signal Processing (ICASSP), pp. 2307–2311. IEEE (2019)
30. Nirkin, Y., Wolf, L., Keller, Y., Hassner, T.: Deepfake detection based on discrepancies between faces and their context. IEEE Trans. Pattern Anal. Mach. Intell. **44**(10), 6111–6121 (2021)
31. Perez, L., Wang, J.: The effectiveness of data augmentation in image classification using deep learning. arXiv preprint arXiv:1712.04621 (2017)
32. Qian, Y., Yin, G., Sheng, L., Chen, Z., Shao, J.: Thinking in frequency: face forgery detection by mining frequency-aware clues. In: European Conference on Computer Vision, pp. 86–103. Springer (2020)
33. Rossler, A., Cozzolino, D., Verdoliva, L., Riess, C., Thies, J., Nießner, M.: Faceforensics++: learning to detect manipulated facial images. In: Proceedings of the IEEE/CVF International Conference on Computer Vision, pp. 1–11 (2019)
34. Sun, Z., Han, Y., Hua, Z., Ruan, N., Jia, W.: Improving the efficiency and robustness of deepfakes detection through precise geometric features. In: Proceedings of the IEEE/CVF Conference on Computer Vision and Pattern Recognition, pp. 3609–3618 (2021)
35. Thies, J., Zollhöfer, M., Nießner, M.: Deferred neural rendering: image synthesis using neural textures. ACM Trans. Graph. (TOG) **38**(4), 1–12 (2019)
36. Thies, J., Zollhofer, M., Stamminger, M., Theobalt, C., Nießner, M.: Face2Face: real-time face capture and reenactment of RGB videos. In: Proceedings of the IEEE Conference on Computer Vision and Pattern Recognition, pp. 2387–2395 (2016)
37. Wang, C., Deng, W.: Representative forgery mining for fake face detection. In: Proceedings of the IEEE/CVF Conference on Computer Vision and Pattern Recognition, pp. 14923–14932 (2021)
38. Wang, F., Cheng, J., Liu, W., Liu, H.: Additive margin Softmax for face verification. IEEE Sig. Process. Lett. **25**(7), 926–930 (2018)
39. Williams, R.J.: Simple statistical gradient-following algorithms for connectionist reinforcement learning. Mach. Learn. **8**, 229–256 (1992)
40. Yan, Z., Zhang, Y., Fan, Y., Wu, B.: UCF: uncovering common features for generalizable deepfake detection. In: Proceedings of the IEEE/CVF International Conference on Computer Vision, pp. 22412–22423 (2023)
41. Yang, X., Li, Y., Lyu, S.: Exposing deep fakes using inconsistent head poses. In: ICASSP 2019-2019 IEEE International Conference on Acoustics, Speech and Signal Processing (ICASSP), pp. 8261–8265. IEEE (2019)
42. Zhao, H., Zhou, W., Chen, D., Wei, T., Zhang, W., Yu, N.: Multi-attentional deepfake detection. In: Proceedings of the IEEE/CVF Conference on Computer Vision and Pattern Recognition, pp. 2185–2194 (2021)
43. Zhao, T., Xu, X., Xu, M., Ding, H., Xiong, Y., Xia, W.: Learning self-consistency for deepfake detection. In: Proceedings of the IEEE/CVF International Conference on Computer Vision, pp. 15023–15033 (2021)
44. Zhou, P., Han, X., Morariu, V.I., Davis, L.S.: Two-stream neural networks for tampered face detection. In 2017 IEEE Conference on Computer Vision and Pattern Recognition Workshops (CVPRW), pp. 1831–1839. IEEE (2017)

Exposing Audio-Visual Forgeries in Frequency Domain

Yuanfei Wan[1], Jian Wang[2], Jinrong Cui[3], and Yunlian Sun[1(✉)]

[1] School of Computer Science and Engineering, Nanjing University of Science and Technology, Nanjing, China
{wanyuanfei,yunlian.sun}@njust.edu.cn
[2] School of Computer Science, Nanjing University of Posts and Telecommunications, Nanjing, China
jwang.cs@njupt.edu.cn
[3] South China Agricultural University, Guangzhou, China

Abstract. Recently, the rapid development of deepfake technology attracted strong attention from the community. Some previous work on deepfake detection achieved good results in the frequency domain, which inspires us to combine frequency-domain information with temporal and spatial domains of visual to detect deepfakes. In addition, the audio signal can be represented in the frequency domain, so we can explore multimodal frequency-domain cues by combining audio and visual modalities. In this paper, we propose a Frequency-aware Audio-Visual Deepfake Detection(FAVDD) method. Specifically, we design a Frequency-Temporal-Spatial(FTS) visual encoder that extracts spatial, frequency, and temporal forgery cues and embeds them into visual features to form a unified representation. In addition, we project the audio signal into the frequency domain by Fourier transform and capture the forgery traces, which are later combined with visual features for deepfake detection. The results show that our proposed framework effectively combines multiple cues and achieves good results on three multimodal deepfake datasets.

Keywords: Deepfake Detection · Multimodal · Audio-Visual · Frequency

1 Introduction

In the past decades, deep learning and computer vision rapidly evolved to provide new techniques and tools for multimedia manipulation. While these techniques and tools are primarily used for legitimate applications in areas such as entertainment and education, they can also be utilized by malicious users for illegal activities. In December 2017, a Reddit user named "Deepfakes" released the

---

Supported by National Natural Science Foundation of China under Grant 62076131 and Postdoctoral Fellowship Program of CPSF under Grant Number GZC20240743.

first faked indecent video generated by the deep neural network, which attracted widespread attention. Since then, Deepfake has become synonymous with deep forgery technology.

To detect deepfakes [1–3], researchers did a lot of studies and proposed many detection methods. Many previous methods used the anomalies of deepfake videos in the RGB domain or temporal domain, extracted features from deep neural networks and performed detection. Some work made good progress in the frequency domain, Qian et al. [4] found that the artifacts brought by the forgery method can be well mined in the frequency domain. Li et al. [5] mined frequency information in a learnable way. PEL [6] used Progressive Enhancement Learning to extract fine-grained frequency features.

The generalization ability of the detector is an important criterion because in real scenarios, the detector is likely to be able to detect only known forgery methods, and the detector fails for unknown forgery methods. It was found that generalization ability can be improved by revealing potential correlations and inconsistencies between audio and visual modalities [7,8].

In this paper, we propose a Frequency-aware Audio-Visual Deepfake Detection(FAVDD) method. Our method consists of a Frequency-Temporal-Spatial (FTS) visual encoder, an audio encoder, and a fusion strategy. Where the FTS visual encoder embeds spatial, frequency, and temporal information into the visual features. The audio signal is Fourier transformed into a mel-spectrogram, which is then fed into the audio encoder to extract the frequency information and obtain the audio features. The audio features are combined with visual features through a fusion strategy for multimodal deepfake detection. Extensive experiments show that our approach achieves effective performance. Our main contributions can be summarised as follows:

- We design the FAVDD to detect deepfakes by effectively combining visual and audio frequency information. Extensive experiments demonstrate the effectiveness of our proposed method.
- We explore the spatial, frequency, and temporal forgery cues in the visual modality, uncover the connection between these three, and propose the FTS visual encoder. By embedding these three visual cues into visual features, we obtain a unified visual representation. The ablation studies demonstrate that our proposed method effectively utilizes these three visual cues.

2 Related Work

In recent years, researchers worked on developing various detection techniques to identify whether an image or video was manipulated through deepfake techniques. Generalization ability to unknown forgery techniques, robustness to various attacks (e.g., adversarial attacks, perturbations), and providing interpretable detection results are three key factors for detectors.

Previously, the researcher worked on detecting deepfakes using spatial or temporal cues. CLRNet [9] captured temporal information in continuous frames to detect deepfakes. Wang et al. [10] proposed SI-Net to improve the detection performance by spatial interaction of global and local features. LiSiam [11] located forgery regions in images with different quality degradation and enforced forgery localization consistency to improve generalization ability.

Some researchers made good progress in deepfake detection using frequency-domain information. Frank et al. [12] found that the up-sampling operation in GAN introduces artifacts in the frequency domain, and they also investigated the artifacts revealed by different GAN architectures in the frequency domain. They demonstrated experimentally that satisfactory results can be achieved using simple classifiers in the frequency domain. Luo et al. [13] proposed a multi-scale high-frequency feature extraction module and a residual-guided spatial attention module to guide the RGB feature extractor to pay more attention to forgery traces. They adopted a cross-modality attention module to fuse high-frequency information with RGB information. Li et al. [5] designed an adaptive frequency feature generation module to mine the frequency information in a learnable way. Jeong et al. [14] designed dual high-pass filters to amplify the effect of frequency-level artifacts.

Some work exploited audio-visual information for deepfake detection with good results. LipForensics [7] assumed that fake videos break the continuity of lips between adjacent frames. The model was first pre-trained for lip-reading and subsequently fine-tuned on the deepfake detection dataset. RealForensics [8] learned the natural correspondence between faces and voices in real videos in a self-supervised manner and was also fine-tuned on the deepfake detection dataset. AVAD [15] proposed an audio-visual anomaly detection framework for detecting deepfakes.

3 Method

Our proposed FAVDD consists of three key components: a FTS visual encoder, an audio encoder, and a fusion strategy. The FTS visual encoder contains multiple FTS blocks with a three-branch structure. The FTS blocks embed spatial, temporal, and frequency information into the visual features. We transform the audio signal into a mel-spectrogram by Fourier transform and input it into the audio encoder to extract the audio features. The visual and audio features are fused by a fusion strategy and the fused features are fed into the classifier for deepfake detection.

3.1 FTS Visual Encoder

Previous work demonstrated that spatial, temporal, and frequency domain cues can be used as strong evidence for detecting face forgery. The goal of our proposed FTS visual encoder is to unify and summarise these cues into a unified visual representation. The FTS visual encoder contains multiple FTS blocks. The FTS blocks adopt a three-branch structure to process spatial, temporal, and frequency information respectively. We assume a video input of $\mathbf{V} \in \mathbb{R}^{(T \times H \times W \times C)}$

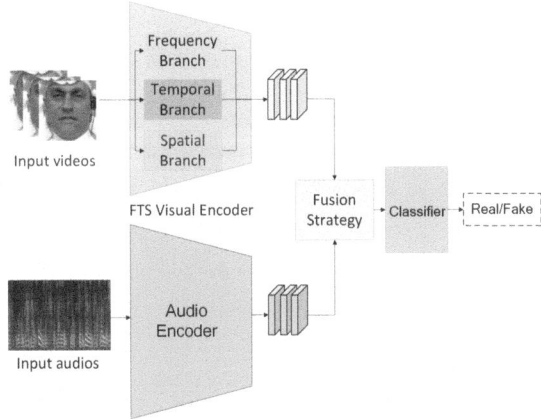

Fig. 1. Overview of our proposed FAVDD. The FTS visual encoder embeds spatial, frequency, and temporal information into visual features. The audio signal is Fourier transformed into a mel-spectrogram, which is then fed into the audio encoder to extract the audio features. We combine the visual and audio features, and input to the classifier through a fusion strategy.

where T is the frames of video, C is the number of channels, H and W are the height and width of the input.

Frequency Branch. Our proposed frequency branch uses a learnable frequency filter to learn the frequency information that favors deepfake detection. Specifically, we first map the input visual features into the frequency domain by performing a 3D fast Fourier transform(FFT). Then the whole frequency features are filtered using a learnable frequency filter to filter some information that is not relevant to forgery detection and enhance the frequency information that is useful for distinguishing between real and fake. Later, in order to facilitate the fusion with other branches of visual features, we map the frequency features back into the original feature domain by 3D inverse fast Fourier transform(IFFT), followed by batch normalization(BN) and ReLU activation. This process can be represented as:

$$\tilde{F}^V_{l-1} = FFT(F^V_{l-1}), \tag{1}$$

$$F^V_{f_l} = ReLU(BN(IFFT(\Theta \odot \tilde{F}^V_{l-1}))), \tag{2}$$

where F^V_{l-1} is the global visual feature extracted from the previous FTS block, and l denotes the lth block. $\tilde{F}^V_{l-1}$ is the frequency representation of F^V_{l-1}, FFT denotes the 3D fast Fourier transform along spatial and temporal dimensions, $IFFT$ is the 3D inverse fast Fourier transform. Θ denotes the learnable frequency filter, $\odot$ is the element-wise multiplication and $F^V_{f_l}$ is the frequency visual features. BN is the batch normalization, and $ReLU$ is the activation function.

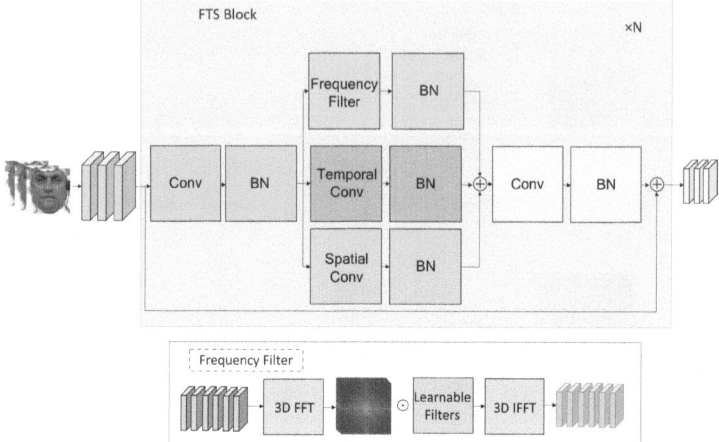

Fig. 2. The FTS visual encoder. This module contains multiple FTS blocks. The FTS block adopts a three-branch structure to process spatial, temporal, and frequency information respectively.

Temporal Branch. Most of the existing deepfake videos are made by forging each frame of the real video individually and then stitching these forged frames into a video. This approach inevitably leads to inter-frame inconsistencies, such as lighting, texture, and facial motion between adjacent frames. We use temporal convolution to capture these inconsistency cues in the temporal domain.

$$F_{t_l}^V = ReLU(BN(Conv_t(F_{l-1}^V))), \tag{3}$$

where $F_{t_l}^V$ is the temporal visual feature and $Conv_t$ denotes the temporal convolution along the temporal dimension.

Spatial Branch. Even the most advanced deepfake methods might inevitably leave forgery traces on the spatial domain. Similar to the temporal branch, we use spatial convolution to capture fine-grained spatial clues. This process can be represented as:

$$F_{s_l}^V = ReLU(BN(Conv_s(F_{l-1}^V))), \tag{4}$$

where $F_{s_l}^V$ is the spatial visual feature from the spatial branch. Here, $Conv_s$ denotes the spatial convolution along the spatial dimension.

Global Visual Features. After obtaining the visual features of the three branches, we represent them as a unified, global form. This process can be represented as:

$$F_l^V = ReLU(BN(Conv(F_{f_l}^V + F_{t_l}^V + F_{s_l}^V))) + F_{l-1}^V, \tag{5}$$

where F_l^V is the output feature of the lth FTS block, and $Conv$ represents the 3D convolution.

3.2 Audio Encoder

The audio signal can be represented in the frequency domain, so we can capture multimodal frequency domain cues by combining audio-visual. Specifically, we perform a Fourier transform of the audio input to obtain a mel-spectrogram, which can be represented by $\mathbf{A} \in \mathbb{R}^{(H \times W)}$. Afterwards, it is fed into the audio encoder to learn audio feature F^A that contains frequency information.

3.3 Fusion Strategy

After obtaining the visual features and audio features, we use a fusion strategy to obtain the multimodal features, which are later input into the classifier to obtain the final prediction scores. In this paper, we try several simple fusion strategies, more complex and effective fusion strategies are to be explored in future research.

4 Experiments

In this section, we first introduce the dataset we use as well as some experimental settings and details. After that, we make an extensive comparison with existing methods. Based on this, we conduct ablation studies to validate the effectiveness of our proposed modules.

4.1 Datasets

Deepfake Detection Challenge (DFDC) [16] dataset is a publicly available deepfake detection dataset. It was made publically available at the Deepfake Detection Challenge in 2020. It contains 23,654 real videos recorded from 960 identities and 104,500 fake videos.

FakeAVCeleb [17] is a multimodal deepfake detection dataset proposed by Khalid et al. It contains deepfake videos and corresponding lip-synchronized synthesized audios, where the real video data is taken from the VoxCeleb2 [18] dataset. It contains 500 real videos and 19500 fake videos.

AVD-TIMIT is a private multimodal deepfake dataset proposed by us. It contains 640 real videos and 2560 fake videos. The real videos are derived from the VidTIMIT dataset, and the corresponding fake videos are generated using FSGAN, Wav2Lip, and SV2TTS. AVD-TIMIT contains four video types: Real Video and Real Audio(RVRA), Real Video and Fake Audio(RVFA), Fake Video and Real Audio(FVRA), and Fake Video and Fake Audio(FVFA) (Table 1).

4.2 Implementation Details

For the visual, we use video clips containing 25 frames each. Then we center-crop these video clips to 160 × 160 and resize them to 112 × 112 as visual input. For audio, we sample the audio using a sampling rate of 16kHz and transform it into 100 × 80 mel-spectrogram as audio input.

Table 1. Details of the datasets used in the experiment.

Dataset	Video number Real/Fake	Visual forgery types	Audio forgery types	Real audio	Train/Test split
DFDC [16]	23654/104500	7	Unknown	✓	✓
FakeAVCeleb [17]	500/19500	3	1	✓	✗
AVD-TIMIT	640/2560	3	1	✓	✓

Our model is implemented using the Pytorch library. For learning parameter settings, we use the AdamP optimizer with a learning rate of 7e-4 and a weight decay of 1e-3. We train our model for 50 epochs using two NVIDIA GTX3090 GPUs, and the batch size is 24.

To evaluate the detection performance of our models and comparative methods, we use Accuracy (ACC) and Area Under Curve (AUC) as evaluation metrics.

4.3 Comparison with Prior Work

To evaluate the performance of the proposed method, we compare it with other unimodal as well as multimodal deepfake detection methods. For a fair comparison, we train these methods from scratch on the dataset. For unimodal methods, we consider only visual labels, i.e., RVRA and RVFA are considered as real and FVRA and FVFA are considered as fake. For multimodal methods, we consider both visual and audio labels, i.e., RVRA is real and the rest are fake.

In this section of experiments, we simply use concatenation as a fusion strategy, i.e., we directly concatenate visual features with audio features as fusion features. More fusion strategies are discussed in the ablation studies.

Intra-Dataset Evaluation. We perform intra-testing on two datasets: AVD-TIMIT and DFDC, i.e., training and testing on the same dataset. Table 2 shows the comparison results. Observing the results, we can see that the multimodal methods show better performance than the unimodal methods whether using pre-training or not. In addition, using a pre-training strategy can improve the detection performance. Our method beats all the other methods on AVD-TIMIT. It should be noted that we do not use a pre-training strategy. This is a strong argument for the superiority of our framework.

Cross-Dataset Evaluation. We perform cross-dataset evaluation on FakeAVCeleb and AVD-TIMIT to evaluate the generalization ability of the model, which is important for deepfake detection methods. As shown in Table 3, all the deepfake detectors show poorer performance than the intra-dataset evaluation. The results show that the generalization ability of our method exceeds that of other methods. Instead of capturing specific forgery artifacts, our method combines clues from multiple domains and thus exhibits better generalization ability.

Table 2. Performance comparison among different methods in intra-dataset evaluation. AVDT refers to the abbreviation for AVD-TIMIT. $\mathcal{M}$ and $\mathcal{P}$ indicate Modality and Pre-Training, respectively.

Method	$\mathcal{M}$	$\mathcal{P}$	AVDT ACC	AVDT AUC	DFDC ACC	DFDC AUC	AVG ACC	AVG AUC
MesoNet [19]	$\mathcal{V}$	×	68.00	68.75	56.37	61.07	62.19	64.91
ViT-Base [20]	$\mathcal{V}$	×	54.75	87.32	65.14	71.18	59.95	79.25
Xception [21]	$\mathcal{V}$	✓	87.88	93.31	73.19	85.58	80.54	89.45
Capsule-forensics [22]	$\mathcal{V}$	✓	90.00	93.54	74.59	81.92	82.30	87.73
Efficientnet [23]	$\mathcal{V}$	✓	89.25	93.75	82.08	90.53	85.67	92.14
LiSiam-C [11]	$\mathcal{V}$	✓	90.00	93.77	82.12	91.37	86.06	92.57
MMCNN-LT1 [24]	$\mathcal{AV}$	×	86.00	92.83	70.11	77.04	78.06	84.94
MMCNN-IA1 [24]	$\mathcal{AV}$	×	86.12	91.67	70.30	79.21	78.21	85.44
AVD-DDL [25]	$\mathcal{AV}$	×	88.38	93.58	-	-	-	-
RealForensics [8]	$\mathcal{AV}$	✓	90.00	93.75	**88.04**	**94.07**	**89.02**	93.91
FAVDD(Ours)	$\mathcal{AV}$	×	**93.50**	**98.62**	76.48	91.17	84.99	**94.90**

Table 3. Performance comparison among different methods in cross-dataset evaluation. FAVC and AVDT refer to the abbreviations for FakeAVCeleb and AVD-TIMIT, respectively. $\mathcal{M}$ and $\mathcal{P}$ indicate Modality and Pre-Training, respectively.

Method	$\mathcal{M}$	$\mathcal{P}$	Training in AVDT ACC	Training in AVDT AUC	Training in FAVC ACC	Training in FAVC AUC	AVG ACC	AVG AUC
MMCNN-LT1 [24]	$\mathcal{AV}$	×	59.38	65.58	80.56	80.38	69.97	72.98
MMCNN-IA1 [24]	$\mathcal{AV}$	×	55.12	61.82	81.31	80.06	68.22	70.94
AVD-DDL [25]	$\mathcal{AV}$	×	62.24	67.57	88.09	92.83	75.17	80.20
RealForensics [8]	$\mathcal{AV}$	✓	**63.58**	81.45	84.19	93.40	73.89	87.43
FAVDD(Ours)	$\mathcal{AV}$	×	58.71	**86.78**	**94.56**	**98.63**	**76.64**	**92.71**

4.4 Ablation Studies

In this section, we discuss the impact of each component in the proposed framework. The results are shown in Table 4, where FAVC is used as the training set and AVDT is used as the test set. From the results, we can see that the proposed FTS visual encoder effectively captures the cues from the three domains and effectively fuses this information to improve the detection performance of our model. Apart from checking the contribution of each visual branch, we further investigate different fusion strategies. The results are shown in Table 5.

Table 4. Ablation study result of the FTS visual encoder. $\mathcal{M}$ indicate Modality.

Ablation Model	$\mathcal{M}$	Training in FAVC	
		ACC	AUC
Only Spatial Branch	$\mathcal{V}$	77.34	91.12
Spatial + Frequency Branch	$\mathcal{V}$	79.06	92.57
Spatial + Frequency + Temporal Branch	$\mathcal{V}$	**80.18**	**93.13**

Table 5. Ablation study result of the Fusion Strategy. $\mathcal{M}$ indicate Modality. Linear means that the fusion weights are generated using the Linear layer.

Fusion Strategy	$\mathcal{M}$	Training in FAVC	
		ACC	AUC
Concatenate	$\mathcal{AV}$	**94.56**	**98.63**
Summation	$\mathcal{AV}$	81.81	91.25
Linear	$\mathcal{AV}$	86.59	98.15

5 Conclusion

In this paper, we proposed the FAVDD. Our approach combined information from multiple domains of vision to form visual features, while combining them with audio features. In future work, we will consider more effective fusion strategies, as well as more challenging situations.

References

1. Sun, Y., Tang, J., Sun, Z., Tistarelli, M.: Facial age and expression synthesis using ordinal ranking adversarial networks. IEEE Trans. Inf. Forensics Secur. **15**, 2960–2972 (2020)
2. Sun, Y., Tang, J., Shu, X., Sun, Z., Tistarelli, M.: Facial age synthesis with label distribution-guided generative adversarial network. IEEE Trans. Inf. Forensics Secur. **15**, 2679–2691 (2020)
3. Li, Z., Lv, X., Yu, W., Liu, Q., Lin, J., Zhang, S.: Face shape transfer via semantic warping. Vis. Intell. **2**(1), 1–11 (2024)
4. Qian, Y., Yin, G., Sheng, L., Chen, Z., Shao, J.: Thinking in frequency: face forgery detection by mining frequency-aware clues. In: European Conference on Computer Vision, pp. 86–103. Springer (2020)
5. Li, J., Xie, H., Li, J., Wang, Z., Zhang, Y.: Frequency-aware discriminative feature learning supervised by single-center loss for face forgery detection. In: Proceedings of the IEEE/CVF Conference on Computer Vision and Pattern Recognition, pp. 6458–6467 (2021)
6. Gu, Q., Chen, S., Yao, T., Chen, Y., Ding, S., Yi, R.: Exploiting fine-grained face forgery clues via progressive enhancement learning. Proc. AAAI Conf. Artif. Intell. **36**, 735–743 (2022)
7. Haliassos, A., Vougioukas, K., Petridis, S., Pantic, M.: Lips don't lie: a generalisable and robust approach to face forgery detection. In: Proceedings of the IEEE/CVF Conference on Computer Vision and Pattern Recognition, pp. 5039–5049 (2021)

8. Haliassos, A., Mira, R., Petridis, S., Pantic, M.: Leveraging real talking faces via self-supervision for robust forgery detection. In: Proceedings of the IEEE/CVF Conference on Computer Vision and Pattern Recognition, pp. 14950–14962 (2022)
9. Tariq, S., Lee, S., Woo, S.S.: A convolutional LSTM based residual network for deepfake video detection. arXiv preprint arXiv:2009.07480 (2020)
10. Wang, J., Du, X., Cheng, Y., Sun, Y., Tang, J.: SI-Net: spatial interaction network for deepfake detection. Multimedia Syst. **29**(5), 3139–3150 (2023)
11. Wang, J., Sun, Y., Tang, J.: LiSiam: localization invariance Siamese network for deepfake detection. IEEE Trans. Inf. Forensics Secur. **17**, 2425–2436 (2022)
12. Frank, J., Eisenhofer, T., Schönherr, L., Fischer, A., Kolossa, D., Holz, T.: Leveraging frequency analysis for deep fake image recognition. In: International Conference on Machine Learning, pp. 3247–3258. PMLR (2020)
13. Luo, Y., Zhang, Y., Yan, J., Liu, W.: Generalizing face forgery detection with high-frequency features. In: Proceedings of the IEEE/CVF Conference on Computer Vision and Pattern Recognition, pp. 16317–16326 (2021)
14. Jeong, Y., Kim, D., Min, S., Joe, S., Gwon, Y., Choi, J.: BiHPF: bilateral high-pass filters for robust deepfake detection. In: Proceedings of the IEEE/CVF Winter Conference on Applications of Computer Vision, pp. 48–57 (2022)
15. Feng, C., Chen, Z., Owens, A.: Self-supervised video forensics by audio-visual anomaly detection. In: Proceedings of the IEEE/CVF Conference on Computer Vision and Pattern Recognition, pp. 10491–10503 (2023)
16. Dolhansky, B., et al.: The deepfake detection challenge (dfdc) dataset. arXiv preprint arXiv:2006.07397 (2020)
17. Khalid, H., Tariq, S., Kim, M., Woo, S.S.: Fakeavceleb: a novel audio-video multi-modal deepfake dataset. arXiv preprint arXiv:2108.05080 (2021)
18. Chung, J.S., Nagrani, A., Zisserman, A.: VoxCeleb2: deep speaker recognition. arXiv preprint arXiv:1806.05622 (2018)
19. Afchar, D., Nozick, V., Yamagishi, J., Echizen, I.: Mesonet: a compact facial video forgery detection network. In: 2018 IEEE International Workshop on Information Forensics and Security, pp. 1–7. IEEE (2018)
20. Dosovitskiy, A., et al.: An image is worth 16x16 words: transformers for image recognition at scale. arXiv preprint arXiv:2010.11929 (2020)
21. Rossler, A., Cozzolino, D., Verdoliva, L., Riess, C., Thies, J., Nießner, M.: Faceforensics++: learning to detect manipulated facial images. In: Proceedings of the IEEE/CVF International Conference on Computer Vision, pp. 1–11 (2019)
22. Nguyen, H.H., Yamagishi, J., Echizen, I.: Capsule-forensics: using capsule networks to detect forged images and videos. In: ICASSP 2019-2019 IEEE International Conference on Acoustics, Speech and Signal Processing, pp. 2307–2311. IEEE (2019)
23. Tan, M., Le, Q.: Efficientnet: rethinking model scaling for convolutional neural networks. In: International Conference on Machine Learning, pp. 6105–6114. PMLR (2019)
24. Chumachenko, K., Iosifidis, A., Gabbouj, M.: Self-attention fusion for audiovisual emotion recognition with incomplete data. In: 2022 26th International Conference on Pattern Recognition, pp. 2822–2828. IEEE (2022)
25. Chugh, K., Gupta, P., Dhall, A., Subramanian, R.: Not made for each other-audio-visual dissonance-based deepfake detection and localization. In: Proceedings of the 28th ACM International Conference on Multimedia, pp. 439–447 (2020)

Synergistic Alignment-Based Domain Adaptation For Gaze Estimation

Yushan Han, Haoxiang Ying, Honggang Zhu, Feiyang Gao, and Wanting Zhou[✉]

School of Artificial Intelligence, Beijing University of Posts and Telecommunications, Beijing, China
`wanting.zhou@bupt.edu.cn`

Abstract. Most appearance-based gaze estimation methods aim to predict gaze direction using a single dataset setting, and tend to suffer performance degradation when crossing domains. The existing domain adaptation solutions either produce noisy pseudo labels or require extra computational resources for domain alignment. In this paper, we propose a synergistic alignment-based method for gaze estimation, enhancing the capability of domain alignment from the category level and feature level. First, we employ a hybrid network consisting of local convolutions and self-attention layers to generate refined pseudo-labels, which captures both local and global gaze related features. Second, resorting to Kullback-Leibler (KL) divergence, we derive a united loss to facilitate the alignment to reduce the mismatch of categories and feature distributions in an effective and efficient way. The experimental results on ETH-XGaze, Gaze360, EyeDiap and MPIIGaze datasets demonstrate that our proposed method achieves significant improvement on the gaze estimation compared with state-of-the-art domain adaptation methods.

Keywords: Gaze Estimation · Unsupervised Domain Adaptation · Pseudo-label

1 Introduction

With the development of deep learning, gaze estimation has been widely used in a variety of applications, such as VR/AR games, intelligent cockpits, medical analysis, human-robot interaction, etc. Traditionally, this has been done through corneal-reflection methods which rely on small eye features to compute the gaze direction [1]. However, this method has limitations of the high requirements on specific hardware for illumination and capture which is expensive and cumbersome. In contrast, appearance-based gaze estimation does not relay on small eye feature extraction under special illumination. Instead, they can work with just a single ordinary camera to capture the eye appearance to learn a mapping function that predicts the gaze direction from the eye appearance directly which greatly enlarges the applicability and can introduce large datasets [8,9].

However, current datasets are mostly collected under controlled laboratory conditions that are characterized by limited variability in appearance and illumination which violate the identical independent distribution nature. While appearance-based gaze estimation methods require the introduction of large, diverse datasets, the difference between training and test datasets is often shown as a person-specific bias which contributes to the rapid performance degradation across multiple datasets. To address this problem, unsupervised domain adaptation (UDA) approaches aim to find a gaze-relevant constraint generalizing the model to the target domain without label. In recent years, many UDA methods for gaze estimation have been proposed. Kellnhofer et al. used domain discrimination and left-right symmetry to adapt gaze models to new domains [10]. Wang et al. developed a UDA method utilizing adversarial learning and Bayesian inference to improve generalization performance by addressing appearance variation, head pose variation, and over-fitting of point estimates [11]. Bao et al. proposed a method based on rotational consistency property in gaze estimation and introduce the 'sub-label' for unsupervised domain adaptation [3]. The backbone of these methods is pure CNN, which has a weak ability to focus on global information. Meanwhile, the production of pseudo labels with a single CNN is usually too noisy for the target domain. In addition, existing feature alignment techniques, e.g., GANs [2], often demand extra computational resources, resulting in a costly and potentially unstable process.

In this paper, we propose a synergistic alignment-based domain adaptation method for gaze estimation, which enhances the capability of domain alignment from the category level and feature level. We first generate refined pseudo-labels using a hybrid network of local convolutions and self-attentions pre-trained on the source domain. Compared with pure CNN, the hybrid network can not only focus on local information, but also capture global patch relationship, facilitating the extraction of gaze related texture and structural features. It provides promising supervision information to guarantee the cross-domain gaze consistency at the category level. In addition, inspired by [22], we introduce Kullback-Leibler (KL) divergence to reduce the mismatch in the distribution of gaze features without extra computation. Together with category level loss functions, we derive a united loss to facilitate the alignment in the feature space and enforce the category consistency between source and target domains in an effective and efficient way. Experiments show that our method achieves an average 37.5% improvement over the baseline on the UDA task of gaze estimation, and achieves competitive results compared with state-of-the-art methods.

2 Related Work

Typical Appearance-Based Gaze Estimation. Typical appearance-based gaze estimation aims to predict gaze direction using eye [5] or face [4] images. Compared with early studies estimating gaze by reconstructing 3D eyeball models and calculate gaze direction [1] which rely on professional cameras and takes a lot of time, the appearance-based gaze estimation method requires fewer hardware conditions. In recent years, with the popularization of deep learning, many gaze estimation methods based on appearance have emerged [8,9]. However, most methods only estimate gaze within a single dataset setting, which usually suffer performance degradation when tested on unseen domain. Domain adaptation for gaze estimation is still a challenging work.

Unsupervised Domain Adaptation (UDA). UDA techniques are employed to adapt models to target domains using a few unlabeled target domain samples. Previous UDA approaches can be categorized into generative adversarial network (GAN) [19,21] and self-training [14]. Recent studies still mostly use these two methods. Kellnhofer et al. used domain discrimination and left-right symmetry to adapt gaze models to new domains [10]. Wang et al. developed a UDA method utilizing adversarial learning and Bayesian inference [11]. Guo et al. introduced target domain representation embedding mechanisms with prediction consistency [12]. Liu et al. used network ensemble methods with momentum and outlier guidance for gaze UDA [13]. In this study, we propose a synergistic alignment based UDA method for gaze estimation.

3 Proposed Method

3.1 Hybrid Network

We introduce a hybrid network consisting of residual blocks [15] and self-attention layers for the domain adaptation of gaze estimation. The hybrid network is used to extract features from the input image $I \in \mathbb{R}^{H \times W \times C}$ and obtain the 2D gaze $G \in \mathbb{R}^2$. The residual block can deepen the network structure to improve training efficiency by introducing skip connections to solve the problem of gradient vanishing. However, due to the inherent problems such as the size limitations of convolution kernels, CNNs only focus on local information such as monocular gaze direction, and pay little attention to global information such as binocular position and head pose. Self-attention layer has a strong information extraction ability, and it can capture dependencies at any position in the sequence regardless of distance, which is impossible to do with CNNs that focus on local information. The two components focus on both local and global information to improve the performance of gaze estimation.

Given a face image $I \in \mathbb{R}^{H \times W \times C}$, first we use residual blocks to process the it and acquire feature maps $\boldsymbol{f}_{img} \in \mathbb{R}^{h \times w \times c}$. The residual block uses the skip connection method, which adds the input to the target output, to alleviate the vanishing gradient problem in deep neural networks. Suppose our input is $\mathbf{x}$ and output is $\mathcal{F}(\mathbf{x}, \{W_i\})$ in a traditional CNN, where W_i represents the weight parameters of each layer. The output of a residual block can be presented as:

$$\boldsymbol{f}_{img} = \mathcal{F}(\mathbf{x}, \{W_i\}) + W_s \mathbf{x}. \tag{1}$$

Since our feature maps get smaller during the convolution process, we apply a linear transformation W_s to the input to match the dimension of the output. Then the feature maps $\boldsymbol{f}_{img} \in \mathbb{R}^{h \times w \times c}$ will be flattened into 1D features $\boldsymbol{f}_p \in$

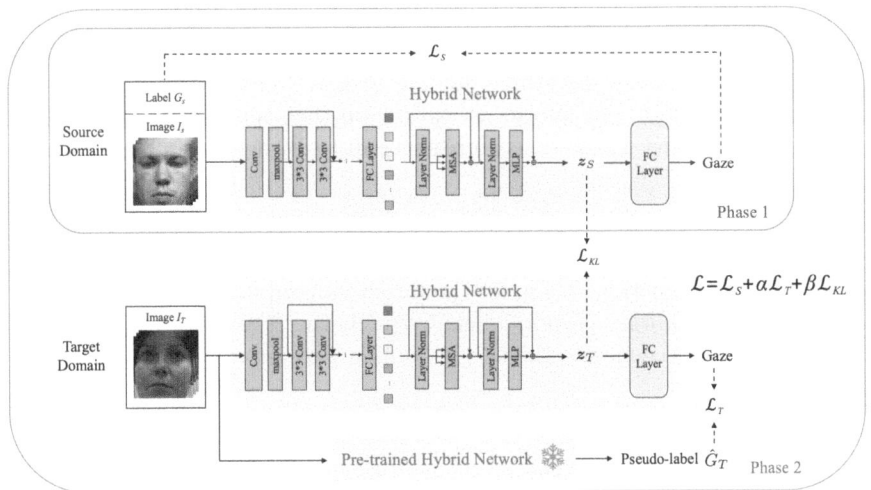

Fig. 1. Overall framework of the synergistic alignment-based domain adaptation method. The hybrid network with local convolutions and self-attentions is responsible for extracting gaze features and generating refined pseudo-labels. A united loss is designed to optimize the model, where Kullback-Leibler (KL) divergence facilitates the alignment in the feature space and gaze losses are used to enforce the category consistency between source and target domains.

$\mathbb{R}^d$, where $d = h \cdot w \cdot c$, and be fed into self-attention layers, which is used to capture global information. The 1D features $\boldsymbol{f_p} \in \mathbb{R}^d$ are represented into a feature matrix $X \in \mathbb{R}^d$, then the feature is projected into queries $Q \in \mathbb{R}^d$, keys $K \in \mathbb{R}^d$, values $V \in \mathbb{R}^d$. The output of self-attention module can be presented as:

$$\text{Attention}(\boldsymbol{Q}, \boldsymbol{K}, \boldsymbol{V}) = \text{softmax}\left(\frac{\boldsymbol{Q}\boldsymbol{K}^\mathrm{T}}{\sqrt{\mathrm{d}}}\right)\boldsymbol{V}. \qquad (2)$$

And we can formulate a self-attention layer as:

$$\boldsymbol{z} = \text{MSA}(\text{LN}(\boldsymbol{X})) + \boldsymbol{X}, \qquad (3)$$

where LN represents the layer normalization and the output z usually has the same dimension as the input X, so it can be stacked for multi-layer self-attention layers. After a series of self-attention layers processes, the d-dimensional features z of image I can be obtained. finally, through a linear layer, we can get the 2D gaze direction $G \in \mathbb{R}^2$ of image I:

$$G = wz + b. \qquad (4)$$

3.2 Pseudo-Label Based Gaze Domain Adaptation

The pseudo-label method solves the problem that the real label of the target domain is invisible. By using the pre-trained hybrid network Φ_p, we predict the gaze direction from the target domain data and obtain the pseudo-label $\hat{G}_T$, providing supervision information for target domain. Firstly, as shown in the Phase 1 of Fig. 1, we use the source domain images I_S and their corresponding gaze labels G_S to train our hybrid network Φ on the source domain and obtain the pre-trained model Φ_p. The loss function can be presented as:

$$\mathcal{L}_S = \|\Phi(I_S) - G_S\|_1, \tag{5}$$

where the model Φ predicts the gaze direction of the input image and $\|\ \|_1$ represents L_1 loss function. Then, for the target domain images I_T without their gaze direction, we obtain pseudo-labels by predicting the images with the pre-trained model Φ_p to generate the target domain gaze pseudo-labels $\hat{G}_T$:

$$\hat{G}_T = \Phi_p(I_T). \tag{6}$$

Note that the parameters of the pre-trained model Φ_p are fixed in the domain adaptation training phase. Then the domain adaptation training on the target domain can be performed with images I_T and pseudo-labels $\hat{G}_T$, and the loss function can be presented as:

$$\mathcal{L}_T = \left\|\Phi(I_T) - \hat{G}_T\right\|_1. \tag{7}$$

3.3 Alignment for Gaze Feature Distributions

In the gaze estimation UDA tasks, data from the source and target domains may differ significantly in the appearance of the image and the distribution of gaze directions. By aligning the distribution of features in the model, the features of the source and target domains can be mapped to a common distribution in an abstract feature space, thus improving the cross-domain generalization ability of the model. Kullback-Leibler (KL) divergence is an asymmetry measure used to measure the difference between two probability distributions, described as the amount of additional information required to go from one probability distribution to the other. We use KL divergence to measure the difference between gaze features and minimize it to align the feature distribution. Suppose we have two d-dimensional probability distributions p and q, and their KL divergence can be calculated as follows:

$$\mathrm{KL}(p\|q) = \sum_d p(d) \log \frac{p(d)}{q(d)}. \tag{8}$$

When we predict the gaze direction with the model Φ, we can get the d-dimensional feature z in the process. Now suppose we have got d-dimensional features z_S, z_T from source domain and target domain, we use KL divergence to measure the difference of gaze feature distributions:

$$\mathcal{L}_{\mathrm{KL}} = \sum_n Softmax(z_S(n)) \log \frac{Softmax(z_S(n))}{Softmax(z_T(n))}. \tag{9}$$

Before the calculation, we add Softmax activation to make it meet the probability distribution. The alignment for gaze feature distributions can be achieved by minimizing $\mathcal{L}_{\text{KL}}$.

3.4 United Loss

In order to achieve the adaptation of the source domain and target domain simultaneously, and improve the performance of our model on the UDA task by aligning gaze from the category level and feature level, we take a linear combination of the source domain gaze loss $\mathcal{L}_S$, target domain gaze loss $\mathcal{L}_T$ and KL divergence loss $\mathcal{L}_{\text{KL}}$ as the loss function for training. The united loss function can be presented as:

$$\mathcal{L} = \mathcal{L}_S + \alpha(\mathcal{L}_T) + \beta(\mathcal{L}_{\text{KL}}). \tag{10}$$

The training process of our method consists of two phases. Phase 1 is shown in the upper part of Fig. 1, we only use the source domain gaze loss $\mathcal{L}_S$ to train the hybrid network on the source domain and get pre-trained model Φ_p. Phase 2 achieves adaptation between the source domain and the target domain. In this phase, we first predict the gaze directions from target domain I_T with pre-trained model Φ_p to get pseudo-labels $\hat{G}_T$, then use the images I_S, I_T and gaze directions G_S, $\hat{G}_T$ of the source domain and target domain for training (note that the labels of target domain $\hat{G}_T$ is pseudo-labels). In addition, the features of both domains, z_S and z_T, can be obtained from the last layer of the transformer in the hybrid network. We use the KL divergence loss function $\mathcal{L}_{KL}$ to measure the difference of gaze feature distributions between the source domain and target domain. Through the integration of three components, our proposed method seeks to overcome domain shift and facilitate the alignment across domains, addressing the challenges of unsupervised domain adaptation tasks.

4 Experiments

4.1 Setup

Datasets. We employ four gaze datasets as four domains: ETH-XGaze($\mathcal{D}_E$) [16], Gaze360($\mathcal{D}_G$) [10], EyeDiap($\mathcal{D}_D$) [17], MPIIGaze($\mathcal{D}_M$) [9]. We choose ETH-XGaze and Gaze360 as the source domains and test on EyeDiap and MPIIGaze. ETH-XGaze contains 1.1M eye, binocular, and face images of 110 subjects. It contains 2D gaze labels such as fixation point coordinates, head pose angles, and 3D gaze labels such as gaze vectors and eye center coordinates. We use training set, which contains 756K images of 80 subjects. Gaze360 contains 84K images of 54 subjects for training and 16K images of 15 subjects for testing. It provides eye and face images and the same 3D gaze labels as ETH-XGaze and does not provide 2D labels. We use its training part for this experiment. EyeDiap contains 16K images of 14 subjects. It provides eye and face images, both 2D and 3D gaze labels, and head pose information. MPIIFaceGaze contains 45K images of 15 subjects. It provides eye and face images, both 2D and 3D gaze labels and head pose direction. We select the face images and 2D gaze label of each domain for the experiment. Note that Gaze360 does not provide 2D labels, and we follow the method of [7] to generate 2D labels. ETH-XGaze provides the normalized data. We directly use the provided data for training and follow [7] to process the other three datasets to unify the evaluation criteria.

Implementation Details. In phase 1, we train the hybrid network on ETH-XGaze with 512 batch sizes and 50 epochs, setting the learning rate to 0.001 and the weight decay to 0.5, with decay step set at 40 epochs. We train the hybrid network on Gaze360 with a batch size of 64 and 50 epochs. The learning rate is set to 0.001 and weight decay is set to 0.5. The decay step is set as 40 epochs. In phase 2, we train the hybrid network on source and target domains with 50 epochs, the learning rate is set to 0.0005. The weights α and β of the united loss function are 2 and 10 respectively. We use the Adam optimizer [18] to train the network with $\beta = 0.999$. In addition, we use a linear learning rate warmup setting as 5 epochs. We use mean angular error as the evaluation metric as most of gaze estimation methods. A smaller error represents a better method.

4.2 Comparison with SOTA

Baseline. We utilize the ResNet18 network and a fully connected layer for gaze regression as our baseline. We train our baseline model using the source domain data with the $\mathcal{L}_S$ gaze estimation loss function only.

Comparison Results. We compare five SOTA methods with our method, which are Adversarial Learning (ADL) [10], Full-Face [9], ADDA [19], UMA [20], and PureGaze [6]. ADL has been proven to be a reliable method for gaze estimation. Full-Face applies no domain adaptation method but performs well in within-dataset evaluation. ADDA uses adversarial learning to decrease the domain gap. UMA is a method proposed for hand segmentation, which uses self-training to decrease the domain gap. We report the performance of these methods from [6,13] for reference. The results are shown in Table 1.

With our method, results show competitive performance in domain adaptation tasks. Compared with our baseline, proposed method achieves an improvement of 69.0%, 60.7%, 6.1%, and 14.2% on $\mathcal{D}_E \rightarrow \mathcal{D}_M$, $\mathcal{D}_E \rightarrow \mathcal{D}_D$, $\mathcal{D}_G \rightarrow \mathcal{D}_M$ and $\mathcal{D}_G \rightarrow \mathcal{D}_D$ tasks, note that where $A \rightarrow B$ means A is source domain and B is target domain. Among them, our method achieves the best results among all methods on $\mathcal{D}_E \rightarrow \mathcal{D}_D$, $\mathcal{D}_G \rightarrow \mathcal{D}_M$ and $\mathcal{D}_G \rightarrow \mathcal{D}_D$ tasks, with a $0.14°(1.9\%)$, $0.29°(3.4\%)$ and $0.50°(5.4\%)$ improvement over the second best method, and also achieves the second best result, slightly inferior to the best result method, ADL, on the $\mathcal{D}_E \rightarrow \mathcal{D}_M$ task. This demonstrates that our approach of focusing on both local and global features and aligning at both category and feature levels is effective.

Table 1. Performance comparison with SOTA methods. Angular gaze gaze error (°) is used as evaluation metric. Bold denote the best result of each column.

Method	$\mathcal{D}_E \to \mathcal{D}_M$	$\mathcal{D}_E \to \mathcal{D}_D$	$\mathcal{D}_G \to \mathcal{D}_M$	$\mathcal{D}_G \to \mathcal{D}_D$
Baseline	20.35°	18.68°	8.75°	11.96°
ADL [10]	**5.48°**	16.11°	9.70°	10.28°
Full-Face [9]	12.35°	30.15°	11.13°	14.42°
ADDA [19]	6.33°	7.90°	8.76°	14.80°
UMA [20]	7.52°	12.37°	8.51°	19.32°
PureGaze [6]	7.08°	7.48°	9.28°	9.32°
Ours	6.30°	**7.34°**	**8.22°**	**8.82°**

4.3 Ablation Study

We conduct an ablation study to evaluate the effectiveness of different components in the proposed method on $\mathcal{D}_G \to \mathcal{D}_M$ and $\mathcal{D}_G \to \mathcal{D}_D$ tasks. Since the network of our method is a hybrid structure and the loss function has three components, we drop some of these components for the experiment, and the results are presented in Table 2.

Table 2. Results of ablation study. Evaluation with different backbones and loss functions. Angular gaze error (°) is used as evaluation metric.

No.	Methods	Components			Testing	
		$\mathcal{L}_S$	$\mathcal{L}_T$	$\mathcal{L}_{KL}$	$\mathcal{D}_G \to \mathcal{D}_M$	$\mathcal{D}_G \to \mathcal{D}_D$
ResNet						
0	ResNet+$\mathcal{L}_S$(Baseline)	✓			8.75°	11.96°
1	ResNet+$\mathcal{L}_S$+$\mathcal{L}_T$	✓	✓		9.43°	12.78°
2	ResNet+$\mathcal{L}_S$+$\mathcal{L}_T$+$\mathcal{L}_{KL}$	✓	✓	✓	9.40°	12.84°
Hybrid network						
3	Hybrid network+$\mathcal{L}_S$	✓			8.86°	9.55°
4	Hybrid network+$\mathcal{L}_S$+$\mathcal{L}_T$	✓	✓		8.65°	9.51°
5	Hybrid network+$\mathcal{L}_S$+$\mathcal{L}_T$+$\mathcal{L}_{KL}$(Ours)	✓	✓	✓	**8.22°**	**8.82°**

It is obvious that both the self-attention part of the hybrid network and every part of the united loss function have an important impact on the accuracy of domain adaptation for the gaze estimation task. Moreover, it can be found that $\mathcal{L}_{KL}$ has a greater impact. With the same loss function, the hybrid network generally shows better performance than the ResNet with an average improvement of 0.61°(6.6%), which illustrates the effectiveness of the self-attention part of the hybrid network. Comparing different loss functions when using the hybrid network, it can be found that each of $\mathcal{L}_S$, $\mathcal{L}_T$, and $\mathcal{L}_{\mathrm{KL}}$ can effectively improve the performance of the UDA task of gaze estimation. When using $\mathcal{L}_S$ unchanged, adding $\mathcal{L}_T$ and $\mathcal{L}_{\mathrm{KL}}$ improves performance by $0.21°(2.4\%)$ and $0.43°(5.0\%)$, which indicates that $\mathcal{L}_{\mathrm{KL}}$ has a greater improvement effect than $\mathcal{L}_T$. On the other hand, when we tested ResNet, $\mathcal{L}_S$ and $\mathcal{L}_T$ did not improve performance but slightly decreased it. This may be because they have less impact on the model performance of ResNet or, more seriously, have a negative impact. In any case, the results demonstrate the effectiveness of the self-attention layer in our model and the effectiveness of $\mathcal{L}_S$ and $\mathcal{L}_T$ to align the domains from the category level and feature level.

5 Conclusion

In this paper, we introduce a synergistic alignment method for the UDA gaze estimation task. We use a hybrid network mainly composed of convolutional and self-attention layers which focuses on both local and global information, and achieve synergistic alignment of domains from both the category level and the feature level. Experimental results show that our method achieves stable and competitive improvements in four cross-domain tasks.

Acknowledgements. This work was partially supported by the National Natural Science Foundation of China (62376037, 62006227) and the Open Project Program of the Key Laboratory of Artificial Intelligence for Perception and Understanding, Liaoning Province (AIPU)(No.20230006).

References

1. Ishikawa, A.: Passive Driver Gaze Tracking with Active Appearance Models. Carnegie Mellon University (2004)
2. Ganin, Y., et al.: Domain-adversarial training of neural networks. J. Mach. Learn. Res. **17**(59), 1–35 (2016)
3. Bao, Y., Liu, Y., Wang, H., Lu, F.: Generalizing gaze estimation with rotation consistency. In: Proceedings of the IEEE/CVF Conference on Computer Vision and Pattern Recognition, pp. 4207–4216 (2022)
4. Bao, Y., Cheng, Y., Liu, Y., Lu, F.: Adaptive feature fusion network for gaze tracking in mobile tablets. In: 2020 25th International Conference on Pattern Recognition (ICPR), pp. 9936–9943. IEEE (2021)
5. Zhang, X., Sugano, Y., Fritz, M., Bulling, A.: Appearance-based gaze estimation in the wild. In: Proceedings of the IEEE Conference on Computer Vision and Pattern Recognition, pp. 4511–4520 (2015)
6. Cheng, Y., Bao, Y., Lu, F.: Puregaze: purifying gaze feature for generalizable gaze estimation. In: Proceedings of the AAAI Conference on Artificial Intelligence, vol. 36, no. 1, pp. 436–443 (2022)
7. Cheng, Y., Wang, H., Bao, Y., Lu, F.: Appearance-based gaze estimation with deep learning: a review and benchmark. In: IEEE Transactions on Pattern Analysis and Machine Intelligence (2024)

8. Cheng, Y., Lu, F.: Gaze estimation using transformer. In: 2022 26th International Conference on Pattern Recognition (ICPR), pp. 3341–3347. IEEE (2022)
9. Zhang, X., Sugano, Y., Fritz, M., Bulling, A.: It's written all over your face: full-face appearance-based gaze estimation. In: Proceedings of the IEEE Conference on Computer Vision and Pattern Recognition Workshops, pp. 51–60 (2017)
10. Kellnhofer, P., Recasens, A., Stent, S., Matusik, W., Torralba, A.: Gaze360: physically unconstrained gaze estimation in the wild. In: Proceedings of the IEEE/CVF International Conference on Computer Vision, pp. 6912–6921 (2019)
11. Wang, K., Zhao, R., Su, H., Ji, Q.: Generalizing eye tracking with Bayesian adversarial learning. In: Proceedings of the IEEE/CVF Conference on Computer Vision and Pattern Recognition, pp. 11907–11916 (2019)
12. Guo, Z., Yuan, Z., Zhang, C., Chi, W., Ling, Y., Zhang, S.: Domain adaptation gaze estimation by embedding with prediction consistency. In: Proceedings of the Asian Conference on Computer Vision (2020)
13. liu, Y., Liu, R., Wang, H., Lu, F.: Generalizing gaze estimation with outlier-guided collaborative adaptation. In: Proceedings of the IEEE/CVF International Conference on Computer Vision, pp. 3835–3844 (2021)
14. Lee, D., et al.: Pseudo-label: the simple and efficient semi-supervised learning method for deep neural networks. In: Workshop on Challenges in Representation Learning, ICML, vol. 3, no. 2, p. 896. Atlanta (2013)
15. he, K., Zhang, X., Ren, S., Sun, J.: Deep residual learning for image recognition. In: Proceedings of the IEEE Conference on Computer Vision and Pattern Recognition, pp. 770–778 (2016)
16. Zhang, X., Park, S., Beeler, T., Bradley, D., Tang, S., Hilliges, O.: ETH-XGaze: a large scale dataset for gaze estimation under extreme head pose and gaze variation. In: Vedaldi, A., Bischof, H., Brox, T., Frahm, J.-M. (eds.) ECCV 2020. LNCS, vol. 12350, pp. 365–381. Springer, Cham (2020). https://doi.org/10.1007/978-3-030-58558-7_22
17. Funes Mora, K., Monay, F., Odobez, J.: EYEDIAP: a database for the development and evaluation of gaze estimation algorithms from RGB and RGB-D cameras. In: Proceedings of the Symposium on Eye Tracking Research and Applications, pp. 255–258 (2014)
18. Kingma, D., Ba, J.: Adam: a method for stochastic optimization. arXiv preprint arXiv:1412.6980 (2014)
19. Tzeng, E., Hoffman, J., Saenko, K., Darrell, T.: Adversarial discriminative domain adaptation. In: Proceedings of the IEEE Conference on Computer Vision and Pattern Recognition, pp. 7167–7176 (2017)
20. Cai, M., Lu, F., Sato, Y.: Generalizing hand segmentation in egocentric videos with uncertainty-guided model adaptation. In: Proceedings of the IEEE/CVF Conference on Computer Vision and Pattern Recognition, pp. 14392–14401 (2020)
21. Goodfellow, I., et al.: Generative adversarial nets. In: Advances in Neural Information Processing Systems, vol. 27 (2014)
22. Nguyen, A., Tran, T., Gal, Y., Torr, P., Baydin, A.: Kl guided domain adaptation. arXiv preprint arXiv:2106.07780 (2021)

Towards Fast Face Image Quality Assessment via Latent Diffusion Model

Zheyu Yan[1,3], Weisong Zhao[5,6], Xiangyu Zhu[1,3], Li Gao[2], Xiao-Yu Zhang[5,6], and Zhen Lei[1,3,4(✉)]

[1] State Key Laboratory of Multimodal Artificial Intelligence Systems, Institute of Automation, Chinese Academy of Sciences, Beijing, China
yanzheyu2024@ia.ac.cn, xiangyu.zhu@ia.ac.cn
[2] China Mobile Financial Technology Co., Ltd., Beijing, China
gaolids@chinamobile.com
[3] School of Artificial Intelligence, University of Chinese Academy of Sciences, Beijing, China
[4] Centre for Artificial Intelligence and Robotics, Hong Kong Institute of Science and Innovation, Chinese Academy of Sciences, Hong Kong, China
zhen.lei@ia.ac.cn
[5] Institute of Information Engineering, Chinese Academy of Sciences, Beijing, China
zhaoweisong@iie.ac.cn, zhangxiaoyu@iie.ac.cn
[6] School of Cyber Security, University of Chinese Academy of Sciences, Beijing, China

Abstract. Face recognition technology has gradually come into wide application in real life. However, in real-life unconstrained scenarios, low-quality images could be matched to unpredictable individuals, thereby affecting the stability of recognition and even causing security problems. Conducting quality assessment on face images before facial recognition can help alleviate these problems by rejecting low-quality samples. In this paper, we propose a Fast Diffusion-model-based Face Image Quality Assessment method (FDif-FIQA). It uses a diffusion model to perturb face images and measures image quality based on the similarity of features before and after the perturbation. The denoising process is transferred from the pixel space to the latent space, thereby reducing the computational cost. We evaluated the performance of this method with multiple mainstream face recognition models on various public datasets. Compared to state-of-the-art methods, our approach demonstrates highly competitive performance and significant improvements in computational efficiency.

Keywords: face recognition · face image quality assessment

1 Introduction

With the rapid development of artificial intelligence, face recognition (FR) has come into wide application. Although existing methods can achieve high accuracy under controlled conditions, real-life unconstrained environments often produce low-quality samples, leading to reduced recognition accuracy and potential mismatches. For instance, in access control systems, low-quality images of individuals not registered might be incorrectly matched to registered individuals, which could raise security concerns and cause financial losses. To solve the above problem, face images can be assessed for quality before recognition to filter out low-quality samples. Face Image Quality Assessment (FIQA) methods typically consider quality as the utility of an image for FR tasks, as defined in ISO/IEC 29794-1 [1]. Quality is expressed as a numerical value called the *quality score*, with higher scores indicating better quality. Recent state-of-the-art (SOTA) FIQA methods either generate pseudo-quality labels to train regression models for predicting quality scores or directly derive scores based on image or embedding properties. While the latter usually achieves better performance, they serve as analytical approaches to compute scores from human-defined rules, which may not precisely reflect the utility of samples for FR algorithms, and tend to be computationally expensive. For instance, DifFIQA [2], a SOTA method, uses a diffusion model to perturb image embeddings and assess their stability. However, this approach is computationally expensive due to the resolution of images and the iterative denoising process, posing challenges for practical applications. Our design, in contrast, significantly enhances computational efficiency.

We believe that the representations of higher-quality images are more stable in the latent space and less likely to be disturbed by a diffusion model. Therefore, the quality of samples is measured by the similarity before and after perturbation. We consider migrating the diffusion process from the pixel space to the latent space to avoid extensive computation. In the proposed method, we first add noise to the image and then reconstruct its embedding from that of the noisy image. This is because experiments show adding noise in the pixel space and denoising in the latent space significantly outperforms the method of adding and removing noise in the latent space. The similarity of embeddings before and after perturbation is used to reflect the quality of the sample. Our approach not only achieves highly competitive performance compared to SOTA methods but also offers a significant advantage in terms of computational efficiency.

In summary, the contributions of this paper include:

- We introduce FDif-FIQA, a novel method that utilizes a latent diffusion model to perturb face image embeddings, evaluating their stability in the latent space of a given FR model.
- The proposed FDif-FIQA enables the forward process to be conducted in the pixel space while the backward process is in the latent space.
- The extensive experiments on popular FR benchmarks show that our method achieves highly competitive performance compared to SOTA methods while significantly reducing computational load.

2 Related Work

2.1 Supervised FIQA

Supervised FIQA approaches train a regression model to generate a quality score for each sample. They differ from each other in the way the pseudo-quality labels are generated. Early works used manually annotated quality scores as pseudo-quality labels [3], but such an approach can make the performance susceptible to human factors, as humans might not fully understand the factors affecting quality for specific FR systems. Recent works often use automated methods to obtain pseudo-quality labels based on certain properties of the face image or its embedding. For example, FaceQnet [4] assumes an ICAO-compliant image is of perfect quality and derives labels by comparing the sample's embedding with the highest quality image of the same identity. PCNet [5] generates labels from the similarity of positive sample pairs, assuming it to be dependent on the lower-quality one in the pair. SDD-FIQA [6] calculates the Wasserstein distance between intra-class and inter-class similarity distribution to obtain pseudo-quality labels. LightQNet [7] derives labels from various image comparisons and uses an identification quality loss to train a lightweight model. CR-FIQA [8] defines the pseudo-quality labels as the ratio between a sample's distance to its positive class center and the nearest negative class center. Such FIQA approaches only involve minimal computational effort. However, the process of generating labels can introduce biases due to the FR model and dataset used.

2.2 Unsupervised FIQA

Unsupervised FIQA approaches analyze the quality of a sample based on the characteristics of samples in the pixel space or the latent space. Early methods typically relied on face image features such as illumination and pose [9,10]. However, these manually selected features often fail to reflect the utility of a face image to an FR model. Recent approaches mostly rely on properties in the latent space, usually based on the assumption that the embeddings of higher-quality samples are more stable. If some perturbation is applied to these samples or their embeddings, the embeddings will show smaller variations. SER-FIQ [11] generates different embeddings through different random patterns of dropout layers. MagFace [12] uses the magnitude of the embedding as an estimate of sample quality. FaceQAN [13] generates a series of adversarial samples by adding adversarial noise to the input image and then compares their embeddings to obtain the quality score. DifFIQA [2] introduces perturbations by the forward and backward processes for a diffusion model. Such FIQA approaches need to extract features from multiple instances for each input and tend to involve significant computational overhead, leading to longer processing times.

3 Methodology

3.1 Preliminaries

Denoising diffusion probabilistic models (DDPMs) [14] consist of a forward process and a backward process. The **forward process** gradually adds Gaussian noise to the input image x_0 to generate noisy images x_T over the time series $\{0, 1, \ldots, T\}$. The process is fixed to be the following Markov chain:

$$q(x_t \mid x_{t-1}) = \mathcal{N}\left(x_t; \sqrt{1 - \beta_t}\, x_{t-1}, \beta_t I\right), \tag{1}$$

where β_t controls the amount of noise added to the sample at time t. The noisy image x_t can be directly calculated from:

$$x_t = \sqrt{\bar{\alpha}_t}\, x_0 + \sqrt{1 - \bar{\alpha}_t}\, \epsilon, \tag{2}$$

where $\bar{\alpha}_t = \prod_{i=0}^{t}(1 - \beta_i)$ and $\epsilon \sim \mathcal{N}(0, I)$.

The **backward process**, iteratively removes noise predicted by a model ϵ_θ with parameters θ. At each time step t, the estimation of x_0 is as follows:

$$x_0' = \frac{x_t - \sqrt{1 - \bar{\alpha}_t}\, \epsilon_\theta(x_t)}{\sqrt{\bar{\alpha}_t}}. \tag{3}$$

The denoising diffusion implicit model (DDIM) [15] is a prominent denoising method known for its efficiency and deterministic output, which is also used in our implementation. It conducts each denoising step as:

$$x_{t-1} = \sqrt{\bar{\alpha}_{t-1}}\, x_0' + \sqrt{1 - \bar{\alpha}_{t-1}}\, \epsilon_\theta(x_t). \tag{4}$$

Latent diffusion models (LDMs) [16] shifts the diffusion process from pixel space to latent space with a fixed autoencoder, achieving excellent performance with substantially reduced computational costs. Our method extends the idea of LDM to FIQA. By replacing the encoder in LDM with an FR model, we map face images from pixel space to features in latent space. The backward process is operated on these features, improving performance and computational efficiency.

3.2 FDif-FIQA

Our method uses the forward and backward processes of the diffusion model to perturb image embeddings and quantifies the degree of change in embeddings as a quality score. An overview of our method is shown in Fig. 1. It can be divided into two steps: (i) embedding perturbation and (ii) quality score calculation.

In the embedding perturbation step, the forward process of the diffusion model adds noise to the input image x, producing a noisy image x_t. A pre-trained FR model, partitioned into two parts $M = \{M_1, M_2\}$, is then used to extract the embeddings, where M_2 denotes the last layer. Thus, we obtain $z = M_1(x)$ from the original image and $z_t = M_1(x_t)$ from the noisy image. The backward process reconstructs the denoised embedding $\hat{z}$ from z_t. To capture pose-related information, the horizontally flipped image x^f undergoes the same process to obtain z^f, z_t^f, and $\hat{z}^f$. In the quality score calculation step, the quality score is computed based on the similarity between z and the other embeddings.

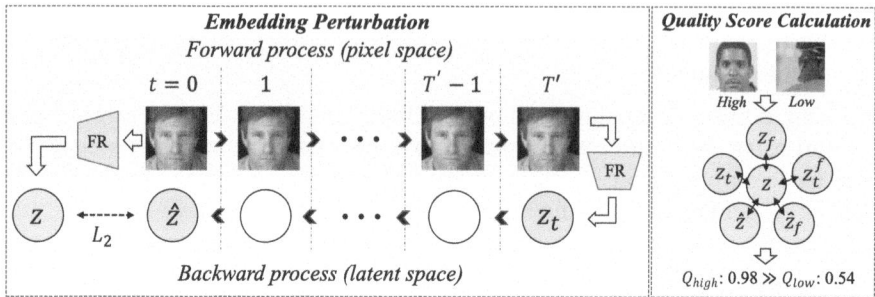

Fig. 1. Overview of the proposed FDif-FIQA. It can be divided into two steps: embedding perturbation and quality score calculation. A diffusion model is used to disturb the embeddings, with its forward process in the pixel space and backward process in the latent space. The process is repeated on a horizontally flipped image to capture the effect of the head pose. The quality score Q is calculated from the similarity of embeddings before and after the perturbation.

Embedding Perturbation. We use a diffusion model to perturb the embeddings of face images, conducting the forward process in pixel space and the backward process in latent space. First, we add noise to the input image x to obtain x_t. Next, M_1 extracts features z and z_t from them. We then use a noise prediction model ϵ_θ, implemented using DiT [17] in our approach, to estimate the noise from z_t. The reconstructed $\hat{z}$ are computed as follows:

$$\hat{z} = \frac{1}{\sqrt{\bar{\alpha}_t}} \left(z_t - \sqrt{1 - \bar{\alpha}_t} \, \epsilon_\theta \left(z_t, t \right) \right), \quad (5)$$

where $\bar{\alpha}_t$ is the cumulative product of noise schedule parameter, and $\epsilon_\theta(z_t, t)$ is the estimated noise at time step t by the noise prediction model. The noise prediction model is trained using the following loss function:

$$L_2 = \| z - \hat{z} \|_2^2. \quad (6)$$

Since head pose is a crucial factor in face quality to an FR model, we horizontally flip the original image x to obtain x^f. We repeat the aforementioned steps to compute the embeddings z^f, z_t^f, and $\hat{z^f}$ for x^f.

Quality-Score Calculation. The quality score is computed based on z and the other embeddings $\mathcal{D} = \{z_t, \hat{z}, z^f, z_t^f, \hat{z^f}\}$. These embeddings are first processed through the last layer of the FR model, denoted as M_2, transforming them from $C \times H \times W$ to C, following the practice of using C-dimensional features in face recognition. We denote the transformed embeddings as $M_2(\mathcal{D}) = \{M_2(z_t), M_2(\hat{z}), M_2(z^f), M_2(z_t^f), M_2(\hat{z^f})\}$. We believe that the embeddings of higher-quality images are more stable in the latent space, so the similarity between $M_2(z)$ and the embeddings in $M_2(\mathcal{D})$ should be higher. The quality score Q is defined as the average cosine similarity between these embeddings:

$$Q = \frac{1}{n|\mathcal{D}|} \sum_{i=1}^{n} \sum_{z_j \in M_2(\mathcal{D})} \frac{M_2(z)^T z_j}{\|M_2(z)\| \cdot \|z_j\|}. \tag{7}$$

For each sample, we repeat the whole embedding perturbation process n times to reduce the impact of randomly generated noise in the diffusion model.

Table 1. Comparison to the SOTA methods. The table reports pAUC scores at a discard rate of 0.3 and an FMR of 10^{-3} and shows the average results across all datasets in $\overline{\text{pAUC}}$. The best result for each dataset is shown in bold.

(a) ArcFace

Method	year	CALFW	CFP-FP	CPLFW	LFW	$\overline{\text{pAUC}}$
FaceQnet[4]	2019	0.955	0.693	0.878	0.884	0.853
SDD-FIQA[6]	2021	0.901	0.491	0.734	0.808	0.734
PFE[18]	2019	0.932	0.524	0.738	0.779	0.743
PCNet[5]	2020	1.006	0.868	0.783	**0.623**	0.820
MagFace[12]	2021	0.902	0.549	0.717	0.635	0.701
LightQNet[7]	2021	0.913	0.612	0.752	0.745	0.756
SER-FIQA[11]	2020	0.903	0.416	0.656	0.935	0.728
FaceQAN[13]	2022	0.941	0.373	0.677	0.624	0.654
CR-FIQA[8]	2023	0.891	0.358	0.689	0.675	0.653
FaceQgen[19]	2021	0.985	0.784	0.701	0.802	0.818
DifFIQA[2]	2023	0.900	0.399	0.647	0.695	0.660
DifFIQA(R)[2]	2023	**0.898**	**0.389**	0.646	0.708	0.660
Ours	2024	**0.898**	0.413	**0.544**	0.675	**0.633**

(b) CosFace

Method	year	CALFW	CFP-FP	CPLFW	LFW	$\overline{\text{pAUC}}$
FaceQnet[4]	2019	0.955	0.693	0.879	0.884	0.853
SDD-FIQA[6]	2021	0.901	0.491	0.735	0.808	0.734
PFE[18]	2019	0.932	0.524	0.748	0.779	0.746
PCNet[5]	2020	1.006	0.868	0.835	0.623	0.833
MagFace[12]	2021	0.902	0.549	0.724	0.635	0.703
LightQNet[7]	2021	0.913	0.612	0.753	0.745	0.756
SER-FIQA[11]	2020	0.903	0.416	0.711	0.935	0.741
FaceQAN[13]	2022	0.941	**0.373**	0.667	0.624	0.651
CR-FIQA[8]	2023	**0.891**	0.358	0.681	0.675	0.651
FaceQgen[19]	2021	0.985	0.784	0.702	0.802	0.818
DifFIQA[2]	2023	0.900	0.399	0.669	0.695	0.666
DifFIQA(R)[2]	2023	0.900	0.389	0.669	0.695	0.663
Ours	2024	0.914	0.385	**0.642**	**0.583**	**0.631**

(c) CurricularFace

Method	year	CALFW	CFP-FP	CPLFW	LFW	$\overline{\text{pAUC}}$
FaceQnet[4]	2019	0.947	0.601	0.867	0.908	0.831
SDD-FIQA[6]	2021	0.900	0.409	0.696	0.821	0.707
PFE[18]	2019	0.923	0.415	0.691	0.785	0.704
PCNet[5]	2020	0.996	0.887	0.899	0.656	0.860
MagFace[12]	2021	0.892	0.477	0.689	0.661	0.680
LightQNet[7]	2021	0.910	0.462	0.704	0.767	0.711
SER-FIQA[11]	2020	0.883	0.389	0.625	0.942	0.710
FaceQAN[13]	2022	0.931	0.343	0.637	0.644	0.639
CR-FIQA[8]	2023	**0.877**	0.318	0.615	0.693	0.626
FaceQgen[19]	2021	0.974	0.662	0.698	0.845	0.795
DifFIQA[2]	2023	0.884	0.384	0.624	0.711	0.651
DifFIQA(R)[2]	2023	0.892	0.358	0.622	0.724	**0.649**
Ours	2024	0.895	0.536	**0.604**	**0.633**	0.667

(d) AdaFace

Method	year	CALFW	CFP-FP	CPLFW	LFW	$\overline{\text{pAUC}}$
FaceQnet[4]	2019	0.938	0.717	0.887	0.884	0.857
SDD-FIQA[6]	2021	0.871	0.500	0.688	0.825	0.721
PFE[18]	2019	0.890	0.566	0.681	0.771	0.727
PCNet[5]	2020	0.979	0.862	0.898	0.661	0.850
MagFace[12]	2021	0.866	0.524	0.664	0.666	0.680
LightQNet[7]	2021	0.894	0.641	0.684	0.777	0.749
SER-FIQA[11]	2020	0.892	0.475	0.626	0.935	0.732
FaceQAN[13]	2022	0.919	**0.383**	0.619	0.656	0.644
CR-FIQA[8]	2023	**0.851**	0.391	0.588	0.707	0.634
FaceQgen[19]	2021	0.970	0.718	0.694	0.834	0.804
DifFIQA[2]	2023	0.900	0.416	0.608	0.719	0.661
DifFIQA(R)[2]	2023	0.895	0.412	0.601	0.708	0.654
Ours	2024	0.906	0.440	**0.546**	**0.633**	**0.631**

4 Experiments and Results

4.1 Experimental Setup

Experimental Setting. Our method is compared with 11 SOTA FIQA methods, namely: (i) supervised methods including FaceQnet [4], PCNet [5], SDD-FIQA [6], and LightQnet [7], and (ii) unsupervised methods including CR-FIQA

[8], SER-FIQ [11], MagFace [12], FaceQAN [13], DifFIQA [2], PFE [18], and FaceQgen [19]. We test on four mainstream FR datasets, including CrossAge Labeled Faces in the Wild (CALFW) [20], Celebrities in Frontal-Profile in the Wild (CFP-FP) [21], CrossPose Labeled Faces in the Wild (CPLFW) [22], and Labeled Faces in the Wild (LFW) [23]. Since the performance of FIQA methods is influenced by the FR models used, we select four SOTA FR models CosFace [24], ArcFace [25], CurricularFace [26], and AdaFace [27] for testing to explore the generalization of the method across different FR models. We use the officially released pre-trained ResNet-100 models, of which AdaFace and ArcFace are trained on MS1MV3, CurricularFace on MS1MV2, and CosFace on Glint360K. In replicating CR-FIQA and DifFIQA, we utilized their official codebases and adhered to their use of the ResNet-100 backbone.

Experimental Methodology. Following standard evaluation methods [2,8], we assess the performance of the method using the Error-versus-Discard Characteristic (EDC) curve and the partial Area Under the Curve (pAUC) values calculated from it. The EDC curve plots the discard rate on the x-axis against the False Non-Match Rate (FNMR) on the y-axis for a predefined False Match Rate (FMR). For an FMR of 10^{-3}, we evaluate test images using the FIQA method and progressively discard low-quality images. As the discard rate increases, the FNMR of the FR model gradually decreases. A more accurate FIQA method results in a more rapid decline in the FNMR curve. Thus, the area under the curve can be used to measure the method's performance, with a smaller area indicating better performance. Since discarding a large proportion of samples is impractical in real-world scenarios, we follow the testing protocol of [2] and focus on performance at lower discard rates. Specifically, we calculate the pAUC based on the curve segment where the discard rate is below 30%. To facilitate comparison across different datasets, we normalize the computed pAUC values using the FNMR at a discard rate of zero.

Implementation Details. During the training of the diffusion model, the maximum number of steps is set to $T = 1000$. The number of noise addition steps in training is limited to $t \in [1, T']$, where $T' < T$, to keep the perturbation within a smaller range so that the information related to FR will not be destroyed. For inference, the noise addition step t adheres to the upper limit of T', which is set to 100 in this paper. The diffusion process is repeated $n = 10$ times to reduce the random effects of sampling noise. Training is performed using the Adam optimizer with a learning rate of 1.0×10^{-6}, and a cosine learning rate scheduler with a warm-up epoch of 5. The batch size is set to 128, and an Exponential Moving Average (EMA) model is used with a decay rate of 0.995. The model is trained on the MS1MV3 [28] dataset.

4.2 Comparison with the State-of-the-Art

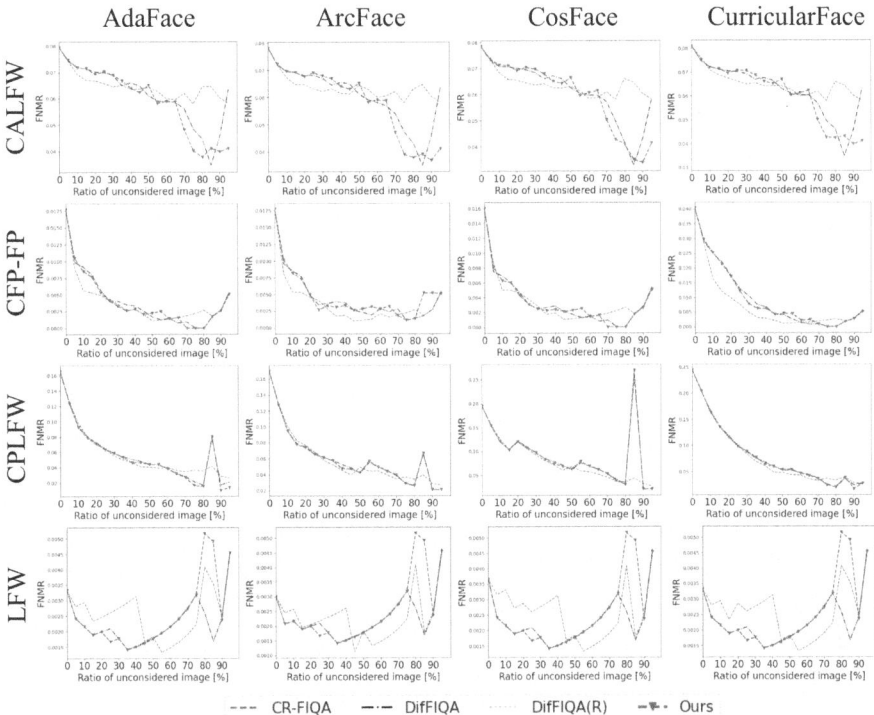

Fig. 2. ERC curves at FMR=10^{-3} compared to SOTA methods. Our method achieves lower FNMR, especially at a low rejection rate.

Performance Analysis. The EDC curves obtained by testing our method on different datasets and FR models are shown in Fig. 2. Based on these curves, the pAUC values calculated for discard rates less than or equal to 0.3 and comparisons with SOTA methods are presented in Table 1, where a smaller pAUC indicates better performance. It can be seen that our proposed FDif-FIQA method demonstrates highly competitive performance across all datasets and FR models. It demonstrates particularly superior performance on CPLFW and LFW, achieving the best $\overline{\text{pAUC}}$ values across three FR models.

Ablation Study. Our method differs from common diffusion models in that the forward process is conducted in the pixel space and the backward process is conducted in the latent space. We explored changing the spaces for the forward and backward processes, as shown in Table 2. The approach with the forward process in the latent space and the backward process in the pixel space is not feasible because the features extracted by an FR model cannot be reconstructed into face images, thus not considered. We performed inference tests on the LFW, CPLFW, and CALFW datasets using the ArcFace FR model and recorded the time taken. The experiments were conducted on an Intel Xeon Gold 6330 CPU

Table 2. Ablation studies on varying the forward and backward processes across different spaces. Results for both processes conducted in pixel space are sourced from DifFIQA. The time represents the average processing time per sample.

Forward process		Backward process		Time(ms)	CALFW	CPLFW	LFW	Avg
Pixel	Latent	Pixel	Latent					
✓		✓		2380	0.900	0.647	0.695	0.747
	✓		✓	**769**	0.936	0.607	0.859	0.801
✓			✓	875	**0.898**	**0.544**	**0.675**	**0.706**

with an NVIDIA M40 GPU. The results show that our design outperforms the other two designs in terms of performance and is nearly optimal in terms of time efficiency. The approach where both noise addition and denoising are conducted in the latent space achieves poor performance, which might be because adding Gaussian noise directly in the latent space does not align with the distribution patterns of features in that space, whereas adding Gaussian noise in the pixel space aligns with real-world conditions, which explains why our method work.

5 Conclusion

We propose a novel FIQA method named FDif-FIQA that leverages a diffusion model to perturb the embeddings of face images, exploring their stability in the embedding space of a given FR model. Experiments on multiple datasets and FR models demonstrate that our method exhibits competitive performance compared to SOTA methods while significantly reducing computational cost. In the future, we consider performing both noise addition and denoising in the latent space to further explore the application of LDM in FIQA.

Acknowledgments. This work was supported in part by Chinese National Natural Science Foundation Projects U23B2054, 62276254, 62106264, the Youth Innovation Promotion Association CAS Y2021131 and InnoHK program.

References

1. International Organization for Standardization: ISO/IEC 29794–1:2024 information technology - biometric sample quality - part 1: framework, Technical report, ISO (2024)
2. Babnik, Ž., Peer, P., Štruc, V.: DifFIQA: face image quality assessment using denoising diffusion probabilistic models. In: 2023 IEEE International Joint Conference on Biometrics (IJCB), pp. 1–10. IEEE (2023)
3. Best-Rowden, L., Jain, A.K.: Learning face image quality from human assessments. IEEE Trans. Inf. Forensics Secur. **13**(12), 3064–3077 (2018)
4. Hernandez-Ortega, J., Galbally, J., Fierrez, J., Haraksim, R., Beslay, L.: FaceQnet: quality assessment for face recognition based on deep learning. In: 2019 International Conference on Biometrics (ICB), pp. 1–8. IEEE (2019)

5. Xie, W., Byrne, J., Zisserman, A.: Inducing predictive uncertainty estimation for face verification. In: BMVC (2020)
6. Ou, F.Z., et al.: SDD-FIQA: unsupervised face image quality assessment with similarity distribution distance. In: Proceedings of the IEEE/CVF Conference on Computer Vision and Pattern Recognition, pp. 7670–7679 (2021)
7. Chen, K., Yi, T., Lv, Q.: LightQNet: lightweight deep face quality assessment for risk-controlled face recognition. IEEE Sig. Process. Lett., pp. 1878–1882 (2021)
8. Boutros, F., Fang, M., Klemt, M., Fu, B., Damer, N.: CR-FIQA: face image quality assessment by learning sample relative classifiability. In: Proceedings of the IEEE/CVF Conference on Computer Vision and Pattern Recognition (2023)
9. Gao, X., Li, S.Z., Liu, R., Zhang, P.: Standardization of face image sample quality. In: Lee, S.-W., Li, S.Z. (eds.) ICB 2007. LNCS, vol. 4642, pp. 242–251. Springer, Heidelberg (2007). https://doi.org/10.1007/978-3-540-74549-5_26
10. Nasrollahi, K., Moeslund, T.B.: Extracting a good quality frontal face image from a low-resolution video sequence. IEEE Trans. Circuits Syst. Video Technol. **21**(10), 1353–1362 (2011)
11. Terhorst, P., Kolf, J.N., Damer, N., Kirchbuchner, F., Kuijper, A.: SER-FIQ: unsupervised estimation of face image quality based on stochastic embedding robustness. In: Proceedings of the IEEE/CVF Conference on Computer Vision and Pattern Recognition, pp. 5651–5660 (2020)
12. Meng, Q., Zhao, S., Huang, Z., Zhou, F.: MagFace: a universal representation for face recognition and quality assessment. In: Proceedings of the IEEE/CVF Conference on Computer Vision and Pattern Recognition, pp. 14225–14234 (2021)
13. Babnik, Ž., Peer, P., Štruc, V.: FaceQAN: face image quality assessment through adversarial noise exploration. In: 2022 26th International Conference on Pattern Recognition (ICPR), pp. 748–754. IEEE (2022)
14. Ho, J., Jain, A., Abbeel, P.: Denoising diffusion probabilistic models. Adv. Neural. Inf. Process. Syst. **33**, 6840–6851 (2020)
15. Song, J., Meng, C., Ermon, S.: Denoising diffusion implicit models. arXiv preprint arXiv:2010.02502 (2020)
16. Rombach, R., Blattmann, A., Lorenz, D., Esser, P., Ommer, B.: High-resolution image synthesis with latent diffusion models. In: Proceedings of the IEEE/CVF Conference on Computer Vision and Pattern Recognition, pp. 10684–10695 (2022)
17. Peebles, W., Xie, S.: Scalable diffusion models with transformers. In: Proceedings of the IEEE/CVF International Conference on Computer Vision, pp. 4195–4205 (2023)
18. Shi, Y., Jain, A.K.: Probabilistic face embeddings. In: Proceedings of the IEEE/CVF International Conference on Computer Vision, pp. 6902–6911 (2019)
19. Hernandez-Ortega, J., Fierrez, J., Serna, I., Morales, A.: FaceQgen: semi-supervised deep learning for face image quality assessment. In: 2021 16th IEEE International Conference on Automatic Face and Gesture Recognition (FG 2021), pp. 1–8. IEEE (2021)
20. Zheng, T., Deng, W., Hu, J.: Cross-Age LFW: a database for studying cross-age face recognition in unconstrained environments. arXiv preprint arXiv:1708.08197 (2017)
21. Sengupta, S., Chen, J.C., Castillo, C., Patel, V.M., Chellappa, R., Jacobs, D.W.: Frontal to profile face verification in the wild. In: 2016 IEEE Winter Conference on Applications of Computer Vision (WACV), pp. 1–9. IEEE (2016)
22. Zheng, T., Deng, W.: Cross-Pose LFW: a database for studying cross-pose face recognition in unconstrained environments. Beijing University of Posts and Telecommunications, Techical report, vol. 5, no. 7, p. 5(2018)

23. Huang, G.B., Mattar, M., Berg, T., Learned-Miller, E.: Labeled faces in the wild: a database for studying face recognition in unconstrained environments. In: Workshop on Faces in Real-Life Images: Detection, Alignment, and Recognition (2008)
24. Wang, H., et al.: CosFace: large margin cosine loss for deep face recognition. In: Proceedings of the IEEE Conference on Computer Vision and Pattern Recognition, pp. 5265–5274 (2018)
25. Deng, J., Guo, J., Xue, N., Zafeiriou, S.: ArcFace: additive angular margin loss for deep face recognition. In: Proceedings of the IEEE/CVF Conference on Computer Vision and Pattern Recognition, pp. 4690–4699 (2019)
26. Huang, Y., et al.: CurricularFace: adaptive curriculum learning loss for deep face recognition. In: Proceedings of the IEEE/CVF Conference on Computer Vision and Pattern Recognition, pp. 5901–5910 (2020)
27. Kim, M., Jain, A.K., Liu, X.: AdaFace: quality adaptive margin for face recognition. In: Proceedings of the IEEE/CVF Conference on Computer Vision and Pattern Recognition, pp. 18750–18759 (2022)
28. Deng, J., Guo, J., Zhang, D., Deng, Y., Lu, X., Shi, S.: Lightweight face recognition challenge. In: Proceedings of the IEEE/CVF International Conference on Computer Vision Workshops, pp. 2638–2646 (2019)

Unknown-Aware Diverse Prompt Learning for Open-Set Single Domain Generalization-Based Face Anti-spoofing

Fangling Jiang[1], Qi Li[2,3(✉)], Weining Wang[2], Bing Liu[1], and Zhenan Sun[2,3]

[1] School of Computer Science, University of South China, Hengyang 421001, China
{jfl,bingliu}@usc.edu.cn
[2] NLPR, MAIS, CASIA, Beijing 100190, China
{qli,weining.wang,znsun}@nlpr.ia.ac.cn
[3] School of Artificial Intelligence, UCAS, Beijing 100190, China

Abstract. Recently, the generalization capability of face anti-spoofing models has taken the attention of both industry and academia. Among all the problems, domain shift and unknown attacks are the most serious problems affecting generalization performance. Existing work usually focuses on dealing with one of the above problems. In this paper, we address a challenging but practical problem, open-set single domain generalization-based (OSSDG-based) face anti-spoofing, simultaneously addressing these two problems with limited training data. We propose a novel unknown-aware diverse prompt learning framework, which mines the visual-language pre-training knowledge for OSSDG-based face anti-spoofing by text prompt generation and unknown-aware learning regularization. Extensive experimental results demonstrate that the proposed method achieves state-of-the-art performance on both known classes and unknown attacks in cross-scenario domains with a single training domain.

Keywords: face anti-spoofing · unknown attack detection · generalized feature learning

1 Introduction

Face anti-spoofing is a crucial technique for the security of face recognition, which aims to prevent spoof faces (e.g., printed photos, replayed videos, or 3D masks) from being verified by face recognition systems. Through the efforts of industry and academia in recent years, excellent performance has been achieved in intra-domain scenarios. However, existing methods still fail to generalize well to cross-domain scenarios [1]. Unseen domains and unknown attacks are the main problems that lead to poor generalization ability in cross-domain scenarios. The unseen domains represent domains that have domain shift, which is caused by changes in extrinsic factors that are spoof-irrelevant but affect the appearance of captured images (e.g., acquisition devices, illumination conditions, and background settings). Unknown attacks refer to new attack types with intrinsic spoof-relevant physical properties that have never been present in the training data (e.g., material and geometry) [1].

Existing work usually focuses on dealing with one of the above problems [2,3]. However, unseen domains and unknown attacks usually appear together in practical applications. To simultaneously address both issues, recent studies [4] have leveraged open-set single-domain generalization (OSSDG) techniques to enhance the generalization ability of face anti-spoofing system to both known and unknown attack types in unseen test domains based a single source domain. OSSDG-based face anti-spoofing is more universal and applicable to real-world scenarios; however, it still offers significant potential for performance enhancement due to the task complexity.

Vision-language pre-training models (e.g., CLIP [5]) show strong zero-shot transfer capability, they are exploited for face anti-spoofing by grounding visual representations with the help of natural language [6,7]. However, conventional deterministic hand-crafted prompts (e.g., A photo of a live/spoof face) not only require expert experience, which is tedious and time-consuming, but also are difficult to adequately adapt to face anti-spoofing tasks. To mine the pre-training knowledge better, the prompts for live faces and various attack types are expected to be diverse, semantic, unknown-aware, automatically generated, and thus can provide richer contextual information corresponding to variants of live faces and attack types.

In this paper, we propose an unknown-aware diverse prompt learning framework for OSSDG-based face anti-spoofing, as illustrated in Fig. 1. The proposed framework mines the rich visual-language multi-modal knowledge to improve the generalizability of the learned model by text prompt generation and unknown-aware learning regularization. Specifically, we design a learnable prompt generator to generate diverse prompts for each class with injected class prior information. The prior information is extracted from a pre-trained language model and modeled as a learnable Gaussian distribution to ensure semantic consistency and diversity of the generated prompts. Consequently, the automatically optimized prompts can provide a more powerful representation of different types of faces. In addition, an unknown-aware learning regularization is designed to constrain the prompt generator to be aware of both known classes and unknown attacks. For a given sample, it constrains the output of the image-text similarity vector by giving the highest prediction probability to the ground truth and the second highest probability to the unknown label. In this way, generalizability over known classes is ensured while allowing the detection of unknown attacks without other predefined category systems. The main contributions of this paper include:

1. We propose a novel unknown-aware diverse prompt learning framework, which mines the rich visual-language pre-training knowledge for OSSDG-based face anti-spoofing by automatic prompt generation.
2. We design an unknown-aware learning regularization to constrain the prompt generator to detect unknown attack types.

3. Experimental results on 8 benchmarks show that the proposed method achieves state-of-the-art performance on both known and unknown classes in unseen domains using a single training domain only.

2 Related Work

Face Anti-spoofing. Considering the real-world application of face anti-spoofing, the problem of poor generalization capability on cross-domain scenarios has received much attention [1,8]. On one hand, the physical discrepancy existing in depth maps [9], rPPG signals [9], and multimodal images [10] between live and spoof faces are exploited to learn generalized features. On the other hand, feature learning-based methods such as domain adaptation [11] and domain generalization [7] are employed to learn domain-invariant features, which aims to reduce the impact of domain shift. In addition, considering the unpredictability of the unknown attack types in the test scenarios, few-shot learning, zero-shot learning, and anomaly detection [3] are also presented to detect rare or unknown attacks for face anti-spoofing. Unlike the previous ones, open-set single-domain generalization is explored to address both domain shift and unknown attacks for face anti-spoofing in [4]. In this paper, we mine the visual-language multi-modal knowledge to improve the generalizability of OSSDG-based face anti-spoofing models.

Prompt Learning. Prompt learning aims to learn optimal context descriptions for downstream visual tasks [12,13] with pre-trained vision-language models [14–16]. Most existing work focuses on text prompt learning. For instance, CoOp [17] designs learnable word vectors to learn context information for different classes. CoCoOp [18] extends CoOp and generates image-specific text prompts by a meta-learning paradigm to mitigate the overfitting on known classes. In contrast to text prompt learning, VPL [19] learns an image perturbation, which is added on input images, as visual prompts. Moreover, unified prompt tuning [20] performs text and visual prompt learning simultaneously, which combines the advantages of both prompts. In this paper, we design a learnable prompt generator equipped with injected class prior knowledge and unknown-aware learning regularization to generate diverse, semantic, and unknown-aware text prompts. These prompts serve the purpose of adequately describing task-specific context information for face anti-spoofing.

3 Method

3.1 Prompt Generation with Injected Category Information

Deterministic prompts or prompts where all categories share the same context [17] cannot fully describe the complex attack types of face anti-spoofing. To mine the rich visual-language multi-modal knowledge in pre-training models for face anti-spoofing, we design a learnable prompt generator G to automatically generate diverse prompts for each class with injected class prior knowledge.

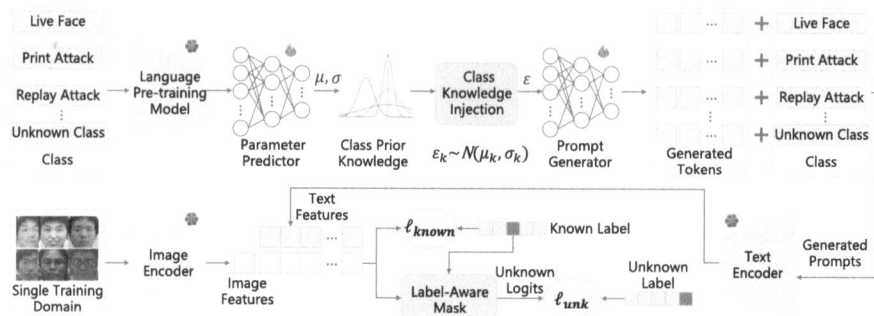

Fig. 1. Overview of the unknown-aware diverse prompt learning framework.

Considering the significant differences between different attack types, each type of known attack is regarded as a separate class. In this paper, we select two common attack types as known attacks. Adding the class of live faces, the total number of known classes K is three. The class name set $\mathcal{C}_n$ corresponding to $\mathcal{C}$ is designed as $\{live\ face,\ print\ attack,\ replay\ attack\}$. Given the k-th class name c_k in $\mathcal{C}_n$ ($k \in \{1, 2, ..., K\}$), its prompt t_k consists of token embedding of the prefix context sequence and the class name. Formally, $t_k = [v_1^k][v_2^k]...[v_L^k][c_k]$, where L is the number of context tokens and $[v_i^k]$ ($i \in \{1, 2, ..., L\}$) represents the i-th context vector for class c_k. It is well known that the same type of sample (live faces or attack types) will vary in the specific image appearance depending on the acquisition equipment, lighting conditions, and acquisition background. Moreover, the same type of attack usually has many variants, which differ in some minor physical attributes. For instance, the exact implementation of print attacks can be attacks from photos printed on plain paper, photos printed on coated paper, photos with localized areas cropped out, and bent printed photos. To allow prompts to generalize to these two types of variants in face anti-spoofing, the prompt generator generates diverse context vectors according to different semantic input vectors for each class. Suppose that ε_k represents the input vector of c_k. The context vectors are generated as $[v_1^k][v_2^k]...[v_L^k] = G(\varepsilon_k)$. The learnable prompt generator is designed as a lightweight network for efficient training, which can be simply implemented as two fully connected layers.

In order to ensure the diversity and preserve the semantic meaning of the generated prompts, we inject class prior information into the input vector. The prior information associated with a class is extracted from a pre-training language model M (e.g., the text encoder of CLIP), which is trained on large-scale real-world data samples. M takes class names as input and outputs class-related prior knowledge. We model the prior knowledge by a learnable Gaussian distribution. Support that μ_k, σ_k represents the mean and variance of the Gaussian distribution d_k of the class c_k. μ_k, σ_k are generated by a learnable parameter predictor P, which takes the output of M as input. The learnable parameter predictor P is also designed as a lightweight network, which can be simply implemented as two fully connected layers. The element of the output vector

$P(M(c_k)) \in \mathbb{R}^2$ represents μ_k and σ_k, respectively. We randomly sample from the Gaussian distribution d_k and encode class prior information into the semantic input vector ε_k as follows: $\varepsilon_k \sim N(\mu_k, \sigma_k)$.

Consequently, the diversity and the semantic meaning of the generated prompts are preserved. Since the generated prompts can describe the context for different types of faces more adequately, our method can adapt visual-language models to fit face anti-spoofing tasks more effectively and efficiently. During training, the parameters of the image encoder and text encoder are frozen. Only the parameters of the prompt generator and parameter predictor are optimized to generate optimal prompts.

3.2 Unknown-Aware Learning Regularization

In face anti-spoofing, the unseen domains usually present unknown attack types. In order to improve the generalization ability of face anti-spoofing models, we train the model to detect the unknown attack types, rather than arbitrarily judge unknown attack types as one of the known classes and cause performance degradation as in previous work. Specifically, we add the 'Unknown Class' to the class name set $\mathcal{C}_n$. Thus, the number of classes in $\mathcal{C}_n$ and $\mathcal{C}$ is extended to $K+1$. The optimization of the prompt generator and parameter predictor is constrained by an unknown-aware learning regularization, which consists of known and unknown discrimination regularization.

The known and unknown discrimination regularization is simply implemented via cross-entropy loss. We forward the input image to the image encoder I and text prompts to the text encoder E, respectively. Then, we compute the similarity between the training sample (x^s, y^s) and the generated text prompts t_k as follows:

$$d_k(\boldsymbol{x}^s, t_k) = \boldsymbol{I}(\boldsymbol{x}^s) \cdot E\left(\boldsymbol{t}_k\right)^{\mathrm{T}} \quad (1)$$

where $k \in \{1, 2, ..., K+1\}$, d_k represents the k-th element of the similarity vector $d \in \mathbb{R}^{K+1}$. The similarity vector d is used as logits in the known and unknown discrimination regularization.

The known discrimination regularization constrains the similarity vector giving the highest predictive probability to the class corresponding to the sample. It is defined as follows:

$$\ell_{known}(x^s, y^s) = \sum_{i=1}^{K+1} y_i \log \frac{e^{d_i}}{\sum_{j=1}^{K+1} e^{d_j}}, \quad (2)$$

where y_i is a binary indicator, $y_i = 1$ if y^s is the i-th class of $\mathcal{C}$, and $y_i = 0$ otherwise.

Meanwhile, the unknown discrimination regularization constrains the similarity vector giving the second highest predictive probability to the unknown label. Specifically, we remove the output dimension corresponding to the sample class in the similarity vector d, and get a masked K-dimensional similarity vector $\widehat{d} \in \mathbb{R}^K$. Since the input sample does not belong to any class in $\mathcal{C}\backslash y^s$ and it is practically unknown to all the classes in $\mathcal{C}\backslash y^s$, the unknown discrimination regularization can be designed as constraining the masked similarity vector $\widehat{d}$ to give the highest predictive probability to the unknown label (the K-th class of $\mathcal{C}\backslash y^s$) as follows:

$$\ell_{unk}(x^s, y^s) = log \frac{e^{\widehat{d}_K}}{\sum_{j=1}^{K} e^{\widehat{d}_j}}. \qquad (3)$$

In this way, the trained face anti-spoofing model will have the ability to detect unknown attack types without other predefined category systems and complex threshold settings.

Combining the known and unknown discrimination regularization, the highest probability will occur in the dimension where the ground truth is located, and the second highest probability will occur in the dimension where the unknown label is located. That is, the model is capable of classifying known class samples along with detecting unknown attack types. This improves the generalization capability of our method on both known classes and unknown attacks of unseen domains at the same time.

3.3 Overall Objective and Inference

In summary, the parameters of the prompt generator and parameter predictor are optimized to minimize the overall loss $\ell_{known} + \ell_{unk}$ during training. During inference, given a testing sample from $\{\mathcal{D}_j^t\}_{j=1}^{J}$, we first use the well-trained prompt generator and parameter predictor to generate prompts for all classes name in the extended $\mathcal{C}_n$. Then, we compute the similarity vector d according to Eq. 1. The predicted probability vector is obtained by performing a softmax operation on the similarity vector d. During inference, we regard face anti-spoofing as a binary classification problem. We sum the probabilities of all attack types as the final predicted probability of the spoof face class.

4 Experiments

4.1 Experimental Setup

Evaluation Protocols and Metrics. We evaluate the effectiveness of the proposed method on six widely used datasets: CASIA-MFSD [21] (C for short), Replay-Attack [22] (I), MSU-MFSD [23] (M), OULU-NPU [24] (O), HQ-WMCA [25] (H) and Rose-Youtu [11] (R). The half total error rate (HTER) and area under the curve (AUC) are employed to quantitatively evaluate the performance of models. Class activation maps (CAMs) are utilized to qualitatively analyze the proposed method.

Implementation Details. We randomly select one frame from each original video to train and test models. All aligned face images are resized to a resolution of 224 × 224 pixels and undergone a random rotation within a range of 0 to 45°. The known classes of the training domain comprise live faces, print attacks, and replay attacks. We choose the CLIP model (backbone network is ViT-B/32) as the vision-language pre-training model. The batch size is set to 32. The number of context tokens L is set to 4. To optimize the prompt generator and parameter predictor, we utilize an Adam with betas of (0.9, 0.999) as the optimizer. The initial learning rate is 0.05 and is adjusted through exponential decay.

Table 1. Comparison with state-of-the-art face anti-spoofing methods using HQ-WMCA dataset as the testing domain.

Method	C to H		I to H		M to H		O to H	
	HTER (%)	AUC (%)	HTER (%)	AUC (%)	HTER (%)	AUC (%)	HTER (%)	AUC (%)
Color texture [26]	43.66	61.70	49.63	50.00	50.00	50.00	42.20	60.07
DR-UDA [27]	40.43	62.23	43.84	57.19	42.70	59.40	39.82	64.09
USDAN [2]	38.96	66.30	38.30	66.40	40.64	62.80	29.09	75.60
PatchCNN [28]	39.54	64.54	35.03	73.24	38.21	67.28	34.24	65.77
CGRL [4]	27.24	78.81	28.03	79.37	34.79	71.26	27.23	80.75
ViTAF* [29]	26.98	76.46	28.07	79.61	39.73	63.42	28.90	76.41
Proposed method	**23.53**	**83.13**	**17.88**	**90.14**	**32.22**	**70.32**	**27.08**	**80.40**

Table 2. Comparison with state-of-the-art face anti-spoofing methods using Rose-Youtu dataset as the testing domain.

Method	C to R		I to R		M to R		O to R	
	HTER (%)	AUC (%)	HTER (%)	AUC (%)	HTER (%)	AUC (%)	HTER (%)	AUC (%)
Color texture [26]	54.59	47.06	48.35	52.00	43.50	60.54	40.13	64.23
DR-UDA [27]	35.35	70.05	39.66	61.80	38.94	62.18	38.87	63.70
USDAN [2]	21.44	83.37	34.15	69.00	28.90	67.65	19.43	85.60
PatchCNN [28]	20.86	81.91	28.14	73.20	33.81	67.18	19.85	83.79
CGRL [4]	20.11	86.00	27.57	75.87	29.26	76.55	**17.87**	87.40
ViTAF* [29]	19.18	89.32	31.93	73.51	33.28	72.04	22.43	86.75
Proposed method	**16.29**	**90.71**	**24.10**	**84.46**	**24.32**	**83.13**	18.39	**90.10**

4.2 Comparison with State-of-the-Art Methods

Tables 1 and 2 present the comparison results among previous state-of-the-art face anti-spoofing methods and the proposed method on HQ-WMCA and Rose-Youtu datasets. The proposed method achieves significant performance improvements on most protocols compared to the previous state-of-the-art method, where 5 of them have an improvement rate exceeding 10% in terms of HTER (36.21% on I to H, 16.88% on M to R, and 15.06% on C to R). The proposed method outperforms previous methods by a large margin on the two testing domains, regardless of whether the unknown attack types are simple or complex.

The significant performance improvements indicate that the proposed unknown-aware diverse prompt learning framework is effective in learning face anti-spoofing models that can generalize well to unseen domains with known and unknown attacks. Note that both the proposed method and ViTAF* use ViT-B as the backbone of the image feature extractor. The performance improvements demonstrate that the proposed text prompt learning paradigm is conducive to mining the knowledge in visual-language pre-training models, which is effective in improving the generalization performance for OSSDG-based face anti-spoofing.

4.3 Ablation Studies

Effectiveness of The Unknown Discrimination Regularization. Table 3 gives the evaluation results about the effectiveness of different components of the proposed method on protocol C to H. We remove ℓ_{unk} during training to evaluate the contribution of the unknown discrimination regularization. Without ℓ_{unk}, the performance is reduced by 10.26%. This indicates that unknown-aware prompt learning is critical for generalized feature learning in OSSDG-based face anti-spoofing.

Table 3. Evaluation of the effectiveness of different components of the proposed method.

Method	HTER (%)	AUC (%)
w/o ℓ_{unk}	26.22	80.55
CoOP	25.46	81.37
CoOP+CSC	28.68	77.02
Proposed method	23.53	83.13

Effectiveness of The Prompt Generation Paradigm. We use learnable word vectors as designed in CoOP and CoOP+CSC to replace the prompt generation module to evaluate the effectiveness of the proposed prompt generation module. In CoOP, all types of faces share the same word vector. In CoOP+CSC, different types of faces have different word vectors. As shown in Table 3, for the OSSDG-based face anti-spoofing task, the generated prompts are more conducive to the mining of pre-trained knowledge than learnable word vectors. Simply learning class-specific word vectors for prompts achieves relatively poor performance. One of the main reasons is that it is difficult for the word vectors to adequately fit task-specific fine-grained information for different types of faces. In contrast, the diverse, semantic, and unknown-aware prompts generated by our prompt generator can better describe the complex context information in face anti-spoofing.

4.4 Visualization Analysis

We perform Grad-CAM visualization to analyze the results of our method. The results on protocol C to H are shown in Fig. 2. From top to bottom, each row is original live face images, class activation maps of the live face images, original spoof face images, and class activation maps of the spoof face images. The spoof face images belong to ten different attack types.

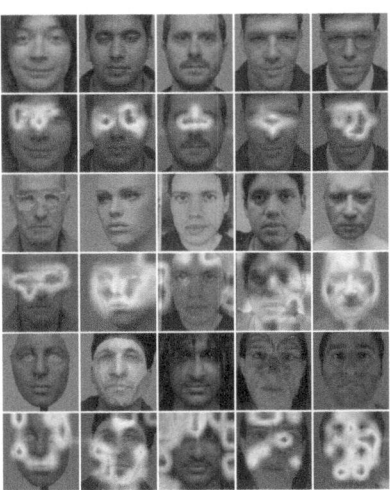

Fig. 2. Grad-CAM results of the proposed method based on protocol C to H.

We can see that for live face images, the model focuses on areas with richly varied three-dimensional structures such as eyes and noses. For spoof face images, the model focuses on areas where the spoof patterns emerge. The focused areas depend on attack types. For instance, the area where the funny glasses are located in a glass attack image, the border area of a printed photo, the unnatural texture on a mask, and the paint in a tattoo are all important information captured by the model. There is a clear difference in the areas of live and spoof faces. This indicates that our model learns discriminative and generalized features for unseen testing domains with both known and unknown attack types.

5 Conclusion

In this paper, we propose an unknown-aware diverse prompt learning framework, which mines the multi-modal knowledge in visual-language pre-training models to simultaneously address the domain shift and unknown attacks for OSSDG-based face anti-spoofing. The learned models generalize well not only to live faces and known attack types but also to unknown attack types, including some high-fidelity unknown attack types. Extensive experiments on 8 protocols demonstrate the effectiveness of the proposed method.

Acknowledgments. This work was supported in part by the National Key Research and Development Program of China (Grant No. 2022YFC3310400), in part by the Natural Science Foundation of China (Grant Nos. U23B2054, 62076240, 62102419, 62276263 and 62406133), in part by the Beijing Municipal Natural Science Foundation (Grant No. 4222054), in part by the Natural Science Foundation of Hunan Province (Grant No.2024JJ6389) and in part by the Hengyang Science and Technology Plan Project (Grant No.202330046190).

References

1. Yu, Z., Qin, Y., Li, X., Zhao, C., Lei, Z., Zhao, G.: Deep learning for face anti-spoofing: a survey. TPAMI **45**(5), 5609–5631 (2023)
2. Jia, Y., Zhang, J., Shan, S., Chen, X.: Unified unsupervised and semi-supervised domain adaptation network for cross-scenario face anti-spoofing. PR **115**, 107888 (2021)
3. Liu, Y., Stehouwer, J., Jourabloo, A., Liu, X.: Deep tree learning for zero-shot face anti-spoofing. In: CVPR, pp. 4680–4689 (2019)
4. Jiang, F., et al.: Open-set single-domain generalization for robust face anti-spoofing. IJCV, 1–22 (2024)
5. Radford, A., et al.: Learning transferable visual models from natural language supervision. In: ICML, pp. 8748–8763 (2021)
6. Srivatsan, K., Naseer, M., Nandakumar, K.: Flip: cross-domain face anti-spoofing with language guidance. In: ICCV, pp. 19 685–19 696 (2023)
7. Liu, A., et al.: CFPL-FAS: class free prompt learning for generalizable face anti-spoofing. In: CVPR, pp. 222–232 (2024)
8. Yan, P., Liu, X., Zhang, P., Lu, H.: Learning convolutional multi-level transformers for image-based person re-identification. Vis. Intell. **1**(1), 24 (2023)
9. Liu, Y., Jourabloo, A., Liu, X.: Learning deep models for face anti-spoofing: binary or auxiliary supervision. In: CVPR, pp. 389–398 (2018)
10. Yu, Z., Cai, R., Cui, Y., Liu, A., Chen, C.: Visual prompt flexible-modal face anti-spoofing. arXiv preprint arXiv:2307.13958 (2023)
11. Li, H., Li, W., Cao, H., Wang, S., Huang, F., Kot, A.C.: Unsupervised domain adaptation for face anti-spoofing. TIFS **13**(7), 1794–1809 (2018)
12. Li, Q., Wang, W., Xu, C., Sun, Z., Yang, M.-H.: Learning disentangled representation for one-shot progressive face swapping. In: TPAMI (2024)
13. Li, Q., Sun, Z., He, R., Tan, T.: Deep supervised discrete hashing. In: NeurIPS, pp. 2479–2488 (2017)
14. Zhang, J., Huang, J., Jin, S., Lu, S.: Vision-language models for vision tasks: a survey. arXiv preprint arXiv:2304.00685 (2023)
15. Li, Z., Lv, X., Yu, W., Liu, Q., Lin, J., Zhang, S.: Face shape transfer via semantic warping. Vis. Intell. **2**(1), 1–11 (2024)
16. Peng, S., Zhu, X., Yi, D., Qian, C., Lei, Z.: Formulating facial mesh tracking as a differentiable optimization problem: a backpropagation-based solution. Vis. Intell. **21**(1), 1–12 (2024)
17. Zhou, K., Yang, J., Loy, C.C., Liu, Z.: Learning to prompt for vision-language models. IJCV **130**(9), 2337–2348 (2022)
18. Zhou, K., Yang, J., Loy, C.C., Liu, Z.: Conditional prompt learning for vision-language models. arXiv preprint arXiv:2203.05557 (2022)
19. Bahng, H., Jahanian, A., Sankaranarayanan, S., Isola, P.: Exploring visual prompts for adapting large-scale models. arXiv preprint arXiv:2203.17274 (2022)

20. Zang, Y., Li, W., Zhou, K., Huang, C., Loy, C.C.: Unified vision and language prompt learning. arXiv preprint arXiv:2210.07225 (2022)
21. Zhang, Z., Yan, J., Liu, S., Lei, Z., Yi, D., Li, S.Z.: A face antispoofing database with diverse attacks. In: ICB, pp. 26–31 (2012)
22. Chingovska, I., Anjos, A., Marcel, S.: On the effectiveness of local binary patterns in face anti-spoofing. In: Proceedings of International Conference of the Biometrics Special Interest Group, pp. 1–7 (2012)
23. Wen, D., Han, H., Jain, A.K.: Face spoof detection with image distortion analysis. TIFS **10**(4), 746–761 (2015)
24. Boulkenafet, Z., Komulainen, J., Li, L., Feng, X., Hadid, A.: OULU-NPU: a mobile face presentation attack database with real-world variations. In: FG, pp. 612–618 (2017)
25. Heusch, G., George, A., Geissbühler, D., Mostaani, Z., Marcel, S.: Deep models and shortwave infrared information to detect face presentation attacks. TBIOM **2**(4), 399–409 (2020)
26. Boulkenafet, Z., Komulainen, J., Hadid, A.: Face spoofing detection using colour texture analysis. TIFS **11**(8), 1818–1830 (2016)
27. Wang, G., Han, H., Shan, S., Chen, X.: Unsupervised adversarial domain adaptation for cross-domain face presentation attack detection. TIFS **16**, 56–69 (2020)
28. Wang, C.-Y., Lu, Y.-D., Yang, S.-T., Lai, S.-H.: PatchNet: a simple face anti-spoofing framework via fine-grained patch recognition. In: CVPR, pp. 20 281–20 290 (2022)
29. Huang, H.-P., et al.: Adaptive transformers for robust few-shot cross-domain face anti-spoofing. In: ECCV, pp. 37–54 (2022)

Author Index

B
Bao, Yongtang II-25
Ben, Xianye II-35
Bi, Yingzhou II-228
Bian, Weixin I-25

C
Cao, Chen II-219
Cao, Zhicheng II-177
Chen, Guang I-68
Chen, Lixi I-220
Chen, Runzhang I-89
Chen, Xianbiao I-200
Chen, Zengqiang I-231
Chen, Zhentao II-3
Cui, Jinrong I-244, II-187
Cui, Zhe I-121

D
Ding, Ruiyang II-159
Dong, Gang II-49
Dong, Jing I-187
Dong, Xingbo II-145

E
El-Yacoubi, Mounim A. II-112

F
Fang, Wei I-220
Fei, Lunke I-46, I-153

G
Gao, Ce II-177
Gao, Chengrui I-14
Gao, Feiyang I-254
Gao, Li I-264
Guo, Dongcai II-219
Guo, Songhui II-159
Guo, Yingying II-35

H
Han, Yushan I-254
He, Jinrong II-228
He, Zhaofeng II-59, II-69
He, Zhipeng II-187
Hou, Chunxia II-103
Hu, Jianian I-46
Hu, Junlin II-3
Hu, Yao I-25
Hu, Yiwei II-209
Huang, Chenyu II-272
Huang, Jiyi I-142
Huang, Junqin I-131, I-142
Huang, Siyu I-174

J
Jia, Wei I-164
Jia, Wenqiang II-35
Jia, Yuwei I-121
Jiang, Fangling I-275
Jiang, Guoxin II-272
Jiang, Jinzhe II-49
Jin, Xin II-112
Jin, Zhe II-145

K
Kang, Wenxiong I-68, I-89, I-100, I-131, I-142

L
Lei, Zhen I-264
Li, Junyu II-133
Li, Qi I-275
Li, Shujie II-133
Li, Shuyi I-46, I-153
Li, Yinghua II-187
Li, Yu II-133
Li, Yuezun I-231
Li, Yuxing II-177
Liang, Hailun II-238
Liang, Qi I-110

© The Editor(s) (if applicable) and The Author(s), under exclusive license to Springer Nature Singapore Pte Ltd. 2025
S. Yu et al. (Eds.): CCBR 2024, LNCS 15352, pp. 287–289, 2025.
https://doi.org/10.1007/978-981-96-1068-6

Liang, Yanyan II-238
Liao, Hongchao II-112
Lin, Chenglin II-123
Lin, Haoheng I-131, I-142
Liu, Bing I-275
Liu, Bojie II-93
Liu, Daming II-93
Liu, Fan II-272
Liu, Feng II-79
Liu, Pudu II-13
Liu, Yongji II-69
Liu, Zhanli I-220
Lu, Huimin II-123
Lu, Hao I-164
Lu, Lihua II-49
Luo, Chaoqi II-248
Luo, Dacan I-89, I-100, I-131, I-142
Luo, Feng I-25

M
Ma, Hui II-238
Ma, Shuai II-228
Ma, Songzhe II-123
Meng, Qinggang I-36
Meng, Qingguo II-145

P
Peng, Bo I-187
Peng, Yuhang II-282

Q
Qi, Xiaolong I-210
Qiang, Sunyuan II-238
Qin, Huafeng II-112

R
Ren, Yani I-79
Ru, Yiwei II-59

S
Shan, Caifeng II-25
Shang, Dongxu II-282
Shao, Huikai I-57, I-79
Sheng, Cunyu I-164
Shi, Binmeng I-110
Shi, Siyu I-57
Song, Shuaichao II-159
Song, Yikang II-3
Su, Fei I-121

Su, Jiajun II-13
Su, Le I-153
Sun, Haohao I-3
Sun, Yunlian I-210, I-244, II-197
Sun, Yuren I-174
Sun, Zhenan I-275

T
Tan, Hai II-260
Tang, Chaoying I-174
Tang, Zhenmin II-103
Teng, Zhan I-220
Teoh, Andrew Beng Jin I-14
Tian, Feng I-68
Tistarelli, Massimo II-197

W
Wan, Hao I-100
Wan, Jun II-238
Wan, Minghua II-260
Wan, Yuanfei I-244
Wang, Binqiang II-49
Wang, Cong II-209
Wang, Haixia I-3
Wang, Huabin II-282
Wang, Huiling I-210
Wang, Jian I-210, I-244, II-197
Wang, Jianbin I-89
Wang, Lei II-79
Wang, Wei I-187
Wang, Weining I-275
Wang, Weiwei II-177
Wang, Xudong I-231
Wang, Yao II-228
Wang, Zilin II-282
Wei, Jia I-153
Wen, Jinchang II-197
Wu, Huijia II-59, II-69
Wu, Lifang I-46
Wu, Yifan II-103

X
Xia, Weijie II-219
Xiang, Yan II-112
Xie, Miner II-79
Xie, Tianming I-68
Xie, Tingxuan II-35

Xie, Xiaohua I-200
Xie, Yiping II-248
Xing, Jing I-121
Xu, Sen II-35
Xu, Shengxiang II-272
Xu, Zhenbo II-59
Xu, Zilong I-25
Xue, Feng II-133

Y

Yan, Zheyu I-264
Yang, Gongping I-36
Yang, Guowei II-260
Yang, Hujiang II-59
Yang, Jinfeng I-110
Yang, Li II-228
Yang, Lu I-36
Yang, Shaocong I-210
Yang, Xu I-68
Yang, Yeming II-159
Yang, Zekai I-100
Yang, Zhangjing II-260
Yang, Ziyuan I-14
Yao, Liang II-272
Ye, Xingjian II-282
Ye, Ziyun I-110
Ying, Haoxiang I-254
Ying, Shuangshuang II-69
You, Weike I-187
Yu, Churan II-59, II-69
Yu, Miao II-159
Yu, Zitong II-248

Z

Zeng, Huanqiang II-13
Zeng, Ming I-100, I-131
Zhan, Simin II-13
Zhang, Dongsen II-69
Zhang, Erhua II-103
Zhang, Gang II-209
Zhang, Hui II-145
Zhang, Mengxin II-282
Zhang, Peng II-25
Zhang, Qiuli II-187
Zhang, Xiao-Yu I-264
Zhang, Yilong I-3
Zhang, Yufei I-187
Zhang, Zexing II-123
Zhao, Heng II-177
Zhao, Qingxin II-123
Zhao, Shuping I-46, I-153, II-187
Zhao, Weisong I-264
Zhao, Zihao I-110
Zheng, Hao II-25
Zhong, Dexing I-57, I-79
Zhou, Jianru I-3
Zhou, Lizhen I-36
Zhou, Wanting I-254
Zhou, Ying II-145
Zhou, Yixuan II-260
Zhu, Honggang I-254
Zhu, Hongyu II-112
Zhu, Jianqing II-13
Zhu, Min I-14
Zhu, Xiangyu I-264
Zhu, Xingzheng I-110

The manufacturer's authorised representative in the EU is Springer Nature Customer Service Centre GmbH, Europaplatz 3, 69115 Heidelberg, Germany. If you have any concerns regarding our products, please contact ProductSafety@springernature.com

Printed and bound by CPI Group (UK) Ltd, Croydon, CR0 4YY

26/03/2026

02078973-0005